双语名著无障碍阅读丛书

经典集锦

福尔摩斯探案经典之

巴斯克维尔的猎犬

The Hound of the Baskervilles

［英国］柯南·道尔 著

潘华凌 译

中国出版集团

中译出版社

图书在版编目（CIP）数据

福尔摩斯探案经典．巴斯克维尔的猎犬：英汉对照/（英）柯南道尔
著；潘华凌译．—北京：中译出版社，2014.8（2023.2 重印）
（双语名著无障碍阅读丛书）
ISBN 978-7-5001-3270-7

Ⅰ.①福… Ⅱ.①柯… ②潘… Ⅲ.①英语—汉语—对照读物
②侦探小说—英国—现代 Ⅳ.①H319.4：Ⅰ

中国版本图书馆 CIP 数据核字（2014）第 151402 号

出版发行/中译出版社
地　　址/北京市西城区新街口外大街 28 号普天德胜主楼四层
电　　话/(010) 68359827；68359303（发行部）；68359725（编辑部）
邮　　编/100044
传　　真/(010) 68357870
电子邮箱/book@ ctph.com.cn
网　　址/http：//www.ctph.com.cn

责任编辑/范祥镇　王诗同　杨佳特
封面设计/潘　峰

排　　版/杰瑞腾达科技发展有限公司
印　　刷/永清县晔盛亚胶印有限公司
经　　销/新华书店

规　　格/710 毫米×1000 毫米　1/16
印　　张/20.5
字　　数/262 千字
版　　次/2014 年 8 月第一版
印　　次/2023 年 2 月第七次

ISBN 978-7-5001-3270-7　　　　　　定价：69.00 元

多年以来，中译出版社有限公司（原中国对外翻译出版有限公司）凭借国内一流的翻译和出版实力及资源，精心策划、出版了大批双语读物，在海内外读者中和业界内产生了良好、深远的影响，形成了自己鲜明的出版特色。

二十世纪八九十年代出版的英汉（汉英）对照"一百丛书"，声名远扬，成为一套最权威、最有特色且又实用的双语读物，影响了一代又一代英语学习者和中华传统文化研究者、爱好者；还有"英若诚名剧译丛""中华传统文化精粹丛书""美丽英文书系"，这些优秀的双语读物，有的畅销，有的常销不衰反复再版，有的被选为大学英语阅读教材，受到广大读者的喜爱，获得了良好的社会效益和经济效益。

"双语名著无障碍阅读丛书"是中译专门为中学生和英语学习者精心打造的又一品牌，是一个新的双语读物系列，具有以下特点：

选题创新——该系列图书是国内第一套为中小学生量身打造的双语名著读物，所选篇目均为教育部颁布的语文新课标必读书目，或为中学生以及同等文化水平的社会读者喜闻乐见的世界名著，重新编译为英汉（汉英）对照的双语读本。这些书既给青少年读者提供了成长过程中不可或缺的精神食粮，又让他们领略到原著的精髓和魅力，对他们更好地学习英文大有裨益；同时，丛书中入选的《论语》《茶馆》《家》等汉英对照读物，亦是热爱中国传统文化的中外读者所共知的经典名篇，能使读者充分享受阅读经典的无限乐趣。

无障碍阅读——中学生阅读世界文学名著的原著会遇到很多生词和文化难点。针对这一情况，我们给每一本读物原文中的较难词汇和不易理解之处都加上了注释，在内文的版式设计上也采取英汉（或汉英）对照方式，扫清了学生阅读时的障碍。

优良品质——中译双语读物多年来在读者中享有良好口碑，这得益于作者和出版者对于图书质量的不懈追求。"双语名著无障碍阅读丛书"继承了中译双语读物的优良传统——精选的篇目、优秀的译文、方便实用的注解，秉承着对每一个读者负责的精神，竭力打造精品图书。

愿这套丛书成为广大读者的良师益友，愿读者在英语学习和传统文化学习两方面都取得新的突破。

目录 CONTENTS

Chapter 1　Mr. Sherlock Holmes

Mr. Sherlock Holmes, who was usually very late in the mornings, **save**[①] upon those not infrequent occasions when he was up all night, was seated at the breakfast table. I stood upon the hearth-rug and picked up the stick which our visitor had left behind him the night before. It was a fine, thick piece of wood, **bulbous**[②]-headed, of the sort which is known as a "Penang lawyer." Just under the head was a broad silver band, nearly an inch across. "To James Mortimer, M.R.C.S., from his friends of the C.C.H.," was engraved upon it, with the date "1884." It was just such a stick as the old-fashioned family **practitioner**[③] used to carry–dignified, solid, and **reassuring**[④].

"Well, Watson, what do you **make of**[⑤] it?"

Holmes was sitting with his back to me, and I had given him no sign of my occupation.

"How did you know what I was doing? I believe you have eyes in the back of your head."

"I have, at least, a well-polished, silver-plated coffee-pot in front of me," said he."But, tell me, Watson, what do you make of our visitor's stick? Since we have been so unfortunate as to miss him and have no notion of his **errand**[⑥], this accidental souvenir becomes of importance. Let me hear you reconstruct the man by an examination of it."

"I think," said I, following as far as I could the methods of my companion, "that Dr. Mortimer is a successful, elderly medical man, **well-esteemed**[⑦], since those who know him give him this mark of their **appreciation**[⑧]."

第一章　夏洛克·福尔摩斯先生

① save [seiv] *conj.* 除了

② bulbous ['bʌlbəs] *a.* 球茎状的，鳞茎状的，鼓凸的

③ practitioner [præk'tiʃənə] *n.*（尤指医生、律师等）开业者；从业者

④ reassuring [,riːə'ʃuəriŋ] *a.* 安慰的；鼓励的

⑤ make of 对…有某种看法；理解；解释

⑥ errand ['erənd] *n.* 特殊的任务，使命

⑦ esteem [i'stiːm] *v.* 尊敬，尊重

⑧ appreciation [ə,priːʃi'eiʃən] *n.* 感激，感谢

夏洛克·福尔摩斯先生坐在餐桌边用早餐。他除了那些并不在少数的彻夜不眠的日子之外，早晨通常很晚起床。我站在壁炉前的地毯上，拿起了头天晚上我们的客人落下的手杖。这是一根木制手杖，制作精巧，很有分量，顶端呈圆球状，木料产于槟榔屿，叫做"山槟榔木手杖"。靠近手杖顶端处扎了一圈很宽的银箍，差不多有一英寸宽，上面刻着"赠予M.R.C.S.詹姆斯·莫蒂默，C.C.H.的朋友们敬赠"字样，还附上了"1884"这个日期。这种手杖通常是那种旧式私人医生使用的——显得高贵儒雅，沉稳体面，温和友爱。

"对啦，华生，你怎么看这根手杖呢？"

福尔摩斯背朝我坐着，再说，我先前并没有弄出什么动静来。

"你怎么知道我在干什么事情呢？我看你的后脑勺上也长了一双眼睛吧。"

"我面前至少还摆着一把锃亮的镀银咖啡壶吧，"他说，"不过，请告诉我，华生，你从我们客人的手杖上都看出了什么端倪呢？很遗憾啊，我们没能见到手杖的主人，也就不知道他此行的目的，因此，这件意外的纪念物就至关重要了。你已经细心地观察过手杖了，给我描述一下它主人的情况吧。"

"我觉得，"我说，尽可能遵循我同伴的推理方法，"这位莫蒂默医生必定在医学上成就卓著，接近老年，所以，那些认识他的人士这才把这个纪念物赠送给了

"Good!" said Holmes. "Excellent!"

"I think also that the probability is in favour of his being a country practitioner who does a great deal of his visiting on foot."

"Why so?"

"Because this stick, though originally a very handsome one, has been so knocked about that I can hardly imagine a town practitioner carrying it. The thick iron **ferrule**① is worn down, so it is **evident**② that he has done a great amount of walking with it."

"Perfectly sound!" said Holmes.

"And then again, there is the 'friends of the C.C.H.' I should guess that to be the Something Hunt, the local **hunt**③ to whose members he has possibly given some surgical assistance, and which has made him a small **presentation**④ in return."

"Really, Watson, you **excel**⑤ yourself," said Holmes, pushing back his chair and lighting a cigarette. "I **am bound to**⑥ say that in all the **accounts**⑦ which you have been so good as to give of my own small achievements you have habitually **underrated**⑧ your own abilities. It may be that you are not yourself **luminous**⑨, but you are a conductor of light. Some people without possessing genius have a remarkable power of stimulating it. I confess, my dear fellow, that I am very much in your debt."

He had never said as much before, and I must admit that his words gave me **keen**⑩ pleasure, for I had often been **piqued**⑪ by his indifference to my admiration and to the attempts which I had made to give publicity to his methods. I was proud, too, to think that I had so far mastered his system as to apply it in a way which earned his approval. He now took the stick from my hands and examined it for a few minutes with his naked eyes. Then with an expression of interest he laid down his cigarette, and carrying the cane to the window, he looked over it again with a **convex**⑫ lens.

"Interesting, though elementary," said he as he returned to his favourite corner of the settee. "There are certainly one or two indications upon the stick. It gives us the basis for several deductions."

"Has anything escaped me?" I asked with some self-importance. "I trust that there is nothing of consequence which I have **overlooked**⑬?"

他，以表达他们的敬意。"

"很好！"福尔摩斯说，"好极了！"

"我还觉得，他很可能是一位在乡村行医的医生，出诊时，多数时候要靠步行。"

"何以见得？"

"因为这根手杖原本很漂亮，但现在下端已经被敲碰得很厉害了，我很难想象一位在城里行医的医生会携带这样一根手杖。包在下端的厚铁包头也已磨损了，很显然，他曾经拄着手杖走很远的路程。"

"很有道理啊！"福尔摩斯说。

"还有就是，上面还刻着'C.C.H.的朋友们'。于是我猜测，那是当地的一个狩猎协会，他很可能曾经给该协会的会员提供过一些外科救助，因此，他们送了这件小礼物给他以表谢意。"

"实际上，华生，你真了不起啊，"福尔摩斯说着，把椅子向后推了一下，点燃一支烟，"我必须得说，你在费脑伤神叙述我的那些微不足道的所谓成就时，总是习惯性地忽略了你自己的本领。你可能本身并不能发光，但一定是个光的传导体。有些人自身并没有什么天分，但却有着非凡的激发天分的能力。我承认，亲爱的朋友，我真是幸亏有了你啊。"

他可从未说过我这么多好话啊。我承认，他的话令我听了很受用，因为我先前每每对他表露钦佩之意并且试图将他的推理方法公之于众时，他总是抱着不以为然的态度。我琢磨着，自己现在已经掌握了他的那套方法，而且还在实际中较好地加以运用了，所以这才得到了他的赞许。想到这儿，我心里洋溢着自豪感。这时，他把手杖从我的手里拿了过去，用肉眼审视了几分钟。随即显露出一副兴致勃勃的神情，他放下手里的烟卷，拿起手杖走到窗前，再用放大镜仔细观察起来。

"虽说简单，但挺有意思啊，"他说着，坐回到了长椅上他喜爱的那一角，"手杖上的确有一两处能够说明问题的地方，我们可以据此做出几点推断。"

"我遗漏了什么情况吗？"我问，有点自以为是，"我相信，没有忽略掉重要的情况吧？"

"亲爱的华生，你的结论恐怕大多数都不正确呢！

---

① ferrule ['feru:l] *n.* （伞、棍、棒等工具顶端的）金属箍，金属环，金属包头

② evident ['evidənt] *n.* 显而易见的，明显的，显然的

③ hunt [hʌnt] *n.* 猎区，猎场

④ presentation [,prezən'teiʃən] *n.* 礼物，赠品

⑤ excel [ik'sel] *v.* （在成就等方面）优于，胜过，超过

⑥ be bound to 应当，理应；有义务要

⑦ account [ə'kaunt] *n.* 记述；报道；记事

⑧ underrate [ʌndə'reit] *v.* 低估

⑨ luminous ['lju:minəs] *a.* 发光的，发亮的

⑩ keen[ki:n] *a.* （感觉）强烈的，激烈的，深切的

⑪ pique [pi:k] *v.* 使生气；伤害…的自尊心

⑫ convex [kɔn'veks] *a.* 凸面的，凸形的，凸圆的

⑬ overlook [,əuvə'luk] *v.* 漏看；忽视，忽略

"I am afraid, my dear Watson, that most of your conclusions were **erroneous**[①]. When I said that you stimulated me I meant, to be frank, that in **noting**[②] your **fallacies**[③] I was occasionally guided towards the truth. Not that you are entirely wrong in this instance. The man is certainly a country practitioner. And he walks a good deal."

"Then I was right."

"To that **extent**[④]."

"But that was all."

"No, no, my dear Watson, not all—by no means all. I would suggest, for example, that a presentation to a doctor is more likely to come from a hospital than from a hunt, and that when the initials 'C.C.' are placed before that hospital the words 'Charing Cross' very naturally suggest themselves."

"You may be right."

"The probability lies in that direction. And if we take this as a working **hypothesis**[⑤] we have a fresh basis from which to start our construction of this unknown visitor."

"Well, then, supposing that 'C.C.H.' does stand for 'Charing Cross Hospital,' what further inferences may we draw?"

"Do none suggest themselves? You know my methods. Apply them!"

"I can only think of the obvious conclusion that the man has practised in town before going to the country."

"I think that we might venture a little farther than this. Look at it in this light. On what occasion would it be most probable that such a presentation would be made? When would his friends unite to give him a **pledge**[⑥] of their good will? Obviously at the moment when Dr. Mortimer **withdrew**[⑦] from the service of the hospital in order to start in practice for himself. We know there has been a presentation. We believe there has been a change from a town hospital to a country practice. Is it, then, stretching our inference too far to say that the presentation was on the occasion of the change?"

"It certainly seems probable."

"Now, you will observe that he could not have been on the staff of the hospital, since only a man well-established in a London practice could hold such a position, and such a one would not drift into the country. What was he,

① erroneous [i'rəuniəs] *a.* 含有（或基于）错误的，谬误的，不正确的
② note [nəut] *v.* 注意，留心
③ fallacy ['fæləsi] *n.* 谬见，错误

④ extent [ik'stent] *n.* 程度；限度

⑤ hypothesis [hai'pɔθisis] *n.* 假说，假设

⑥ pledge [pledʒ] *n.* 信物，祝愿
⑦ withdraw [wið'drɔ:] *v.* 离开，引退

坦率地说，我刚才说你激发了我的灵感，其真正的含意是，通过发现你的谬误之处，我可以偶尔找到真相。但这并不是说你这次完全错了。那人肯定是一位在乡村行医的医生，他确实要步行走很远的路程。"

"那我就是说对了。"

"仅在这个方面。"

"但是，全部情况也就这么多啊。"

"不，不，亲爱的华生，根本不是全部——绝对不是全部。我给你提示一下，比如说，给一位医生赠送纪念品的人很有可能是医院的，而不是什么狩猎协会的。而在医院（Hospital）前面加上字母C.C.自然就是查令十字（Charing Cross）两个单词的首字母了。"

"你或许是对的。"

"有这方面的可能性。如果我们把这当成一种有效的假设，那就有了一个推测我们的客人身份的新依据了。"

"行啊，我们就假定C.C.H.代表查令十字医院，那又如何据此做进一步的推断呢？"

"难道没有一点结论凸显出来吗？你了解我的推理方法，使用一下吧！"

"我只能得出一个显而易见的结论，那就是，那人先是在城里行医，然后才到乡村去的。"

"我觉得，我们可以大胆地往深里探讨一下这个问题。如此看来，我们就要考虑，这件纪念品最有可能是在什么样的情形下赠送出的呢？他那些朋友在什么时候会联合赠送给他一件礼物以表达他们良好的祝愿呢？很显然，是在莫蒂默医生辞去医院职务，去当开业医生时。我们听说过有这种馈赠的情况。我们相信，他是从城里医院转到乡下行医的。那么，我们由此推断该礼物正是在他事业转变之时送给他的，这应该不算太牵强吧？"

"看起来确实有这种可能啊。"

"是啊，你会注意到，他不可能是一名医院的主治医师，因为只有在伦敦行医相当有名望的人才能享有这样的地位，但这样的人是不会流落到乡村的。那么，他是做什么的呢？如果他是在医院工作，但又不在主治医

then? If he was in the hospital and yet not on the staff he could only have been a house-surgeon or a house-physician–little more than a senior student. And he left five years ago–the date is on the stick. So your grave, middle-aged family practitioner vanishes into thin air, my dear Watson, and there emerges a young fellow under thirty, **amiable**①, unambitious, absent-minded, and the possessor of a favourite dog, which I should describe roughly as being larger than a **terrier**② and smaller than a **mastiff**③."

I laughed **incredulously**④ as Sherlock Holmes leaned back in his settee and blew little wavering rings of smoke up to the ceiling.

"As to the latter part, I have no means of **checking**⑤ you," said I, "but at least it is not difficult to find out a few particulars about the man's age and professional career." From my small medical shelf I took down the Medical Directory and turned up the name. There were several Mortimers, but only one who could be our visitor. I read his record aloud.

"Mortimer, James, M.R.C.S., 1882, Grimpen, Dartmoor, Devon. House-surgeon, from 1882 to 1884, at Charing Cross Hospital. Winner of the Jackson prize for Comparative Pathology, with essay entitled 'Is Disease a Reversion?' Corresponding member of the Swedish Pathological Society. Author of 'Some Freaks of Atavism' (*LANCET,* 1882). 'Do We Progress?' (*JOURNAL OF PSYCHOLOGY*, March, 1883). Medical Officer for the parishes of Grimpen, Thorsley, and High Barrow."

"No mention of that local hunt, Watson," said Holmes with a mischievous smile, "but a country doctor, as you very **astutely**⑥ observed. I think that I am fairly justified in my inferences. As to the adjectives, I said, if I remember right, amiable, unambitious, and absent-minded. It is my experience that it is only an amiable man in this world who receives **testimonials**⑦, only an unambitious one who abandons a London career for the country, and only an absent-minded one who leaves his stick and not his visiting-card after waiting an hour in your room."

"And the dog?"

"Has been in the habit of carrying this stick behind his master. Being a heavy stick the dog has held it tightly by the middle, and the marks of his teeth

师之列，那他就只可能是一个外科住院医生，或者是内科住院医生——地位和医学院高年级的学生差不多。况且，他是在五年前离开医院的——这一日期被刻在手杖上了。因此，亲爱的华生，你推测的那位神情庄重的中年家庭诊所医生就化为乌有了，取而代之的是一位三十岁不到的青年人。他亲切和蔼，缺少抱负，健忘马虎，还养了一条心爱的犬，我可以大致描述出犬的体型比狸犬大，但比獒犬小。"

我满腹狐疑，哈哈笑了起来。夏洛克·福尔摩斯则靠在他的长椅上，对着天花板吐着飘荡不定的小烟圈。

"至于后面那部分，我无法核实你是否准确，"我说，"但我们至少可以根据他的年龄和从业经历来找出几个可能的对象，这一点是不难做到的。"我从放医学书籍的小书架上把那本医疗手册拿下来，翻到了人名栏所在的页码。里面有好几位姓莫蒂默的医生，但与我们的来客情况相仿的却只有一位。我大声念出了有关他的记载：

"詹姆斯·莫蒂默，德文郡达特穆尔的格林彭人，1882年成为皇家外科医师学会的会员，1882至1884年期间在查令十字医院任外科住院医生。因撰写了题为《疾病会隔代遗传吗？》的论文而获得杰克逊比较病理学奖，是瑞典病理学协会的通讯会员。曾撰写过《几种隔代遗传的畸形症》（1882年刊载于《柳叶刀》），《我们在前进吗？》（1883年3月刊载于《心理学学刊》），并担任过格林彭、索斯利和高冈等教区的医务官。

"没提到那个当地的狩猎协会吧，华生，"福尔摩斯说，揶揄地微笑着，"但正如你目光敏锐地观察到的那样，他是个乡村医生。我认为自己的推论是站得住脚的。至于那几个形容词，如果我没记错的话，我用的是'亲切和蔼，缺少抱负，健忘马虎'。因为以我的经验来看，在这个世界上，只有待人亲切和蔼的人才能收到纪念品，只有安于现状且不贪功名的人才会放弃伦敦的事业，而跑到乡下去，也只有健忘马虎的人才会在你屋里等了一个小时后，没留下自己的名片，却落下了自己的手杖。"

"那条犬呢？"

"它养成了叼着手杖跟在主人后面的习惯。因为这

① amiable ['eimjəbl] *a.* 令人愉悦的，悦人的，友善的
② terrier ['teriə] *n.* 狸犬
③ mastiff ['mæstif] *n.*（耳、唇下垂的）猛犬，獒
④ incredulous [in'kredjuləs] *a.* 不相信的；怀疑的
⑤ check [tʃek] *v.* 检查，检验

⑥ astute [ə'stju:t] *a.* 精明的，机敏的，敏锐的

⑦ testimonial [,testi'məuniəl] *n.* 纪念品

are very **plainly**① visible. The dog's jaw, as shown in the space between these marks, is too broad in my opinion for a terrier and not broad enough for a mastiff. It may have been–yes, by Jove, it *is* a curly-haired spaniel."

He had risen and paced the room as he spoke. Now he **halted**② in the **recess**③ of the window. There was such a ring of **conviction**④ in his voice that I glanced up in surprise.

"My dear fellow, how can you possibly be so sure of that?"

"For the very simple reason that I see the dog himself on our very door-step, and there is the ring of its owner. Don't move, I beg you, Watson. He is a professional brother of yours, and your presence may be of assistance to me. Now is the dramatic moment of fate, Watson, when you hear a step upon the stair which is walking into your life, and you know not whether for good or ill. What does Dr. James Mortimer, the man of science, ask of Sherlock Holmes, the specialist in crime? Come in!"

The appearance of our visitor was a surprise to me, since I had expected a typical country practitioner. He was a very tall, thin man, with a long nose like a beak, which **jutted**⑤ out between two keen, gray eyes, set closely together and sparkling brightly from behind a pair of gold-rimmed glasses. He was clad in a professional but rather **slovenly**⑥ fashion, for his frock-coat was **dingy**⑦ and his trousers **frayed**⑧. Though young, his long back was already bowed, and he walked with a forward thrust of his head and a general air of peering benevolence. As he entered his eyes fell upon the stick in Holmes's hand, and he ran towards it with an exclamation of joy. "I am so very glad," said he. "I was not sure whether I had left it here or in the Shipping Office. I would not lose that stick for the world."

"A presentation, I see," said Holmes.

"Yes, sir."

"From Charing Cross Hospital?"

"From one or two friends there on the occasion of my marriage."

"Dear, dear, that's bad!" said Holmes, shaking his head.

Dr. Mortimer blinked through his glasses in mild astonishment.

"Why was it bad?"

"Only that you have **disarranged**⑨ our little **deductions**⑩. Your marriage,

① plain[plein] *a.* 明白的，
显而易见的

② halt [hɔ:lt] *v.* 停住，停止
③ recess [ri'ses] *n.*（墙壁等
的）凹进之处
④ conviction [kən'vikʃən] *n.*
深信，确信

⑤ jut [dʒʌt] *v.* 突出，伸出

⑥ slovenly ['slʌvənli] *a.* 不
修边幅的，邋遢的
⑦ dingy [dindʒi] *a.* 不干净
的；褪色的
⑧ frayed [freid] *a.* 磨损的

⑨ disarrange [,disə'reindʒ] *v.*
扰乱，弄乱
⑩ deduction [di'dʌkʃən] *n.*
推论，推断

根木手杖很有分量，犬只得紧紧地咬着其中间部位，这
样一来，上面的犬齿印就非常清晰了。从齿印间的空隙
来看，我认为犬的下巴比狸犬的宽，比獒犬的窄，估计
是……对了，一定是一条卷毛长耳猎犬。"

他已经站起了身，说话时一直在屋里来回踱步。话
音刚落，他就在向外突出的窗台前停了下来。他的声音
里充满了自信，这让我觉得很奇怪，便抬头瞥了他一眼。

"亲爱的朋友，你对那条犬的事情怎么能这么肯定呢？"

"原因很简单，我现在看到了那条犬在我们大门口
的台阶上呢，而且其主人按门铃的声音也已经响起来了。
不要走开，我请求你啦，华生。他是你的同行，你在场
肯定会对我有所帮助。命运之中充满戏剧性的时刻到了，
华生，你听到的楼梯上传来的脚步声正一步一步地走进
你的生活，然而，你却无法知道这是福还是祸。詹姆
斯·莫蒂默医生，医学界的人物，要向夏洛克·福尔摩
斯——犯罪问题专家——请教些什么问题呢？请进！"

我们的客人的外表令我吃了一惊，因为我先前料想
他是一位典型的乡村医生。他是个极高极瘦的人，一个
长长的鸟嘴似的鼻子凸显在两只距离很近的眼睛之间。
他的眼睛呈灰色，锐利的目光在金边眼镜的后面闪烁。
他穿着一身职业装，但样子显得很邋遢，因为他的外衣
已经弄脏，裤子也已磨损。尽管他还很年轻，但长长的
后背却已经弯曲，走路时脑袋向前倾着，一副凝视关注
着什么的神情。他一进门就看到了福尔摩斯手里拿着的
那根手杖，高兴得大叫了一声，径直向福尔摩斯跑去。
"我太开心了！"他说，"我不能确定，是落在您这儿，
还是落在轮船公司了。我无论如何也不能丢失这根手杖
啊。"

"我看，是一件人家送的礼物。"福尔摩斯说。

"是啊，先生。"

"是查令十字医院的同事们送的吗？"

"是我结婚时那儿的两个朋友送的。"

"天哪，天哪，真是糟糕！"福尔摩斯摇了摇头说。

莫蒂默医生有些吃惊，眼睛在镜片后面眨了眨。

"怎么会很糟糕呢？"

"因为您打乱了我们刚才做的几点小小的推断，您

you say?"

"Yes, sir. I married, and so left the hospital, and with it all hopes of a consulting practice. It was necessary to make a home of my own."

"Come, come, we are not so far wrong, after all," said Holmes. "And now, Dr. James Mortimer ――"

"Mister, sir, Mister–a humble M.R.C.S."

"And a man of precise mind, evidently."

"A **dabbler**① in science, Mr. Holmes, a picker up of shells on the shores of the great unknown ocean. I presume that it is Mr. Sherlock Holmes whom I am **addressing**② and not ――"

"No, this is my friend Dr. Watson."

"Glad to meet you, sir. I have heard your name mentioned in connection with that of your friend. You interest me very much, Mr. Holmes. I had hardly expected so **dolichocephalic**③ a skull or such well-marked **supra-orbital**④ development. Would you have any objection to my running my finger along your **parietal**⑤ **fissure**⑥? A cast of your skull, sir, until the original is available, would be an ornament to any anthropological museum. It is not my intention to be **fulsome**⑦, but I confess that I covet your skull."

Sherlock Holmes waved our strange visitor into a chair. "You are an enthusiast in your line of thought, I perceive, sir, as I am in mine," said he. "I observe from your forefinger that you make your own cigarettes. Have no hesitation in lighting one."

The man drew out paper and tobacco and twirled the one up in the other with surprising **dexterity**⑧. He had long, quivering fingers as **agile**⑨ and restless as the **antennae**⑩ of an insect.

Holmes was silent, but his little **darting**⑪ glances showed me the interest which he took in our curious companion.

"I presume, sir," said he at last, "that it was not merely for the purpose of examining my skull that you have done me the honour to call here last night and again to-day?"

"No, sir, no; though I am happy to have had the opportunity of doing that as well. I came to you, Mr. Holmes, because I recognized that I am myself an unpractical man and because I am suddenly confronted with a most serious and

是说您结婚的时候，对吧？"

"是的，先生，我一结完婚就离开了医院，同时也远离了成为咨询医师的希望。但建立一个属于自己的家庭是很有必要的。"

"是啊，是啊，我们毕竟还是没有错得离谱，"福尔摩斯说，"对啦，詹姆斯·莫蒂默医生——"

"叫我'先生'吧，先生，叫我'先生'——只是区区一个英国皇家外科医师学会会员而已。"

"很显然，您是个凡事讲究精准的人。"我说。

"一个对科学稍有涉猎的人，福尔摩斯先生，一个在未知的浩瀚海洋边拾贝壳的人。我猜想，自己是在同夏洛克·福尔摩斯先生说话，而不是——"

"不，这是我的朋友华生医生。"

"很高兴见到您，先生，听到人们提起您朋友大名的时候，也听到过您的大名。您让我产生了极大的兴趣，福尔摩斯先生。没想到您的颅骨这么长，额头这么高，您不介意我用手指触碰一下您的头顶骨缝吧？在没有您的颅骨实物之前，如果按您的颅骨做出一具模型，对任何人类学博物馆而言，都会是一具出色的标本。不是我曲意奉承，但说句心里话，我觊觎您的颅骨。"

夏洛克·福尔摩斯挥了挥手，示意我们这位怪异的客人坐到椅子上。"我看得出来，您对自己本行的问题非常执着用心啊，先生，这一点和我相似，"他说，"看到您的食指，知道您是自己卷烟抽的，如果想抽烟，就请自便吧。"

客人掏出了纸和烟丝，三下两下就卷成了烟卷，动作娴熟得惊人。他那修长的手指抖动着，像昆虫的触须那样细巧、敏捷。

福尔摩斯沉默不语，不过，他迅速移动的目光告诉我，他对我们这位怪异离奇的客人颇感兴趣。

"我估计，先生，"他终于开口说话了，"您昨晚大驾光临，今天又再度造访，不仅仅是为了来仔细观察一番我的颅骨吧？"

"不是，先生，不是的。不过，我很高兴，顺便也赶上了这样的好机会。我来找您，福尔摩斯先生，是因

① dabbler ['dæblə] n. 涉猎者，浅尝者

② address [ə'dres] v. 与…说话

③ dolichocephalic [ˌdɔlikəuse'fælik] a. 头形狭长的
④ supra-orbital 眉骨的
⑤ parietal [pə'raiitəl] a.【解剖学】体壁的；腔壁的；顶骨的
⑥ fissure ['fiʃə]【解剖学】（如大脑皮质的）裂纹，裂隙，沟
⑦ fulsome ['fulsʌm] a.（恭维等）过分的；虚伪的
⑧ dexterity [dek'steriti] n.（身、手等的）敏捷，灵敏，灵巧，熟练

⑨ agile ['ædʒail] a. 灵活的，敏捷的
⑩ antenna [æn'tenə] n. 触角，触须
⑪ dart [dɑ:t] v. 急速移动

extraordinary problem. Recognizing, as I do, that you are the second highest expert in Europe --"

"Indeed, sir! May I inquire who has the honour to be the first?" asked Holmes with some **asperity**①.

"To the man of precisely scientific mind the work of Monsieur Bertillon must always **appeal**② strongly."

"Then had you not better consult him?"

"I said, sir, to the precisely scientific mind. But as a practical man of affairs it is acknowledged that you stand alone. I trust, sir, that I have not **inadvertently**③ --"

"Just a little," said Holmes. "I think, Dr. Mortimer, you would do wisely if without more **ado**④ you would kindly tell me plainly what the exact nature of the problem is in which you demand my assistance."

为我意识到，自己是个毫无实践经验的人，却又偏偏突然遇到了非常严重而又非常离奇的问题。我同时也知道，您是全欧洲名列第二的权威专家——"

"可不是嘛，先生！敢问荣登榜首的那位是谁呢？"福尔摩斯问了一声，语气有点刻薄。

"要论最具严密科学头脑的人，贝蒂荣先生占有很大的优势。"

"那您去请教他不是更好吗？"

"我说的是，先生，针对最具严密科学头脑的。但在处理实际问题的经验方面，人们公认，您是独一无二的。先生，我想，我该不是无意中——"

"有一点点，"福尔摩斯说，"我认为，莫蒂默医生，您不要多说不相干的事情了，还是直截了当地告诉我您在什么问题上想要我效劳吧。"

① asperity [æ'sperəti] *n.* 粗暴，严厉

② appeal [ə'pi:l] *v.* （迫切）要求；呼吁，吁请（某人帮助、同情等）

③ inadvertent [,inəd'və:tənt] *a.* 非故意的，出于无心的

④ ado [ə'du:] *n.* 麻烦，费力

Chapter 2　The Curse of the Baskervilles

"I have in my pocket a manuscript," said Dr. James Mortimer.

"I observed it as you entered the room," said Holmes.

"It is an old manuscript."

"Early eighteenth century, unless it is a **forgery**[①]."

"How can you say that, sir?"

"You have presented an inch or two of it to my examination all the time that you have been talking. It would be a poor expert who could not give the date of a document within a decade or so. You may possibly have read my little **monograph**[②] upon the subject. I put that at 1730."

"The exact date is 1742." Dr. Mortimer drew it from his breast-pocket. "This family paper was committed to my care by Sir Charles Baskerville, whose sudden and tragic death some three months ago created so much excitement in Devonshire. I may say that I was his personal friend as well as his medical attendant. He was a strong-minded man, sir, **shrewd**[③], practical, and as unimaginative as I am myself. Yet he took this document very seriously, and his mind was prepared for just such an end as did eventually **overtake**[④] him."

Holmes stretched out his hand for the manuscript and flattened it upon his knee.

"You will observe, Watson, the alternative use of the long s and the short. It is one of several indications which enabled me to fix the date."

第二章　巴斯克维尔家族的祸根

① forgery ['fɔːdʒəri] *n.* 伪造品，赝品

② monograph ['mɔnəgrɑːf] *n.* 专题论著（书，文章或论文）

③ shrewd [ʃruːd] *a.* 精明的

④ overtake [ˌəuvə'teik] *v.* 突然降临；意外地碰上；突然袭击

"我衣服口袋里有一份手稿。"詹姆斯·莫蒂默医生说。

"您走进房间时我就看出来了。"福尔摩斯回答说。

"这是一份陈旧的手稿。"

"是十八世纪早期的，如果不是伪造的话。"

"您是怎么判断出的，先生？"

"您在说话的当儿，手稿露出了一两英寸，让我看到了。如果一位专家不能把文件的日期估计得误差在十年之内，那他就太蹩脚了。我曾就这个问题写过一篇小论文，想必您看到过的。我觉得您这份手稿是1730年写成的。"

"确切的年份是1742年，"莫蒂默医生从前胸口袋里拿出手稿，"这是一份祖传家书，是查尔斯·巴斯克维尔爵士托付给我的。三个月前，他突然去世了，死得很悲惨，引起了整个德文郡的震动。可以说，我既是他的保健医生，又是他的私交朋友。先生，他那个人意志很坚强，精明灵活，讲求实际，并且和我一样，从不胡思乱想。但是，他对这份家书却很重视，心里早就准备好了这样一个结局，而这样的厄运最终真的降落到了他的头上。"

福尔摩斯伸出手拿过手稿，然后在膝盖上把它展开。

"华生，你注意看，长短S交替使用。这便是使我

I looked over his shoulder at the yellow paper and the faded script. At the head was written: "Baskerville Hall," and below, in large, **scrawling**[1] figures: "1742."

"It appears to be a statement of some sort."

"Yes, it is a statement of a certain legend which runs in the Baskerville family."

"But I understand that it is something more modern and practical upon which you wish to consult me?"

"Most modern. A most practical, pressing matter, which must be decided within twenty-four hours. But the manuscript is short and is **intimately**[2] connected with the affair. With your permission I will read it to you."

Holmes leaned back in his chair, placed his finger-tips together, and closed his eyes, with an air of **resignation**[3]. Dr. Mortimer turned the manuscript to the light and read in a high, **cracking**[4] voice the following curious, old-world narrative:

Of the origin of the Hound of the Baskervilles there have been many statements, yet as I come in a direct line from Hugo Baskerville, and as I had the story from my father, who also had it from his, I have **set it down**[5] with all belief that it occurred even as is here set forth. And I would have you believe, my sons, that the same Justice which punishes sin may also most graciously forgive it, and that no ban is so heavy but that by prayer and repentance it may be removed. Learn then from this story not to fear the fruits of the past, but rather to be **circumspect**[6] in the future, that those foul passions whereby our family has suffered so grievously may not again be loosed to our **undoing**[7].

"Know then that in the time of the Great Rebellion (the history of which by the learned Lord Clarendon I most earnestly **commend**[8] to your attention) this Manor of Baskerville was held by Hugo of that name, nor can it be **gainsaid**[9] that he was a most wild, **profane**[10], and godless man. This, in truth, his neighbours might have pardoned, seeing that saints have never flourished in those parts, but there was in him a certain **wanton**[11] and cruel humour which made his name a **byword**[12] through the West. It chanced that this Hugo came to love (if, indeed, so dark a passion may be known

① scrawl [skrɔːl] v. 涂写；乱写，乱画

② intimate ['intimət] a. 深入的，深刻的

③ resignation [,rezig'neiʃən] n. 顺从；屈从
④ cracking ['krækiŋ] a. 生气勃勃的；敏捷的

⑤ set down 记下，写下

⑥ circumspect ['sə:kəmspekt] a. 谨慎的，小心的，慎重的
⑦ undoing [ʌn'duːiŋ] n. 毁灭
⑧ commend [kə'mend] v. 委托，把…交托给
⑨ gainsay [gein'sei] v. 否认；反驳
⑩ profane [prəu'fein] a. 不敬神的；好咒骂的
⑪ wanton ['wɔntən] a. 轻浮的；放荡的，淫乱的
⑫ byword ['baiwə:d] n. 众人鄙视（或指责）的人（或物）

能够确定手稿年代的几个特征中的一个。"

我站在他背后，看着那张泛黄的纸张和褪了色的字迹。手稿的顶上写着："巴斯克维尔庄园"，紧接着就是大而潦草的数字"1742"。

"看上去像是在叙述一件什么事情。"

"对啊，是在叙述一个巴斯克维尔家族流传下来的传说。"

"但是，我知道，您希望和我商议的是一件关系当前的、更具实际意义的事情，对吧？"

"最近发生的。一桩很有实际意义、迫在眉睫的事情，必须得在二十四小时之内决定。但是，这份简短的手稿与该事件有非常密切的关联。如果您允许，我就把它念给您听听。"

福尔摩斯靠在椅子背上，把两只手的指尖对顶在一起，然后闭上眼睛，露出一副悠然自得的神情。莫蒂默医生把手稿拿到光亮处，用高亢、急促的声音朗读了下面这段离奇而又年代久远的故事：

关于巴斯克维尔家族猎犬的由来，已有许多叙述。然而，由于我是雨果·巴斯克维尔的嫡系后代，我从我父亲那儿听说了这个故事，而我父亲又是他父亲告诉他的。因此，我把故事记录了下来，完全相信，故事就像这里所叙述的那样发生过。我希望你们能够相信，孩子们啊，惩罚那些有罪之人的公正的神明也会大度地宽恕他们的。只要他们真心悔改，不断祈祷，再深重的罪孽都能够豁免。由此，你们就会懂得：不要惧怕前辈所种下的恶果，但你们将来行事一定要谨小慎微，尽力避免我们家族过去所受的深重苦难再次降临在家族败落的后代身上。

你们应当知道，大叛乱时期（我要郑重其事地向你们推荐，去阅读一下饱学之士克拉伦登撰写的关于该时期的历史著作），巴斯克维尔庄园的主人是雨果·巴斯克维尔。不可否认，此人凶蛮卑鄙，目无上帝。事实上，如果他只有这一点缺点的话，乡邻们本是可以谅解他的，因为在该区域，圣教从来就没有兴旺过。但是，他狂妄自大，残忍无度，令他在西部地区臭名远扬。一个偶然机会，雨果先生爱上了（如果如此阴暗的情欲也

under so bright a name) the daughter of a **yeoman**[①] who held lands near the Baskerville estate. But the young maiden, being discreet and of good repute, would ever avoid him, for she feared his evil name. So it came to pass that one Michaelmas this Hugo, with five or six of his idle and wicked companions, **stole**[②] down upon the farm and carried off the maiden, her father and brothers being from home, as he well knew. When they had brought her to the Hall the maiden was placed in an upper chamber, while Hugo and his friends sat down to a long **carouse**[③], as was their nightly custom. Now, the poor **lass**[④] upstairs was like to have her wits turned at the singing and shouting and terrible oaths which came up to her from below, for they say that the words used by Hugo Baskerville, when he was in wine, were such as might blast the man who said them. At last in the stress of her fear she did that which might have **daunted**[⑤] the bravest or most active man, for by the aid of the growth of ivy which covered (and still covers) the south wall she came down from under the eaves, and so homeward across the moor, there being three leagues betwixt the Hall and her father's farm.

"It chanced that some little time later Hugo left his guests to carry food and drink–with other worse things, perchance–to his captive, and so found the cage empty and the bird escaped. Then, as it would seem, he became as one that hath a devil, for, rushing down the stairs into the dining-hall, he **sprang**[⑥] upon the great table, **flagons**[⑦] and **trenchers**[⑧] flying before him, and he cried aloud before all the company that he would that very night render his body and soul to the Powers of Evil if he might but overtake the **wench**[⑨]. And while the **revellers**[⑩] stood **aghast**[⑪] at the fury of the man, one more wicked or, it may be, more drunken than the rest, cried out that they should put the hounds upon her. **Whereat**[⑫] Hugo ran from the house, crying to his grooms that they should saddle his mare and **unkennel**[⑬] the pack, and giving the hounds a kerchief of the maid's, he swung them to the line, and so off full cry in the moonlight over the moor.

"Now, for some space the revellers stood **agape**[⑭], unable to understand all that had been done in such haste. But **anon**[⑮] their bemused wits awoke to the nature of the deed which was like to be done upon the moorlands. Everything was now in an uproar, some calling for their pistols, some for

① yeoman ['jəumən] *n.* 小地主

② steal [sti:l] *v.* 偷偷地行动

③ carouse [kə'rauz] *n.* 狂欢的宴会

④ lass [læs] *n.* 少女

⑤ daunt [dɔ:nt] *v.* 使畏缩，使胆怯

⑥ spring [spriŋ] *v.* 跳，跃起

⑦ flagon ['flægən] *n.* 酒壶

⑧ trencher ['trentʃə] *n.* 木盘

⑨ wench [wentʃ] *n.* 女孩，少女

⑩ reveller['revələ] *n.* 饮酒狂欢者；摆设酒宴者

⑪ aghast [ə'gɑ:st] *a.* 惊骇的，吓呆的

⑫ whereat [hwεə'æt] *conj.* 因之，于是

⑬ unkennel [ʌn'kenəl] *v.* 把…从窝中放出

⑭ agape [ə'geip] *a.* 目瞪口呆的

⑮ anon [ə'nɔn] *ad.* 不久

可以冠以如此阳光的字眼的话）一位美丽的少女，她是一个在巴斯克维尔庄园附近有几亩地产的庄稼汉的女儿。但是，少女向来谨言慎行，名声极佳，她还惧怕他的恶名，自然就躲避他了。后来，在米迦勒节那天，那位雨果先生得知她的父亲、兄弟都外出了，便和五六个游手好闲的恶棍朋友一同偷偷跑到了她家里，把她抢了回去。他们把她弄到了庄园的别墅后，把她关在楼上的一间小屋里。雨果和他那些狐朋狗友围坐在一起狂欢痛饮起来，这是他们夜晚常有的消遣。这时，楼上的可怜姑娘听到了楼下的狂歌乱吼声，还有那些不堪入耳的污言秽语，早已惶恐万分，惊慌失措。因为听人说，雨果·巴斯克维尔醉酒时说出的话，无论是谁，只要重说一遍都可能会遭天谴的。最后，在极其恐惧的情形下，姑娘竟然干了一件让最勇敢或者最敏捷的人都会为之咋舌的事情。她从窗口爬出，攀缘着南墙上的蔓藤（至今仍爬满了）从房檐上一路爬了下来，然后横过荒原径直往回家的方向跑去，庄园的别墅离她父亲的农场有大概三里格的路程。

事情凑巧的是，过后不久，雨果撇下客人，自己带着酒食——或者兼具邪恶之意——去找他那位囚禁的姑娘，结果发现，鸟笼已空，囚鸟飞离。紧接着，他像魔鬼附身了一样，冲下楼进入餐厅，一跃身跳上大餐桌，把上面的东西——酒瓶，木盘——全都踢飞了。他在朋友面前大声嚷嚷，说只要他当晚能追上姑娘，情愿把自己的肉体和灵魂全都献给恶魔，任其摆布。那些纵酒狂欢的浪子们被他的暴怒吓得目瞪口呆，这时，一个更邪恶的家伙，也可能是一个喝得比别人更醉的人，大声叫喊着说，他们应当放猎犬出去追捕她。雨果一听，立刻跑出了别墅，高喊马夫，要他们牵马备鞍，并把犬舍里的狗全部放出。他把那少女落下的头巾给那些猎犬嗅了嗅，随即便一窝蜂地把它们赶了出去。猎犬们发出一片狂吠声，在月光的照耀下，向荒原狂奔而去。

是啊，浪子们目瞪口呆地站在原地，都没回过神儿来，不知道刚才匆匆忙忙干的是什么事。过了一会儿，那些醉醺醺的头脑清醒了，明白了去荒原上所要干的事

their horses, and some for another flask of wine. But **at length**① some sense came back to their crazed minds, and the whole of them, thirteen in number, took horse and started in pursuit. The moon shone clear above them, and they rode swiftly **abreast**②, taking that course which the maid must needs have taken if she were to reach her own home.

"They had gone a mile or two when they passed one of the night shepherds upon the moorlands, and they cried to him to know if he had seen the hunt. And the man, as the story goes, was so crazed with fear that he could **scarce**③ speak, but at last he said that he had indeed seen the unhappy maiden, with the hounds upon her track. 'But I have seen more than that,' said he, 'for Hugo Baskerville passed me upon his black mare, and there ran **mute**④ behind him such a hound of hell as God forbid should ever be at my heels.' So the drunken squires cursed the shepherd and rode onward. But soon their skins turned cold, for there came a galloping across the moor, and the black mare, **dabbled**⑤ with white froth, went past with trailing bridle and empty saddle. Then the revellers rode close together, for a great fear was on them, but they still followed over the moor, though each, had he been alone, would have been right glad to have turned his horse' s head. Riding slowly in this fashion they came at last upon the hounds. These, though known for their valour and their breed, were **whimpering**⑥ in a **cluster**⑦ at the head of a deep **dip**⑧ or goyal, as we call it, upon the moor, some **slinking**⑨ away and some, with starting **hackles**⑩ and staring eyes, gazing down the narrow valley before them.

"The company had come to a halt, more sober men, as you may guess, than when they started. The most of them would by no means advance, but three of them, the boldest, or it may be the most drunken, rode forward down the goyal. Now, it opened into a broad space in which stood two of those great stones, still to be seen there, which were set by certain forgotten peoples in the days of old. The moon was shining bright upon the clearing, and there in the centre lay the unhappy maid where she had fallen, dead of fear and of fatigue. But it was not the sight of her body, nor yet was it that of the body of Hugo Baskerviile lying near her, which raised the hair upon the heads of these three dare-devil **roysterers**⑪, but it was that, standing over Hugo, and plucking at his throat, there stood a foul thing, a great, black

① at length 最终

② abreast [ə'brest] ad. 并肩地

③ scarce [skɛəs] ad. 几乎不，简直不

④ mute [mju:t] a. 沉默的，无声的

⑤ dabble ['dæbl] v. 浸湿

⑥ whimper ['hwimpə] v. 抽泣，呜咽

⑦ cluster ['klʌstə] n. 群集，一群，一帮

⑧ dip [dip] n. 凹地，洼地

⑨ slink [sliŋk] v. 偷偷溜走

⑩ hackles ['hækls] n.（特指犬发怒时）颈背部竖起的毛

⑪ roysterer ['rɔistərə] n. 喝酒喧闹者

情。于是，大家又大喊大叫起来，有人喊着要带手枪，有人高呼自己的坐骑，有人大叫要再带一瓶酒。最后，他们恢复了一些理智，13个人一同上马追了上去。皎洁的月光照在他们头上，他们并肩前行，沿着少女回家的必经之路急速地奔跑。

他们跑了一二英里路时，遇到了一个荒原上的夜间放牧人，便大声问，他是否看到了他们要追赶的人。听说那牧人被吓得差点儿连话都说不出来了，后来，他终于开了口，说他确实看到了那个可怜的少女，她身后有一群猎犬在追赶。"不过我看到的远不止这些，"他说，"我还碰到了雨果·巴斯克维尔，他骑着那匹黑马从这里跑过，后面悄无声息地跟着一条魔鬼似的大猎犬。上帝啊，但愿不要让那样的狗跟在我的后面！"那些醉鬼们咒骂了那牧人一通后又骑马往前追了。但很快，他们就被吓得浑身发冷，因为荒原上传来了马匹奔跑的声音，随后一匹黑马就从他们身边跑了过去。马的嘴里流着白沫，缰绳拖在地上，马鞍上却空无一人。当时，浪子们挤成一堆，因为他们感到无比恐惧，但他们还是继续向荒原上前行。如果他们是各自单独去追的话，那一个个早就掉转马头往回跑了。他们就这样缓缓地前行，最后终于赶上了那群猎犬。猎犬尽管以骁勇和优种而闻名，但此时却挤在荒原上一段峡谷的尽头处竟相哀鸣，有些已经逃了出来了，有些则颈毛直竖，两只发亮的眼睛直勾勾地盯着他们前面那片窄窄的谷地。

那伙人停了下来，你们可以想象得到，他们此时比出发时要清醒得多了。他们中的大多数都绝对不想再往前了，但有三个是胆大妄为的，或者说可能是醉酒最严重的。他们继续策马向峡谷前行。少顷，出现了一片宽阔的平地，中间立着两块巨石，现在仍在原地，不知道是古时候哪个先人立下的。皎洁的月光倾洒在那片空地上，他们在空地的中间看到了那个可怜的少女，她因恐惧疲乏致死后便倒在了那里。但让三个胆大包天的酒鬼感到毛发直竖的却不是那少女的尸体，也不是躺在她近旁的雨果·巴斯克维尔的尸体，而是站在雨果身旁，正撕扯他喉咙的魔兽。那是一只体形巨大的黑毛畜生，样子像猎犬，但活人

beast, shaped like a hound, yet larger than any hound that ever mortal eye has rested upon. And even as they looked the thing tore the throat out of Hugo Baskerville, on which, as it turned its blazing eyes and dripping jaws upon them, the three shrieked with fear and rode for dear life, still screaming, across the moor. One, it is said, died that very night of what he had seen, and the other twain were but broken men for the rest of their days.

"Such is the tale, my sons, of the coming of the hound which is said to have plagued the family so sorely ever since. If I have set it down it is because that which is clearly known hath less terror than that which is but **hinted**[①] at and guessed. Nor can it be denied that many of the family have been unhappy in their deaths, which have been sudden, bloody, and mysterious. Yet may we shelter ourselves in the infinite goodness of Providence, which would not forever punish the innocent beyond that third or fourth generation which is threatened in Holy Writ. To that Providence, my sons, I hereby commend you, and I counsel you by way of caution to **forbear**[②] from crossing the moor in those dark hours when the powers of evil are **exalted**[③].

"[This from Hugo Baskerville to his sons Rodger and John, with instructions that they say nothing **thereof**[④] to their sister Elizabeth.]"

When Dr. Mortimer had finished reading this **singular**[⑤] narrative he pushed his spectacles up on his forehead and stared across at Mr. Sherlock Holmes. The latter yawned and tossed the end of his cigarette into the fire.

"Well?" said he.

"Do you not find it interesting?"

"To a collector of fairy tales."

Dr. Mortimer drew a folded newspaper out of his pocket.

"Now, Mr. Holmes, we will give you something a little more recent. This is the *Devon County Chronicle* of May 14th of this year. It is a short account of the facts **elicited**[⑥] at the death of Sir Charles Baskerville which occurred a few days before that date."

My friend leaned a little forward and his expression became **intent**[⑦]. Our visitor readjusted his glasses and began:

谁也没亲眼见过体形如此硕大的猎犬。正当他们看着那东西扯出雨果·巴斯克维尔的喉咙的时候，它那闪亮的眼睛和鲜血直滴的大嘴向他们转了过来。三个人一看，吓得尖叫了起来，赶紧策马逃命了，横过荒原时还一路惊呼。据说，三人中的一个因为看到的一切当晚便吓死了，另外两个也吓破了胆，后半辈子在疯疯癫癫中度过。

此乃猎犬传说的由来。亲爱的孩子们，据说从那以后，那只猎犬便一直搅得我们的家族不得安宁。我之所以要把它记录下来，那是因为，对于一件恐怖可怕的事情而言，仅凭暗示或者猜测，还不如完完全全地知晓。不可否认，我们家族的很多人都没有得到善终，他们死得突然，死得凄惨而神秘。我们乞求得到上帝那无限慈爱的庇护，不会无休止地惩罚下去，不会让这样的灾难降罚在我们家族第三、第四代笃信《圣经》的人头上。孩子们啊，我借上帝之名嘱咐你们，真心地劝告你们，务必要多加小心，邪恶势力甚嚣尘上的黑暗时刻，要避开荒原。

［这是雨果·巴斯克维尔写给他的儿子罗杰、约翰的家书，并叮嘱二人切勿将此事告诉他们的妹妹伊丽莎白］

莫蒂默医生念完了这篇不可思议的记述之后，便把眼镜推到前额上，眼睛盯着福尔摩斯。而福尔摩斯却打了个哈欠，把烟头扔进了壁炉里。

"呃？"他呃了一声。

"您难道不觉得这很有意思吗？"

"对搜集神话故事的人而言，确实如此。"

莫蒂默医生把手伸进衣服口袋里，掏出一张折叠的报纸。

"对啦，福尔摩斯先生，我要告诉您一件近段时间发生的事情。这是今年5月14日的《德文郡纪事报》。上面有一则简短的报道，叙述的是那之前几天查尔斯·巴斯克维尔爵士死亡一事。"

我朋友上身稍稍前倾，神色也变得专注了起来。我们的客人重新戴好眼镜，开始大声念了起来：

近日，查尔斯·巴斯克维尔爵士猝亡，这事给本郡蒙上了一层阴影。据说，他本来有可能会在下届

① hint [hint] v. 暗示

② forbear ['fɔ:'bɛə] v. 避免

③ exalt [ig'zɔ:lt] v. 增强，强调…的作用（或效果）

④ thereof [ˌðɛər'ɔv] ad. 关于那

⑤ singular ['siŋgjulə] a. 非凡的；异常的

⑥ elicit [i'lisit] v. 使谈出，使透露

⑦ intent [in'tent] a. （注意力等）集中的

"The recent sudden death of Sir Charles Baskerville, whose name has been mentioned as the probable **Liberal**[1] candidate for Mid-Devon at the next election, has cast a gloom over the county. Though Sir Charles had resided at Baskerville Hall for a comparatively short period his amiability of character and extreme generosity had won the affection and respect of all who had been brought into contact with him. In these days of **nouveaux riches**[2] it is refreshing to find a case where the **scion**[3] of an old county family which has fallen upon evil days is able to make his own fortune and to bring it back with him to restore the fallen **grandeur**[4] of his line. Sir Charles, as is well known, made large sums of money in South African speculation. More wise than those who go on until the wheel turns against them, he realized his gains and returned to England with them. It is only two years since he took up his residence at Baskerville Hall, and it is common talk how large were those schemes of reconstruction and improvement which have been interrupted by his death. Being himself childless, it was his openly expressed desire that the whole countryside should, within his own lifetime, profit by his good fortune, and many will have personal reasons for **bewailing**[5] his untimely end. His generous donations to local and county charities have been frequently **chronicled**[6] in these columns.

"The circumstances connected with the death of Sir Charles cannot be said to have been entirely cleared up by the **inquest**[7], but at least enough has been done to dispose of those rumours to which local superstition has given rise. There is no reason whatever to suspect **foul play**[8], or to imagine that death could be from any but natural causes. Sir Charles was a widower, and a man who may be said to have been in some ways of an eccentric habit of mind. In spite of his considerable wealth he was simple in his personal tastes, and his indoor servants at Baskerville Hall consisted of a married couple named Barrymore, the husband acting as butler and the wife as housekeeper. Their evidence, **corroborated**[9] by that of several friends, tends to show that Sir Charles's health has for some time been impaired, and points especially to some affection of the heart, manifesting itself in changes of colour, breathlessness, and acute attacks of nervous depression. Dr. James Mortimer, the friend and medical attendant of the **deceased**[10], has given evidence to the same effect.

"The facts of the case are simple. Sir Charles Baskerville was in the habit every night before going to bed of walking down the famous **yew**[11] alley of Baskerville Hall. The evidence of the Barrymores shows that this had been his custom. On the fourth

① Liberal ['libərəl] n. 自由党

② nouveaux riches 暴发户
③ scion ['saiən] n. （尤指贵族等的）子孙，后裔
④ grandeur ['grændʒə] n. 豪华的排场

⑤ bewail [bi'weil] v. 为…而悲伤
⑥ chronicle ['krɔnikl] v. 记述
⑦ inquest ['inkwest] n. （有陪审团参加的调查死因的）讯问；验尸

⑧ foul play 暴行（尤指谋杀）

⑨ corroborate [kə'rɔbə,reit] v. 确证，证实

⑩ deceased [di'si:st] a. 已故的

⑪ yew [ju:] n. 紫杉

选举中被选为德文郡自由党的候选人。查尔斯爵士在巴斯克维尔庄园居住时间短暂，但他为人厚道，慷慨大方，深得同他打交道的人们的喜爱与尊敬。在此充斥着暴发新贵的年代，查尔斯这样一位名门之后竟也能衣锦还乡，恢复因厄运而中衰的家族荣耀，这确实是一件可喜之事。众所周知，查尔斯爵士是在南非做投机生意发家的。他比那些做投机做到倒霉为止的人聪明得多，他见好就收，带着变卖了的资财返回了英伦。他迁居至巴斯克维尔庄园才两年，人们都在谈论他那庞大的重建和修缮计划，但因他本人逝世，此计划也被中断。因他本人并无子嗣，他曾公开表示，有生之年，整个郡区都将从他的巨额财富中受益。因此，很多人因他猝亡而表达哀思是有缘由的。至于他对本郡慈善机构的慷慨捐赠，本报的专栏昔日常有刊载。

死因调查已告结束，有关查尔斯爵士的死亡原因虽不能说已经完全弄清楚了，但至少足以消除当地因迷信所引起的各种传言。没有任何理由怀疑爵士之死是由暴行所致，或者想象其死亡并非自然原因。查尔斯爵士是个鳏夫，据说，他在有些方面，思维显得怪异。尽管他拥有巨额财富，但他平时却清心寡欲，生活简朴。巴斯克维尔庄园的仆人只有巴里摩尔夫妇二人，丈夫是庄园总管，妻子是管家。他们二人的证词得到了查尔斯爵士几个朋友的证实：一段时间以来，查尔斯爵士出现了健康状况不佳的征兆，尤其有罹患心脏病的症状，症状为脸色骤变、呼吸困难和神经系统严重衰弱。死者的朋友兼私人医生詹姆斯·莫蒂默也提供了相似的证明。

情况很简明。巴斯克维尔庄园内有条著名的两边是紫杉树篱的小道，查尔斯·巴斯克维尔爵士有个习惯，每晚睡觉前都要在小道上散步。这一习惯也得到了巴里摩尔夫妇的证实。5月4日，查尔斯爵士宣布他将于次日启程去伦敦，并吩咐巴里摩尔替自己打点好行装。当晚，他照例去散步了，同时还抽了支雪茄，这是他的另一个习惯。但这一回却去而未返。十二点钟时，巴里摩尔发现大厅的门依然敞开着，大惊失

of May Sir Charles had declared his intention of starting next day for London, and had ordered Barrymore to prepare his luggage. That night he went out as usual for his **nocturnal**[1] walk, in the course of which he was in the habit of smoking a cigar. He never returned. At twelve o'clock Barrymore, finding the hall door still open, became alarmed, and, lighting a lantern, went in search of his master. The day had been wet, and Sir Charles's footmarks were easily traced down the alley. Halfway down this walk there is a gate which leads out on to the moor. There were indications that Sir Charles had stood for some little time here. He then proceeded down the alley, and it was at the far end of it that his body was discovered. One fact which has not been explained is the statement of Barrymore that his master's footprints altered their character from the time that he passed the moor-gate, and that he appeared from **thence**[2] onward to have been walking upon his toes. One Murphy, a **gipsy**[3] horse-dealer, was on the moor at no great distance at the time, but he appears by his own confession to have been the worse for drink. He declares that he heard cries but is unable to state from what direction they came. No signs of violence were to be discovered upon Sir Charles's person, and though the doctor's evidence pointed to an almost incredible facial distortion–so great that Dr. Mortimer refused at first to believe that it was indeed his friend and patient who lay before him–it was explained that that is a symptom which is not unusual in cases of **dyspnoea**[4] and death from **cardiac**[5] exhaustion. This explanation was **borne out**[6] by the **post-mortem**[7] examination, which showed long-standing organic disease, and the coroner's jury returned a verdict in accordance with the medical evidence. It is well that this is so, for it is obviously of the utmost importance that Sir Charles's heir should settle at the Hall and continue the good work which has been so sadly interrupted. Had the **prosaic**[8] finding of the coroner not finally put an end to the romantic stories which have been whispered in connection with the affair, it might have been difficult to find a tenant for Baskerville Hall. It is understood that the next of kin is Mr. Henry Baskerville, if he be still alive, the son of Sir Charles Baskerville's younger brother. The young man when last heard of was in America, and inquiries are being **instituted**[9] with a view to informing him of his good fortune."

Dr. Mortimer refolded his paper and replaced it in his pocket.

"Those are the public facts, Mr. Holmes, in connection with the death of Sir Charles Baskerville."

① nocturnal [nɔk'tə:nəl] a.
夜间的

② thence [ðens] ad. 从那里
起；从那一点
③ gipsy ['dʒipsi] a. 吉卜赛
人的

④ dyspnoea [disp'ni:ə] n. 呼
吸困难
⑤ cardiac ['kɑ:diæk] a. 心脏
的
⑥ bear out 证实，支持
⑦ post-mortem ['pəust'm
ɔ:tem] a. 验尸的

⑧ prosaic [prəu'zeiik] a. 平
淡无奇的；乏味的

⑨ institute ['institjut] v. 开
始；实行

色，立刻掌灯外出寻找主人。当天地面潮湿，顺着树
篱中间的小道很容易找到查尔斯爵士的脚印。走到道
路的一半处，边上有一个栅门，通向外面的荒原。种
种迹象表明，查尔斯爵士曾在栅门边停留了许久，然
后才顺着林荫道往前走，一直走到了尽头，他的尸体
也正是在那儿被发现的。有一个情节尚未得到解释：
据巴里摩尔陈述，主人的脚印自通向荒原的栅门处后
就发生了变化，他随后好像都是踮着脚尖走路的。事
发当时，有个名叫默菲的吉卜赛马贩，正好在荒原上
距事发地不远处，但他自称当时酩酊大醉，不省人事
了。他承认确实听见了喊叫声，但无法弄清声音来自
何方。未发现查尔斯爵士身遭暴力的痕迹，不过医生
证明，其面部扭曲得很严重，简直难以辨认，就连莫
蒂默医生乍一看，也不能确认躺在他面前的确实就是
他的朋友——据解释，此乃因呼吸困难和心脏衰竭而
猝死时的正常症状之一。这一解释也为尸体解剖的结
果所证实。尸检表明，死者患有这种官能性疾病为时
已久。死因调查陪审团做出的判决和医学鉴定的结果
完全一致。依照事实，如此结案实属妥善。很显然，
此事至关重要的是，查尔斯爵士的后人将在此庄园居
住，继续进行不幸被中断的善行义举。假若死因调查
结果的报告无法消除邻里间对此事件所产生的各种荒
谬的谣传，那势必难以再度找到巴斯克维尔庄园的住
户。众所周知，查尔斯·巴斯克维尔爵士的胞弟之子
亨利·巴斯克维尔先生如若健在，则是爵士最近的亲
属。最近一次听闻，此年轻人现在美洲，已派人询问
其下落，以通知其前来继承这笔巨额遗产。

　　莫蒂默医生重新叠好报纸，放回到衣服口袋里。
　　"有关查尔斯·巴斯克维尔爵士之死，福尔摩斯先
生，这些就是已经公之于众的事实。"
　　"我必须得感谢您啊，"夏洛克·福尔摩斯说，"您
引起了我对这桩颇有意思的案件的注意。我当时也曾从
报纸上看过一些评论，但当时正全力以赴破解梵蒂冈宝
石案那桩小案件，急于想使教皇满意，所以忽略了发生
在英国的几桩很有意思的案件。您说，这则报道包括了

"I must thank you," said Sherlock Holmes, "for calling my attention to a case which certainly presents some features of interest. I had observed some newspaper comment at the time, but I was **exceedingly**[1] **preoccupied**[2] by that little affair of the Vatican **cameos**[3], and in my anxiety to **oblige**[4] the Pope I lost touch with several interesting English cases. This article, you say, contains all the public facts?"

"It does."

"Then let me have the private ones." He leaned back, put his finger-tips together, and assumed his most **impassive**[5] and judicial expression.

"In doing so," said Dr. Mortimer, who had begun to show signs of some strong emotion, "I am telling that which I have not **confided**[6] to anyone. My motive for **withholding**[7] it from the coroner's inquiry is that a man of science shrinks from placing himself in the public position of seeming to indorse a popular superstition. I had the further motive that Baskerville Hall, as the paper says, would certainly remain **untenanted**[8] if anything were done to increase its already rather grim reputation. For both these reasons I thought that I was **justified**[9] in telling rather less than I knew, since no practical good could result from it, but with you there is no reason why I should not be perfectly frank.

"The moor is very **sparsely**[10] inhabited, and those who live near each other are thrown very much together. For this reason I saw a good deal of Sir Charles Baskerville. With the exception of Mr. Frankland, of Lafter Hall, and Mr. Stapleton, the naturalist, there are no other men of education within many miles. Sir Charles was a retiring man, but the chance of his illness brought us together, and a **community**[11] of interests in science kept us so. He had brought back much scientific information from South Africa, and many a charming evening we have spent together discussing the comparative anatomy of the Bushman and the Hottentot.

"Within the last few months it became increasingly plain to me that Sir Charles's nervous system was strained to the breaking point. He had taken this legend which I have read you exceedingly to heart–so much so that, although he would walk in his own grounds, nothing would induce him to go out upon the moor at night. Incredible as it may appear to you, Mr. Holmes, he was honestly convinced that a dreadful fate **overhung**[12] his family, and certainly

所有公之于众的事实是吗？"

"包括了。"

"那就让我知道一些私下里的情况吧。"他向后靠在椅背上，两手的指尖对顶在一起，显露着他那最冷峻漠然和明辨慎思的神情。

"要做到这一点，"莫蒂默医生说着，情绪开始有点激动起来了，"我就要把没有向任何人透露过的情况讲述出来，我之所以向死因调查陪审团也隐瞒下来，那是因为，作为一个从事科学工作的人，不至于让公众觉得，我这样做还有更深层次的原因，那就是，巴斯克维尔庄园本来就名声在外，是个阴郁恐怖的所在，如果再火上浇油，那就会正如报纸上所说的那样，肯定无人敢于入住了。由于上述原因，我认为，不把自己知道的情况全部说出来是明智的，即便全说了也不会有什么实际的益处。不过现在和您在一起，我就没有任何理由藏着掖着了。

"荒原上人烟极为稀少，如果人们相互之间成为邻居的话，那来往就会很密切。因此，我和查尔斯·巴斯克维尔爵士见面的机会很多。方圆数英里之内，除了拉夫特尔庄园的弗兰克兰先生和生物学家斯塔普尔顿先生之外，没有别的什么受过教育的人了。查尔斯爵士是个离群索居的人，但由于他生病，我们才有了见面的机会。还有，对科学的共同兴趣使我们保持联系。他从南非带回了大量的科学资料，我们共度了很多美好的夜晚，共同讨论对布希曼人和霍屯督人的比较解剖学问题。

"最近几个月之内，我越来越清楚地意识到，查尔斯爵士的神经系统已经紧张到快要崩溃的地步了。关于我刚才念给您听的那个传说，他深信不疑。尽管时常自己在庄园里面散步，但每到了夜间，无论如何也不会走出宅邸到荒原上去的。您可能会觉得那个传说难以置信，福尔摩斯先生，但查尔斯爵士却坚信有一种可怕的宿命正笼罩着他的家族。诚然，他从祖辈那里获知的传说确实让人情绪沮丧。他总觉得会有可怕的怪物出现，这种想法阴魂不散，不断困扰着他。他不止一次问我，夜间出诊时是否看到过什么怪异的东

① exceedingly [ik'si:diŋli] ad. 极其，非常；过度地
② preoccupied [pri:'ɔkjupaid] a. 全神贯注的
③ cameo ['kæmiəu] n. 浮雕玉石（宝石或贝壳）
④ oblige [ə'blaidʒ] v. 使感恩，帮…的忙
⑤ impassive [im'pæsiv] a. 冷漠的；无动于衷的
⑥ confide [kən'faid] v. 吐露秘密
⑦ withhold ['wið'həuld] v. 隐瞒
⑧ untenanted ['ʌn'tenəntid] a. 无人租赁的；未被租用的
⑨ justified ['dʒʌstifaid] a. 合乎情理的
⑩ sparse [spɑ:s] a. 稀疏的，不密的
⑪ community [kə'mju:niti] n. 共有，共享
⑫ overhang [,əuvə'hæŋ] v. （危险、邪恶等）逼近；威胁

the records which he was able to give of his ancestors were not encouraging. The idea of some **ghastly**① presence constantly **haunted**② him, and on more than one occasion he has asked me whether I had on my medical journeys at night ever seen any strange creature or heard the **baying**③ of a hound. The latter question he put to me several times, and always with a voice which vibrated with excitement.

"I can well remember driving up to his house in the evening some three weeks before the fatal event. He chanced to be at his hall door. I had descended from my **gig**④ and was standing in front of him, when I saw his eyes fix themselves over my shoulder and stare past me with an expression of the most dreadful horror. I **whisked**⑤ round and had just time to catch a glimpse of something which I took to be a large black calf passing at the head of the drive. So excited and alarmed was he that I was compelled to go down to the spot where the animal had been and look around for it. It was gone, however, and the incident appeared to make the worst impression upon his mind. I stayed with him all the evening, and it was on that occasion, to explain the emotion which he had shown, that he confided to my keeping that narrative which I read to you when first I came. I mention this small episode because it assumes some importance in view of the tragedy which followed, but I was convinced at the time that the matter was entirely **trivial**⑥ and that his excitement had no justification.

"It was at my advice that Sir Charles was about to go to London. His heart was, I knew, affected, and the constant anxiety in which he lived, however **chimerical**⑦ the cause of it might be, was evidently having a serious effect upon his health. I thought that a few months among the distractions of town would send him back a new man. Mr. Stapleton, a mutual friend who was much concerned at his state of health, was of the same opinion. At the last instant came this terrible **catastrophe**⑧.

"On the night of Sir Charles's death Barrymore the butler, who made the discovery, sent Perkins the **groom**⑨ on horseback to me, and as I was sitting up late I was able to reach Baskerville Hall within an hour of the event. I checked and corroborated all the facts which were mentioned at the inquest. I followed the footsteps down the yew alley, I saw the spot at the moor-gate where he

① ghastly ['gɑːstli] *a.* 令人
毛骨悚然的，可怕的，
恐怖的
② haunt [hɔːnt] *v.* 萦绕在…
心中；缠扰
③ bay [bei] *v.* 吠叫

④ gig [gig] *n.* 轻便双轮马
车

⑤ whisk [hwisk] *v.* 迅速移
动

⑥ trivial ['triviəl] *a.* 无足轻
重的

⑦ chimerical [kai'miərikəl]
a. 荒诞的，不可能的

⑧ catastrophe [kə'tæstrəfi] *n.*
灾祸

⑨ groom [gruːm] *n.* 马夫

西，是否听到过猎犬的狂吠。后一个问题他问过我好
几次，每次提出这个问题时，他的声音都会因为情绪
紧张而颤抖。

"我清楚地记得，惨剧发生前的三个礼拜，有一
天傍晚，我坐着马车去他家。他正好伫立在厅堂门
口。我刚从轻便马车上下来，站在他跟前，就看到他
目光越过我的肩膀，牢牢盯着我身后看，充满了极度
的恐惧。我急速转过身去，正好看见了一个体形像大
牛犊似的黑东西消逝在路的尽头。他情绪激动，惶恐
不安，我不得不走到那动物刚滞留过的地方，并在四
周寻找了一番。但是，它已经不见了踪影。这件事情
好像给了他心理上一个非常沉重的打击，我整个夜晚
都陪伴着他。正是在那种情形下，为了解释他所表现
出来的情绪，他托付我保存那封我一开始念给您听的
家书。我之所以提到这个小插曲，是因为它在随后发
生的悲剧中可能发挥了一些作用。但在当晚，我认为
那只是一件微不足道的小事，觉得他惊恐不安是毫无
理由的。

"正是因为有了我的劝告，查尔斯爵士这才打算去
伦敦。我知道，他的心脏已经受到了影响，加上时刻处
在焦虑不安的状态中，不管其原因有多么荒诞不经，但
显然对他的健康已经产生了严重影响。我认为，几个月
的城市生活可能会分散他的注意力，使他恢复健康。我
们共同的朋友——斯塔普尔顿先生非常关心他的健康状
况，完全赞同我的意见。临行前的最后一晚，竟然发生
了可怕的灾祸。

"查尔斯爵士猝亡当晚，总管巴里摩尔发现了情况，
立刻派了马夫珀金斯骑马来找我。因为那天我很晚都没
睡，所以出事后的一个小时内就赶到了巴斯克维尔庄
园。我对调查过程中提到过的所有细节都验证和核实过
了。我顺着紫杉林荫小道往前走，到达了栅门附近的一
处地方，他似乎曾在那儿等待过什么人。我注意到，从
那个地方向前，他的脚印发生了变化。我还发现，除
了巴里摩尔留在松软地面上的脚印外，再没有其他足迹
了。最后，我对遗体进行了仔细检查，遗体在我到达前
没有人动过。查尔斯爵士俯卧倒地，两臂往外伸出，十

seemed to have waited, I remarked the change in the shape of the prints after that point, I noted that there were no other footsteps save those of Barrymore on the soft **gravel**[①], and finally I carefully examined the body, which had not been touched until my arrival. Sir Charles lay on his face, his arms out, his fingers dug into the ground, and his features **convulsed**[②] with some strong emotion to such an extent that I could hardly have **sworn**[③] to his identity. There was certainly no physical injury of any kind. But one false statement was made by Barrymore at the inquest. He said that there were no traces upon the ground round the body. He did not observe any. But I did–some little distance off, but fresh and clear."

"Footprints?"

"Footprints. "

"A man's or a woman's?"

Dr. Mortimer looked strangely at us for an instant, and his voice sank almost to a whisper as he answered:

"Mr. Holmes, they were the footprints of a **gigantic**[④] hound!"

① gravel ['grævəl] n. 碎石；
沙砾

② convulse [kən'vʌls] v. 痉
挛

③ swear [swɛə] v. 肯定地
说，保证

④ gigantic [,dʒai'gæntik] a.
巨大的，庞大的

指插在泥土里，面部因强烈的情绪变化而扭曲，有点面
目全非了，连我都认不出来了。可以肯定，他身上没有
任何的伤痕。但是，调查过程中，巴里摩尔有一点说错
了，他说在遗体附近没有任何痕迹。他没有发现任何情
况，但是，我发现了痕迹——就在不远处，是新留下
的，非常清晰。"

"脚印吗？"

"脚印。"

"男人的还是女人的？"

莫蒂默医生神情怪异地看了看我们，像说悄悄话似
的压低嗓音回答说：

"福尔摩斯先生，是一只巨型猎犬的爪印。"

Chapter 3   The Problem

I confess that at these words a shudder passed through me. There was a thrill in the doctor's voice which showed that he was himself deeply moved by that which he told us. Holmes leaned forward in his excitement and his eyes had the hard, dry **glitter**[①] which shot from them when he was keenly interested.

"You saw this?"

"As clearly as I see you."

"And you said nothing?"

"What was the use?"

"How was it that no one else saw it?"

"The marks were some twenty yards from the body and no one gave them a thought. I don't suppose I should have done so had I not known this legend."

"There are many sheep-dogs on the moor?"

"No doubt, but this was no sheep-dog."

"You say it was large?"

"**Enormous**[②]. "

"But it had not **approached**[③] the body?"

"No."

"What sort of night was it?"

"Damp and **raw**[④]."

"But not actually raining?"

"No."

"What is the alley like?"

第三章　疑案呈现

我承认，听到这句话之后，我浑身感到不寒而栗。医生说话的声音也颤抖着，说明他自己也深受说出来了情况的影响。福尔摩斯身子前倾着，兴奋不已，两眼闪烁着坚定敏锐的光芒，说明他产生了强烈的兴趣。

"您真的看到那个了吗？"

"如同我现在看到您一样，清清楚楚。"

"而您却没有声张，对吧？"

"说出来了能起什么作用呢？"

"怎么就没有别的什么人看见它呢？"

"爪印在离尸体大概有二十码的样子，没有人会注意的。我觉得，如果不知道那个传说，我看我也不会去注意的。"

"荒原上有很多牧羊犬吗？"

"毫无疑问，但那一只不是牧羊犬。"

"您说它体形巨大，对吧？"

"非常大。"

"不过，没有靠近尸体，对吧？"

"对啊。"

"当晚的天气情况如何？"

"潮湿阴冷。"

"但实际上没有下雨，对吧？"

"对啊。"

"那条树篱中间的小道是怎么样的？"

"两边是紫杉构成的树篱，高达十二英尺，紫杉种

① glitter ['glitə] *n.* 闪光

② enormous [i'nɔ:məs] *n.* 巨大的，庞大的
③ approach [ə'prəutʃ] *v.* 靠近，迫近

④ raw [rɔ:] *a.* （天气等）湿冷的；阴凉的

· 037 ·

"There are two lines of old yew **hedge**[①], twelve feet high and **impenetrable**[②]. The walk in the centre is about eight feet across."

"Is there anything between the hedges and the walk?"

"Yes, there is a strip of grass about six feet broad on either side."

"I understand that the yew hedge is penetrated at one point by a gate?"

"Yes, the **wicket-gate**[③] which leads on to the moor."

"Is there any other opening?"

"None."

"So that to reach the yew alley one either has to come down it from the house or else to enter it by the moor-gate?"

"There is an exit through a summer-house at the far end."

"Had Sir Charles reached this?"

"No; he lay about fifty yards from it."

"Now, tell me, Dr. Mortimer–and this is important–the marks which you saw were on the path and not on the grass?"

"No marks could show on the grass."

"Were they on the same side of the path as the moor-gate?"

"Yes; they were on the edge of the path on the same side as the moor-gate."

"You interest me exceedingly. Another point. Was the wicket-gate closed?"

"Closed and **padlocked**[④]."

"How high was it?"

"About four feet high."

"Then anyone could have got over it?"

"Yes."

"And what marks did you see by the wicket-gate?"

"None in particular."

"Good heaven! Did no one examine?"

"Yes, I examined, myself."

"And found nothing?"

"It was all very confused. Sir Charles had evidently stood there for five or ten minutes."

"How do you know that?"

"Because the ash had twice dropped from his cigar."

① hedge [hedʒ] *n.* 树篱

② impenetrable [im'penit rəbl] *a.* 不能通过的

③ wicket-gate 小门；边门

④ padlock ['pædlɔk] *v.* （用挂锁）锁上；把…锁上

植得很密，人不能从树篱缝中通过，中间是一条大概八英尺宽的人行道。"

"在树篱和人行道之间还有什么东西吗？"

"在人行道两旁各有一条绿草带，大约六英尺宽。"

"我认为，那树篱的某处应该有个缺口，用来装栅门的吧？"

"对，就是那道通往荒原的边门。"

"还有别的出口吗？"

"没有。"

"这么说来，到紫杉树篱中间的小道去有两条途径，从宅邸往前走，或者从通向荒原的那道边门，对吧？"

"不对，在另一头的凉亭处还有一个出口。"

"查尔斯爵士走到了那儿了吗？"

"没有，他倒下的地方距离那儿差不多有五十码远。"

"对啦，莫蒂默医生，请您告诉我——这一点非常重要——您看见的脚印是在小道上，而不是在草地上，对吧？"

"草地上看不出有任何脚印。"

"脚印是在那道门所在的小道那一边吗？"

"对，是在边门那一侧的路边上。"

"您激发了我对案件的兴趣。还有一点，当时栅门是关着的吗？"

"是关着的，还上了锁呢。"

"门有多高？"

"大概四英尺高吧。"

"那么，人可以跨过去了？"

"可以。"

"您在边门处看到什么痕迹了吗？"

"没有什么特别的痕迹。"

"天哪！难道就没人检查一下？"

"不，我检查过了，我亲自检查的。"

"什么都没发现？"

"一切都令人感到迷惑不解。但显然，查尔斯爵士在那里站了五到十分钟。"

"这个您是怎么知道的呢？"

"因为他抽的雪茄掉下过两次烟灰。"

"妙极了！他简直就是我们的同行，华生，思路和

"Excellent! This is a colleague, Watson, after our own heart. But the marks?"

"He had left his own marks all over that small patch of gravel. I could **discern**① no others."

Sherlock Holmes struck his hand against his knee with an impatient gesture.

"If I had only been there!" he cried. "It is evidently a case of extraordinary interest, and one which presented **immense**② opportunities to the scientific expert. That gravel page upon which I might have read so much has been long **ere**③ this **smudged**④ by the rain and defaced by the **clogs**⑤ of curious peasants. Oh, Dr. Mortimer, Dr. Mortimer, to think that you should not have called me in! You have indeed much to answer for."

"I could not call you in, Mr. Holmes, without disclosing these facts to the world, and I have already given my reasons for not wishing to do so. Besides, besides ——"

"Why do you hesitate?"

"There is a realm in which the most acute and most experienced of detectives is helpless."

"You mean that the thing is supernatural?"

"I did not positively say so."

"No, but you evidently think it."

"Since the tragedy, Mr. Holmes, there have come to my ears several incidents which are hard to **reconcile with**⑥ the settled order of Nature."

"For example?"

"I find that before the terrible event occurred several people had seen a creature upon the moor which **corresponds with**⑦ this Baskerville demon, and which could not possibly be any animal known to science. They all agreed that it was a huge creature, **luminous**⑧, ghastly, and **spectral**⑨. I have **cross-examined**⑩ these men, one of them a hard-headed countryman, one a **farrier**⑪, and one a moorland farmer, who all tell the same story of this dreadful **apparition**⑫, exactly corresponding to the hell-hound of the legend. I assure you that there is a reign of terror in the district, and that it is a **hardy**⑬ man who will cross the moor at night."

我们的一样。那么脚印呢？"

"他的脚印都出现在那一小片沙砾地面上，我没发现其他人的脚印。"

福尔摩斯的一只手在一条膝盖上打了一下，做出了一个不耐烦的动作。

"如果我当时在场多好啊！"他大声说，"很明显，这是一桩奇特而又很有意思的案件，给科学研究的专家提供了极好机会。我本可以从那片沙砾地面找出很多线索的，但案发距今已经过了一段时间了，那里肯定被雨水冲刷，被好奇农夫们的木鞋踩踏得不成样了。噢！莫蒂默医生，莫蒂默医生，多遗憾啊，您怎么就没想到要叫我呢！您真的难辞其咎啊。"

"我不可能把您找来，福尔摩斯先生，又不向公众公布这些事实。而我为何不愿意这样做，已经陈述自己的理由了。还有，还有——"

"您为何要犹豫呢？"

"有那么一个领域，即便是最最机敏睿智和最最富有经验的侦探也是无能为力的。"

"您的意思是说，事情涉及到超自然现象？"

"我也不能完全肯定是这样的。"

"您是没有完全肯定，不过很明显，您是这样认为的。"

"悲剧发生之后，福尔摩斯先生，我听到了几桩已知的自然规律难以解释的事件。"

"比如说？"

"我发现，悲惨事件发生之前，曾有几个人在荒原上看到过一只跟传说中的巴斯克维尔怪物的特征相吻合的动物，而且该动物肯定不是科学界所已知的兽类。他们异口同声地说那是一只大家伙，会发光，像魔鬼一样可怕。我曾询问过那几个人，一个是头脑聪明的乡下人，一个是马掌铁匠，还有一个是荒原上的佃户。他们三人对那个可怕幽灵的描述是一致的，与传说中那只令人恐惧的猎犬外形完全一样。我明确地告诉您，恐惧笼罩在这片区域，只有英勇无畏的人才敢于夜间穿越荒原。"

"而您，一个受过科学训练的人，竟然会相信那是超自然现象？"

---

① discern [di'sə:n] v. 辨出；识别

② immense [i'mens] a. 极好的

③ ere [ɛə] prep. 在…之前
④ smudge [smʌdʒ] v. 把…弄模糊
⑤ clog [klɔg] n. 木底鞋，木屐

⑥ reconcile with 使与…一致

⑦ correspond with 符合，一致
⑧ luminous ['lju:minəs] a. 发光的；发亮的
⑨ spectral ['spektrəl] a.恶魔的，幽灵的
⑩ cross-examine ['krɔ:sig'zæmin] v. 盘问
⑪ farrier ['færiə] n. 蹄铁匠
⑫ apparition [,æpə'riʃən] n. 幽灵
⑬ hardy ['hɑ:di] a.大胆的，勇敢的

"And you, a trained man of science, believe it to be supernatural?"

"I do not know what to believe."

Holmes shrugged his shoulders.

"I have **hitherto**[1] confined my investigations to this world," said he. "In a modest way I have combated evil, but to take on the Father of Evil himself would, perhaps, be too ambitious a task. Yet you must admit that the footmark is material."

"The original hound was material enough to tug a man's throat out, and yet he was **diabolical**[2] as well."

"I see that you have quite gone over to the supernaturalists. But now, Dr. Mortimer, tell me this. If you hold these views, why have you come to consult me at all? You tell me **in the same breath**[3] that it is useless to investigate Sir Charles's death, and that you desire me to do it."

"I did not say that I desired you to do it."

"Then, how can I assist you?"

"By advising me as to what I should do with Sir Henry Baskerville, who arrives at Waterloo Station"–Dr. Mortimer looked at his watch– "in exactly one hour and a quarter."

"He being the heir?"

"Yes. On the death of Sir Charles we inquired for this young gentleman and found that he had been farming in Canada. From the accounts which have reached us he is an excellent fellow in every way. I speak now not as a medical man but as a **trustee**[4] and executor of Sir Charles's will."

"There is no other **claimant**[5], I presume?"

"None. The only other **kinsman**[6] whom we have been able to trace was Rodger Baskerville, the youngest of three brothers of whom poor Sir Charles was the elder. The second brother, who died young, is the father of this lad Henry. The third, Rodger, was the black sheep of the family. He came of the old masterful Baskerville strain and was the very image, they tell me, of the family picture of old Hugo. He made England too hot to hold him, fled to Central America, and died there in 1876 of yellow fever. Henry is the last of the Baskervilles. In one hour and five minutes I meet him at Waterloo Station. I have had a **wire**[7] that he arrived at Southampton this morning. Now, Mr.

① hitherto [ˌhiðə'tuː] *ad.* 迄今，至今

② diabolical ['daiə'bɔlikəl] *a.* 残忍的，凶暴的

③ in the same breath 同时

④ trustee [ˌtrʌs'tiː] *n.* （财产）受托人，受托管理人

⑤ claimant ['kleimənt] *n.* 要求权利的人

⑥ kinsman ['kinzmən] *n.* 男性家属（或亲属）

⑦ wire ['waiə] *n.* 电报

"我都不知道该相信什么了。"

福尔摩斯耸了耸肩膀。

"迄今为止，我把自己的侦案工作范围限制在人世间，"他说，"尽着自己的一份绵力，同邪恶势力作斗争，但是，要同罪恶之神本人较量，任务过于宏大，我胜任不了。不过，您得承认，脚印确实真实存在。"

"那只怪异的猎犬的确真实存在，它撕碎了人的喉咙，但它也是妖魔的化身。"

"我明白了，您现在站在超自然论者的立场上了。但是，莫蒂默医生，请您现在告诉我，既然您坚持这样的看法，那您为什么还来找我商量呢？您对我说调查查尔斯爵士之死是没有一点儿用处的，但同时您又希望我去调查。"

"我并没说过希望您去调查啊。"

"那我该如何帮助您呢？"

"给我提点建议，我该如何同亨利·巴斯克维尔爵士打交道，他很快就要到达滑铁卢车站了，"——莫蒂默医生看了看自己的怀表——"正好还差一个小时零一刻钟。"

"他就是那位遗产继承人吗？"

"对啊，查尔斯爵士亡故后，我们查找了这位年轻绅士，发现他一直在加拿大经营农场。根据我们了解到的情况，这位先生无论在哪个方面都非常优秀。我不仅仅是以一位医生，现在还是以查尔斯爵士遗嘱的受托人和执行人的身份同您说话。"

"我估计，没有别的遗产继承申请者吧？"

"没有。我们所知道的查尔斯爵士的亲属就只有罗杰·巴斯克维尔一人。亡故的查尔斯爵士三兄弟，他本人是老大，罗杰最小，老二亨利年轻时去世了，留下了这个叫亨利的儿子。最小的罗杰是家族的害群之马。他遗传到了专横的老巴斯克维尔的品性，我听说，他和家族中老雨果的画像简直一模一样。他在英格兰折腾得待不下去了，便逃到了中美洲，1876年得黄热病暴死在那儿了。亨利是巴斯克维尔家族的最后一个子嗣，再过一小时零五分钟，我就会在滑铁卢车站见到他。我接到一封电报，说他今天早晨已经到了南安普敦。福尔摩斯先生，您会给我提些什么建议，我该如何应对他呢？"

Holmes, what would you advise me to do with him?"

"Why should he not go to the home of his fathers?"

"It seems natural, does it not? And yet, consider that every Baskerville who goes there meets with an evil fate. I feel sure that if Sir Charles could have spoken with me before his death he would have warned me against bringing this, the last of the old race, and the heir to great wealth, to that **deadly**① place. And yet it cannot be denied that the prosperity of the whole poor, **bleak**② countryside depends upon his presence. All the good work which has been done by Sir Charles will crash to the ground if there is no tenant of the Hall. I fear lest I should be **swayed**③ too much by my own obvious interest in the matter, and that is why I bring the case before you and ask for your advice."

Holmes considered for a little time.

"Put into plain words, the matter is this," said he. "In your opinion there is a diabolical **agency**④ which makes Dartmoor an unsafe **abode**⑤ for a Baskerville—that is your opinion?"

"At least I might **go the length of**⑥ saying that there is some evidence that this may be so."

"Exactly. But surely, if your supernatural theory be correct, it could work the young man evil in London as easily as in Devonshire. A devil with merely local powers like a **parish**⑦ **vestry**⑧ would be too inconceivable a thing."

"You put the matter more **flippantly**⑨, Mr. Holmes, than you would probably do if you were brought into personal contact with these things. Your advice, then, as I understand it, is that the young man will be as safe in Devonshire as in London. He comes in fifty minutes. What would you recommend?"

"I recommend, sir, that you take a cab, call off your spaniel who is scratching at my front door, and proceed to Waterloo to meet Sir Henry Baskerville."

"And then?"

"And then you will say nothing to him at all until I have made up my mind about the matter."

"How long will it take you to make up your mind?"

"Twenty-four hours. At ten o'clock to-morrow, Dr. Mortimer, I will be

"为什么不让他回到他祖先世代都居住的宅邸里去呢？"

"似乎理应如此，难道不是吗？不过，我们也要掂量一下，因为每个到那里去的巴斯克维尔家族的人都遭受了可怕的厄运。我敢肯定，如果查尔斯爵士亡故前还能够和我说话，他一定会提醒我，不要把亨利——古老家族的最后一根独苗，还是巨额财富的继承者，带到那个要命的地方去。但不可否认，那个贫困而荒凉的乡区的繁荣昌盛都有赖于他的到来。如果庄园没主人居住，查尔斯爵士所做过的一切善行就会烟消云散。我担心自己会对利益问题考虑得过多，从而让自己对此事的看法有失偏颇。正因为如此，我才把事情的来龙去脉全都告诉您，并征求您的意见。"

福尔摩斯思忖了片刻。

"简单说起来吧，事情是这么回事，"他说，"按照您的看法，存在着一种魔鬼般邪恶的力量，令达特穆尔荒原成了个巴斯克维尔家族无法安居的所在——这就是您的看法，对吧？"

"我至少可以说，有迹象表明，这种可能性还是存在的。"

"一点没错，但是，毫无疑问，如果您那套关于超自然力量的说法站得住脚的话，那么它要在伦敦伤害那个年轻人和在德文郡伤害他一样轻而易举。如果说魔鬼像是教区委员会一样，其权力只是限制在当地的范围内，那简直就是不可想象的事情啊。"

"您把这件事看得太过轻巧了，福尔摩斯先生。如果您亲历了那件事情，您就不会这样认为了。我是这样理解您的意见的：那个年轻人在德文郡和在伦敦是同样安全的。五十分钟后他就到了，您还有什么建议吗？"

"我建议，先生，您叫一辆马车，带上您的那条猎犬——它正在抓挠我们家前门呢，速去滑铁卢车站接亨利·巴斯克维尔爵士。"

"然后呢？"

"然后，不要对他说任何情况，直到我对事情有了判断再说。"

"您要多长时间才能想好呢？"

"二十四小时吧，莫蒂默医生，明天上午十点，您

---

① deadly ['dedli] a. 致命的

② bleak [bli:k] a. 荒凉的，光秃秃的

③ sway [swei] v. 影响

④ agency ['eidʒənsi] n. 力量
⑤ abode [ə'bəud] n. 住处，寓所

⑥ go the length of 不惜；甚至于

⑦ parish ['pæriʃ] n. 教区
⑧ vestry ['vestri] n. 教区委员会
⑨ flippant ['flipənt] a. 轻率的

much obliged to you if you will call upon me here, and it will be of help to me in my plans for the future if you will bring Sir Henry Baskerville with you."

"I will do so, Mr. Holmes." He scribbled the appointment on his shirt-cuff and hurried off in his strange, peering, absent-minded fashion. Holmes stopped him at the head of the stair.

"Only one more question, Dr. Mortimer. You say that before Sir Charles Baskerville's death several people saw this apparition upon the moor?"

"Three people did."

"Did any see it after?"

"I have not heard of any."

"Thank you. Good-morning."

Holmes returned to his seat with that quiet look of inward satisfaction which meant that he had a **congenial**[①] task before him.

"Going out, Watson?"

"Unless I can help you."

"No, my dear fellow, it is at the hour of action that I turn to you for aid. But this is splendid, really unique from some points of view. When you pass Bradley's, would you ask him to send up a pound of the strongest **shag**[②] tobacco? Thank you. It would be as well if you could make it convenient not to return before evening. Then I should be very glad to compare impressions as to this most interesting problem which has been submitted to us this morning."

I knew that **seclusion**[③] and solitude were very necessary for my friend in those hours of intense mental concentration during which he weighed every particle of evidence, constructed **alternative**[④] theories, balanced one against the other, and made up his mind as to which points were **essential**[⑤] and which **immaterial**[⑥]. I therefore spent the day at my club and did not return to Baker Street until evening. It was nearly nine o'clock when I found myself in the sitting-room once more.

My first impression as I opened the door was that a fire had broken out, for the room was so filled with smoke that the light of the lamp upon the table was blurred by it. As I entered, however, my fears were set at rest, for it was the **acrid**[⑦] fumes of strong coarse tobacco which took me by the throat and set me coughing. Through the haze I had a vague vision of Holmes in his dressing-

如果能来这儿找我，我会非常感激的。如果领着亨利·巴斯克维尔爵士一道来，那将更加有助于我做以后的各种计划。"

"我一定做到，福尔摩斯先生。"他把约定的时间写在衬衫的袖口上，然后匆匆地离去，其时，表情怪异，目光凝滞，一副心不在焉的样子。他刚走到楼梯口，福尔摩斯又把他叫住了。

"还有最后一个问题，莫蒂默医生，您说查尔斯·巴斯克维尔爵士亡故之前，有几个人曾在荒原上看见过那只怪兽，对吧？"

"三个人看见过。"

"出事后，还有人看见过吗？"

"我没听说过。"

"谢谢您，再见。"

福尔摩斯回到座位上，表情安宁，内心满足，说明他遇上感兴趣的案件了。

"到外面去走走怎么样，华生？"

"除非待在这儿能够帮上你的忙。"

"不，亲爱的朋友，到了要采取行动的时候，我才会需要你的协助。这件事情很奇妙，从某种程度上来说，确实是独一无二的。华生，你路过布莱德雷店铺时，请叫他们给我送一磅浓烈的板烟过来好吗？先谢谢你了。如果方便，你黄昏之前不回来，那简直就太好了。到时，我会很乐意表达看法，谈谈我们今天上午接到的这桩很有意思的案件。"

我知道，在我朋友精神高度集中地思考问题时，闭门独处对他来说非常重要。这样，他就能权衡点滴的证据，做出不同的假设，并将其进行对比以确定哪些是重点，哪些是经不住推敲的。因此，我整个白天都待在俱乐部里，直到傍晚才回贝克大街。接近九点钟时，我再次走进了休息室。

刚一打开门，我的第一反应是屋里着火了，因为满房间都是浓烟，连桌子上台灯的灯光都变得模糊不清了。不过，我走进房内后，心就放下了，因为呛进我喉咙，弄得我咳嗽的只不过是浓烈的粗板烟的烟雾而已。透过烟雾，我隐隐约约看见福尔摩斯穿着晨衣正蜷卧在

① congenial [kən'dʒi:njəl] a. 适意的，相宜的

② shag [ʃæg] n. 粗烟丝，劣质烟丝

③ seclusion [si'klu:ʒən] n. 隔离，隔绝；孤立

④ alternative [ɔ:l'tə:nətiv] a. 两者（或两者以上）择一的

⑤ essential [i'senʃəl] a. 很重要的

⑥ immaterial [,imə'tiəriəl] a. 无关紧要的；不重要的

⑦ acrid ['ækrid] a. （味道或气味等）辛辣的；刺激的

gown **coiled**① up in an armchair with his black clay pipe between his lips. Several rolls of paper lay around him.

"Caught cold, Watson?" said he.

"No, it's this poisonous atmosphere."

"I suppose it is pretty thick, now that you mention it."

"Thick! It is intolerable."

"Open the window, then! You have been at your club all day, I perceive."

"My dear Holmes!"

"Am I right?"

"Certainly, but how ––?"

He laughed at my **bewildered**② expression.

"There is a delightful freshness about you, Watson, which makes it a pleasure to exercise any small powers which I possess at your expense. A gentleman goes forth on a showery and **miry**③ day. He returns **immaculate**④ in the evening with the **gloss**⑤ still on his hat and his boots. He has been a fixture therefore all day. He is not a man with intimate friends. Where, then, could he have been? Is it not obvious?"

"Well, it is rather obvious."

"The world is full of obvious things which nobody by any chance ever observes. Where do you think that I have been?"

"A fixture also."

"On the contrary, I have been to Devonshire."

"In spirit?"

"Exactly. My body has remained in this armchair and has, I regret to observe, **consumed**⑥ in my absence two large pots of coffee and an incredible amount of tobacco. After you left I sent down to Stamford's for the Ordnance map of this portion of the moor, and my spirit has **hovered**⑦ over it all day. I flatter myself that I could find my way about."

"A large-scale map, I presume?"

"Very large." He unrolled one section and held it over his knee. "Here you have the particular district which concerns us. That is Baskerville Hall in the middle."

"With a wood round it?"

① coil [kɔil] v. 盘成圈

② bewildered [bi'wildəd] a. 困惑的；不知所措的

③ miry ['maiəri] a. 泥泞的
④ immaculate [i'mækjulət] a. 无污点的
⑤ gloss [glɔs] n.（表面的）光泽，色彩

⑥ consume [kən'sjuːm] v. 耗尽；用掉

⑦ hover ['hɔvə] v. 盘旋，翱翔

安乐椅里，嘴里叼着黑色的陶制烟斗，周围放着好几卷卷烟纸。

"感冒啦，华生？"他问。

"没有，都是这里的毒气闹的。"

"你都这样说，那一定是浓得够可以的了。"

"很浓啊！简直令人受不了。"

"那就把窗户打开吧！我猜想，你是在俱乐部待了一整天吧。"

"亲爱的福尔摩斯！"

"我猜对了吧？"

"非常正确，不过你是怎么——"

他看到我一脸疑惑，笑了起来。

"你全身上下都透着轻松愉快，华生，我要要要小把戏拿你开开心了。有位绅士在泥泞的雨天出了门，晚上回家时，身上却干干净净的，帽子，鞋子还依旧发亮。那他肯定是一整天呆坐着没动。他身边又没什么亲朋好友。那可能会待在什么地方呢？这不是明摆着的吗？"

"是啊，是很明显。"

"这世上有很多明摆着的事情，人们却看不见。你觉得我今天待在什么地方？"

"你也是一整天坐着没动。"

"恰恰相反，我去了德文郡。"

"是你的'灵魂'去了吧？"

"一点不错。我的身子一直坐在这张安乐椅里，遗憾的是，它趁我的'灵魂'不在，竟喝掉了两大壶咖啡，抽掉了多得令人难以置信的烟卷。你出门后，我派人去斯坦福德的店铺买来了一幅绘有荒原上那一片区域的全国地形图，我的'灵魂'便在地图上方遨游了一整天。我很满意，对那个地区的地形已经了如指掌了。"

"我估计，是一幅大比例尺的地图吧？"

"比例尺很大啊，"他打开地图的一个角，然后把它放在膝盖上，"这一片就是我们非常关注的地区，中间部分就是巴斯克维尔庄园。"

"四周是一片树林吗？"

"一点不错，我想象得到，紫杉树篱林荫小道虽然

"Exactly. I fancy the yew alley, though not marked under that name, must stretch along this line, with the moor, as you perceive, upon the right of it. This small clump of buildings here is the hamlet of Grimpen, where our friend Dr. Mortimer has his headquarters. Within a **radius**[①] of five miles there are, as you see, only a very few scattered dwellings. Here is Lafter Hall, which was mentioned in the narrative. There is a house indicated here which may be the residence of the naturalist–Stapleton, if I remember right, was his name. Here are two moorland farmhouses, High Tor and Foulmire. Then fourteen miles away the great convict prison of Princetown. Between and around these scattered points extends the desolate, lifeless moor. This, then, is the stage upon which tragedy has been played, and upon which we may help to play it again."

"It must be a wild place."

"Yes, the setting is a worthy one. If the devil did desire to have a hand in the affairs of men --"

"Then you are yourself **inclining**[②] to the supernatural explanation."

"The devil's agents may be of flesh and blood, may they not? There are two questions waiting for us **at the outset**[③]. The one is whether any crime has been committed at all; the second is, what is the crime and how was it committed? Of course, if Dr. Mortimer's **surmise**[④] should be correct, and we are dealing with forces outside the ordinary laws of Nature, there is an end of our investigation. But we are bound to exhaust all other hypotheses before falling back upon this one. I think we'll shut that window again, if you don't mind. It is a singular thing, but I find that a concentrated atmosphere helps a concentration of thought. I have not pushed it to the **length**[⑤] of getting into a box to think, but that is the logical outcome of my convictions. Have you turned the case over in your mind?"

"Yes, I have thought a good deal of it in the course of the day."

"What do you make of it?"

"It is very bewildering."

"It has certainly a character of its own. There are points of **distinction**[⑥] about it. That change in the footprints, for example. What do you make of that?"

"Mortimer said that the man had walked on tiptoe down that portion of the alley."

没有标出名称，但它一定是沿着这条线往下延伸的，你看得出，小道的右侧就是荒原。这一片房舍就是格林彭村。我们的朋友莫蒂默医生的住宅就在那里。你也看到了，在这方圆五英里的区域内，只有寥寥落落的几幢住房。这里就是医生叙述时提到过的拉夫特尔庄园，上面标明的房屋可能就是那位生物学家的住宅，如果我没记错的话，他名叫斯塔普尔顿。这里是两幢荒原的农舍：海托尔和福尔米尔。然后，十四英里开外的地方就是王子镇的大监狱。在这些零散的屋舍之间，以及四周，是一片广袤的凄凉萧疏、毫无声息的荒原，也就是悲剧曾经上演的舞台。我们要试图还原悲剧上演的过程。"

"那一定是一片蛮荒之地。"

"是啊，这个背景很理想。如果魔鬼真想要插手人间事务的话——"

"这么说来，你自己也开始认同超自然因素的说法啦。"

"魔鬼的代言人可能就是血肉之躯，难道没有这种可能吗？我们从一开始就面临着这么两个问题：第一，这其中是否真的存在犯罪行为？第二，是什么性质的犯罪，如何实施的犯罪？当然啦，如果莫蒂默医生的猜测正确，我们就要和自然规律之外的非同寻常的势力打交道了，那我们的调查就只能到此为止。但是，我们一定要在全部假设都被推翻之后，才可以再回到这条思路上来。你如果不介意的话，我想把窗户重新关闭起来。这可真是件不可思议的事情，但我发现，浓稠的空气有助于我集中思想。迄今为止，我虽说还没有到一定要钻进盒子里面去才能思考问题的地步，但是，我相信，照此下去，迟早会到那一步的。你今天仔细想过本案的事情了吗？"

"想过了，白天一直想来着。"

"有什么想法了吗？"

"很令人迷惑不解。"

"本案确实很独特，有几个与众不同的地方。比如说，边门附近的脚印的变化。你是怎么看的呢？"

"莫蒂默医生说过，从边门处开始，那人就是用足尖走路的。"

① radius ['reidiəs] *n.* 半径

② incline [in'klain] *v.* 倾向于；赞同

③ at the outset 开始；起初

④ surmise ['sə:maiz] *n.* 猜测

⑤ length [leŋθ] *n.* 程度，极端

⑥ distinction [dis'tiŋkʃən] *n.* 特征；特别

"He only repeated what some fool had said at the inquest. Why should a man walk on tiptoe down the alley?"

"What then?"

"He was running, Watson-running desperately, running for his life, running until he burst his heart and fell dead upon his face."

"Running from what?"

"There lies our problem. There are indications that the man was **crazed**[①] with fear before ever he began to run."

"How can you say that?"

"I am presuming that the cause of his fears came to him across the moor. If that were so, and it seems most probable, only a man who had lost his wits would have run *from* the house instead of towards it. If the gipsy's evidence may be taken as true, he ran with cries for help in the direction where help was least likely to be. Then, again, whom was he waiting for that night, and why was he waiting for him in the yew alley rather than in his own house?"

"You think that he was waiting for someone?"

"The man was elderly and **infirm**[②]. We can understand his taking an evening stroll, but the ground was damp and the night **inclement**[③]. Is it natural that he should stand for five or ten minutes, as Dr. Mortimer, with more practical sense than I should have **given** him **credit for**[④], deduced from the cigar ash?"

"But he went out every evening."

"I think it unlikely that he waited at the moor-gate every evening. On the contrary, the evidence is that he avoided the moor. That night he waited there. It was the night before he made his departure for London. The thing takes shape, Watson. It becomes coherent. Might I ask you to hand me my violin, and we will postpone all further thought upon this business until we have had the advantage of meeting Dr. Mortimer and Sir Henry Baskerville in the morning."

"他只不过是把一个傻瓜在对死因进行调查时说过的话重复了一遍而已。哪个人会在那条小道上踮着脚走路呢？"

"那是怎么回事呢？"

"他是在奔跑，华生——拼着命奔跑，为逃命而奔跑，一直跑到心脏爆裂，扑倒在地。"

"那么跑着，要逃离什么呢？"

"这就是我们面临的问题。有迹象表明，他在开始奔跑之前已经被吓得失去理智了。"

"你是怎么知道的？"

"我推测，让他受到惊吓的那个东西是从荒原那边过来的。如果情况如此，我们就很有把握断定，只有失去理智的人才会朝着离家相反的方向跑，而不是朝着家里跑。如果吉卜赛人的证词真实可信，那他一定是边跑边高喊着救命，但他跑的方向却是最不可能获得援救的地方。此外，那天傍晚他在等谁呢？他为何不在自己家里等，而偏偏跑到紫杉树篱小道边等呢？"

"你认为他是在等待某个人吗？"

"死者上了年纪，身体虚弱，傍晚出去散散步，这我们是可以理解的。出事当晚地面潮湿，室外寒冷，但莫蒂默医生——他的智慧远远超出了我们对他的估计——根据地上的雪茄烟灰得出他在那里站了五到十分钟，这正常吗？"

"但是，他每天傍晚都要外出散步的。"

"我认为，他不大可能每天傍晚都会在通向荒原的边门处伫立等待。恰恰相反，有证据表明，他竭力要避开荒原。但那天晚上他却在荒原边上等人，而那晚又恰好是他动身去伦敦的前夕。华生，案件的始末已经初步成形，前后已经贯通了。请帮我把小提琴拿过来，这件事情我们不要再考虑了，等到明天早上，我们同莫蒂默医生和亨利·巴斯克维尔爵士见面后再看吧！"

---

① crazed [kreizd] *a.* 发狂的，疯狂的

② infirm [in'fə:m] *a.* （尤指因年迈而）虚弱的，体弱的，衰弱的

③ inclement [in'klemənt] *a.* 严寒的；狂风暴雨的

④ give sb credit for 为…而称赞某人；相信某人具有

Chapter 4　Sir Henry Baskerville

Our breakfast table was cleared early, and Holmes waited in his dressing-gown for the promised interview. Our clients were punctual to their appointment, for the clock had just struck ten when Dr. Mortimer was shown up, followed by the young **baronet**①. The latter was a small, alert, dark-eyed man about thirty years of age, very **sturdily**② built, with thick black eyebrows and a strong, **pugnacious**③ face. He wore a ruddy-tinted tweed suit and had the weather-beaten appearance of one who has spent most of his time in the open air, and yet there was something in his steady eye and the quiet assurance of his bearing which indicated the gentleman.

"This is Sir Henry Baskerville," said Dr. Mortimer.

"Why, yes," said he, "and the strange thing is, Mr. Sherlock Holmes, that if my friend here had not proposed coming round to you this morning I should have come **on my own account**④. I understand that you think out little puzzles, and I've had one this morning which wants more thinking out than I am able to give it."

"Pray take a seat, Sir Henry. Do I understand you to say that you have yourself had some remarkable experience since you arrived in London?"

"Nothing of much importance, Mr. Holmes. Only a joke, as like as not. It was this letter, if you can call it a letter, which reached me this morning."

He laid an envelope upon the table, and we all bent over it. It was of common quality, grayish in colour. The address, "Sir Henry Baskerville, Northumberland Hotel," was printed in rough characters; the post-mark "Charing

第四章　亨利·巴斯克维尔爵士

我们用过早餐后，餐桌早早地就收拾好了。福尔摩斯穿着晨衣，等待约好的来客。客人很准时，时钟刚敲响十点，莫蒂默医生便出现了，身后跟着那位年轻的从男爵。从男爵身材矮小，神态机警，黑色眼睛，三十岁的样子，身板很是结实，眉毛又浓又黑，面容显得坚毅强悍。他身穿红色粗花呢衣裤，从外表看，是一个久经风霜、在户外活动的时间居多的人。但同时，他眼神沉稳，举止安详，充满自信，一派绅士风度。

“这位是亨利·巴斯克维尔爵士。”莫蒂默医生说。

“啊，是的，”亨利爵士说，“事情蹊跷的是，福尔摩斯先生，即便我的这位朋友今天早上没有建议我来这里拜访您，我自己也会来的。我听说您是一个善解谜团的人。我今天早上就遇到了一个谜团，自己无法解开，只有求您帮助了。”

“请坐，亨利爵士，您是说，您到伦敦后遇到了不可思议的情况，对吧？”

“没什么大不了的情况，福尔摩斯先生。我觉得，可能是有人在跟我闹着玩吧。如果您能称之为信的话，我今天早上收到了这封信。”

他把信封放在桌上，我们都弓着身子看。信封的质地很普通，呈暗灰色。地址栏上用潦草的字迹写着“诺森伯兰旅馆，亨利·巴斯克维尔爵士”，邮戳盖的是“查令十字”，邮寄时间是头一天傍晚。

① baronet ['bærənit] *n.* 准男爵（低于男爵的爵位，被称为“Sir”）
② sturdy ['stə:di] *a.* 强壮的，结实的
③ pugnacious [pʌg'neiʃəs] *a.* 好斗的，好战的；爱吵架的
④ on one's own account 为自身利益

Cross," and the date of posting the **preceding**[1] evening.

"Who knew that you were going to the Northumberland Hotel?" asked Holmes, glancing keenly across at our visitor.

"No one could have known. We only decided after I met Dr. Mortimer."

"But Dr. Mortimer was no doubt already stopping there?"

"No, I had been staying with a friend," said the doctor. "There was no possible **indication**[2] that we intended to go to this hotel."

"Hum! Someone seems to be very deeply interested in your movements." Out of the envelope he took a half-sheet of **foolscap**[3] paper folded into four. This he opened and spread flat upon the table. Across the middle of it a single sentence had been formed by the **expedient**[4] of **pasting**[5] printed words upon it. It ran:

As you value your life or your reason keep away from the moor.

The word "moor" only was printed in ink.

"Now," said Sir Henry Baskerville, "perhaps you will tell me, Mr. Holmes, what **in thunder**[6] is the meaning of that, and who it is that takes so much interest in my affairs?"

"What do you make of it, Dr. Mortimer? You must allow that there is nothing supernatural about this, at any rate?"

"No, sir, but it might very well come from someone who was convinced that the business is supernatural."

"What business?" asked Sir Henry sharply. "It seems to me that all you gentlemen know a great deal more than I do about my own affairs."

"You shall share our knowledge before you leave this room, Sir Henry. I promise you that," said Sherlock Holmes. "We will confine ourselves for the present with your permission to this very interesting document, which must have been put together and posted yesterday evening. Have you yesterday's *Times*, Watson?"

"It is here in the corner."

"Might I trouble you for it—the inside page, please, with the leading articles?" He glanced swiftly over it, running his eyes up and down the columns. "Capital article this on free trade. Permit me to give you an **extract**[7] from it.

① preceding [priˈsiːdiŋ] *a.* 在前的，在先的

② indication [ˌindiˈkeiʃən] *n.* 暗示，预示

③ foolscap [ˈfuːlˌskæp] *n.* 大裁（不同尺寸的书写纸张，尤指美国为13×16英寸的纸张）

④ expedient [ikˈspiːdiənt] *n.* 应急的手段（或办法）

⑤ paste [ˈpeist] *v.* 用糨糊粘贴

⑥ in thunder　到底，究竟

⑦ extract [ikˈstrækt] *n.* 摘录

"有谁知道您打算住在诺森伯兰旅馆吗？"福尔摩斯一边问道，一边用锐利的目光打量着我们这位来客。

"不可能会有人知道。这是我见到莫蒂默医生之后，我们一同决定的。"

"但是，莫蒂默医生无疑已经下榻在那儿了吧？"

"没有，我之前同一个朋友住在一起的，"医生解释说，"我们根本没表示过要去那家旅馆住的意思。"

"哼！这样看来，有人对您的一举一动很感兴趣啊。"福尔摩斯说着，一边从信封里抽出了半张折成四折的大裁纸，把它打开后平铺在桌面上。信笺的中间位置是用剪下来的铅字拼凑贴成的一句话："如果您珍惜自己的生命，或是您还有理性，那就请远离荒原。"

只有"荒原"这个词是用墨水写的。

"对啦，"亨利·巴斯克维尔爵士说，"您或许可以告诉我，福尔摩斯先生，这句话到底是什么意思，谁又会对我的事情如此上心呢？"

"莫蒂默医生，您是怎么看这件事情的呢？不管怎么说，您必须得认可，这其中并不存在着什么超自然的因素，对吧？"

"对啊，先生，不过，写信的人很可能相信，这事情超自然。"

"什么事情？"亨利·巴斯克维尔爵士问，显得很急切，"我感觉，关于我自己的事情，你们几位先生比我知道的还要多呢。"

"亨利爵士，您离开这个房间前，我会把我们知道的事情全部告诉您，我向您保证。"福尔摩斯说，"眼下，请您允许我们把注意力全部集中在这封非常有趣的信件上。它应该是昨晚拼贴好寄出的。华生，你有昨天的《泰晤士报》吗？"

"放在那边角落里呢。"

"麻烦你去拿一下——请翻到里面一个版面，有大标题的，好吗？"他眼睛从上到下，把内容快速浏览了一遍，"头篇文章是谈自由贸易的。请允许我选一段念给大家听。

您或许会被花言巧语哄骗，从而相信保护性关税将

"You may be **cajoled**① into imagining that your own special trade or your own industry will be encouraged by a protective **tariff**②, but it stands to reason that such legislation must in the long run keep away wealth from the country, diminish the value of our imports, and lower the general conditions of life in this island.

"What do you think of that, Watson?" cried Holmes in high **glee**③, rubbing his hands together with satisfaction. "Don't you think that is an admirable sentiment?"

Dr. Mortimer looked at Holmes with an air of professional interest, and Sir Henry Baskerville turned a pair of puzzled dark eyes upon me.

"I don't know much about the tariff and things of that kind," said he, "but it seems to me we've got a bit **off the trail**④ so far as that note is concerned."

"On the contrary, I think we are particularly **hot**⑤ upon the trail, Sir Henry. Watson here knows more about my methods than you do, but I fear that even he has not quite grasped the significance of this sentence."

"No, I confess that I see no connection."

"And yet, my dear Watson, there is so very close a connection that the one is extracted out of the other.'You,' 'your,' 'your,' 'life,' 'reason,' 'value,' 'keep away,' 'from the.' Don't you see now **whence**⑥ these words have been taken?"

"By thunder, you're right! Well, if that isn't smart!" cried Sir Henry.

"If any possible doubt remained it is settled by the fact that 'keep away' and 'from the' are cut out in one piece."

"Well, now—so it is!"

"Really, Mr. Holmes, this exceeds anything which I could have imagined," said Dr. Mortimer, gazing at my friend in amazement. "I could understand anyone saying that the words were from a newspaper; but that you should name which, and add that it came from the leading article, is really one of the most remarkable things which I have ever known. How did you do it?"

"I presume, Doctor, that you could tell the skull of a negro from that of an **Esquimau**⑦?"

"Most certainly."

"But how?"

① cajole [kə'dʒəul] v. 劝诱；
哄骗
② tariff ['tærif] n. 关税

③ glee ['gli:] n. 欢乐，高兴

④ off the trail 迷失方向
⑤ hot [hɔt] a. 紧跟的；接近
的

⑥ whence [hwens] ad. 从何
处

⑦ Esquimaux ['eskiməu(z)]
n. 爱斯基摩人

给您自己的特殊贸易或者特殊产业带来强心剂。但理智地分析一下便可知道：从长远来看，此项立法将会导致财富远离本国，出口总值锐减，从而降低岛国民众的总体生活水平。

"你怎么看这一段话，华生？"福尔摩斯大声说，他兴致勃勃，满意地搓着双手，"你难道不觉得这种态度令人钦佩吗？"

莫蒂默医生以其职业的敏感性审视福尔摩斯，而亨利·巴斯克维尔爵士的那双茫然的黑眼睛却盯着我看。

"我对税收之类的事情一窍不通。不过，我觉得，我们离纸条涉及的问题相距甚远啊。"

"恰恰相反，亨利爵士，我觉得，我们正好找到了他们之间的关联。华生比您更加了解我看问题的方法，不过，现在恐怕连他也看不到这段文字的重要性。"

"对啊，实话实说，我看不出存在什么关系。"

"不过啊，亲爱的华生，关系密切得很呢，信上的文字都是从这一段话里摘剪下来的。'您'，'您的'，'您的'，'生命'，'理性'，'珍视'，'远离'，'离'，你还看不出这些词都是从这里面剪下来的吗？"

"天啊，您还真说对了！啊，真高明啊！"亨利爵士大声说。

"如果还有什么疑惑的话，看看这个事实，'远离'和'离'这几个字是从同一个地方剪下来的，那就足以打消疑虑了。"

"是啊，可不是嘛——确实如此啊！"

"说真格的，福尔摩斯先生，这超乎了我的想象啊，"莫蒂默医生说，惊诧不已，眼睛盯着我的朋友看，"如果有人说这封信上的字都是从报纸上剪下来的，我还能理解。但是，您却能直接说出是哪份报纸，还附带说明是从头篇文章里剪下来的，真是神奇了，这样的本事我连听都没听说过呢。您是怎么做到的呢？"

"我猜想，医生，您一定能够把黑人的颅骨和爱斯基摩人的区别开来，对吧？"

"Because that is my special hobby. The differences are obvious. The supra-orbital crest, the facial angle, the **maxillary**[①] curve, the --"

"But this is my special hobby, and the differences are equally obvious. There is as much difference to my eyes between the leaded bourgeois type of a *Times* article and the slovenly print of an evening half-penny paper as there could be between your negro and your Esquimau. The detection of types is one of the most elementary branches of knowledge to the special expert in crime, though I confess that once when I was very young I confused the *Leeds Mercury* with the *Western Morning News*. But a *Times* leader is entirely **distinctive**[②], and these words could have been taken from nothing else. As it was done yesterday the strong probability was that we should find the words in yesterday's issue."

"So far as I can follow you, then, Mr. Holmes," said Sir Henry Baskerville, "someone cut out this message with a scissors --"

"Nail-scissors," said Holmes. "You can see that it was a very short-bladed scissors, since the cutter had to take two snips over'keep away.'"

"That is so. Someone, then, cut out the message with a pair of short-bladed scissors, pasted it with paste --"

"Gum," said Holmes.

"With gum on to the paper. But I want to know why the word 'moor' should have been written?"

"Because he could not find it in print. The other words were all simple and might be found in any issue, but 'moor' would be less common."

"Why, of course, that would explain it. Have you read anything else in this message, Mr. Holmes?"

"There are one or two indications, and yet the utmost pains have been taken to remove all clues. The address, you observe is printed in rough characters. But the *Times* is a paper which is seldom found in any hands but those of the highly educated. We may take it, therefore, that the letter was composed by an educated man who wished to pose as an uneducated one, and his effort to conceal his own writing suggests that that writing might be known, or come to be known, by you. Again, you will observe that the words are not gummed on in an accurate line, but that some are much higher than others. 'Life,' for example,

① maxillary ['mæksiləri] *a.*
【解剖学】上颌的；上
颌骨的

"毫无疑问。"

"但那是如何区分的呢？"

"因为那是我的特别爱好，两者的区别显而易见，
眉骨的隆起，脸部的轮廓，腭骨的曲线，还有——"

"但这也是我的特别爱好啊，两者的区别同样显而
易见啊。《泰晤士报》用五号字排印出的文章和半个便
士一份的晚报草率印刷之间的区别，我一眼就能看出
来，就像您一眼就能看出两种颅骨之间的区别一样。对
于一个破案专家来说，识别不同字体只是必须掌握的基
本知识的一部分。当然，我得承认，我年轻时曾有一次
把《利兹信使报》和《西部晨报》上的字体给弄混淆
了。但《泰晤士报》上的字体同其他报刊所用字体的区
别很大，这些字不可能是从别的报纸上剪下来的。因为
信是昨天剪拼的，因此我们就很有可能可以从昨天的报
纸上找到这些字。"

② distinctive [dis'tiŋktiv] *a.*
有特色的，与众不同的

"那么，按照我的理解，福尔摩斯先生，"亨利·巴
斯克维尔爵士说，"您是说信上的字是有人用剪刀从那
份报纸上剪下来的——"

"用指甲剪，"福尔摩斯说，"您看，'远离'这两个
字剪了两下才剪下来，这说明剪刀的刀刃很短。"

"确实如此。这么说，有人是用短刃剪刀把字一个
个地剪下来，然后用浆糊把它们贴在——"

"是用胶水。"福尔摩斯说。

"用胶水把它们贴在这张纸上。但我不明白，'荒
原'这个词为何又用手写呢？"

"因为他在报上找不到那个词啊，其他的字都很简
单常用，在任何文章里都可以找到，但'荒原'一词就
没那么常用了。"

"啊，当然，这样就解释得通了。您从这封信上还
看出了别的什么信息吗，福尔摩斯先生？"

"还有一两处蛛丝马迹，不过，写信人为了清除所
有痕迹可谓煞费苦心。您看，这地址栏上的字体很是
潦草，但《泰晤士报》是有相当文化程度的人才看的，
并不是人手一份。据此，我们便可以推断，写信的人
具有较高的文化程度，但他却装成没有文化的样子，
想方设法要掩盖自己的笔迹，说明他的字迹可能会被

is quite out of its proper place. That may point to carelessness or it may point to **agitation**① and hurry upon the part of the cutter. On the whole I incline to the latter view, since the matter was evidently important, and it is unlikely that the composer of such a letter would be careless. If he were in a hurry it opens up the interesting question why he should be in a hurry, since any letter posted up to early morning would reach Sir Henry before he would leave his hotel. Did the composer fear an interruption–and from whom?"

"We are coming now rather into the region of guesswork," said Dr. Mortimer.

"Say, rather, into the region where we balance probabilities and choose the most likely. It is the scientific use of the imagination, but we have always some material basis on which to start our speculation. Now, you would call it a guess, no doubt, but I am almost certain that this address has been written in a hotel."

"How in the world can you say that?"

"If you examine it carefully you will see that both the pen and the ink have given the writer trouble. The pen has **spluttered**② twice in a single word and has run dry three times in a short address, showing that there was very little ink in the bottle. Now, a private pen or ink-bottle is seldom allowed to be in such a state, and the combination of the two must be quite rare. But you know the hotel ink and the hotel pen, where it is rare to get anything else. Yes, I have very little hesitation in saying that could we examine the waste-paper baskets of the hotels around Charing Cross until we found the remains of the **mutilated**③ *Times* leader we could lay our hands straight upon the person who sent this singular message. Halloa! Halloa! What's this?"

He was carefully examining the foolscap, upon which the words were pasted, holding it only an inch or two from his eyes.

"Well?"

"Nothing," said he, throwing it down. "It is a blank half-sheet of paper, without even a water-mark upon it. I think we have drawn as much as we can from this curious letter; and now, Sir Henry, has anything else of interest happened to you since you have been in London?"

"Why, no, Mr. Holmes. I think not."

"You have not observed anyone follow or watch you?"

"I seem to have walked right into the **thick**④ of a dime novel," said our

① agitation [ˌædʒi'teiʃən] n.
（情绪等的）纷乱，骚
动，激动不安

② splutter ['splʌtə] v.（液
体）溅泼

③ mutilated ['mju:tileitid] a.
残缺的；破坏的

④ thick [θik] n. 最激烈处

您认出来，或者会被您查出来。还有一点，您看到了，这些字贴得并不整齐一致，而是高低不一。例如，'生命'这个词就贴得很不是地方。这说明剪贴的人要么粗心大意，要么激动慌张。总体上看，我倾向于后一种猜测，因为此事显然至关重要，写这封信的人不大可能会粗心大意。如果他匆忙行事，那就出现了一个很有意思的问题，他为何要匆忙行事？因为任何信件只要清早发出，亨利爵士都可以在离开旅馆前收到信件。难道写信人是害怕被人打扰——害怕什么人打扰呢？"

"我们至此这是在猜谜语啊。"莫蒂默医生说。

"确切地说，我们这是在比较权衡各种可能性，从中选择可能性最大的。这是科学地运用想象力，但我们自始至终都是以事实作为思考问题的基础的。是啊，您会说这是在猜谜语，但是，毫无疑问，我几乎可以肯定，信封上的地址是在旅馆里面写的。"

"您到底凭什么这么说呢？"

"您如果仔细观察一下，就可以看得出，笔尖和墨水都给写信人带来了不少麻烦。每写一个字，笔尖就溅出了两次墨水。写一个这么简短的地址，墨水就干了三次，这说明墨水瓶里的墨水已经所剩无几了。您想想看，私人的钢笔和墨水瓶很少会出现这种情况，而这两种情况同时发生的概率更是少之又少了。但您知道，旅馆里的钢笔和墨水却很少不是这个样子的。事实上，我可以断定，我们到查令十字附近的旅馆里去查查废纸篓，找到那份被抠剪过的《泰晤士报》，那就可以直接找出那位寄出奇特信件的人了。嘿！嘿！这是什么啊？"

他拿起信纸，把它凑到离眼睛仅有一两英寸处，仔细端详起来。

"呃？"

"没什么，"他说，放下信纸，"这是半张白底信笺，上面连水印都没有。我看，我们从这封无头信中能找到的线索也就只有这些了。亨利爵士，我想问问您，您到伦敦后，是否遇到过别的什么怪事？"

"啊，没有，福尔摩斯先生，感觉没有啊。"

visitor. "Why in thunder should anyone follow or watch me?"

"We are coming to that. You have nothing else to report to us before we go into this matter?"

"Well, it depends upon what you think worth reporting."

"I think anything out of the ordinary **routine**^{①} of life well worth reporting." Sir Henry smiled.

"I don't know much of British life yet, for I have spent nearly all my time in the States and in Canada. But I hope that to lose one of your boots is not part of the ordinary routine of life over here."

"You have lost one of your boots?"

"My dear sir," cried Dr. Mortimer, "it is only mislaid. You will find it when you return to the hotel. What is the use of troubling Mr. Holmes with **trifles**^{②} of this kind?"

"Well, he asked me for anything outside the ordinary routine."

"Exactly," said Holmes, "however foolish the incident may seem. You have lost one of your boots, you say?"

"Well, mislaid it, anyhow. I put them both outside my door last night, and there was only one in the morning. I could get no sense out of the **chap**^{③} who cleans them. The worst of it is that I only bought the pair last night in the Strand, and I have never had them on."

"If you have never worn them, why did you put them out to be cleaned?"

"They were **tan**^{④} boots and had never been **varnished**^{⑤}. That was why I put them out."

"Then I understand that on your arrival in London yesterday you went out at once and bought a pair of boots?"

"I did a good deal of shopping. Dr. Mortimer here went round with me. You see, if I am to be **squire**^{⑥} down there I must dress the part, and it may be that I have got a little careless in my ways out West. Among other things I bought these brown boots–gave six dollars for them–and had one stolen before ever I had them on my feet."

"It seems a **singularly**^{⑦} useless thing to steal," said Sherlock Holmes. "I confess that I share Dr. Mortimer's belief that it will not be long before the missing boot is found."

① routine [ruːˈtiːn] n. 日常事务

"有没有注意到有什么人跟踪您或者监视您？"

"我似乎觉得自己走进了一部廉价纸面小说里面了，"我们的客人说，"到底是怎么回事，怎么会有人跟踪或监视我呢？"

"我们马上就会谈到这件事，但在此之前，您确实没有什么事情要对我们说吗？"

"呃，这要看您认为什么是值得说的东西了。"

"我认为，日常生活中任何反常的情况都值得说一说。"亨利爵士露出了微笑。

"我对英国人的生活状况还不是很熟悉，因为我从小就住在美国和加拿大。不过，我觉得，丢失一只靴子在这里不算是正常的生活现象吧！"

② trifle [ˈtraifl] n. 琐事，小事

"您丢了一只靴子？"

"尊敬的爵士啊，"莫蒂默大声说，"它只是放错了地方，等您回到旅馆之后就可以找到了。这种鸡毛蒜皮的小事何必劳福尔摩斯先生的神呢？"

"啊，是他要我说任何超出常规的情况的。"

③ chap [tʃæp] n. 家伙

"一点没错，"福尔摩斯说，"无论情况看起来是多么荒唐可笑。您是说您丢失了一只靴子，对吧？"

"是啊，随随便便放错地方了。我昨天晚上把一双靴子放在房门口，早上起来却只剩下一只了。我问过擦鞋的人，他也说不出个所以然来。最让人生气的是，靴子是我昨晚在斯特兰德大街买的，还没有穿过呢。"

④ tan [tæn] a. 棕褐色的
⑤ varnish [ˈvɑːniʃ] v. 给…上清漆

"您没穿过的新靴子为何要放到外面叫人擦呢？"

"那是一双棕褐色的靴子，还没上过油，因此我就把它搁置在外面了。"

"那我知道了，您昨天一到伦敦就立刻出门上街，还买了一双靴子，对吧？"

⑥ squire [ˈskwaiə] n. 乡绅

"我买了好多东西呢。这位莫蒂默医生陪我一道去的。您想想看，我都要回老家定居了，总要穿得体面些吧。也许是因为我在美国西部待过，对穿着打扮一直不是很讲究。除了一堆别的东西，我买了那双棕褐色的高筒靴子——给了六个五先令的硬币呢——但还没来得及穿到脚上就被人偷掉了一只。"

⑦ singularly [ˈsiŋgjuləli] ad. 异常地；非常地

"这样偷东西毫无用处，看起来很是蹊跷啊，"夏洛

"And, now, gentlemen," said the baronet with decision, "it seems to me that I have spoken quite enough about the little that I know. It is time that you kept your promise and gave me a full account of what we are all driving at."

"Your request is a very reasonable one," Holmes answered. "Dr. Mortimer, I think you could not do better than to tell your story as you told it to us."

Thus encouraged, our scientific friend drew his papers from his pocket and presented the whole case as he had done upon the morning before. Sir Henry Baskerville listened with the deepest attention and with an occasional exclamation of surprise.

"Well, I seem to have come into an inheritance with a **vengeance**[①]," said he when the long narrative was finished. "Of course, I've heard of the hound ever since I was in the **nursery**[②]. It's the **pet**[③] story of the family, though I never thought of taking it seriously before. But as to my uncle's death–well, it all seems boiling up in my head, and I can't get it clear yet. You don't seem quite to have made up your mind whether it's a case for a policeman or a clergyman."

"Precisely."

"And now there's this affair of the letter to me at the hotel. I suppose that fits into its place."

"It seems to show that someone knows more than we do about what goes on upon the moor," said Dr. Mortimer.

"And also," said Holmes, "that someone is not **ill-disposed**[④] towards you, since they warn you of danger."

"Or it may be that they wish, for their own purposes, to scare me away."

"Well, of course, that is possible also. I am very much indebted to you, Dr. Mortimer, for introducing me to a problem which presents several interesting alternatives. But the practical point which we now have to decide, Sir Henry, is whether it is or is not advisable for you to go to Baskerville Hall."

"Why should I not go?"

"There seems to be danger."

"Do you mean danger from this family **fiend**[⑤] or do you mean danger from human beings?"

"Well, that is what we have to find out."

"Whichever it is, my answer is fixed. There is no devil in hell, Mr. Holmes,

克·福尔摩斯说，"我赞同莫蒂默医生的看法，那只丢失的靴子很快就可以找到。"

"行啊，先生们，"从男爵语气坚定地说，"我自己知道的小事情都讲出来了。现在是该您兑现承诺的时候了，请您把我们大家关心的那件事情的原委告诉我吧。"

"您的要求合情合理，"福尔摩斯回答说，"莫蒂默医生，我看，您最好还是像昨天对我们讲述的那样再讲述一遍。"

受到这个鼓励之后，我们喜爱科学的朋友从自己的衣服口袋里掏出了那份手稿和报纸，像头天上午那样把事情的原委完整地讲述了一遍。亨利·巴斯克维尔爵士聚精会神地听着，时不时地因为惊讶而发出几声感叹。

"啊，看来我继承的遗产当中含有仇怨呢，"他听完长篇叙述后说，"当然啦，我孩提时候曾听说过关于猎犬的事情。那是我们家族中的人经常会讲述的故事，但我以前没有把它当成一回事。不过，想到我伯父的离世——啊，事情在我脑袋里像是开了锅似的翻腾着，至今都还没有弄明白这到底是怎么一回事。现在看来，你们好像也不能肯定，这件事情究竟是该由警察来管，还是牧师来管。"

"确实如此啊。"

"对啦，还有把信件寄到我下榻的旅馆里来的事情，我看这是其中的一个环节吧。"

"看起来，关于荒原的情况，有人知道得比我们还要多啊。"莫蒂默医生说。

"还有就是，"福尔摩斯说，"寄信人对您并无恶意，因为他提醒您有危险。"

"说不定他们为了自己的某种目的想把我吓走呢。"

"是啊，当然，也有这种可能。莫蒂默医生，非常感谢您给我介绍了一个具有多种可能性的有趣案件。但亨利爵士，我们眼下有个问题必须要做出决断，您是去巴斯克维尔庄园好呢，还是不去好？"

"我为何不该去呢？"

"好像有危险啊。"

"您说的危险是来自于家族的恶魔呢，还是来自于人？"

① vengeance ['vendʒəns] n.
报仇，复仇

② nursery ['nəːsəri] n. 保育室；儿童室

③ pet [pet] a. 特别喜爱的

④ ill-disposed ['ildi'spəuzd]
a. 敌视的

⑤ fiend [fiːnd] n. 魔鬼，恶魔

and there is no man upon earth who can prevent me from going to the home of my own people, and you may take that to be my final answer." His dark brows knitted and his face flushed to a **dusky**① red as he spoke. It was evident that the **fiery**② temper of the Baskervilles was not extinct in this their last representative. "Meanwhile," said he, "I have hardly had time to think over all that you have told me. It's a big thing for a man to have to understand and to decide at one sitting. I should like to have a quiet hour by myself to make up my mind. Now, look here, Mr. Holmes, it's half-past eleven now and I am going back right away to my hotel. Suppose you and your friend, Dr. Watson, **come round**③ and lunch with us at two. I'll be able to tell you more clearly then how this thing strikes me."

"Is that convenient to you, Watson?"

"Perfectly."

"Then you may expect us. Shall I have a cab called?"

"I'd prefer to walk, for this affair has **flurried**④ me rather."

"I'll join you in a walk, with pleasure," said his companion.

"Then we meet again at two o'clock. Au revoir, and good-morning!"

We heard the steps of our visitors descend the stair and the bang of the front door. In an instant Holmes had changed from the **languid**⑤ dreamer to the man of action.

"Your hat and boots, Watson, quick! Not a moment to lose!" He rushed into his room in his dressing-gown and was back again in a few seconds in a frock-coat. We hurried together down the stairs and into the street. Dr. Mortimer and Baskerville were still visible about two hundred yards ahead of us in the direction of Oxford Street.

"Shall I run on and stop them?"

"Not for the world, my dear Watson. I am perfectly satisfied with your company if you will tolerate mine. Our friends are wise, for it is certainly a very fine morning for a walk."

He quickened his pace until we had decreased the distance which divided us by about half. Then, still keeping a hundred yards behind, we followed into Oxford Street and so down Regent Street. Once our friends stopped and stared into a shop window, upon which Holmes did the same. An instant afterwards he gave a little cry of satisfaction, and, following the direction of his eager eyes, I

① dusky ['dʌski] *a.* 暗淡的

② fiery ['faiəri] *a.* 易怒的，暴躁的

③ come round 顺道拜访

④ flurry ['flʌri] *v.* 使激动

⑤ languid ['læŋgwid] *a.* 倦怠的

"对啊，这正是我必须要弄明白的问题。"

"不管是什么，我的回答是确定无疑的，福尔摩斯先生，无论是地狱里的魔鬼，还是世界上的什么人，都无法阻止我回老家去。这就是我的回答。"他说话的时候，浓眉紧锁，脸色红得发紫。很显然，巴斯克维尔家人那暴躁的脾气在这个家族最后一位后裔身上还没有完全消除。"况且，"他接着说，"我还没来得及仔细思考你们所告诉我的这些事实。这是一件大事，我无法在短时间内全部理解并即刻做出决定。我想单独待一个小时，然后再来决定。啊，福尔摩斯先生，您看，现在已经是十一点半了，我得立刻回旅馆去。您和您的朋友，华生医生，两点钟时到旅馆来同我们一道用午餐吧。到时，我就能够更加清楚地告诉你们，我对这件事情的想法了。"

"你到时方便吗，华生？"

"完全没问题。"

"那您就等着我们吧。要我给您叫辆马车来吗？"

"我更想要走一走，这件事情把我给弄得挺心烦意乱的。"

"我很乐意陪同您一道走。"他的同伴说。

"那我们就两点钟再见面，再见。"

我们听着两位来客下楼的脚步声，还有随后大门砰的一声关上的声音。刹那间，福尔摩斯不再是一副慵懒倦怠、睡眼蒙眬的模样了，变成了一个行动利索的人。

"戴上帽子，穿好靴子，华生，赶快！刻不容缓！"他穿着晨衣冲进卧室，片刻之后，又冲了出来，身上已经换成了礼服。我们一同匆匆下楼，走到了街上，看到莫蒂默医生和巴斯克维尔在前面。他们正向牛津大街方向走去，和我们大约相距两百码远。

"我们要跑上去把他们叫住吗？"

"不，亲爱的华生，千万不要。如果你不嫌弃与我做伴，我有你做伴，心里面就觉得很满足了。我们的朋友很明智，上午的天气这么好，正适合步行。"

他加快了脚步，我们和前面两个人的距离很快就缩短了一半。随后，我们保持着一百码的距离，跟着他们走进了牛津大街，后又转入了摄政街。有一次，

saw that a **hansom**① cab with a man inside which had halted on the other side of the street was now proceeding slowly onward again.

"There's our man, Watson! Come along! We'll have a good look at him, if we can do no more."

At that instant I was aware of a bushy black beard and a pair of piercing eyes turned upon us through the side window of the cab. Instantly the **trapdoor**② at the top flew up, something was screamed to the driver, and the cab flew madly off down Regent Street. Holmes looked eagerly round for another, but no empty one was in sight. Then he dashed in wild pursuit amid the stream of the traffic, but the start was too great, and already the cab was out of sight.

"There now!" said Holmes bitterly as he emerged panting and white with **vexation**③ from the tide of vehicles. "Was ever such bad luck and such bad management, too? Watson, Watson, if you are an honest man you will record this also and set it against my successes!"

"Who was the man?"

"I have not an idea."

"A spy?"

"Well, it was evident from what we have heard that Baskerville has been very closely shadowed by someone since he has been in town. How else could it be known so quickly that it was the Northumberland Hotel which he had chosen? If they had followed him the first day I argued that they would follow him also the second. You may have observed that I twice strolled over to the window while Dr. Mortimer was reading his legend."

"Yes, I remember."

"I was looking out for **loiterers**④ in the street, but I saw none. We are dealing with a clever man, Watson. This matter cuts very deep, and though I have not finally made up my mind whether it is a benevolent or a **malevolent**⑤ agency which is in touch with us, I am conscious always of power and **design**⑥. When our friends left I at once followed them in the hopes of marking down their invisible attendant. So **wily**⑦ was he that he had not trusted himself upon foot, but he had **availed himself of**⑧ a cab so that he could loiter behind or dash past them and so escape their notice. His method had the additional advantage that if they were to take a cab he was all ready to follow them. It has, however,

① hansom ['hænsəm] *n.* （御座高居在后的）双轮双座单马车

② trapdoor ['træp'dɔː] *n.* 活板门

③ vexation [vek'seiʃən] *n.* 烦恼，苦恼

④ loiterer ['lɔitərə] *n.* 闲荡的人

⑤ malevolent [mə'levələnt] *a.* 敌意的，恶毒的
⑥ design [di'zain] *n.* 阴谋，诡计

⑦ wily ['waili] *a.* 狡猾的；狡诈的；诡计多端的
⑧ avail of 利用

我们的朋友停下脚步，盯着橱窗看了一会儿，福尔摩斯也学着他们的样儿。没过一会儿，他轻轻地欢呼了一声。我顺着他那急切的目光看到了一辆本来停在街对面的很气派的马车，里面坐着一位男士，此时正开始慢慢地向前移动。

"那就是我们要寻找的人，华生！快跟上！我们顾不上别的什么事情，至少应该看清楚他。"

霎时间，我看到马车的侧窗中有个面孔向我们转过来，面孔上长着浓密的黑胡子和一双炯炯逼人的眼睛。他突然打开车顶的滑动窗，向马车夫大声吼了些什么，然后马车就沿着摄政街狂奔而去。福尔摩斯焦急地四下张望，想找一辆马车，但看不到一辆空车。于是，他冲进车马的洪流里拼命追赶，但那马车跑得太快，片刻就不见了踪影。

"哎呀！"福尔摩斯喘着粗气，脸色煞白，痛心地说，"我们可曾有过这样坏的运气，可曾做过如此糟糕的布局？华生，华生，如果你是一个诚实的人，就请你把今天的事情也记录下来，作为我破案的反面教材吧！"

"那人是谁呢？"

"我还不知道呢。"

"是来盯梢的吧？"

"是啊，根据亨利爵士刚才的陈述，他显然是一到伦敦就被人死死地盯上了。不然的话，他住的那家旅馆不可能这么快就被人知道了。既然他刚到的第一天就被盯上了，我便推断，他第二天还会处在他人的监视之下。你或许注意到了，在莫蒂默医生讲述那个传说的时候，我曾两次走到窗户边去察看。"

"是啊，我注意到了。"

"当时，我透过窗户在大街上寻找盯梢的人，但一无所获。华生，我们这一次的对手是个精明的角色。这件事情隐藏得很深，到目前为止我不能最终确定和我们接触的这个人是善意还是恶意，但我始终觉得他是一个有能力而且是有谋略的人。我们的朋友告别后，我立刻尾随而出，就是想找出暗中跟踪他们的人。他非常狡猾，知道走路可能不可靠，便为自己叫好了马车，这样他就能随意地跟在他们后面，或者从他们的身边飞奔而

one obvious disadvantage."

"It puts him in the power of the cabman."

"Exactly."

"What a pity we did not get the number!"

"My dear Watson, clumsy as I have been, you surely do not seriously imagine that I neglected to get the number? No. 2704 is our man. But that is no use to us for the moment."

"I fail to see how you could have done more."

"On observing the cab I should have instantly turned and walked in the other direction. I should then at my leisure have hired a second cab and followed the first at a respectful distance, or, better still, have driven to the Northumberland Hotel and waited there. When our unknown had followed Baskerville home we should have had the opportunity of playing his own game upon himself and seeing where he made for. As it is, by an **indiscreet**[①] eagerness, which was taken advantage of with extraordinary quickness and energy by our opponent, we have betrayed ourselves and lost our man."

We had been **sauntering**[②] slowly down Regent Street during this conversation, and Dr. Mortimer, with his companion, had long vanished in front of us.

"There is no object in our following them," said Holmes. "The shadow has departed and will not return. We must see what further cards we have in our hands and play them with decision. Could you swear to that man's face within the cab?"

"I could swear only to the beard."

"And so could I–from which I gather that in all probability it was a false one. A clever man upon so delicate an errand has no use for a beard save to conceal his features. Come in here, Watson!"

He turned into one of the district messenger offices, where he was warmly greeted by the manager.

"Ah, Wilson, I see you have not forgotten the little case in which I had the good fortune to help you?"

"No, sir, indeed I have not. You saved my good name, and perhaps my life."

"My dear fellow, you exaggerate. I have some **recollection**[③], Wilson, that you had among your boys a lad named Cartwright, who showed some ability during the investigation."

去，还不会引起他们的注意。他的这种做法还有一个特别的好处，那就是，如果他们是坐马车走的，那他也可以轻而易举地追上。不过，这种做法也有一个非常明显的缺陷。"

"他这样会受到马车夫的牵制。"

"一点没错。"

"真是很可惜啊，没有记下马车的车号。"

"亲爱的华生，我虽然有些愚钝，但你不至于真的会认为，我会粗心大意到连车号都没记下吧？我们要找的车号是2704。不过，眼下对我们没有什么用处。"

"我看不出，你刚才还有别的什么选择。"

"我当时一看到那辆马车，就应该立刻转身，朝着另外一个方向走，然后再不慌不忙地雇另外一辆跟踪，保持一定的距离，或者，更好的办法是，我们乘车先到诺森伯兰旅馆，在那儿等候他。等那个陌生人尾随巴斯克维尔回旅馆的时候，我们就有机会学着他的样儿，搞清楚他到底想干什么。而实际情况是，我们刚才太过疏忽冒失了，以致我们的对手充分利用了这个疏忽。我们暴露了自己，还跟丢了目标。"

我们两人一边交谈，一边沿着摄政街慢慢向前走。在我们前面的莫蒂默医生和他的同伴早已不见了踪影。

"我们再跟踪他们两个人已经没有意义了，"福尔摩斯说，"可疑的人影消失了，就不会再回来了。我们必须看看手里还有些什么王牌，然后再果断地出牌。你看清了坐在马车里的那人的模样了吗？"

"我只看清了他的胡子。"

"我和你一样——但觉得那很可能是假胡子。一个头脑机灵的人在做这么细致的事情时，胡子没有别的任何用处，只能用来伪装自己的面目。进来吧，华生。"

他转身进了一家区域信差事务所，里面的经理热情地跟他打招呼。

"啊，威尔逊，我在那桩小案件中有幸能够帮上您的忙，我看您还没有忘记吧？"

"没有忘记啊，先生，确实忘不了，您拯救了我的良好声誉，可以说也拯救了我的生命啊。"

"好伙伴，您过奖了。我隐约记得，威尔逊，您的

"Yes, sir, he is still with us."

"Could you ring him up?–thank you! And I should be glad to have change of this five-pound note."

A lad of fourteen, with a bright, keen face, had obeyed the summons of the manager. He stood now gazing with great **reverence**[①] at the famous detective.

"Let me have the Hotel Directory," said Holmes. "Thank you! Now, Cartwright, there are the names of twenty-three hotels here, all in the immediate neighbourhood of Charing Cross. Do you see?"

"Yes, sir."

"You will visit each of these in turn."

"Yes, sir."

"You will begin in each case by giving the outside **porter**[②] one shilling. Here are twenty-three shillings."

"Yes, sir."

"You will tell him that you want to see the waste-paper of yesterday. You will say that an important telegram has miscarried and that you are looking for it. You understand?"

"Yes, sir."

"But what you are really looking for is the centre page of the *Times* with some holes cut in it with scissors. Here is a copy of the *Times*. It is this page. You could easily recognize it, could you not?"

"Yes, sir."

"In each case the outside porter will send for the hall porter, to whom also you will give a shilling. Here are twenty-three shillings. You will then learn in possibly twenty cases out of the twenty-three that the waste of the day before has been burned or removed. In the three other cases you will be shown a heap of paper and you will look for this page of the *Times* among it. The odds are enormously against your finding it. There are ten shillings over in case of emergencies. Let me have a report by wire at Baker Street before evening. And now, Watson, it only remains for us to find out by wire the identity of the cabman, No. 2704, and then we will drop into one of the Bond Street picture galleries and fill in the time until we are **due**[③] at the hotel."

投递员中有个少年名叫卡特赖特，他在调查当中显示了能力。"

"是啊，先生，他还在我们这儿呢。"

"您能把他叫过来吗？——谢谢您！另外，有劳您帮我把这五英镑换成零钱。"

一个十四岁的少年应经理的召唤来到了我们面前，他一脸阳光，相貌机灵，正以极大的敬意注视着眼前的大侦探。

"请把旅馆指南拿给我，"福尔摩斯说，"谢谢您！对啦，卡特赖特，这里是二十三家旅馆的名字，全都在查令十字附近。你明白了吗？"

"看见了，先生。"

"你挨家到这些旅馆去走一趟。"

"好的，先生。"

"你每到一家，就先给看门人一个先令。这儿有二十三个先令。"

"好的，先生。"

"然后你再告诉他，你想看看昨天的废纸。你就跟他们说有一份重要的电报被送错了地方，现在要找到它。明白了吗？"

"明白了，先生。"

"但是，你真正要寻找的是《泰晤士报》的中心页，上面有一些用剪刀剪出来的洞洞。这一份就是《泰晤士报》。你要找的就是这个版面，很容易就能认出来，对吧？"

"是的，先生。"

"每当这个时候，大门的守门人就会叫来客房部的门卫，你也给他一个先令。这里是二十三个先令。你可能会了解到，在二十三家旅馆中有二十家的废纸都在昨天被烧掉了，或者被拿走了。另外的三四家可能会把一大堆废报纸指给你看，你就要在里面找寻《泰晤士报》的这个版面。你很有可能什么都找不到。这里有十个先令，给你备着急需用。天黑之前把结果发电报到贝克大街告诉我。好啦，华生，还剩下一件事情：我们要去发封电报，查出2704号马车夫的身份，然后去参观一下邦德大街的画廊，在那里打发一点儿时间，等到了约定的时间再去旅馆。"

① reverence ['revərəns] *n.* 尊敬，尊重

② porter ['pɔːtə] *n.* 守门人，门房

③ due [djuː] *a.* 应到达的，应出席的

Chapter 5 Three Broken Threads

Sherlock Holmes had, in a very remarkable degree, the power of **detaching**① his mind at will. For two hours the strange business in which we had been involved appeared to be forgotten, and he was entirely absorbed in the pictures of the modern Belgian masters. He would talk of nothing but art, of which he had the **crudest**② ideas, from our leaving the gallery until we found ourselves at the Northumberland Hotel.

"Sir Henry Baskerville is upstairs expecting you," said the clerk. "He asked me to show you up at once when you came."

"Have you any objection to my looking at your register?" said Holmes.

"Not in the least."

The book showed that two names had been added after that of Baskerville. One was Theophilus Johnson and family, of Newcastle; the other Mrs. Oldmore and maid, of High Lodge, Alton.

"Surely that must be the same Johnson whom I used to know," said Holmes to the porter. "A lawyer, is he not, gray-headed, and walks with a limp?"

"No, sir, this is Mr. Johnson, the coal-owner, a very active gentleman, not older than yourself."

"Surely you are mistaken about his trade?"

"No, sir! he has used this hotel for many years, and he is very well known to us."

"Ah, that settles it. Mrs. Oldmore, too; I seem to remember the name. Excuse my curiosity, but often in calling upon one friend one finds another."

第五章 三条被掐断的线索

① detach [di'tætʃ] v. （使）
  分离，（使）分开

② crude [kru:d] a. 肤浅的，
  幼稚的

夏洛克·福尔摩斯在转移自己的注意力方面具有非凡的能力，可以做到随心所欲。两个小时时间里，他似乎把我们已经牵扯其中的那桩离奇案件忘记得一干二净了，完全沉浸在现代比利时艺术大师们的作品中，乃至在离开画廊前往诺森伯兰旅馆的路上，他也只谈艺术，不涉及别的任何内容。实际上，他对艺术的见解还是很肤浅的。

"亨利·巴斯克维尔爵士正在楼上等候你们呢，"旅馆雇员说，"他吩咐我说，你们一到就领你们上去。"

"我想看看你们旅馆的登记簿，您不会反对吧？"福尔摩斯说。

"当然不会。"

登记簿上显示，巴斯克维尔名字后面增加了两位住客的名字，一位是来自纽克斯尔的西奥菲勒斯·约翰逊及其家人，另一位是奥尔顿海洛奇宅邸的奥尔德摩尔夫人及其女仆。

"毫无疑问，这一定是我过去认识的那位约翰逊先生，"福尔摩斯对门卫说，"是个律师，头发灰白，走起路来有点跛，对吧？"

"不对，先生，这位约翰逊先生是个煤矿老板，是位行动利索的绅士，年龄不会比您大。"

"关于他的职业，您一定是弄错了吧？"

"没有弄错，先生！他许多年来都是住在这家旅馆里，我跟他很熟悉。"

"She is an **invalid**[①] lady, sir. Her husband was once mayor of Gloucester. She always comes to us when she is in town."

"Thank you; I am afraid I cannot claim her **acquaintance**[②]. We have established a most important fact by these questions, Watson," he continued in a low voice as we went upstairs together. "We know now that the people who are so interested in our friend have not settled down in his own hotel. That means that while they are, as we have seen, very anxious to watch him, they are equally anxious that he should not see them. Now, this is a most **suggestive**[③] fact."

"What does it suggest?"

"It suggests–halloa, my dear fellow, what on earth is the matter?"

As we came round the top of the stairs we had run up against Sir Henry Baskerville himself. His face was flushed with anger, and he held an old and dusty boot in one of his hands. So furious was he that he was hardly **articulate**[④], and when he did speak it was in a much broader and more Western dialect than any which we had heard from him in the morning.

"Seems to me they are playing me for a **sucker**[⑤] in this hotel," he cried. "They'll find they've started in to **monkey**[⑥] with the wrong man unless they are careful. By thunder, if that chap can't find my missing boot there will be trouble. I can take a joke with the best, Mr. Holmes, but they've got a bit **over the mark**[⑦] this time."

"Still looking for your boot?"

"Yes, sir, and mean to find it."

"But, surely, you said that it was a new brown boot?"

"So it was, sir. And now it's an old black one."

"What! you don't mean to say –– ?"

"That's just what I do mean to say. I only had three pairs in the world–the new brown, the old black, and the patent leathers, which I am wearing. Last night they took one of my brown ones, and to-day they have sneaked one of the black. Well, have you got it? Speak out, man, and don't stand staring!"

An agitated German waiter had appeared upon the scene.

"No, sir; I have made inquiry all over the hotel, but I can hear no word of it."

① invalid ['invəli:d] *a.* 有病
的

② acquaintance [ə'kweintəns]
n. （对某人的）相识，
认识

③ suggestive [sə'dʒestiv] *a.*
耐人寻味的

④ articulate [ɑ:'tikjulət] *a.*
能说话的

⑤ sucker ['sʌkə] 笨蛋

⑥ monkey ['mʌŋki] *v.* 胡
闹；捣蛋

⑦ over the mark 过分，超
过限度

"啊，那就不会有什么问题了。奥尔德摩尔夫人也
是，我似乎记得这个名字的。请原谅我的好奇，但是，
人们在拜访一个朋友时往往会遇上另外一个。"

"她是位行动不便的夫人，先生，丈夫曾经是格洛
斯特市的市长。她来了伦敦就会住在我们这儿。"

"谢谢您，我恐怕跟她不熟。通过刚才提出的问题，
我们弄清楚了一个非常重要的事实，华生，"我们一起
上楼时，他低声对我说，"我们现在知道了，那些对我
们的朋友感兴趣的人没有下榻在同一家旅馆，也就是
说，一方面，他们心急火燎，想要监视他，这一点我们
已经看到了。另一方面，他们同样心急火燎，生怕他发
现他们。对啊，这是个很耐人寻味的事实。"

"说明了什么呢？"

"这说明了——嘿，亲爱的朋友，这到底是怎么了？"

我们刚走到楼梯的顶端，便迎面碰上了亨利·巴
斯克维尔爵士本人。他气得满脸通红，一只手上拿着一
只满是灰尘的旧皮靴，简直怒不可遏，连话都说不出来
了。当他终于开口说话时，他声音高亢，美国西部口音
很重，程度远胜过我们上午听到过的。

"我感觉，这家旅馆的人把我当傻瓜笨蛋了，"他大声
嚷嚷着，"他们可得给我当心点，否则，很快就会发现自己
找错了戏弄的对象了。丑话说在前头，那个门卫若是不把
我的靴子找回来，那就有他好受的！我这个人平时很开得
起玩笑的，但这一次，他们玩笑也未免开得太大了点吧。"

"您还在寻找靴子吗？"

"对啊，先生，一定要找到。"

"但是，可以肯定，您说那是一只棕褐色的新靴子啊。"

"是这么回事，先生，而现在是一只黑色的旧靴子。"

"什么啊！您不是要说——？"

"我正想告诉您呢，我总共就只有三双——一双新
的棕褐色，一双旧的黑色，还有现在脚上穿着的黑漆皮
的。昨天夜间，他们拿走了我棕褐色那双中的一只，而
今天，又拿走了一只黑色的。对啦，你找到了吗，伙
计，说话啊，不要站在那儿干瞪眼啊！"

一位情绪不安的德国侍者走了过来。

"没有呢，先生，我把旅馆里的人都问遍了，但没

"Well, either that boot comes back before sundown or I'll see the manager and tell him that I go right straight out of this hotel."

"It shall be found, sir–I promise you that if you will have a little patience it will be found."

"Mind it is, for it's the last thing of mine that I'll lose in this **den**① of thieves. Well, well, Mr. Holmes, you'll excuse my troubling you about such a trifle ––"

"I think it's well worth troubling about."

"Why, you look very serious over it."

"How do you explain it?"

"I just don't attempt to explain it. It seems the very maddest, queerest thing that ever happened to me."

"The queerest perhaps ––" said Holmes thoughtfully.

"What do you make of it yourself?"

"Well, I don't **profess**② to understand it yet. This case of yours is very complex, Sir Henry. When taken **in conjunction with**③ your uncle's death I am not sure that of all the five hundred cases of **capital**④ importance which I have handled there is one which cuts so deep. But we hold several threads in our hands, and the odds are that one or other of them guides us to the truth. We may waste time in following the wrong one, but sooner or later we must come upon the right."

We had a pleasant **luncheon**⑤ in which little was said of the business which had brought us together. It was in the private sitting-room to which we afterwards repaired that Holmes asked Baskerville what were his intentions.

"To go to Baskerville Hall."

"And when?"

"At the end of the week."

"On the whole," said Holmes, "I think that your decision is a wise one. I have **ample**⑥ evidence that you are being **dogged**⑦ in London, and amid the millions of this great city it is difficult to discover who these people are or what their object can be. If their intentions are evil they might do you a mischief, and we should be powerless to prevent it. You did not know, Dr. Mortimer, that you were followed this morning from my house?"

听到一点儿消息。"

"啊，你们可得给我在天黑前把靴子找回来，否则，我就要去找经理了，告诉他我这就直接走人，离开旅馆。"

"会找到的，先生——我向您保证，您只要再耐心等一等，靴子会找到的。"

"但愿如此啊，我可不想在这样一个贼窝里再丢失什么东西了。对啦，对啦，福尔摩斯先生，为这样的一件小事情让您费心劳神的，请您谅解——"

"我认为，这事值得费心劳神。"

"啊，您看起来很看重这一点啊。"

"您如何解释这个情况呢？"

"我压根儿没想过要解释，这是我遇到过的最荒诞可笑和最离奇古怪的事情。"

"或许是最离奇古怪的——"福尔摩斯说，一副若有所思的样子。

"您自己怎么看呢？"

"是啊，我得承认，我自己也还没完全弄明白。您的这桩案件十分复杂，亨利爵士。如果同您伯父的去世联系起来看，恐怕比我经手过的那五百桩大案要案中的任何一桩都更加扑朔迷离啊。不过，我们现在手上掌握了几条线索，其中应该有一两条可以引导我们找出真相。我们或许关注错误的线索，浪费一点儿时间，但迟早会找到那条正确的线索的。"

我们享受了一顿愉快的午餐，席间很少再提把我们集聚到一块儿的那桩案件。午餐后，我们一同到了一间私密的起居室，福尔摩斯在此询问了巴斯克维尔的打算。

"到巴斯克维尔庄园去。"

"什么时候？"

"这个礼拜结束时。"

"总的说起来，"福尔摩斯说，"我认为，您的决定是明智的。我有充分的证据证明，您在伦敦被人注意上了。在这座城市的几百万人口当中，很难弄清楚跟踪您的是什么人，为了什么目的。倘若他们居心不良，恐怕会加害于您。到时，我们就是有心防范也恐怕无能为力。您不知道啊，莫蒂默医生，你们一出我的家门就

① den [den] n. 贼窝

② profess [prəu'fes] v. 伪称；假装
③ in conjunction with 连同，共同
④ capital ['kæpitəl] a. 第一流的

⑤ luncheon ['lʌntʃən] n. 午餐

⑥ ample ['æmpl] a. 足够的
⑦ dog [dɔg] v. 追踪，跟随

Dr. Mortimer started violently.

"Followed! By whom?"

"That, unfortunately, is what I cannot tell you. Have you among your neighbours or acquaintances on Daftmoor any man with a black, full beard?"

"No–or, let me see–why, yes. Barrymore, Sir Charles's butler, is a man with a full, black beard."

"Ha! Where is Barrymore?"

"He is in charge of the Hall."

"We had best ascertain if he is really there, or if by any possibility he might be in London."

"How can you do that?"

"Give me a telegraph form. 'Is all ready for Sir Henry?' That will do. Address to Mr. Barrymore, Baskerville Hall. What is the nearest telegraph-office? Grimpen. Very good, we will send a second wire to the postmaster, Grimpen: 'Telegram to Mr. Barrymore to be delivered into his own hand. If absent, please return wire to Sir Henry Baskerville, Northumberland Hotel.' That should let us know before evening whether Barrymore is at his post in Devonshire or not."

"That's so," said Baskerville. "By the way, Dr. Mortimer, who is this Barrymore, anyhow?"

"He is the son of the old **caretaker**[1], who is dead. They have looked after the Hall for four generations now. So far as I know, he and his wife are as **respectable**[2] a couple as any in the county."

"At the same time," said Baskerville, "it's clear enough that so long as there are none of the family at the Hall these people have a **mighty**[3] fine home and nothing to do."

"That is true."

"Did Barrymore profit at all by Sir Charles's will?" asked Holmes.

"He and his wife had five hundred pounds each."

"Ha! Did they know that they would receive this?"

"Yes; Sir Charles was very fond of talking about the **provisions**[4] of his wlll."

"That is very interesting."

被人跟踪了。"

莫蒂默医生大吃一惊。

"跟踪！什么人？"

"非常遗憾，我也无法告诉您是谁。您在达特穆尔荒原那边的邻居，或者熟人当中，有没有一个留着大黑胡子的人？"

"没有——不，让我想想——啊，有的，巴里摩尔，查尔斯爵士的管家，他就留着一大把黑胡子。"

"哈！巴里摩尔在哪里？"

"他管理着庄园呢。"

"我们最好还是证实一下，看他是不是真的在那里，说不定有可能在伦敦呢。"

"您如何才能证实呢？"

"给我一张电报单。'准备好了迎接亨利爵士吗？'这样写就可以了。电报发给巴斯克维尔庄园的巴里摩尔先生。离庄园最近的电报局在哪里？格林彭，很好啊。此外，我们再发一封电报给格林彭邮政所的所长，'发给巴里摩尔的电报请务必让其亲自签收为盼，如若本人不在，请把电报退回诺森伯兰旅馆，亨利·巴斯克维尔爵士收。'这样一来，我们天黑之前就可以弄清巴里摩尔是否在德文郡坚守职责呢。"

"这样行，"巴斯克维尔说，"顺便问一声，莫蒂默医生，巴里摩尔到底是怎么样的一个人啊？"

"他是已故老管家的儿子。他们一直负责管理着庄园，至今已是第四代了。据我所知，他们夫妻两人在当地是很受人尊敬的。"

"同时，"巴斯克维尔说，"事情很明了了，如果我家族的人都不去庄园住的话，那他们就住着豪宅，一点儿事情都不用做了。"

"确实如此。"

"查尔斯爵士的遗嘱里提到了巴里摩尔的份额吗？"福尔摩斯问。

"他和妻子各得五百英镑。"

"哈！他们知道，自己可以得到这笔遗产吗？"

"知道。查尔斯爵士很喜欢讲在他的遗嘱中每个人可以得到的份额。"

① caretaker ['kɛə,teikə] n. 看门人

② respectable [ri'spektəbl] a. 品行端正的；正派的

③ mighty ['maiti] ad. 很，非常

④ provision [prəu'viʒən] n. 条款

"I hope," said Dr. Mortimer, "that you do not look with suspicious eyes upon everyone who received a legacy from Sir Charles, for I also had a thousand pounds left to me."

"Indeed! And anyone else?"

"There were many insignificant sums to individuals, and a large number of public charities. The **residue**① all went to Sir Henry."

"And how much was the residue?"

"Seven hundred and forty thousand pounds."

Holmes raised his eyebrows in surprise. "I had no idea that so gigantic a sum was involved," said he.

"Sir Charles had the reputation of being rich, but we did not know how very rich he was until we came to examine his **securities**②. The total value of the estate was close on to a million."

"Dear me! It is a **stake**③ for which a man might well play a desperate game. And one more question, Dr. Mortimer. Supposing that anything happened to our young friend here–you will forgive the unpleasant hypothesis!–who would inherit the estate?"

"Since Rodger Baskerville, Sir Charles's younger brother died unmarried, the estate would descend to the Desmonds, who are distant cousins. James Desmond is an elderly clergyman in Westmoreland."

"Thank you. These details are all of great interest. Have you met Mr. James Desmond?"

"Yes; he once came down to visit Sir Charles. He is a man of **venerable**④ appearance and of saintly life. I remember that he refused to accept any **settlement**⑤ from Sir Charles, though he pressed it upon him."

"And this man of simple tastes would be the heir to Sir Charles's thousands."

"He would be the heir to the estate because that is **entailed**⑥. He would also be the heir to the money unless it were willed otherwise by the present owner, who can, of course, do what he likes with it."

"And have you made your will, Sir Henry?"

"No, Mr. Holmes, I have not. I've had no time, for it was only yesterday that I learned how matters stood. But in any case I feel that the money should go with the title and estate. That was my poor uncle's idea. How is the owner

"这很有意思。"

"但愿,"莫蒂默医生说,"您不会怀疑每一个得到过查尔斯爵士遗赠的人吧,因为我本人也得到了一千英镑呢。"

"是吗!还有别的什么人吗?"

① residue ['rezidju] *n*. 剩余物

"很多笔数目不大的金额遗赠给了个人,还有一大笔赠给了公共慈善机构,余下的财产则全归亨利爵士所有。"

"余下的有多少?"

"七十四万英镑。"

福尔摩斯感到很惊讶,眉头竖了起来。"我没想到有这么大的一笔钱。"他说。

② securities [si'kjuəritis] *n*. 证券

"查尔斯爵士是个远近闻名的富翁,但我们直到他去世后查验他的证券时才知道他如此富有,他的资产总值将近一百万英镑。"

③ stake [steik] *n*. 赌金,赌注

"天哪!这么大的赌注,肯定有人拼死也要博它一回。莫蒂默医生,再问您一个问题。假设我们这位年轻的朋友在伦敦惨遭不测——请您谅解我用这个不详的假设——那会由谁来继承那笔遗产呢?"

"因为罗杰·巴斯克维尔——查尔斯爵士的弟弟还未结婚就亡故了,所以遗产就将由德斯蒙德家族继承,他们之间是远表亲关系。詹姆斯·德斯蒙德是威斯特摩兰的一位上了年纪的牧师。"

"谢谢您。这些细节全都大有用途。您见过詹姆斯·德斯蒙德先生吗?"

④ venerable ['venərəbl] *a*. 德高望重的

⑤ settlement ['setlmənt] *n*. 赠予(或转让)的财产

"见过,他有一次来拜访过查尔斯爵士。从外表看,他为人庄重可敬,过着圣洁的生活。我记得,他拒绝从查尔斯爵士那里接受任何产业,尽管查尔斯爵士力劝他接受。"

"这个没什么欲望的人会成为查尔斯爵士巨额财产的继承人吗?"

⑥ entail [in'teil] *v*. 把…按固定的顺序传给(或遗传给)

"他是法定的继承人,除非现在的所有人按照自己的喜好来处理财产,另立遗嘱,按律他将继承遗产。"

"那亨利爵士,您立过遗嘱了吗?"

"没有,福尔摩斯先生,还没有呢。我还没有时间这样做,因为我昨天才知道整件事情。不过,我觉得,无论在什么情况下,钱财都不该与爵位和产业分开。我

going to restore the glories of the Baskervilles if he has not money enough to keep up the property? House, land, and dollars must go together."

"Quite so. Well, Sir Henry, I am **of one mind**① with you as to the **advisability**② of your going down to Devonshire without delay. There is only one provision which I must make. You certainly must not go alone."

"Dr. Mortimer returns with me."

"But Dr. Mortimer has his practice to attend to, and his house is miles away from yours. With all the good will in the world he may be unable to help you. No, Sir Henry, you must take with you someone, a **trusty**③ man, who will be always by your side."

"Is it possible that you could come yourself, Mr. Holmes?"

"If matters came to a crisis I should **endeavour**④ to be present in person; but you can understand that, with my **extensive**⑤ consulting practice and with the constant **appeals**⑥ which reach me from many quarters, it is impossible for me to be absent from London for an indefinite time. At the present instant one of the most revered names in England is being **besmirched**⑦ by a blackmailer, and only I can stop a disastrous scandal. You will see how impossible it is for me to go to Dartmoor."

"Whom would you recommend, then?"

Holmes laid his hand upon my arm.

"If my friend would undertake it there is no man who is better worth having at your side when you are in a tight place. No one can say so more confidently than I."

The proposition took me completely by surprise, but before I had time to answer, Baskerville seized me by the hand and **wrung**⑧ it heartily.

"Well, now, that is real kind of you, Dr. Watson," said he. "You see how it is with me, and you know just as much about the matter as I do. If you will come down to Baskerville Hall and see me through I'll never forget it."

The promise of adventure had always a fascination for me, and I was complimented by the words of Holmes and by the eagerness with which the baronet hailed me as a companion.

"I will come, with pleasure," said I. "I do not know how I could employ my time better."

① of one mind 同心一致

② advisability [əd,vaizə'bi
ləti] *n.* 明智；适当

③ trusty ['trʌsti] *a.* 可信赖的

④ endeavour [in'devə] *v.* 尽
力，竭力
⑤ extensive [ik'stensiv] *a.* 大
量的
⑥ appeal [ə'pi:l] *n.* 要求
（帮助、同情等），恳求
⑦ besmirch [bi'smə:tʃ] *v.* 弄
污

⑧ wring [riŋ] *v.* 拧，绞

那已故的伯父就是这样想的。如果房主没有足以维持产业的现金，那他怎么能够重振巴斯克维尔家族的威望呢？宅邸、土地和现金必须结合在一块儿。"

"是这么回事，对啦，亨利爵士，我和您的想法是一样的：您最好不要拖延，立刻到德文郡去。我只提一个条件：您一定不要一个人单独去。"

"莫蒂默医生陪我一同前往。"

"但是，莫蒂默医生经常要出诊，况且他的住所离您家有好几英里的路程。虽然他热情友善，但关键时刻他可能帮不上您什么忙。不，亨利爵士，您必须贴身带上一个人，一个值得信赖、能经常陪在您身边的人。"

"您亲自陪同我前往，这可能吗，福尔摩斯先生？"

"如果事情到了危急关头，我本人一定会想方设法赶过去的。不过，我的咨询业务很广泛，来自四面八方的请求又接连不断，因此，无限期地离开伦敦是不可能的。这点还希望您能谅解。眼下就有一位名人的事务需要处理，他出身于英国最有名望的家族之一，但他现在被人敲诈，名誉即将被毁坏，非得我出马才能阻止这场灾难性丑闻。您现在知道了，要我和您一起去达特穆尔是不可能的。"

"那您会给我推荐什么人呢？"

福尔摩斯把他的一只手放在我的胳膊上。

"如果我这位朋友愿意的话，那就再好不过了。当您处在紧急关头时，他能在您身边保护您。说到这一点，我比任何人都更加有把握。"

这个提议完全出乎我的意料，但没等我开口回应，巴斯克维尔就已经一把将我的手抓住，热情洋溢地握着不放。

"啊，是啊，您真好啊，华生医生，"他说，"您清楚我目前的处境，对事情的来龙去脉，您和我一样清楚。如果您能屈尊随我去庄园，陪我渡过难关，我将终生不忘。"

面临着的冒险对我总是有吸引力的，此外，我还受到福尔摩斯的一番恭维，从男爵又是那么真挚而热情地欢迎我做他的伙伴。

"非常荣幸，我会去的，"我说，"我不知道还有什

"And you will report very carefully to me," said Holmes. "When a crisis comes, as it will do, I will direct how you shall act. I suppose that by Saturday all might be ready?"

"Would that suit Dr. Watson?"

"Perfectly."

"Then on Saturday, unless you hear to the contrary, we shall meet at the ten-thirty train from Paddington."

We had risen to depart when Baskerville gave a cry, of triumph, and diving into one of the corners of the room he drew a brown boot from under a cabinet.

"My missing boot!" he cried.

"May all our difficulties vanish as easily!" said Sherlock Holmes.

"But it is a very singular thing," Dr. Mortimer remarked. "I searched this room carefully before lunch."

"And so did I," said Baskerville. "Every inch of it."

"There was certainly no boot in it then."

"In that case the waiter must have placed it there while we were lunching."

The German was sent for but professed to know nothing of the matter, nor could any inquiry, clear it up. Another item had been added to that constant and apparently purposeless series of small mysteries which had succeeded each other so rapidly. Setting aside the whole grim story of Sir Charles's death, we had a line of inexplicable incidents all within the limits of two days, which included the receipt of the printed letter, the black-bearded spy in the hansom, the loss of the new brown boot, the loss of the old black boot, and now the return of the new brown boot. Holmes sat in silence in the cab as we drove back to Baker Street, and I knew from his drawn brows and keen face that his mind, like my own, was busy in endeavouring to **frame**[1] some **scheme**[2] into which all these strange and apparently disconnected episodes could be fitted. All afternoon and late into the evening he sat lost in tobacco and thought.

Just before dinner two telegrams were handed in. The first ran:

Have just heard that Barrymore is at the Hall.

BASKERVILLE.

The second:

么方式能更好地支配我的时间。"

"你要仔细地向我汇报情况，"福尔摩斯说，"等到了危急关头，这是迟早的事，我会嘱咐你如何行动的。我想，到了礼拜六,一切都能准备就绪吧？"

"不知道这对华生医生是否方便？"

"非常方便。"

"那就定在礼拜六。如果我没有另行通知，我们就在火车站会面，乘十点三十分的从帕丁顿方向开来的那趟火车。"

我们刚站起身准备离开，这时，巴斯克维尔发出一声胜利的欢呼，并向房间的一个墙角跑过去，随后便从橱柜底下拖出一只棕褐色的靴子。

"我丢失的靴子！"他喊道。

"但愿我们的难题都能这样轻松地解决！"夏洛克·福尔摩斯说。

"但这可真是件怪事，"莫蒂默医生说，"我午餐前还把房间仔仔细细地检查了一遍。"

"我也检查过，"巴斯克维尔说，"一寸地方都没放过。"

"当时靴子肯定没在房间里。"

"这么说，一定是我们午餐时侍者把它放在那里的。"

找来了那个德国人，但他坦言自己对这件事情毫不知情，而且问他什么问题他都不清楚。一桩桩诡秘的小事件接二连三地发生，现在又添了这一桩，但从中又看不出任何意图。除去查尔斯爵士猝亡这个大疑团，在这两天的时间内又发生了一连串无法解释的事情。其中包括：收到用铅字粘贴成的短信，马车里的黑胡子跟踪的人，棕褐色的新靴和黑色旧靴的失踪，还有现在棕褐色新靴的重现。在我和福尔摩斯乘马车返回贝克大街的路上，他一言不发。从他那紧皱着的眉头和严峻的脸色，我知道他和我一样，头脑里正忙着把这些看似毫不相干的桩桩怪事拼串起来，看它们是否互相关联。整个下午，直至深夜，他始终坐着不动，一边抽烟一边沉思。

晚餐前夕，送来了两封电报，第一封的内容是：

刚才得知消息，巴里摩尔在庄园。

巴斯克维尔

① frame [freim] v. 制定，设计

② scheme[ski:m] n. 计划

Visited twenty-three hotels as directed, but sorry to report unable to trace cut sheet of Times.

CARTWRIGHT.

"There go two of my threads, Watson. There is nothing more stimulating than a case where everything goes against you. We must cast round for another scent."

"We have still the cabman who drove the spy."

"Exactly. I have wired to get his name and address from the Official Registry. I should not be surprised if this were an answer to my question."

The ring at the bell proved to be something even more satisfactory than an answer, however, for the door opened and a rough-looking fellow entered who was evidently the man himself.

"I got a message from the head office that a **gent**[1] at this address had been inquiring for No. 2704," said he. "I've driven my cab this seven years and never a word of complaint. I came here straight from the Yard to ask you **to your face**[2] what you had against me."

"I have nothing in the world against you, my good man," said Holmes. "On the contrary, I have half a **sovereign**[3] for you if you will give me a clear answer to my questions."

"Well, I've had a good day and no mistake," said the cabman with a grin. "What was it you wanted to ask, sir?"

"First of all your name and address, in case I want you again."

"John Clayton, 3 Turpey Street, the Borough. My cab is out of Shipley's Yard, near Waterloo Station."

Sherlock Holmes made a note of it.

"Now, Clayton, tell me all about the **fare**[4] who came and watched this house at ten o'clock this morning and afterwards followed the two gentlemen down Regent Street."

The man looked surprised and a little embarrassed. "Why, there's no good my telling you things, for you seem to know as much as I do already," said he. "The truth is that the gentleman told me that he was a detective and that I was

第二封的内容是：

照嘱已走访了二十三家旅馆，但很遗憾，未能找到剪过的《泰晤士报》。

卡特赖特

"我发现的两条线索都被掐断了，华生啊，一桩案件当中，一切都与你作对，没有比这更刺激的了。我们必须得设法寻找别的蛛丝马迹了。"

"我们还可以寻找那位载过盯梢者的马车夫呢。"

"一点不错。我已经发了电报给执照管理局，查寻他的姓名和住址。如果我要的答案现在就送到了，我一点都不会觉得奇怪。"

门铃响了，答复比预想的还要令人满意，因为大门打开后，进来了一个相貌粗俗的人，他显然就是我们要找的马车夫。

"管理局通知我说，住在这儿的一位顾客在打听2704号车，"他说，"我驾车有七个年头儿了，还从来没有顾客说要投诉我。所以我就从车场直接赶到这儿来了，想亲口问问您，您什么地方对我不满意。"

"好伙计，我对您没有任何不满，"福尔摩斯说，"恰恰相反，如果您明确地回答了我提出的问题，我还要送给您半个沙弗林。"

"啊，今天是个好日子，没有出什么差错，"车夫说着，咧开嘴笑了，"先生，您想问什么呢？"

"首先请告诉我您的大名和住址，恐怕以后还要请教您呢。"

"约翰·克莱顿，住在市镇区特皮大街三号。我的马车是从滑铁卢车站附近的希普利车场租的。"

夏洛克·福尔摩斯把这个情况记录了下来。

"行啊，克莱顿，请您把那位乘客的情况原原本本说一说，他今天上午十点钟来监视这所住宅，然后沿着摄政街尾随两位绅士。"

车夫看上去很惊讶，还有一点点尴尬。"啊，我也没什么事情好对您说的，因为您知道的事情好像和我知道的一样多了，"他说，"情况是这样的：乘车的那位先

① gent [dʒent] *n.* 绅士，男子

② to one's face 当面

③ sovereign ['sɔvərin] *n.* 金镑（面值一英镑的英国金币，1914年后停用）

④ fare [fɛə] *n.* 支付旅费的乘客

to say nothing about him to anyone."

"My good fellow; this is a very serious business, and you may find yourself in a pretty bad position if you try to hide anything from me. You say that your fare told you that he was a detective?"

"Yes, he did."

"When did he say this?"

"When he left me."

"Did he say anything more?"

"He mentioned his name."

Holmes cast a swift glance of triumph at me. "Oh, he mentioned his name, did he? That was imprudent. What was the name that he mentioned?"

"His name," said the cabman, "was Mr. Sherlock Holmes."

Never have I seen my friend more completely **taken aback**[①] than by the cabman's reply. For an instant he sat in silent amazement. Then he burst into a hearty laugh.

"A touch, Watson–an undeniable touch!" said he. "I feel a **foil**[②] as quick and **supple**[③] as my own. He got home upon me very prettily that time. So his name was Sherlock Holmes, was it?"

"Yes, sir, that was the gentleman's name."

"Excellent! Tell me where you picked him up and all that occurred."

"He **hailed**[④] me at half-past nine in Trafalgar Square. He said that he was a detective, and he offered me two **guineas**[⑤] if I would do exactly what he wanted all day and ask no questions. I was glad enough to agree. First we drove down to the Northumberland Hotel and waited there until two gentlemen came out and took a cab from the **rank**[⑥]. We followed their cab until it **pulled up**[⑦] somewhere near here."

"This very door," said Holmes.

"Well, I couldn't be sure of that, but I dare say my fare knew all about it. We pulled up halfway down the street and waited an hour and a half. Then the two gentlemen passed us, walking, and we followed down Baker Street and along ––"

"I know," said Holmes.

"Until we got three-quarters down Regent Street. Then my gentleman threw up the trap, and he cried that I should drive right away to Waterloo Station as hard as I could go. I whipped up the mare and we were there under

生告诉我，他是个侦探，要我不要对任何人提起他。"

"好伙计，这是件非常严肃的事情，如果您试图要对我隐瞒什么，您会发现自己的处境非常不利。您刚才是说，乘客告诉您他是一个侦探吗？"

"对，他就是这样说的。"

"他什么时候说的？"

"下车时。"

"他还说了什么？"

"他说了自己的名字。"

福尔摩斯得意地朝我使了个眼色。"噢，他说了自己的名字，对吧？那真是犯傻啊！他说他叫什么名字？"

"他的名字，"车夫说，"叫夏洛克·福尔摩斯先生。"

车夫的回答让我朋友完全愣住了，我还从没见他这样发愣过。一时间他目瞪口呆地坐着，随后便开怀大笑起来。

"碰着了，华生——毋庸置疑地碰着了啊！"他说，"我感触到了一柄利剑，如同我自己这柄一样锐利轻便。上次他可把我耍得团团转呢。他自称是夏洛克·福尔摩斯，对吧？"

"对，先生，这正是那位绅士的大名。"

"妙极了！告诉我他是在哪里上您的车的，后来情况如何？"

"他是九点半钟在特拉法尔加广场叫上我的，说自己是个侦探，如果我一整天严格按照他说的去做，不问任何问题，他就会付两个几尼给我。我很高兴，便满口答应了。我们驱车首先到了诺森伯兰旅馆，然后在那里等待，直到那两位先生出来，并叫了辆停在那儿的马车。我们跟在那辆马车的后面行驶，行进到这附近后便停了下来。"

"就是这个门？"福尔摩斯问。

"呃，我不能肯定，不过，那位乘客心里有数。我们在半道上停下，然后等了一个半小时。后来，两位先生步行从我们马车旁经过，我们就一路跟着，沿着贝克大街走下去——"

"这个我知道。"福尔摩斯说。

"我们一直跟着，走到了摄政街四分之三处。就在那时，我的乘客推开顶窗，大声叫我立刻往滑铁卢车站

① take aback 使吃惊；惊吓

② foil [foil] n. 花剑，轻剑。福尔摩斯为了说明对手思维敏捷，行动迅速，运用了击剑的隐喻。
③ supple ['sʌpl] a. 柔软的，灵活的

④ hail [heil] v. 打信号招呼（车、船等）
⑤ guinea ['gini] n. 几尼（1663年英国发行的一种金币，=21先令，于1813年停止流通）
⑥ rank [ræŋk] n. 行列
⑦ pull up 停住（车等）

the ten minutes. Then he paid up his two guineas, like a good one, and away he went into the station. Only just as he was leaving he turned round and he said: 'It might interest you to know that you have been driving Mr. Sherlock Holmes.' That's how I come to know the name."

"I see. And you saw no more of him?"

"Not after he went into the station."

"And how would you describe Mr. Sherlock Holmes?"

The cabman scratched his head. "Well, he wasn't **altogether**[1] such an easy gentleman to describe. I'd put him at forty years of age, and he was of a middle height, two or three inches shorter than you, sir. He was dressed like a **toff**[2], and he had a black beard, cut square at the end, and a pale face. I don't know as I could say more than that."

"Colour of his eyes?"

"No, I can't say that."

"Nothing more that you can remember?"

"No, sir; nothing."

"Well, then, here is your half-sovereign. There's another one waiting for you if you can bring any more information. Good-night!"

"Good-night, sir, and thank you!"

John Clayton departed **chuckling**[3], and Holmes turned to me with a shrug of his shoulders and a **rueful**[4] smile.

"Snap goes our third thread, and we end where we began," said he. "The cunning **rascal**[5]! He knew our number, knew that Sir Henry Baskerville had consulted me, spotted who I was in Regent Street, **conjectured**[6] that I had got the number of the cab and would lay my hands on the driver, and so sent back this **audacious**[7] message. I tell you, Watson, this time we have got a **foeman**[8] who is **worthy of our steel**[9]. I've been **checkmated**[10] in London. I can only wish you better luck in Devonshire. But I'm not easy in my mind about it."

"About what?"

"About sending you. It's an ugly business, Watson, an ugly, dangerous business, and the more I see of it the less I like it. Yes my dear fellow, you may laugh, but I give you my word that I shall be very glad to have you back **safe and sound**[11] in Baker Street once more."

跑，而且要尽可能快。我甩着鞭子策马，不到十分钟就赶到了车站。随后，他履行了承诺，付了两个几尼给我，然后哗的一下就进车站去了。就在他快要消失不见时，他回过头说，'今天乘坐您这辆车的就是夏洛克·福尔摩斯先生，您听了可能会觉得很有趣吧。'我就是这样知道这个名字的。"

"明白了。您随后就再没有见到过他吗？"

"他进车站后就再也没见着了。"

"那么，您会怎样描述那位夏洛克·福摩斯先生呢？"

车夫挠了挠头。"啊，要说清楚那位先生的长相还真难啊。先生，依我看，他四十岁左右，中等个头儿，比您矮那么两三英寸。他的穿着打扮像个有钱人，长着一大把黑胡子，胡子两端剪得齐平，脸色灰白。我想，我能说的就只有这些了。"

"眼睛是深颜色的？"

"不，我说不准。"

"您能想起其他什么情况吗？"

"没有了，先生，就只有这些。"

"嗯，那好，您拿着这半个沙弗林。您如果今后能给我带来其他消息，我还会奖您半个。晚安！"

"晚安，先生，非常感谢。"

约翰·克莱顿离开时咯咯地笑了。福尔摩斯转身看着我，耸了耸肩，脸上挂着无奈的笑容。

"我们的第三条线索也断了，又回到原点了，"他说，"狡诈的流氓！他清楚我们的路数了。他知道亨利爵士来找我咨询，在摄政街时，他又认出了我，于是，便猜到我会记下马车的车号，然后找到马车夫，所以他故意把我的名字告诉了他，真是岂有此理。华生，你要知道，我们这回可算是遇上了一个值得一争高下的对手了。他在伦敦给我将了一军。我只盼望你到德文郡后能有更好的运气。但这件事情我还是觉得放不下心。"

"对什么不放心？"

"派你去我不放心。华生，一桩棘手又危险的案件。我掌握的情况越多越担心。是啊，亲爱的伙伴，你可能会发笑，但我还是要对你说上一声，如果你能安然无恙地回到贝克大街，我会很高兴的。"

① altogether [,ɔ:ltə'geðə] *ad.*
总起来说

② toff [tɔːf] *n.* 花花公子，纨绔子弟

③ chuckle ['tʃʌkl] *v.* 咯咯地笑

④ rueful ['ruːful] *a.* 可怜的；令人同情的

⑤ rascal ['rɑːskəl] *n.* 流氓，恶棍，无赖

⑥ conjecture [kən'dʒektʃə] *v.* 推测出，猜想出

⑦ audacious [ɔː'deiʃəs] *a.* 放肆的，鲁莽的

⑧ foeman ['fəumən] *n.* 敌人

⑨ be worthy of one's steel 值得某人与之一斗的

⑩ checkmate ['tʃekmeit] *v.* 把…将死；使彻底失败

⑪ safe and sound 安然无恙

Chapter 6   Baskerville Hall

Sir Henry Baskerville and Dr. Mortimer were ready upon the appointed day, and we started as arranged for Devonshire. Mr. Sherlock Holmes drove with me to the station and gave me his last parting **injunctions**① and advice.

"I will not **bias**② your mind by suggesting theories or suspicions, Watson," said he; "I wish you simply to report facts in the fullest possible manner to me, and you can leave me to do the theorizing."

"What sort of facts?" I asked.

"Anything which may seem to have a **bearing**③ however indirect upon the case, and especially the relations between young Baskerville and his neighbours or any fresh particulars concerning the death of Sir Charles. I have made some inquiries myself in the last few days, but the results have, I fear, been negative. One thing only appears to be certain, and that is that Mr. James Desmond, who is the next heir, is an elderly gentleman of a very amiable **disposition**④, so that this persecution does not arise from him. I really think that we may eliminate him entirely from our calculations. There remain the people who will actually surround Sir Henry Baskerville upon the moor."

"Would it not be well in the first place to get rid of this Barrymore couple?"

"**By no means**⑤. You could not make a greater mistake. If they are innocent it would be a cruel injustice, and if they are guilty we should be giving up all chance of **bringing it home to**⑥ them. No, no, we will preserve them upon our list of suspects. Then there is a groom at the Hall, if I remember right. There are two moorland farmers. There is our friend Dr. Mortimer, whom I believe to

第六章　巴斯克维尔庄园

① injunction [in'dʒʌŋkʃən] *n.* 嘱咐
② bias ['baiəs] *v.* 影响，影响…以致产生偏差

③ bearing ['bɛəriŋ] *n.* 关系，关联

④ disposition [,dispə'ziʃən] *n.* 性格，脾气

⑤ by no means 决不

⑥ bring home (to) 证实（某人）犯（某罪）

到了约定的日子，亨利·巴斯克维尔爵士和莫蒂默医生都准备妥当了，我们按照事先的安排启程前往德文郡。夏洛克·福尔摩斯先生同我一道乘车去火车站。他临行前又给了我一些嘱咐和建议。

"我不想做出什么解释或者说出什么疑虑，以免影响你的判断，华生，"他说，"我只要求你把各种事实尽可能如实地向我汇报，然后由我来完成归纳、推理的工作。"

"哪方面的事实？"我问。

"看上去与本案有关的所有事实，不管是多么地间接的，尤其是年轻的巴斯克维尔与他的邻居们的关系，或者是与查尔斯爵士的猝亡有关的任何新疑点。前几天，我亲自做过一些调查，但我担心那些调查结果都是同案件关联不大的。只有一点似乎可以肯定，那就是詹姆斯·德斯蒙德先生，即下一任继承人，是一位年事较高的绅士，他为人非常友善，因此他绝对不会干出这种伤天害理的事情。我真的认为，我们在考虑嫌疑人时可以完全把他排除在外，只考虑那些荒原一带住在亨利·巴斯克维尔附近的人。"

"我们首先辞掉巴里摩尔夫妇不行吗？"

"绝对不行，否则你就犯下了没有比这更大的错误了。如果他们是无辜的，这样做对他们太不公平，而如果他们确实有罪，这样做就等于放弃了判他们应得之罪的机会。不行，不行，我们不如把他们留下列入嫌疑人

be entirely honest, and there is his wife, of whom we know nothing. There is this naturalist, Stapleton, and there is his sister, who is said to be a young lady of attractions. There is Mr. Frankland, of Lafter Hall, who is also an unknown factor, and there are one or two other neighbours. These are the folk who must be your very special study."

"I will do my best."

"You have **arms**[1], I suppose?"

"Yes, I thought it as well to take them."

"Most certainly. Keep your **revolver**[2] near you night and day, and never relax your precautions."

Our friends had already secured a first-class carriage and were waiting for us upon the platform.

"No, we have no news of any kind," said Dr. Mortimer in answer to my friend's questions. "I can swear to one thing, and that is that we have not been **shadowed**[3] during the last two days. We have never gone out without keeping a sharp watch, and no one could have escaped our notice."

"You have always kept together, I presume?"

"Except yesterday afternoon. I usually give up one day to pure amusement when I come to town, so I spent it at the Museum of the College of Surgeons."

"And I went to look at the folk in the park," said Baskerville. "But we had no trouble of any kind."

"It was imprudent, all the same," said Holmes, shaking his head and looking very grave. "I beg, Sir Henry, that you will not go about alone. Some great misfortune will **befall**[4] you if you do. Did you get your other boot?"

"No, sir, it is gone forever."

"Indeed. That is very interesting. Well, good-bye," he added as the train began to glide down the platform. "**Bear in mind**[5], Sir Henry, one of the phrases in that **queer**[6] old legend which Dr. Mortimer has read to us and avoid the moor in those hours of darkness when the powers of evil are exalted."

I looked back at the platform when we had left it far behind and saw the tall, **austere**[7] figure of Holmes standing motionless and gazing after us.

The journey was a swift and pleasant one, and I spent it in making the

名单。对啦，如果我没记错的话，庄园里住着一个马夫和两个荒原上的农夫。还有我们的朋友莫蒂默医生和他的夫人，我相信医生是绝对诚实的，而我们对他夫人却一无所知。还有那位生物学家斯塔普尔顿，以及他的妹妹，据说是位迷人的年轻姑娘。还有住在拉夫特尔庄园的弗兰克兰先生，他也是个情况不明的人物。最后还有一两个别的邻居。所有这些人你都要特别注意观察。"

"我会竭尽所能。"

"我看，你带着枪吧？"

"对，我觉得还是带着的好。"

"毫无疑问。无论白天黑夜，手枪绝对不要离身，千万不要放松警惕啊。"

我们的朋友早已订好了头等车厢的座位，此时正站在站台上等着我们。

"没有，没有任何消息，"莫蒂默医生回答我朋友的问话，"有一点我能肯定，那就是，昨天和前天都没人盯我们的梢。我们每次出去时都高度警惕，谁也逃不出我们的视线。"

"我想，这两天你们一直形影不离吧？"

"除了昨天下午，我每次进城时，总会花上一整天时间来消遣娱乐，所以我昨天下午去参观了外科医师学会博物馆。"

"我去公园看热闹去了，"巴斯克维尔说，"我们都没遇上什么麻烦。"

"不管怎么说，你们还是不够谨慎，"福尔摩斯摇了摇头，板着脸说，"亨利爵士，我请求您，以后不要一个人单独四处走动。不然，您肯定会大祸临头的。您找到另一只靴子了吗？"

"没有啊，先生，永远找不回来了。"

"可不是嘛。这事情很有意思啊。行啊，再见吧，"火车沿着站台徐徐移动时，他补充说，"请记住，亨利爵士，莫蒂默医生给我们念的那个怪异离奇的古老传说中的一句话——邪恶势力甚嚣尘上的黑暗时刻，要避开荒原。"

火车离开站台很远了，我回头望去，看到了福尔摩斯高大严肃的身影，仍然一动不动地仁立在那儿，目不转睛地盯着我们看。

---

① arms [ɑːmz] *n.* 武器

② revolver [riˈvɔlvə] *n.* 左轮手枪

③ shadow [ˈʃædəu] *v.* 跟踪

④ befall [biˈfɔːl] *v.* 降临，发生

⑤ bear in mind 记住

⑥ queer [kwiə] *a.* 异乎寻常的

⑦ austere [ɔˈstiə] *a.* （神色、态度等）严肃的，严峻的

more intimate acquaintance of my two companions and in playing with Dr. Mortimer's spaniel. In a very few hours the brown earth had become **ruddy**[①], the brick had changed to **granite**[②], and red cows **grazed**[③] in well-hedged fields where the **lush**[④] grasses and more **luxuriant**[⑤] vegetation spoke of a richer, if a damper, climate. Young Baskerville stared eagerly out of the window and cried aloud with delight as he recognized the familar features of the Devon scenery.

"I've been over a good part of the world since I left it, Dr. Watson," said he; "but I have never seen a place to compare with it."

"l never saw a Devonshire man who did not **swear by**[⑥] his county," I remarked.

"It depends upon the breed of men quite as much as on the county," said Dr. Mortimer. "A glance at our friend here reveals the rounded head of the **Celt**[⑦], which carries inside it the Celtic enthusiasm and power of attachment. Poor Sir Charles's head was of a very rare type, half Gaelic, half Ivernian in its characteristics. But you were very young when you last saw Baskerville Hall, were you not?"

"I was a boy in my teens at the time of my father's death and had never seen the Hall, for he lived in a little cottage on the South Coast. Thence I went straight to a friend in America. I tell you it is all as new to me as it is to Dr. Watson, and I'm as keen as possible to see the moor."

"Are you? Then your wish is easily granted, for there is your first sight of the moor," said Dr. Mortimer, pointing out of the carriage window.

Over the green squares of the fields and the low curve of a wood there rose in the distance a gray, **melancholy**[⑧] hill, with a strange **jagged**[⑨] summit, dim and vague in the distance, like some fantastic landscape in a dream. Baskerville sat for a long time, his eyes fixed upon it, and I read upon his eager face how much it meant to him, this first sight of that strange spot where the men of his blood had **held sway**[⑩] so long and left their mark so deep. There he sat, with his **tweed**[⑪] suit and his American accent, in the corner of a prosaic railway-carriage, and yet as I looked at his dark and expressive face I felt more than ever how true a descendant he was of that long line of **high-blooded**[⑫], fiery, and masterful men. There were

① ruddy ['rʌdi] a. 发红的

② granite ['grænit] n. 花岗岩
③ graze [greiz] v. 吃草
④ lush [lʌʃ] a. 葱翠的；繁茂的
⑤ luxuriant [lʌg'zjuəriənt] a. 茂盛的，繁茂的

⑥ swear by 认为…极好，对…评价很高

⑦ Celt [kelt] n. 凯尔特人

⑧ melancholy ['melənkəli] a. 令人伤感的；使人忧郁的
⑨ jagged ['dʒægid] a. 凹凸不平的

⑩ hold sway 支配，统治
⑪ tweed [twi:d] n. 粗呢套装

⑫ high-blooded ['hai'blʌdid] a. 血统纯正的；出身良好的

这是一段快捷而又舒适的行程。期间，我同两位同伴的关系进一步密切了，还同莫蒂默医生的长耳猎犬玩耍嬉戏。短短几个小时之后，棕褐色的土地变成了红色，砖瓦房换成了石头建筑，枣红色的牛群在用树篱圈起来的土地上吃草。如茵绿草，更显茂盛的植被，表明了气候更加湿润，甚至更加潮湿。年轻的巴斯克维尔急切地盯着窗外看，当他认出德文郡那熟悉的风光时，他高兴得大叫起来。

"我离开这儿之后，到过世界上的许多地方，华生医生，"他说，"但我却从未见过任何一个能够同这儿相媲美的地方。"

"我也从没见过任何一个不赞美自己故乡的德文郡人呢。"我说。

"这既有赖于本郡的自然环境，也同时有赖于人脉血统啊，"莫蒂默医生说，"请看我们这位朋友，他圆圆的头颅就是属于凯尔特型的，里面充满了凯尔特人的热情洋溢和忠诚不贰。已故的查尔斯爵士的头颅则十分罕见，兼有盖尔人和伊弗尼人的特点。但是，您最后见到巴斯克维尔庄园时，还很年幼，对吧？"

"我父亲去世时，我还是个十多岁的孩子。先前从未见过庄园，因为他居住在南海岸的一幢小别墅里。从那之后，我便直接去投靠了一个在美国的朋友。实话告诉您，我同华生医生一样，对庄园的情况一无所知，热切地期待着去欣赏一番荒原上的风光呢。"

"真的吗？那么，您的愿望很容易就能够实现了，因为那就是呈现在您面前的第一道荒原风光了。"莫蒂默医生边说边指着车窗外面。

眺望远方，在那被分割成一块块方格的绿色田野上，在那由树梢连成的低矮的曲线处，一座灰暗而阴郁、顶端崎岖不平的小山丘慢慢地升起来。远远望去，小山晦暗而朦胧，宛若梦中的幻景。巴斯克维尔久久地坐着，两眼紧盯着窗外，一脸热切的表情。我据此明白了，第一眼看到这个怪异的地方对他的触动很大。毕竟，他的同族家人管理了庄园这么多年，在此留下了深深的印记。他身上穿着苏格兰呢的衣服，说话时带着美洲口音，静坐在一个寻常火车车厢的角落里。但当我看

pride, valour, and strength in his thick brows, his sensitive nostrils, and his large **hazel**① eyes. If on that **forbidding**② moor a difficult and dangerous quest should lie before us, this was at least a comrade for whom one might venture to take a risk with the certainty that he would bravely share it.

The train pulled up at a small wayside station and we all descended. Outside, beyond the low, white fence, a **wagonette**③ with a pair of **cobs**④ was waiting. Our coming was evidently a great event, for station-master and porters clustered round us to carry out our luggage. It was a sweet, simple country spot, but I was surprised to observe that by the gate there stood two soldierly men in dark uniforms who leaned upon their short rifles and glanced keenly at us as we passed. The coachman, a hard-faced, **gnarled**⑤ little fellow, saluted Sir Henry Baskerville, and in a few minutes we were flying swiftly down the broad, white road. Rolling pasture lands curved upward on either side of us, and old **gabled**⑥ houses peeped out from amid the thick green **foliage**⑦, but behind the peaceful and sunlit countryside there rose ever, dark against the evening sky, the long, gloomy curve of the moor, broken by the jagged and **sinister**⑧ hills.

The wagonette swung round into a side road, and we curved upward through deep lanes worn by centuries of wheels, high banks on either side, heavy with dripping moss and fleshy **hart's-tongue**⑨ ferns. Bronzing **bracken**⑩ and mottled **bramble**⑪ gleamed in the light of the sinking sun. Still steadily rising, we passed over a narrow granite bridge and skirted a noisy stream which gushed swiftly down, foaming and roaring amid the gray **boulders**⑫. Both road and stream wound up through a valley dense with scrub oak and fir. At every turn Baskerville gave an exclamation of delight, looking eagerly about him and asking countless questions. To his eyes all seemed beautiful, but to me a tinge of melancholy lay upon the countryside, which bore so clearly the mark of the waning year. Yellow leaves carpeted the lanes and **fluttered**⑬ down upon us as we passed. The rattle of our wheels died away as we drove through drifts of rotting vegetation–sad gifts, as it seemed to me, for Nature to throw before the carriage of the returning heir of the Baskervilles.

"Halloa!" cried Dr. Mortimer, "what is this?"

① hazel ['heizəl] *a.* 淡褐色的

② forbidding[fə'bidiŋ] *a.* 恐怖的，可怕的

③ wagonette [,wægə'net] *n.* 四轮轻便游览马车

④ cob [kɔb] *n.* 结实的短腿马

⑤ gnarled [nɑːld] *a.* （性情）暴躁的，易怒的

⑥ gabled ['geibld] *a.* 有山墙的；有三角墙的

⑦ foliage ['fəuliidʒ] *n.* （一株植物或树的）全部叶子；一簇叶子

⑧ sinister ['sinistə] *a.* 不吉利的，不祥的

⑨ hart's-tongue ['hɑːtstʌŋ] *n.* 羊齿蕨

⑩ bracken ['brækən] *n.* 欧洲蕨

⑪ bramble ['bræmbl] *n.* 荆棘；树莓

⑫ boulder ['bəuldə] *n.* 大圆石；巨砾

⑬ flutter ['flʌtə] *v.* 飘扬，飘落

着他那黝黑而富于表情的面孔时，我就更加真切地意识到，他确是那个古老家族的后代，血统高贵，性情刚烈，高傲专横。他那浓密的眉毛，敏感的鼻子和栗色的大眼睛无不显示着骄傲、豪放和强大。如果我们真会在那令人恐怖的荒原上面临困难和危险情况，至少他会是个可靠的同伴，会勇敢地承担风险。

火车在路边的一个小站停了下来，我们下车了。一辆由两匹短腿小马拉着的四轮马车在低矮的白色栏杆外等候着我们。很显然，我们的到来是一件大事，因为站长和搬运工都向我们围了上来，帮着我们搬运行李。这是一个恬静而朴实的乡村小站。但是，令我感到诧异的是，出站口处，站着两个身穿黑色制服的人，他们像军人那样站着，身体倚在不长的来复枪上，两眼直勾勾地盯着我们走过去。马车夫身材矮小，神情冷酷而粗鲁，他对着亨利·巴斯克维尔爵士行了个礼。几分钟过后，我们沿着宽阔的白色大道疾驰而去。道路的两旁是起伏不平的牧草地。古老的山墙房舍穿透浓密的绿荫，露出屋顶。但在这宁静而又充满阳光的村落后面，却绵延着又长又阴郁的荒原，上面布列着几座参差不齐且险恶的小山，在傍晚天空的衬托下，显得尤为阴暗。

四轮马车拐了个弯，驶入了一条岔路。我们顺着一条路面深陷的——这是几个世纪来被马车车轮轧成的小路曲折前行。道路的两侧是高高的石壁，上面长满了湿漉漉的苔藓和枝叶肥厚的羊齿植物。在落日的余晖中，古铜色的蕨类和色彩斑驳的黑莓闪闪发亮。我们持续往上行驶着，经过了一座窄小的花岗石桥，然后沿着一条喧闹的小河继续前行。小河水流湍急，浪花四溅，从灰色的乱石之间咆哮而过。无论是小河还是道路，他们都在长满了矮小的橡树和枞树的峡谷之中蜿蜒而行。每到一个拐弯处，巴斯克维尔都会高兴得大叫起来，他眼睛急切地环顾四周，嘴里不断问着无数的问题。在他眼里，一切都是那么美丽，但我却觉得这一带的乡村明显呈现出深秋的景象，难免有一点凄凉。枯黄的树叶铺满了整条小路，我们从那儿经过时，还有些树叶翩翩飞落到我们身上。我们的马车从枯叶上走过，此时，辘辘的车轮声也寂静了下来——我隐约觉得，这是造物主撒在

A steep curve of heath-clad land, an outlying **spur**① of the moor, lay in front of us. On the summit, hard and clear like an **equestrian**② statue upon its **pedestal**③, was a mounted soldier, dark and stern, his rifle poised ready over his forearm. He was watching the road along which we travelled.

"What is this, Perkins?" asked Dr. Mortimer.

Our driver half turned in his seat.

"There's a **convict**④ escaped from Princetown, sir. He's been out three days now, and the **warders**⑤ watch every road and every station, but they've had no sight of him yet. The farmers about here don't like it, sir, and that's a fact."

"Well, I understand that they get five pounds if they can give information."

"Yes, sir, but the chance of five pounds is but a poor thing compared to the chance of having your throat cut. You see, it isn't like any ordinary convict. This is a man that would **stick**⑥ at nothing."

"Who is he, then?"

"It is Selden, the Notting Hill murderer."

I remembered the case well, for it was one in which Holmes had taken an interest on account of the peculiar **ferocity**⑦ of the crime and the wanton brutality which had marked all the actions of the assassin. The **commutation**⑧ of his death sentence had been due to some doubts as to his complete sanity, so **atrocious**⑨ was his conduct. Our wagonette had topped a rise and in front of us rose the huge expanse of the moor, mottled with gnarled and **craggy**⑩ **cairns**⑪ and **tors**⑫. A cold wind swept down from it and set us shivering. Somewhere there, on that desolate plain, was lurking this **fiendish**⑬ man, hiding in a burrow like a wild beast, his heart full of **malignancy**⑭ against the whole race which had cast him out. It needed but this to complete the grim suggestiveness of the barren waste, the chilling wind, and the darkling sky. Even Baskerville fell silent and pulled his overcoat more closely around him.

We had left the fertile country behind and beneath us. We looked back on it now, the slanting rays of a low sun turning the streams to threads of

① spur[spə:] n. 山鼻子，山嘴尖坡
② equestrian [i'kwestriən] n. 骑马者
③ pedestal ['pedistəl] n. 基座，底座

④ convict [kən'vikt] n. 罪犯
⑤ warder ['wɔ:də] n. 监狱看守，狱吏

⑥ stick[stik] v. 犹豫，踌躇；有顾虑

⑦ ferocity [fə'rɔsiti] n. 凶恶，残忍
⑧ commutation [,kɔmju:'teiʃən] n. 改刑；减刑
⑨ atrocious [ə'trəuʃəs] a. 残忍的，残暴的

⑩ craggy['krægi] a. 峻峭的；崎岖的
⑪ cairn [kɛən] n. 石冢
⑫ tor [tɔ:] n. 突岩
⑬ fiendish ['fi:ndiʃ] a. 穷凶极恶的
⑭ malignancy [mə'lignənsi] n. 恶意；敌意

重返家园的巴斯克维尔家族后裔车前的不祥之物。

"嘿！"莫蒂默医生大声说，"那是什么？"

我们的前方出现了一处长满欧石南的陡峭的山坡，它突显在荒原的边缘。山顶上可以清楚地看到一个骑在马背上的士兵，就像一具屹立在碑座上的骑士雕像一样。他黝黑而严峻，来复枪搭在伸向前方的手臂上，呈预备发射的姿势。他在监视我们要走的这条道路。

"那是什么啊，珀金斯？"莫蒂默医生问。

车夫在座位上把身子半侧过来。

"有个罪犯从王子镇逃跑了，先生，到现在为止，已经三天了。监狱的看守们正在监视每一条道路，每一个车站，但还没有发现他的踪迹呢。附近的农户们都感到很不安，先生，事情就是这样的。"

"啊，我知道这个，如果有人提供信息，就能得到五英镑的赏金。"

"是的，先生，但同可能会被人割断喉管相比，可能拿到的五镑钱就显得太微不足道了。您知道，他可不是什么普通的罪犯，是个肆无忌惮的家伙。"

"那他到底是谁呢？"

"他叫塞尔登，是诺丁山凶杀案中的那位凶手。"

那桩案件我记得很清楚，罪行极其残暴，罪犯的手段极其残忍，因此引起了福尔摩斯的关注。罪犯之所以逃脱了死刑，是因为其暴行太过残忍，以至让人怀疑他的精神状态是否健全。说话的当儿，我们的马车驶上了坡顶，呈现在我们眼前的是一片广袤的荒原，还有散布其中的嶙峋怪异的突岩和堆垒如冢的乱石。一股寒风从荒原方向吹过来，我们不禁浑身打寒战。渺无人烟的荒原上的某个角落里，一个鬼魅似的人物正像野兽藏身于洞穴一样潜藏着。他的内心充满着憎恨，他恨所有摒弃他的人们。光秃秃的荒地，冷飕飕的寒风，幽黑的夜空，再加上一个杀人逃犯，所有这一切都会令人感到阴森恐怖。就连巴斯克维尔也沉默不语，他把大衣裹得更紧了。

我们很快驶离了丰饶肥沃的乡村。回头遥望，我们看见在夕阳的斜照下，溪水泛着丝丝闪闪的金光，新近翻耕过的红色土地和宽广而葱郁的林地也烁烁发亮。我们前面的道路蜿蜒在棕褐色和橄榄色的坡地上，更显得

gold and glowing on the red earth new turned by the plough and the broad
tangle of the woodlands. The road in front of us grew bleaker and wilder
over huge **russet**① and olive slopes, sprinkled with giant boulders. Now and
then we passed a moorland cottage, walled and roofed with stone, with no
creeper to break its harsh outline. Suddenly we looked down into a cuplike
depression, patched with stunted oaks and firs which had been twisted and
bent by the fury of years of storm. Two high, narrow towers rose over the
trees. The driver pointed with his whip.

"Baskerville Hall," said he.

Its master had risen and was staring with flushed cheeks and shining
eyes. A few minutes later we had reached the lodge-gates, a maze of
fantastic **tracery**② in wrought iron, with weather-bitten pillars on either
side, blotched with **lichens**③, and surmounted by the boars' heads of the
Baskervilles. The lodge was a ruin of black granite and bared ribs of rafters,
but facing it was a new building, half constructed, the first fruit of Sir
Charles's South African gold.

Through the gateway we passed into the avenue, where the wheels were
again hushed amid the leaves, and the old trees shot their branches in a
sombre④ tunnel over our heads. Baskerville shuddered as he looked up the
long, dark drive to where the house glimmered like a ghost at the farther end.

"Was it here?" he asked in a low voice.

"No, no, the yew alley is on the other side."

The young heir glanced round with a gloomy face.

"It's no wonder my uncle felt as if trouble were coming on him in such
a place as this," said he. "It's enough to scare any man. I'll have a row of
electric lamps up here inside of six months, and you won't know it again,
with a thousand candle-power Swan and Edison right here in front of the
hall door."

The avenue opened into a broad expanse of turf, and the house lay
before us. In the fading light I could see that the centre was a heavy block of
building from which a **porch**⑤ **projected**⑥. The whole front was **draped**⑦
in ivy, with a patch clipped bare here and there where a window or **a coat
of arms**⑧ broke through the dark veil. From this central block rose the twin

凄凉荒芜。我们时不时地途经一幢荒原小屋，墙和顶都是用石头砌成的，粗陋的墙体上也没有藤蔓的攀缘和装饰。忽然，我们低头一望，看见到了一处盆状的低洼地，那里四处长着成片的橡树和冷杉，因受长年的风吹雨打，枝干扭曲、弯折了。穿过树林，可以看见两座高耸的尖塔。车夫用马鞭指了指尖塔。

"巴斯克维尔庄园。"他说。

庄园的主人早已站起身来，出神地看着，两颊泛红，眼睛发亮。几分钟过后，我们到达了宅邸大门前。大门是用式样奇异繁复的铁条焊接而成，两边的门柱饱受风雨的侵蚀，上面的地衣苔藓斑驳可见，门柱的顶端各有一个象征巴斯克维尔家族的石雕野猪头标记。门房已破旧成了一堆花岗岩石头，露出了一根光秃的柱椽。但门房的对面却是一座崭新的建筑，刚完成了一半，它是查尔斯爵士从南非淘金回来后兴建的第一幢建筑。

走过大门，我们进入了林荫道，路面铺满了落叶，车轮的辘辘声又寂静了下来。在我们头顶上，老树枝丫交错，形成了一条阴暗的拱道。巴斯克维尔抬头向又长又暗的拱道另一端望去，只见一幢宅邸如幽灵般发出亮光，他不禁打了个哆嗦。

"这儿就是出事地点吗？"他低声问了一句。

"不，不是，是在另一边的紫杉树篱的小道附近。"

年轻继承人脸色阴郁地环顾了一番四周。

"住在这样一个地方，难怪我伯父总有一种要大难临头的感觉，"他说，"这里足以把任何人吓跑。我要在六个月内给小道装上一排一千标准烛光的'斯旺牌'和'爱迪生牌'的灯泡，到那时你们恐怕都不再认得这个地方了。"

走过林荫道尽头进入一片宽阔的草地，宅院就呈现在我们的面前了。昏暗的光线下，我看到宅院的中央是一幢坚实的楼房，前面设有一道门廊。宅邸前部爬满了常春藤，只有在窗户或装有纹章图案的地方剪掉了藤蔓，显出一小块一小块光秃的地方。就像是在黑色面罩的破损处打上了补丁似的。中心楼房的顶上有一对开有枪眼和瞭望孔的古老塔楼。塔楼的左侧和右侧各有一座式样现代的用黑色花岗岩建成的翼楼。暗淡的光线从带有厚重窗棂的窗口透出来，一条黑色的烟柱从安装在陡

① russet ['rʌsit] a. 黄褐色的；赤褐色的

② tracery ['treisəri] n. 窗花格；装饰图案
③ lichen ['laikən] n. 地衣

④ sombre ['sɔmbə] a. 阴沉的，阴暗的

⑤ porch [pɔːtʃ] n. （上有顶棚的）门廊；柱廊
⑥ project ['prɔdʒekt] v. 凸出；突出
⑦ drape [dreip] v. 覆盖
⑧ coat of arms （盾形）纹章，盾徽，盾形徽号

towers, ancient, **crenellated**①, and pierced with many loopholes. To right and left of the turrets were more modern wings of black granite. A dull light shone through heavy **mullioned**② windows, and from the high chimneys which rose from the steep, high-angled roof there sprang a single black column of smoke.

"Welcome, Sir Henry! Welcome to Baskerville Hall!"

A tall man had stepped from the shadow of the porch to open the door of the wagonette. The figure of a woman was **silhouetted**③ against the yellow light of the hall. She came out and helped the man to hand down our bags.

"You don't mind my driving straight home, Sir Henry?" said Dr. Mortimer. "My wife is expecting me."

"Surely you will stay and have some dinner?"

"No, I must go. I shall probably find some work awaiting me. I would stay to show you over the house, but Barrymore will be a better guide than I. Good-bye, and never hesitate night or day to send for me if I can be of service."

The wheels died away down the drive while Sir Henry and I turned into the hall, and the door clanged heavily behind us. It was a fine apartment in which we found ourselves, large, **lofty**④, and heavily **raftered**⑤ with huge **baulks**⑥ of age-blackened oak. In the great old-fashioned fireplace behind the high iron **dogs**⑦ a log-fire crackled and snapped. Sir Henry and I held out our hands to it, for we were numb from our long drive. Then we gazed round us at the high, thin window of old stained glass, the oak panelling, the stags' heads, the coats of arms upon the walls, all dim and sombre in the subdued light of the central lamp.

"It's just as I imagined it," said Sir Henry. "Is it not the very picture of an old family home? To think that this should be the same hall in which for five hundred years my people have lived. It strikes me solemn to think of it."

I saw his dark face lit up with a boyish enthusiasm as he gazed about him. The light beat upon him where he stood, but long shadows trailed down the walls and hung like a black **canopy**⑧ above him. Barrymore had returned from taking our luggage to our rooms. He stood in front of us now with the

① crenellated ['krenəleitid] *a.* 有雉堞的

② mullioned ['mʌljənd] *a.* 有竖框的

③ silhouette [ˌsilu:'et] *v.* 使现出轮廓

④ lofty ['lɔfti] *a.* 极高的
⑤ rafter ['rɑːftə] *v.* 装椽于
⑥ baulk [bɔːk] *n.* 梁木
⑦ dog [dɔg] *v.* 跟踪；尾随

⑧ canopy ['kænəpi] *n.* 天篷；华盖

峭而倾斜的屋顶上的高烟囱里袅袅上升。

"欢迎啊，亨利爵士！欢迎您回巴斯克维尔庄园！"

一个身材高大的男子从门廊的背阴处走过来，打开了马车的车门。大厅里淡黄色的灯光映照着一个女人的身影。她走了出来，帮那个男人把我们的行李袋搬下来。

"我乘车直接回家，您不会介意吧，亨利爵士？"莫蒂默医生说，"我夫人正在家等着我呢。"

"一定要再待一会儿，用过晚餐再走，不可以吗？"

"不行啊，我一定要走。可能家里还有事情等待我去处理呢。我本该留下来领着您看看宅邸的，不过巴里摩尔比我更适合当您的向导。再见吧。无论白天还是黑夜，只要我能帮得上忙，就请您立刻差人来叫我好啦。"

当车轮声消失在林荫道上时，我和亨利爵士走进了大厅，厅门在我们身后发出砰的一声巨响。我们所在的厅堂非常豪华，宽敞高大，橡木是一些因年代久远而变黑了的巨重橡木。高大的铁狗雕像后面是一个巨大的旧式壁炉，木柴在里面噼啪爆裂地燃烧着。因为长途乘车的缘故，我和亨利爵士都冻得全身麻木了，我们便伸手去烤火取暖，想好好休息一下。随后，我们朝四周环顾了一番，看了看那又窄又高的镶嵌着老式彩色玻璃的窗户，橡木做的嵌板，牡鹿头的标本和墙上所挂的纹章图案。一切在中间大吊灯柔和的光映照下，显得格外幽暗阴郁。

"此景恰如我想象中的样子，"亨利爵士说，"这不就是一个古老家族应有的景象吗？想一想，这就是我们家族祖祖辈辈住了五百年的大厅啊。想到这一点，一种庄严神圣的感觉在我心中油然而生。"

他环视着四周时，我看到他那黝黑的面孔上燃起了孩童般的激情。灯光从他站立的地方照射下来，在墙上留下了长长的影像，像天棚似的罩在他头上。巴里摩尔把我们的行李送进各自的卧室后，回到了大厅，谦卑顺从地站立在我们的面前，举止神态一看就是个训练有素的仆人。他是个长相不一般的男人，身材修长，相貌英俊，黑胡须剪得方方正正的，肤色白皙，五官出色。

"打算立刻就用餐吗，先生？"

"准备好了吗？"

"几分钟就好了，先生。你们的房间里准备好了热

subdued[①] manner of a well-trained servant. He was a remarkable-looking man, tall, handsome, with a square black beard and pale, distinguished features.

"Would you wish dinner to be served at once, sir?"

"Is it ready?"

"In a very few minutes, sir. You will find hot water in your rooms. My wife and I will be happy, Sir Henry, to stay with you until you have made your fresh arrangements, but you will understand that under the new conditions this house will require a considerable staff."

"What new conditions?"

"I only meant, sir, that Sir Charles led a very retired life, and we were able to look after his **wants**[②]. You would, naturally, wish to have more company, and so you will need changes in your household."

"Do you mean that your wife and you wish to leave?"

"Only when it is quite convenient to you, sir."

"But your family have been with us for several generations, have they not? I should be sorry to begin my life here by breaking an old family connection."

I seemed to discern some signs of emotion upon the butler's white face.

"I feel that also, sir, and so does my wife. But to tell the truth, sir, we were both very much attached to Sir Charles and his death gave us a shock and made these surroundings very painful to us. I fear that we shall never again be easy in our minds at Baskerville Hall."

"But what do you intend to do?"

"I have no doubt, sir, that we shall succeed in establishing ourselves in some business. Sir Charles's generosity has given us the **means**[③] to do so. And now, sir, perhaps I had best show you to your rooms."

A square **balustraded**[④] gallery ran round the top of the old hall, approached by a double stair. From this central point two long corridors extended the whole length of the building, from which all the bedrooms opened. My own was in the same **wing**[⑤] as Baskerville's and almost next door to it. These rooms appeared to be much more modern than the central part of the house, and the bright paper and numerous candles did something to remove the sombre impression which our arrival had left upon my mind.

① subdued [səb'dju:d] *a.* 服从的，顺从的

② wants [wɔnts] *n.* 需求

③ means[mi:nz] *n.* 财富；资力

④ balustrade [,bæləs'treid] *n.* 栏杆，扶手

⑤ wing [wiŋ] *n.*（建筑物）侧翼

水。亨利爵士，在您做出新的安排之前，我和我的妻子都很愿意伺候您。不过，您可能看出来了，在目前这种新情况下，府上需要相当多的人手。"

"什么新情况？"

"我只是想要说，先生，查尔斯爵士过的是离群索居的生活，我们两个人可以满足得了他的需求。不过您呢，自然会希望有更多的人跟您住在一起，您势必会对府上的规矩做出一些调整。"

"你的意思是，你和你妻子要离去吗？"

"只是在您认为方便的时候，先生。"

"但是，你们家同我们在一起，已经有几代人的时间了，不是吗？如果说我到这儿的生活以断绝一种悠久的家族关系开始，那真会感到遗憾的。"

我从管家苍白的面孔看到了些许激动的情绪。

"我也有这种感觉，先生，我妻子也是如此。但是，实话实说，先生，我们两个人对查尔斯爵士的感情都很深，他的离世让我们非常震惊，这儿周围各处的环境都会让我们感到很痛苦。我担心，只要我们留在巴斯克维尔庄园，我们的内心就再也不会得到安宁了。"

"但是，你们打算干什么呢？"

"我毫不怀疑，先生，我们可以干点营生来自食其力。查尔斯爵士的慷慨大方也给予了我们这样去做的可能。不过现在，先生们，我最好还是领你们去看看你们的房间吧。"

一个装有回栏的方形游廊在古老大厅的上层，要通过一段双叠的楼梯才能走上去。以此为中心，两侧各伸出一条长长的走廊，直通整座建筑，所有卧室的门都朝走廊开着。我的卧室和巴斯克维尔的在同一侧，并且几乎紧挨着。卧室看上去比宅邸中间部分要显得现代多了。里面糊着色调明快的墙纸，点着数不胜数的蜡烛。这令刚到此地时，我的脑海中留下的阴郁印象多少消除掉了一点。

但是，对着大厅而开的餐厅却是一个昏暗阴沉的地方。这是长方形的房间，里面有一个台阶把餐厅隔成高低两部分。高出的一端是主人用餐的地方，低的部分是供下人使用的。餐厅的一端还建有一个演奏台。我们的头顶上横着一些乌黑的梁木，再往上就是被熏黑了的天

But the dining-room which opened out of the hall was a place of shadow and gloom. It was a long chamber with a step separating the **dais**① where the family sat from the lower portion reserved for their dependents. At one end a **minstrel's**② gallery overlooked it. Black beams shot across above our heads, with a smoke-darkened ceiling beyond them. With rows of **flaring**③ torches to light it up, and the colour and rude **hilarity**④ of an old-time banquet, it might have softened; but now, when two black-clothed gentlemen sat in the little circle of light thrown by a shaded lamp, one's voice became hushed and one's spirit subdued. A dim line of ancestors, in every variety of dress, from the Elizabethan knight to the **buck**⑤ of the Regency, stared down upon us and **daunted**⑥ us by their silent company. We talked little, and I for one was glad when the meal was over and we were able to retire into the modern billiard-room and smoke a cigarette.

"My word, it isn't a very cheerful place," said Sir Henry. "I suppose one can **tone down**⑦ to it, but I feel a bit **out of the picture**⑧ at present. I don't wonder that my uncle got a little **jumpy**⑨ if he lived all alone in such a house as this. However, if it suits you, we will retire early to-night, and perhaps things may seem more cheerful in the morning."

I drew aside my curtains before I went to bed and looked out from my window. It opened upon the grassy space which lay in front of the hall door. Beyond, two copses of trees moaned and swung in a rising wind. A half moon broke through the **rifts**⑩ of racing clouds. In its cold light I saw beyond the trees a broken fringe of rocks, and the long, low curve of the melancholy moor. I closed the curtain, feeling that my last impression was in keeping with the rest.

And yet it was not quite the last. I found myself weary and yet **wakeful**⑪, tossing restlessly from side to side, seeking for the sleep which would not come. Far away a chiming clock struck out the quarters of the hours, but otherwise a deathly silence lay upon the old house. And then suddenly, in the very dead of the night, there came a sound to my ears, clear, resonant, and unmistakable. It was the sob of a woman, the **muffled**⑫, **strangling**⑬ gasp of one who is torn by an uncontrollable sorrow. I sat up in bed and listened intently. The noise could not have been far away and was certainly in the house. For half an hour I waited with every nerve on the alert, but there came no other sound save the chiming clock and the rustle of the ivy on the wall.

① dais ['deiis] *n.* （大厅、房间等一端为贵宾设置的）上座
② minstrel ['minstrəl] *n.* 乐师
③ flaring ['flɛəriŋ] *a.* 闪烁的，闪亮的
④ hilarity [hi'lærəti] *n.* 狂欢，欢闹

⑤ buck [bʌk] *n.* 纨绔子弟，花花公子
⑥ daunt [dɔ:nt] *v.* 使畏缩

⑦ tone down 变和谐；和缓
⑧ out of the picture 不相干的
⑨ jumpy ['dʒʌmpi] *a.* 紧张不安的；神经质的

⑩ rift [rift] *n.* 裂缝；裂隙

⑪ wakeful ['weikful] *a.* 醒着的，失眠的

⑫ muffled ['mʌfld] *v.* 抑制的，强压着的
⑬ strangle ['stræŋgl] *v.* 抑制，压制

花板。如果用一排排燃得正旺的火炬把餐厅照亮，并举行一场丰富多彩的狂欢不羁的古老的宴会，餐厅的气氛或许能缓和下来。但是，现在只有两位身着黑衣的绅士坐在从灯罩下面射出的一小圈光晕里，一个人说话的声音都不由得变低了，精神上也觉得很压抑。隐隐约约之中可以看见一排先祖画像，他们的衣着各式各样，有的打扮成伊丽莎白女皇时代的骑士，有的打扮成乔治四世皇子摄政时代的花花公子。他们一个个目不转睛地盯着我们，无声无息地陪伴着我们，令我们胆战心惊。我们没怎么说话。等到用完晚餐时，我倒是感到很高兴，因为我们能够到新式的弹子房吸支烟，休息一下了。

"哎呀，这可真不是个令人感到愉快的地方啊，"亨利爵士说，"我觉得，倒是可以慢慢适应的，只是眼下感觉有点难以融入罢了。我伯父独自一人住在这样一座宅邸里，难怪他会感觉不踏实。啊，如果您愿意的话，我们今晚就早点休息，到了明天早上，这里的一切或许会让人感觉欢快一些。"

我上床睡觉之前拉开了窗帘，站在窗户边朝外眺望。卧室的窗户正好对着大厅门前的草坪。远处，两丛矮树在愈刮愈猛的夜风中呻吟着，摇摆着。云朵在空中竞相翻腾，一轮半月从云隙之间探出头来。清冷的月光下，我看见树丛后面是一堵嶙峋的碎岩，低洼昏暗的荒原绵延起伏。我拉上窗帘，感觉刚才获得的最终印象和先前的没有什么不同。

不过，这还不能算是最终印象。我感到疲惫不堪，但意识很清醒。不停地辗转反侧，想要快点睡着，但就是难以入眠。远处的钟声每到一刻钟时就会敲响，而这古老的宅邸却与此相反，笼罩着一片寂静。突然之间，沉寂的深夜里，我的耳畔突然传来了一个声音，清晰而又深沉，绝非错觉。是个女人的啜泣声，就像一个被无法控制的悲痛所折磨的人发出的那种强忍着的哽噎的喘息声。我从床上坐了起来，全神贯注地倾听，声音离我不可能太远，肯定就在本宅邸。我的每根神经都警觉起来了，等待了半个时辰，但是，除了时钟的敲击声和墙上的常春藤发出的窸窣声之外，再没有听见任何别的声音了。

Chapter 7　The Stapletons of Merripit House

The fresh beauty of the following morning did something to **efface**[①] from our minds the grim and gray impression which had been left upon both of us by our first experience of Baskerville Hall. As Sir Henry and I sat at breakfast the sunlight flooded in through the high mullioned windows, throwing watery patches of colour from the coats of arms which covered them. The dark **panelling**[②] glowed like bronze in the golden rays, and it was hard to realize that this was indeed the chamber which had struck such a gloom into our souls upon the evening before.

"I guess it is ourselves and not the house that we have to blame!" said the baronet. "We were tired with our journey and chilled by our drive, so we took a gray view of the place. Now we are fresh and well, so it is all cheerful once more."

"And yet it was not entirely a question of imagination," I answered. "Did you, for example, happen to hear someone, a woman I think, sobbing in the night?"

"That is curious, for I did when I was half asleep **fancy**[③] that I heard something of the sort. I waited quite a time, but there was no more of it, so I concluded that it was all a dream."

"I heard it **distinctly**[④], and I am sure that it was really the sob of a woman."

"We must ask about this right away." He rang the bell and asked Barrymore

第七章　梅里皮特别墅的斯塔普尔顿一家

① efface [i'feis] v. 抹去，擦去

② panelling ['pænəliŋ] n. 镶板

③ fancy ['fænsi] v. 以为；猜想

④ distinctly [dis'tiŋktli] ad. 清楚地，明显地

翌日早晨，一切都是那么清新美丽。这多少消除了一点我们初到巴斯克维尔庄园时所产生的阴郁灰暗的印象。我和巴斯克维尔爵士坐下来用早餐时，阳光从高高的窗棂中倾泻进来，穿过窗上的纹章窗玻璃，投射出一片片淡淡的波光。在金色阳光的照耀下，深色的护墙板发出青铜色的光辉。我们觉得难以置信，这竟然真真切切是头天晚上在我们的心灵上投下阴影的那个房间。

"我觉得吧，我们要怪就该怪我们自己，而不要怪这幢宅邸！"从男爵说，"昨天我们长途驱车，又累又冷，以致对这个地方产生了不好的印象。而现在，我们都神清气爽，焕然一新，因此，对这里的一切又感觉愉悦了。"

"不过，那也不是凭空想象出来的问题啊，"我回答说，"比如说吧，您是否碰巧也听到过有人，我认为是女人，半夜里在哭泣，对吧？"

"这可真奇怪，因为我的确在半梦半醒的时候听到过哭声。我等了一段时间，但后来什么声音都没有了，因此，我便以为那是在做梦。"

"我听得非常清楚，而且可以肯定，那真的是女人的哭声。"

"我们得马上把这件事问问清楚，"他摇铃唤来了巴里摩尔，问他能否解释我们所听到的声音。我觉得，管

· 115 ·

whether he could account for our experience. It seemed to me that the **pallid**^① features of the butler turned a **shade**^② paler still as he listened to his master's question.

"There are only two women in the house, Sir Henry," he answered. "One is the **scullery**^③-maid, who sleeps in the other wing. The other is my wife, and I can answer for it that the sound could not have come from her."

And yet he lied as he said it, for it **chanced**^④ that after breakfast I met Mrs. Barrymore in the long corridor with the sun full upon her face. She was a large, impassive, heavy-featured woman with a stern set expression of mouth. But her **telltale**^⑤ eyes were red and glanced at me from between swollen lids. It was she, then, who wept in the night, and if she did so her husband must know it. Yet he had taken the obvious risk of discovery in declaring that it was not so. Why had he done this? And why did she weep so bitterly? Already round this pale-faced, handsome, black-bearded man there was gathering an atmosphere of mystery and of gloom. It was he who had been the first to discover the body of Sir Charles, and we had only his word for all the circumstances which led up to the old man's death. Was it possible that it was Barrymore, after all, whom we had seen in the cab in Regent Street? The beard **might well have been**^⑥ the same. The cabman had described a somewhat shorter man, but such an impression might easily have been erroneous. How could I settle the point forever? Obviously the first thing to do was to see the Grimpen postmaster and find whether the test telegram had really been placed in Barrymore's own hands. Be the answer what it might, I should at least have something to report to Sherlock Holmes.

Sir Henry had numerous papers to examine after breakfast, so that the time was **propitious**^⑦ for my **excursion**^⑧. It was a pleasant walk of four miles along the edge of the moor, leading me at last to a small gray **hamlet**^⑨, in which two larger buildings, which proved to be the inn and the house of Dr. Mortimer, stood high above the rest. The postmaster, who was also the village grocer, had a clear recollection of the telegram.

"Certainly, sir," said he, "I had the telegram delivered to Mr. Barrymore exactly as directed."

"Who delivered it?"

① pallid ['pælid] *a.* 无血色的；苍白的
② shade [ʃeid] *n.* 少许，些微，一点

③ scullery ['skʌləri] *n.* 碗碟洗涤室（或存放室）

④ chance [tʃɑːns] *v.* 碰巧

⑤ telltale ['telteil] *a.* 泄露机密的

⑥ might well 很可能

⑦ propitious [prəu'piʃəs] *a.* 合适的
⑧ excursion [ik'skəːʃən] *n.* 远足
⑨ hamlet ['hæmlit] *n.* 小村庄

家在听到主人的问话后，那张苍白的面孔好像变得更加苍白了。

"这座宅邸里就只有两个女人，亨利爵士，"他回答说，"一个是在厨房里干粗活的女仆，她睡在宅邸的另外一侧。另一个就是我妻子，我可以保证，那声音绝对不是她发出来的。"

然而，他说这话时扯了谎，因为早餐后，我碰巧在长长的走廊上遇见了巴里摩尔太太，当时，阳光正照在她的脸上。她身材高大，表情冷漠，面色阴沉，紧绷着嘴唇透着严厉的神情。但是，她两眼通红，眼皮肿起，看我的时候眼睛成了一条小缝，这种情形不言而喻。这样一来，夜里哭泣的人就是她了。如果她确实哭过，她的丈夫就一定会知道。而他竟然冒着显然会被人揭穿的风险说不是她发出的声音。他为何要这样做呢？而她又为何哭得那么伤心呢？一种神秘而阴郁的气氛已经在这个脸色苍白、外表英俊、蓄着黑胡子的人的周围形成了。正是他第一个发现了查尔斯爵士的尸体，而关于将那老人引向死亡的所有相关情况也只是听他来讲述的。有没有可能，我们在摄政街看到的那辆马车里的人就是巴里摩尔呢？他们的胡子差不多是相同的。根据马车夫的描述，那个人身材有些矮小。但一面之交留下的印象是很容易出差错的啊。如何才能彻底弄清楚这个情况呢？显而易见，我要做的第一件事情就是去拜访一下格林彭的邮政所所长，去查证那封试探性的电报是否真的交到了巴里摩尔本人的手上。不管最后结果如何，我至少可以获得一些能够向夏洛克·福尔摩斯报告的东西。

亨利爵士早餐后要审阅大量文件，我正好可以利用这个时间外出了。这是一次舒心惬意的步行之旅，四英里的路程，我一路沿着荒原的边缘前行，最后进入了一座灰暗单调的小村庄。村上有两幢较其他建筑都要更加高的房舍，我后来得知，其中的一幢是旅馆，另一幢是莫蒂默医生的住宅。那个邮政所所长，同时也是村上的杂货商，对那封电报的情况记忆犹新。

"可以肯定，先生，"他说，"我是完全遵照吩咐行事的，派人把那封电报送交给了巴里摩尔先生。"

"谁去送的？"

"My boy here. James, you delivered that telegram to Mr. Barrymore at the Hall last week, did you not?"

"Yes, father, I delivered it."

"Into his own hands?" I asked.

"Well, he was up in the **loft**[①] at the time, so that I could not put it into his own hands, but I gave it into Mrs. Barrymore's hands, and she promised to deliver it at once."

"Did you see Mr. Barrymore?"

"No, sir; I tell you he was in the loft."

"If you didn't see him, how do you know he was in the loft?"

"Well, surely his own wife ought to know where he is," said the postmaster **testily**[②]. "Didn't he get the telegram? If there is any mistake it is for Mr. Barrymore himself to complain."

It seemed hopeless to pursue the inquiry any farther, but it was clear that in spite of Holmes's **ruse**[③] we had no proof that Barrymore had not been in London all the time. Suppose that it were so—suppose that the same man had been the last who had seen Sir Charles alive, and the first to dog the new heir when he returned to England. What then? Was he the agent of others or had he some sinister design of his own? What interest could he have in persecuting the Baskerville family? I thought of the strange warning clipped out of the leading article of the Times. Was that his work or was it possibly the doing of someone who was bent upon counteracting his schemes? The only conceivable motive was that which had been suggested by Sir Henry, that if the family could be scared away a comfortable and permanent home would be secured for the Barrymores. But surely such an explanation as that would be quite inadequate to account for the deep and subtle scheming which seemed to be weaving an invisible net round the young baronet. Holmes himself had said that no more complex case had come to him in all the long series of his sensational investigations. I prayed, as I walked back along the gray, lonely road, that my friend might soon be freed from his **preoccupations**[④] and able to come down to take this heavy burden of responsibility from my shoulders.

Suddenly my thoughts were interrupted by the sound of running feet behind me and by a voice which called me by name. I turned, expecting to see Dr.

① loft [lɔft] *n.* 阁楼；顶楼层

② testily ['testili] *ad.* 暴躁地；易怒地；性急地

③ ruse [ru:z] *n.* 策略，计谋；诡计

④ preoccupation [pri:,ɔkju'peiʃən] *n.* 关注的事物

"我儿子，詹姆斯，上个礼拜是你去给住在庄园的巴里摩尔先生送的电报，对不对？"

"对啊，父亲，我送去的。"

"是交到他本人手上的吗？"我问。

"呃，他当时在楼上，因此，没能把电报交到他本人手上。不过，我把它交给了巴里摩尔太太，她答应即刻送上去给他。"

"你看见了巴里摩尔先生吗？"

"没有，先生，我说了他当时正在楼上。"

"你都没有亲眼看见他，怎么知道他在楼上呢？"

"对啊，他自己的太太肯定知道他在什么地方了，"邮政所所长说，显得有点烦躁，"难道他没有收到那份电报？如果真是出了差错，也应该是由巴里摩尔先生本人来质询啊。"

看起来，再追问下去也不可能有什么结果。不过，有一点很清楚了，尽管福尔摩斯巧用计谋，我们还是不能证明巴里摩尔确实不曾去过伦敦。假定事实就是如此——假定最后一个看见查尔斯爵士还活着的人是他，新继承人回到英国后第一个跟踪的也是他，接下来他会怎样呢？他是受人指使呢，还是自己有什么用心险恶的图谋？残害巴斯克维尔家族的人会给他带来什么好处？我想起了那封从《泰晤士报》评论文章中剪字而拼贴成的奇怪的警示信。是他自己干的，还是哪个要阻碍其阴谋的人干的呢？唯一想得到的动机是，正如亨利爵士所暗示的那样，如果庄园的主人被吓跑了，那么，巴里摩尔一家就能守着这幢永久舒适的宅邸。不过，这样的解释还远远不足以说明，他为何要如此精细谋划，大费周折，仿佛给年轻的从男爵编织了一张无形大网。福尔摩斯亲口说过，他经手过的全部惊人大案中没有一桩如本案一样复杂。走在那条灰暗而孤寂的回家路上，我默默地祈祷，希望我朋友能早日从他手头上的事务中脱身，能到庄园来把我肩上的重任接过去。

突然之间，我的思绪被身后传来的跑步声给打断了，还听见有人在喊我的名字。我想，一定是莫蒂默医生，便转过身去，但让我大吃一惊的是，追赶我的竟然是个陌生人。此人身材矮小，体形瘦削，面部修饰得干

Mortimer, but to my surprise it was a stranger who was pursuing me. He was a small, slim, clean-shaven, **prim-faced**[①] man, **flaxen-haired**[②] and lean-jawed, between thirty and forty years of age, dressed in a gray suit and wearing a straw hat. A tin box for botanical specimens hung over his shoulder and he carried a green butterfly-net in one of his hands.

"You will, I am sure, excuse my presumption, Dr. Watson," said he as he came panting up to where I stood. "Here on the moor we are **homely**[③] folk and do not wait for formal introductions. You may possibly have heard my name from our mutual friend, Mortimer. I am Stapleton, of Merripit House."

"Your net and box would have told me as much," said I, "for I knew that Mr. Stapleton was a naturalist. But how did you know me?"

"I have been calling on Mortimer, and he pointed you out to me from the window of his surgery as you passed. As our road lay the same way I thought that I would overtake you and introduce myself. I trust that Sir Henry is **none the worse**[④] for his journey?"

"He is very well, thank you."

"We were all rather afraid that after the sad death of Sir Charles the new baronet might refuse to live here. It is asking much of a wealthy man to come down and bury himself in a place of this kind, but I need not tell you that it means a very great deal to the countryside. Sir Henry has, I suppose, no superstitious fears in the matter?"

"I do not think that it is likely."

"Of course you know the legend of the fiend dog which haunts the family?"

"I have heard it."

"It is extraordinary how **credulous**[⑤] the peasants are about here! Any number of them are ready to swear that they have seen such a creature upon the moor." He spoke with a smile, but I seemed to read in his eyes that he took the matter more seriously. "The story took a great hold upon the imagination of Sir Charles, and I have no doubt that it led to his tragic end."

"But how?"

"His nerves were so **worked up**[⑥] that the appearance of any dog might have had a fatal effect upon his diseased heart. I fancy that he really did see something of the kind upon that last night in the yew alley. I feared that some

① prim [prim] *a.* 整洁的
② flaxen ['flæksən] *a.* （头发）像亚麻色的，淡黄色的

③ homely ['həumli] *a.* 熟悉的，亲切友好的

④ none the worse 不受影响；依然如故

⑤ credulous ['kredjuləs] *a.* 轻信的，易信的

⑥ work up 使激动

干净净，表情严肃，头发呈淡黄色，下巴尖长，年龄在三十到四十岁之间。他穿着一身灰白色套装，头戴一顶草帽，肩上挂着一只用来装生物标本的镀锡铁皮盒子，一只手上拿着绿色的扑蝶网兜。

"我肯定，您会原谅我的冒昧，华生医生，"他说着，气喘吁吁地走到我的跟前，"在我们荒原这一带，大家都像一家人，都用不着做任何正式的介绍。您可能从我们共同的好朋友莫蒂默那里听过我的名字了。我就是斯塔普尔顿，住在梅里皮特别墅。"

"您的网兜和盒子已经向我做了介绍了，"我说，"因为我知道，斯塔普尔顿先生是位生物学家。但是，您怎么就知道了我的名字呢？"

"我刚才到了莫蒂默医生家里，正好您从他家的窗户外面经过，他便把您指给我看了。因为，我们要走的路相同，我就想追上您，做个自我介绍。我估计，亨利爵士的这趟旅行一切都顺利吧？"

"他很好，谢谢您！"

"我们都很担心，查尔斯爵士的猝亡之后，这位从男爵会不愿到此居住。要求一位有钱的绅士屈尊埋没在这样一处地方，确实有点过分了。不过，不用我说您也知道，在这样偏僻的一隅，其意义是非常重大的。我猜，亨利爵士不会这么迷信，觉得这件事情很恐怖吧？"

"我想，不太可能吧！"

"您肯定听说过有关纠缠这个家族的魔鬼似的猎犬的传说吧？"

"我确实听说过了。"

"确实很奇怪啊，住在这儿的农夫们怎么就轻信了呢！他们中任何人都会发誓说，曾在这片荒原上亲眼看到那样一只畜生，"他说话时脸上露着微笑，但从他的眼神中，我似乎看到了，他心里感觉事态更加严重，"那个传说给查尔斯爵士的心理产生了很大的影响，我毫不怀疑，这事最终导致了他的悲惨结局。"

"但怎么会呢？"

"他的心脏本来就有毛病，加上神经高度紧张，任何猎犬的出现都会给他造成致命的危险。我猜想，最后出事的那天傍晚，他一定是在紫杉树篱小道看见什么类似于

disaster might occur, for I was very fond of the old man, and I knew that his heart was weak."

"How did you know that?"

"My friend Mortimer told me."

"You think, then, that some dog pursued Sir Charles, and that he died of fright in consequence?"

"Have you any better explanation?"

"I have not come to any conclusion."

"Has Mr. Sherlock Holmes?"

The words took away my breath for an instant, but a glance at the **placid**[1] face and **steadfast**[2] eyes of my companion showed that no surprise was intended.

"It is useless for us to pretend that we do not know you, Dr. Watson," said he. "The records of your detective have reached us here, and you could not celebrate him without being known yourself. When Mortimer told me your name he could not deny your identity. If you are here, then it follows that Mr. Sherlock Holmes is interesting himself in the matter, and I am naturally curious to know what view he may take."

"I am afraid that I cannot answer that question."

"May I ask if he is going to honour us with a visit himself?"

"He cannot leave town at present. He has other cases which engage his attention."

"What a pity! He might throw some light on that which is so dark to us. But as to your own researches, if there is any possible way in which I can be of service to you I trust that you will command me. If I had any indication of the nature of your suspicions or how you propose to investigate the case, I might perhaps even now give you some aid or advice."

"I assure you that I am simply here upon a visit to my friend, Sir Henry, and that I need no help of any kind."

"Excellent!" said Stapleton. "You are perfectly right to be wary and discreet. I am justly **reproved**[3] for what I feel was an **unjustifiable**[4] **intrusion**[5], and I promise you that I will not mention the matter again."

We had come to a point where a narrow grassy path struck off from the

猎犬的东西。我先前担心，有可能会发生什么不测，因为我很喜欢那位老人，同时也知道，他的心脏很脆弱。"

"您是怎样知道这个情况的呢？"

"我朋友莫蒂默告诉我的。"

"那么您认为，当时是否有条猎犬在追逐查尔斯爵士，他也因此被吓死了吗？"

"您还能有什么更加理想的解释吗？"

"我还没有得出任何结论呢。"

"夏洛克·福尔摩斯先生呢？"

他这句话让我顿时感到呼吸困难。我看了一眼我的同伴，见他表情平静，目光沉稳，感觉他并非故意要使我感到惊讶。

"要我们假装不认识您，那是无济于事的，华生医生，"他说，"我们这里的人都看过您对侦探案的记述，您在褒扬您的朋友的同时，自己也跟着出了名。当莫蒂默在我面前提到您的名字时，他不可能隐瞒得了您的身份啊。既然您都到这儿来了，由此推测，夏洛克·福尔摩斯先生本人也对本案产生了兴趣。我呢，生来就很好奇，很想知道他对这事的看法。"

"我恐怕无法回答您这个问题。"

"请问一下，他会赏光亲自来我们这儿吗？"

"他目前无法离开伦敦，有些其他案件需要去处理。"

"真是遗憾啊！他本可以把这件我们迷惑不解的怪事看出些端倪来的。不过，您在调查取证时，如果有能够用得上我的地方，请尽管吩咐。如果我能稍稍了解您的疑问或者是您取证的方式方法，我或许能即刻给您提供协助或者提出建议呢。"

"您相信好啦，我来这里仅仅是为了拜访我的朋友亨利爵士，我不需要任何协助。"

"太好啦！"斯塔普尔顿说，"您这样小心谨慎是绝对正确的。我毫无缘由地多管闲事，理应受到训斥。我向您保证，以后再也不提这件事情了。"

我们走到了一个岔口，一条狭窄多草的小路从大道上斜岔出去，弯弯曲曲地向前延伸，一直穿过了荒原。右侧是一座山，地势陡峭，乱石密布，先前是个花岗岩石料场。正对着我们的那面是乌黑的崖壁，上面的罅隙里长着羊齿

① placid ['plæsid] *a.* 平静的；宁静的
② steadfast ['stedfəst] *a.* 方向固定的

③ reprove [ri'pru:v] *v.* 责备
④ unjustifiable [ʌn'dʒʌstɪfaɪəb(ə)l] *a.* 辩护不了的；不能认为是正当的
⑤ intrusion [in'tru:ʒən] *n.* 打扰；干涉；妨碍

road and **wound**① away across the moor. A steep, boulder-sprinkled hill lay upon the right which had in bygone days been cut into a granite quarry. The face which was turned towards us formed a dark cliff, with ferns and brambles growing in its niches. From over a distant rise there floated a gray plume of smoke.

"A moderate walk along this moor-path brings us to Merripit House," said he. "Perhaps you will **spare**② an hour that I may have the pleasure of introducing you to my sister."

My first thought was that I should be by Sir Henry's side. But then I remembered the pile of papers and bills with which his study table was **littered**③. It was certain that I could not help with those. And Holmes had **expressly**④ said that I should study the neighbours upon the moor. I accepted Stapleton's invitation, and we turned together down the path.

"It is a wonderful place, the moor," said he, looking round over the **undulating**⑤ downs, long green **rollers**⑥, with crests of jagged granite foaming up into fantastic surges. "You never tire of the moor. You cannot think the wonderful secrets which it contains. It is so vast, and so barren, and so mysterious."

"You know it well, then?"

"I have only been here two years. The residents would call me a newcomer. We came shortly after Sir Charles settled. But my tastes led me to explore every part of the country round, and I should think that there are few men who know it better than I do."

"Is it hard to know?"

"Very hard. You see, for example, this great plain to the north here with the queer hills breaking out of it. Do you observe anything remarkable about that?"

"It would be a rare place for a **gallop**⑦."

"You would naturally think so and the thought has cost several their lives before now. You notice those bright green spots scattered thickly over it?"

"Yes, they seem more fertile than the rest."

Stapleton laughed.

"That is the great Grimpen Mire," said he. "A false step yonder means death to man or beast. Only yesterday I saw one of the moor ponies wander into

① wind [waind] v. 蜿蜒；曲折而行

② spare [spɛə] v. 留出，抽出

③ litter ['litə] v. 使…到处都是

④ expressly [ik'spresli] ad. 明确地

⑤ undulating ['ʌndjuleitiŋ] v. 起伏的
⑥ roller ['rəulə] n. 巨浪

⑦ gallop ['gæləp] n. 骑马奔驰

草和荆棘。在远处的山顶上，飘荡着一股灰色的烟雾。

"顺着这条荒原小道，再往前走一小段，我们就到梅里皮特别墅了，"他说，"您或许能够抽出一个小时的空闲来，我将十分荣幸地把我妹妹介绍给您认识。"

我心里闪过的第一个念头便是，自己应该陪伴在亨利爵士身边。但是，马上又想起了那一堆散放在他书桌上的文件和证券。对于那些东西，我肯定是帮不上任何忙的。况且，福尔摩斯还特意交待过，要我对荒原上住着的邻居们多加观察，因此，我接受了斯塔普尔顿的邀请，同他一道拐弯走上了小路。

"这是个神奇的地方，我说的是荒原，"他说着，一边环顾四周，看着那起伏的丘陵，连绵的绿浪，还有参差不齐的像浪涛激起的奇形怪状的水花似的花岗岩山巅。"您永远都不可能对荒原感到厌倦。您想象不到，其中蕴藏着怎样神奇的秘密。它如此地广袤辽阔，如此地荒凉萧疏，如此地神秘莫测。"

"这么说来，您对荒原了解得很清楚啦？"

"我才在此地待了两年，本地的居民还会把我当成新来者看呢。查尔斯爵士到此定居不久，我们也来了。不过，由于我个人兴趣爱好的缘故，我踏遍了这片土地上的每一个角落，所以，我有理由相信，没有多少人比我更加熟悉这块地方了。"

"要了解这片地方很艰难吗？"

"非常艰难。您看吧，比如说，这儿北面的平原，幅员辽阔，奇形怪状的山丘点缀其中，您看出了什么不同凡响之处吗？"

"纵马驰骋，这是个少有的好地方啊。"

"您自然会这样想，但至今为止，这一想法已经让好些个人断送性命了。您看到那些密密麻麻呈现在平原上的一块块嫩绿的草地了吗？"

"看到了，那些地方好像比其他地方更肥沃呀。"

斯塔普尔顿哈哈大笑起来。

"那边就是格林彭大泥潭，"他说，"无论是人还是野兽，一旦走错一步，那就必死无疑。就在昨天，我还看见了一匹荒原的小马驹误闯了进去，便再也没出来。我看到它的头拼命地探出泥坑，挣扎了很长时间，但最

it. He never came out. I saw his head for quite a long time **craning**[1] out of the bog-hole, but it sucked him down at last. Even in dry seasons it is a danger to cross it, but after these autumn rains it is an awful place. And yet I can find my way to the very heart of it and return alive. By George, there is another of those miserable ponies!"

Something brown was rolling and tossing among the green sedges. Then a long, agonized, **writhing**[2] neck shot upward and a dreadful cry echoed over the moor. It turned me cold with horror, but my companion's nerves seemed to be stronger than mine.

"It's gone!" said he. "The mire has him. Two in two days, and many more, perhaps, for they get in the way of going there in the dry weather and never know the difference until the mire has them in its clutches. It's a bad place, the great Grimpen Mire."

"And you say you can penetrate it?"

"Yes, there are one or two paths which a very active man can take. I have found them out."

"But why should you wish to go into so horrible a place?"

"Well, you see the hills beyond? They are really islands cut off on all sides by the impassable mire, which has crawled round them in the course of years. That is where the rare plants and the butterflies are, if you have the wit to reach them."

"I shall try my luck some day."

He looked at me with a surprised face.

"For God's sake put such an idea out of your mind," said he. "Your blood would be upon my head. I assure you that there would not be the least chance of your coming back alive. It is only by remembering certain complex landmarks that I am able to do it."

"Halloa!" I cried. "What is that?"

A long, low moan, indescribably sad, swept over the moor. It filled the whole air, and yet it was impossible to say whence it came. From a dull murmur it **swelled**[3] into a deep roar, and then sank back into a melancholy, throbbing murmur once again. Stapleton looked at me with a curious expression in his face.

① crane [krein] v. 伸颈，探头

② writhe [raið] v. （因痛苦而）扭动

终还是陷了下去。即便是在干燥的季节里，要穿过大泥潭也是充满危险的。但是，下过了秋雨之后，那儿就成了个令人望而生畏的地方了。尽管如此，我却能找到通向泥潭中心的路径，而且还能活着回来。天哪，又来了一匹倒霉的小马驹！"

有个棕褐色的东西正在一丛绿色的苔草中翻滚、扭动。它的长脖子痛苦地抽搐，奋力地向上伸举，随后发出了一声恐怖的嘶鸣，声音在荒原上回荡。这一切把我吓得浑身冰凉，但我同伴的神经好像比我的坚强得多。

"没有了，"他说，"葬身泥潭了。两天之内就有两匹马送了命，说不定还有更多，因为马匹在干燥的气候里习惯到那儿去，但绝对不可能知晓情况会有变化，直到最后掉入泥潭。格林彭大泥潭真是个糟糕的地方啊。"

"但您说，您能够穿过去，对吧？"

"对啊，里面有一两条小路，行动敏捷的人可以走过的。我已经把小路找出来了。"

"但是，您怎么会想要到那个可怕的地方去呢？"

"是啊，您看到那边那些山丘了吗？它们真正是孤岛，周围的泥潭长年累月缓慢涌动着，无法到达。如果开动脑筋设法到达那儿的话，便可以收集到珍稀的植物和蝴蝶。"

"哪天我也去碰碰运气吧。"

他看着我，一脸惊讶。

"看在上帝的分儿上，您尽快打消这个念头吧，"他说，"万一您出了什么意外，我可担当不起啊！我敢说，您活着回来的几率微乎其微。我也是记住了那些错综复杂的标识才能到达那里去的。"

"嘿！"我大声说着，"这是什么声音啊？"

荒原上响起一阵悠长而低沉的呻吟声，其凄厉程度难以形容。这声音响彻在空中，但根本无法说清究竟来自何方。开始是低哼声，然后慢慢地增强变成了沉重的狂吼声，随后又回落成悲伤而发颤的哼哼声。斯塔普尔顿看着我，脸上露出好奇的神情。

"荒原，怪异的地方！"他说。

"那到底是什么声音啊？"

"这儿的农夫都说，那是巴斯克维尔猎犬召唤其猎

③ swell [swel] v. （声音、音调等）变响亮

"Queer place, the moor!" said he.

"But what is it?"

"The peasants say it is the Hound of the Baskervilles calling for its prey. I've heard it once or twice before, but never quite so loud."

I looked round, with a chill of fear in my heart, at the huge swelling plain, mottled with the green patches of **rushes**①. Nothing stirred over the vast expanse save a pair of **ravens**②, which **croaked**③ loudly from a tor behind us.

"You are an educated man. You don't believe such nonsense as that?" said I. "What do you think is the cause of so strange a sound?"

"**Bogs**④ make queer noises sometimes. It's the mud settling, or the water rising, or something."

"No, no, that was a living voice."

"Well, perhaps it was. Did you ever hear a **bittern**⑤ **booming**⑥?"

"No, I never did."

"It's a very rare bird–practically extinct–in England now, but all things are possible upon the moor. Yes, I should not be surprised to learn that what we have heard is the cry of the last of the bitterns."

"It's the weirdest, strangest thing that ever I heard in my life."

"Yes, it's rather an **uncanny**⑦ place altogether. Look at the hillside **yonder**⑧. What do you make of those?"

The whole steep slope was covered with gray circular rings of stone, a score of them at least.

"What are they? Sheep-pens?"

"No, they are the homes of our worthy ancestors. Prehistoric man lived thickly on the moor, and as no one in particular has lived there since, we find all his little arrangements exactly as he left them. These are his **wigwams**⑨ with the roofs off. You can even see his hearth and his couch if you have the curiosity to go inside."

"But it is quite a town. When was it inhabited?"

"**Neolithic**⑩ man–no date."

"What did he do?"

"He grazed his cattle on these slopes, and he learned to dig for tin when the bronze sword began to **supersede**⑪ the stone axe. Look at the great trench in

物的吠叫声。我以前也听到过一两次，但声音都没有这一次叫得响亮。"

我环视四周，茫茫原野连绵起伏，一丛丛绿色的灌木点缀其间，心里觉得发冷。广袤的原野上悄无声息，只有几只渡鸦在我们身后的岩岗大声地鸣叫着。

"您是受过教育的人，不会相信那种无稽之谈吧？"我说，"您觉得这种怪声是什么东西发出来的呢？"

"泥潭有时候会发出奇怪的响声来。那是由于淤泥下沉，地下水上冒，或者其他某些原因。"

"不，不，刚才的那个声音是生命体发出的。"

"啊，或许是吧。您过去听过麻鳽鸣叫吗？"

"没有，从没听过。"

"这是英国的一种稀有鸟类——几乎快要绝迹了，但是，到了这荒原地带，什么事情都有可能发生。是啊，如果我们刚才听到的鸣叫声是麻鳽鸟中的最后一只发出来的，我也不会觉得奇怪的。"

"这可是我有生以来听到的最怪异、最奇特的声音啊。"

"是啊，这本来就是个十分怪异离奇的地方。看看那边的山坡，看清那些是什么东西了吗？"

整个陡峭的坡面上全是由灰色石块围成的一个个的圆圈，至少也得有20个吧。

"那是什么东西呢？羊圈吗？"

"不是，那是我们可敬的祖先居住生活的地方。史前时期，荒原上人口稠密。后来就没有人居住了，因此，我们看到的祖先们那些精巧的小设施就原封不动地保存下来了。那些圆圈就是祖先们留下的房屋，只是屋顶没有了。如果您有兴趣到里面去光顾一番，还可以看到他们留下的火炉和床铺呢。"

"但是，那可是够得上一个城镇的规模啊，住在那儿的人们是什么年代的呢？"

"新石器时代吧——没有确切的年代。"

"他们靠什么谋生呢？"

"在那些坡地上放牧。青铜刀器开始代替石斧时，他们学会了挖掘锡矿。请看对面山坡上的那些壕沟，这就是当年挖掘的遗迹。是啊，华生医生，您会发现荒原那些非同寻常的地方的。噢，对不起，失陪一下。这肯

① rush [rʌʃ] n. 灯芯草科植物
② raven ['reivən] n. 渡鸦
③ croak [krəuk] v. 呱呱地叫

④ bog [bɔg] n. 沼泽

⑤ bittern ['bitən] n. 麻鳽
⑥ boom [bu:m] v. 发出深沉、洪亮的声音

⑦ uncanny [ʌnˈkæni] a. 神秘的，可怕的
⑧ yonder [jɔndə] a. 远处的；那边的

⑨ wigwam ['wigwæm] n. 简陋的小屋

⑩ Neolithic [ˌniːəuˈliθik] a. 新石器时代的

⑪ supersede [ˌsjuːpəˈsiːd] v. 代替，取代

the opposite hill. That is his mark. Yes, you will find some very singular points about the moor, Dr. Watson. Oh, excuse me an instant! It is surely Cyclopides."

A small fly or moth had fluttered across our path, and in an instant Stapleton was rushing with extraordinary energy and speed in pursuit of it. To my dismay the creature flew straight for the great mire, and my acquaintance never paused for an instant, bounding from **tuft**[①] to tuft behind it, his green net waving in the air. His gray clothes and jerky, zigzag, irregular progress made him not unlike some huge moth himself. I was standing watching his pursuit with a mixture of admiration for his extraordinary activity and fear lest he should lose his footing in the **treacherous**[②] mire when I heard the sound of steps and, turning round, found a woman near me upon the path. She had come from the direction in which the plume of smoke indicated the position of Merripit House, but the dip of the moor had hid her until she was quite close.

I could not doubt that this was the Miss Stapleton of whom I had been told, since ladies of any sort must be few upon the moor, and I remembered that I had heard someone describe her as being a beauty. The woman who approached me was certainly that, and of a most uncommon type. There could not have been a greater contrast between brother and sister, for Stapleton was neutral **tinted**[③], with light hair and gray eyes, while she was darker than any brunette whom I have seen in England–slim, elegant, and tall. She had a proud, finely cut face, so regular that it might have seemed impassive were it not for the sensitive mouth and the beautiful dark, eager eyes. With her perfect figure and elegant dress she was, indeed, a strange apparition upon a lonely moorland path. Her eyes were on her brother as I turned, and then she quickened her pace towards me. I had raised my hat and was about to make some explanatory remark when her own words turned all my thoughts into a new channel.

"Go back!" she said. "Go straight back to London, instantly."

I could only stare at her in stupid surprise. Her eyes **blazed**[④] at me, and she tapped the ground impatiently with her foot.

"Why should I go back?" I asked.

"I cannot explain." She spoke in a low, eager voice, with a curious **lisp**[⑤] in her **utterance**[⑥]. "But for God's sake do what I ask you. Go back and never set foot upon the moor again."

定是一只独眼蛾。"

一只像是小苍蝇或者小飞蛾一样的东西振翅飞过小路。斯塔普尔顿立刻追赶上去，精力充沛，速度惊人。让我惊愕不已的是，那只小东西径直飞向大泥潭了，而我朋友则刻不容缓，在一丛丛小树中间跳来跳去，紧紧地尾随其后，不时地在空中挥舞那绿色的网兜。他身穿灰色衣服，加上猛然跳跃，曲折前行，连他本人看上去都像是一只大飞蛾了。我站在那里看他追蛾，心情非常复杂，钦佩他动作敏捷，同时又提心吊胆，生怕他不慎掉入那诡异莫测的泥潭。这时，我听到了脚步声，一转身，看到一个女子正在离我不远的路边。我们先前看到那缕缕青烟升起的地方就是梅里皮特别墅所处的位置，她就是从那个方向过来的。刚才我们没有看见她，是因为她行走的地方正好是荒原上的一片低洼地。

我毫不怀疑，眼前这位就是大家在我面前提到过的斯塔普尔顿小姐，因为整个荒原地带所有女士加在一起一定也是寥寥无几，况且我还记得，有人说过的，她是个大美人。而迎面走过来的这位小姐就是个大美人，而且还是那种少见的大美人。没有见过兄妹之间相貌反差如此巨大的。斯塔普尔顿肤色适中，浅色的头发，灰色的眼睛。而她却肤色黝黑，肤色比我在英格兰见过的所有深肤色女子都要深——身材高挑，仪态万方。长着一张高傲而轮廓俊美的脸蛋，五官端正，要不是那性感的双唇和美丽而热切的黑色双眸，整张脸就会显得有点冷淡了。她身段完美无缺，着装高贵优雅，站在这孤寂的小路上，活脱脱是个怪异的幽灵。我转过身看到她时，她两眼盯着她的哥哥看，随即向我快步走了过来。我摘下帽子正想向她解释几句，但她却抢先开口了，把我的思绪引向了一个全新的方向。

"回去吧！"她说，"直接回伦敦去，立刻动身。"

我直呆呆地盯着她，惊讶不已。她也盯着我，两眼冒着火，情绪不安，一只脚不停地跺着地面。

"我为何要回去呢？"我问了一声。

"我无法解释，"她说，声音很小，语气急切，话语听起来有点奇怪，口齿不大清楚，"但是，看在上帝的分儿上，按照我的要求做吧。返回去，再不要涉足荒原了。"

① tuft [tʌft] n. 丛生植物

② treacherous ['tretʃərəs] a. 暗藏危险的

③ tint [tint] v. 给…着淡色

④ blaze [bleiz] v. 发（强）光，发亮

⑤ lisp [lisp] n. 咬舌（发音）

⑥ utterance ['ʌtərəns] n. 发音

"But I have only just come."

"Man, man!" she cried. "Can you not tell when a warning is for your own good? Go back to London! Start to-night! Get away from this place at all costs! Hush, my brother is coming! Not a word of what I have said. Would you mind getting that **orchid**[1] for me among the **mare's-tails**[2] yonder? We are very rich in orchids on the moor, though, of course, you are rather late to see the beauties of the place."

Stapleton had abandoned the chase and came back to us breathing hard and flushed with his exertions.

"Halloa, Beryl!" said he, and it seemed to me that the tone of his greeting was not altogether a cordial one.

"Well, Jack, you are very hot."

"Yes, I was chasing a Cyclopides. He is very rare and seldom found in the late autumn. What a pity that I should have missed him!" He spoke **unconcernedly**[3], but his small light eyes glanced **incessantly**[4] from the girl to me.

"You have introduced yourselves, I can see."

"Yes. I was telling Sir Henry that it was rather late for him to see the true beauties of the moor."

"Why, who do you think this is?"

"I imagine that it must be Sir Henry Baskerville."

"No, no," said I. "Only a humble commoner, but his friend. My name is Dr. Watson."

A flush of vexation passed over her expressive face. "We have been talking **at cross purposes**[5]," said she.

"Why, you had not very much time for talk," her brother remarked with the same questioning eyes.

"I talked as if Dr. Watson were a resident instead of being merely a visitor," said she. "It cannot much matter to him whether it is early or late for the orchids. But you will come on, will you not, and see Merripit House?"

A short walk brought us to it, a bleak moorland house, once the farm of some **grazier**[6] in the old prosperous days, but now put into repair and turned into a modern dwelling. An orchard surrounded it, but the trees, as is usual upon

① orchid ['ɔ:kid] n. 兰花
② mare's tail ['mɛəz,teil] n. 杉叶藻

③ unconcerned [ˌʌnkən'sə:nd] a. 漫不经心的
④ incessantly [in'sesəntli] ad. 不停地

⑤ at cross purposes 互相误解；南辕北辙

⑥ grazier ['greizjə] n. 放牧人，养畜者

"但我这才刚刚到啊。"

"您，您啊！"她大声说，"难道您就听不出来，这个警示全是为了您好吗？返回伦敦去！今晚就动身吧！无论如何，远离这个地方！嘘，我哥哥过来了！我刚才说过的话，决不能在他面前提起。请您把那边杉叶藻丛中的一朵兰花摘给我，好吗？我们这片荒原上有的是兰花，不过，您显然回来得晚了点，领略不到这儿的美妙了。"

斯塔普尔顿已经放弃了追捕，回到了我们的身边，因为追赶得太累，他喘着粗气，满脸通红。

"嘿，贝丽尔！"他说着，我觉得他打招呼的语气并不显得热情。

"啊，杰克，你很热吧。"

"是的，我刚才在追一只独眼蛾。晚秋时节，那可是少见的珍稀物种啊。我竟然让它给跑掉了，太遗憾了！"他漫不经心地说着话，但明亮的小眼睛却不停地在我和姑娘的脸上转来转去。

"看得出来，你们已经互相自我介绍过了。"

"是的，我刚才告诉了亨利爵士，他回来得太晚了些，已经看不到荒原真正的美景了。"

"啊，你以为这位是谁啊？"

"我猜他一定是亨利·巴斯克维尔爵士。"

"不，不是的，"我说，"我只不过是一个微不足道的普通人，是爵士的朋友。我是华生医生。"

她那富于表情的脸泛起了红晕，露出了懊恼的神色。

"我们竟然在误会之中聊起天来了。"她说。

"啊，你们并没谈多久啊。"她哥哥说着，仍然满腹狐疑地打量着我们。

"我和华生医生说话时，把他当成了一个本地居民，而不是当客人看，"她说，"他认为，兰花的早晚都没有什么关系。不过，请您赏光随着我们一道走吧，看看我们的梅里皮特别墅。"

我们行进了一小段路程便到达了梅里皮特别墅。这是一座阴郁冷静的荒原住宅，往昔的繁荣岁月里，曾是某个牧人的农庄，但是，现如今，经过修缮，变成了一幢现代的住所了。住宅的周围是一片果园，不过，园子里面的果树如同荒原上常见的树木一样，树干矮小，生长不茂

the moor, were **stunted**[1] and **nipped**[2], and the effect of the whole place was mean and melancholy. We were admitted by a strange, **wizened**[3], rusty-coated old manservant, who seemed in keeping with the house. Inside, however, there were large rooms furnished with an elegance in which I seemed to recognize the taste of the lady. As I looked from their windows at the interminable granite-flecked moor rolling unbroken to the farthest horizon I could not but **marvel at**[4] what could have brought this highly educated man and this beautiful woman to live in such a place.

"Queer spot to choose, is it not?" said he as if in answer to my thought. "And yet we manage to make ourselves fairly happy, do we not, Beryl?"

"Quite happy," said she, but there was no ring of conviction in her words.

"I had a school," said Stapleton. "It was in the north country. The work to a man of my temperament was mechanical and uninteresting, but the privilege of living with youth, of helping to mould those young minds, and of impressing them with one's own character and ideals was very dear to me. However, the fates were against us. A serious epidemic broke out in the school and three of the boys died. It never recovered from the blow, and much of my capital was irretrievably swallowed up. And yet, if it were not for the loss of the charming companionship of the boys, I could rejoice over my own misfortune, for, with my strong tastes for botany and zoology, I find an unlimited field of work here, and my sister is as devoted to Nature as I am. All this, Dr. Watson, has been brought upon your head by your expression as you surveyed the moor out of our window."

"It certainly did cross my mind that it might be a little dull–less for you, perhaps, than for your sister."

"No, no, I am never dull," said she quickly.

"We have books, we have our studies, and we have interesting neighbours. Dr. Mortimer is a most learned man in his own **line**[5]. Poor Sir Charles was also an admirable companion. We knew him well and miss him more than I can tell. Do you think that I should intrude if I were to call this afternoon and make the acquaintance of Sir Henry?"

"I am sure that he would be delighted."

"Then perhaps you would mention that I propose to do so. We may in our

① stunt [stʌnt] v. 阻碍…的正常成长
② nip [nip] v. 抑制…的成长
③ wizened ['wiznd] a. 干瘪的

④ marvel at 对…惊奇

⑤ line [lain] n. 行业；行当

盛。整个地方让人觉得阴郁萧疏。一位老男仆领着我们进入室内，只见他表情怪异，身躯干瘦，衣衫破旧，同住宅的格调很是相配。然而，里面有几个很宽敞的房间，陈设雅致，我似乎通过室内的陈设看到了小姐的品味。我站在窗口向外望去，看到处处密布着花岗岩石的荒原连绵起伏，毫无间断地一直伸向远方的地平线。这时，我不由得心生疑问，是什么因素促使这位受过高深教育的男子和这位端庄美丽的女子来到这种地方定居呢？

"选择了这样一处怪异离奇的所在，对吧？"他说着，好像是在回答我心中的疑问，"不过，我们有办法让自己在这里过得很舒心愉快，是不是啊，贝丽尔？"

"是很舒心愉快。"她说，但她的话语显得言不由衷。

"我以前办过一所学校，"斯塔普尔顿说，"那是在北方。那份工作对我这种性情的人来说，显得枯燥乏味。不过，那也让我有机会和孩子们一起生活，帮助他们，塑造他们的心灵，用自己的个性和理想来激发他们。这一点对我来说是弥足珍贵的。然而，我们运气不好。学校发生了非常严重的传染病，死了三个男孩。学校遭此一劫便一蹶不振，我的家底全部搭进去了，赔了个精光。不过，如果不是没有了同孩子相处的乐趣，我真可以庆幸自己的不幸了，因为我对植物学和动物学有着强烈的兴趣，在此地找到了一个广阔无垠的天地从事自己的研究。我妹妹也和我一样，痴迷于大自然。华生医生，所有这些疑问在您透过我家窗子向外看时就产生了，我从您脸上的表情就看出来了。"

"我心里刚才确实闪过这样的念头，觉得这儿可能有点枯燥乏味——说不定，您的感受不如您妹妹那样强烈吧。"

"不，不，我从来都没有觉得枯燥乏味。"她急忙说。

"我们有各种书籍，有自己的研究，还有非常有趣的邻居们。莫蒂默医生在自己的专业领域很有造诣。已故的查尔斯爵士过去也是一位可敬可亲的伙伴。我们对他很了解，心中对他的怀念简直是无法言表。我打算下午去拜访亨利爵士，互相认识一下，您觉得这样做会显得冒失吗？"

"我相信，他见到您一定会非常高兴的。"

"这么说，您或许愿意帮我带句话，告知一下我的打算。我们或许能够略尽绵力，给他提供一些便利，让他早

· 135 ·

humble way do something to make things more easy for him until he becomes accustomed to his new surroundings. Will you come upstairs, Dr. Watson, and inspect my collection of *Lepidoptera*? I think it is the most complete one in the south-west of England. By the time that you have looked through them lunch will be almost ready."

But I was eager to get back to my charge. The melancholy of the moor, the death of the unfortunate pony, the weird sound which had been associated with the grim legend of the Baskervilles, all these things **tinged**[①] my thoughts with sadness. Then on the top of these more or less vague impressions there had come the definite and distinct warning of Miss Stapleton, delivered with such intense earnestness that I could not doubt that some grave and deep reason lay behind it. I resisted all pressure to stay for lunch, and I set off at once upon my return journey, taking the grass-grown path by which we had come.

It seems, however, that there must have been some short cut for those who knew it, for before I had reached the road I was **astounded**[②] to see Miss Stapleton sitting upon a rock by the side of the track. Her face was beautifully flushed with her exertions, and she held her hand to her side.

"I have run all the way in order to **cut you off**[③], Dr. Watson," said she. "I had not even time to put on my hat. I must not stop, or my brother may miss me. I wanted to say to you how sorry I am about the stupid mistake I made in thinking that you were Sir Henry. Please forget the words I said, which have no application whatever to you."

"But I can't forget them, Miss Stapleton," said I. "I am Sir Henry's friend, and his **welfare**[④] is a very close concern of mine. Tell me why it was that you were so eager that Sir Henry should return to London."

"A woman's **whim**[⑤], Dr. Watson. When you know me better you will understand that I cannot always give reasons for what I say or do."

"No, no. I remember the thrill in your voice. I remember the look in your eyes. Please, please, be frank with me, Miss Stapleton, for ever since I have been here I have been conscious of shadows all round me. Life has become like that great Grimpen Mire, with little green patches everywhere into which one may sink and with no guide to point the track. Tell me then what it was that you meant, and I will promise to convey your warning to Sir Henry."

日熟悉这儿的新环境。华生医生，您想到楼上去看看我收集的鳞翅目昆虫吗？我认为，那是英国西南部能采集到的最齐全的标本了。等您看完，午饭也准备得差不多了。"

但是，我迫不及待地想要返回去履行自己的使命了。阴郁的荒原，小马驹不幸丧命，让人想起令人毛骨悚然的巴斯克维尔猎犬传说的古怪声音，凡此种种，令我感到忧伤不已，心情沉重。不过，除了这些或多或少有点模糊的印象之外，最重要的还是斯塔普尔顿小姐的警示，那是确凿无疑、清晰透明的。她说话时，态度恳切。毫无疑问，这背后一定隐藏着某些严重的深层原因。我谢绝了主人坚定的邀请，没有留下来午餐，立刻出发返回——踏上了我们来时的那条长满野草的小路。

不过，看起来，这儿一定有一条熟人知道的捷径，我还没有到达那条路边，便惊讶地看见，斯塔普尔顿小姐已经坐在那条小路旁边的一块石头上。可能是行动急迫的缘故，她满脸通红，显得格外美丽，一只手叉在腰间。

"为了拦截住您，我是一路跑着过来的，华生医生，"她说，"连帽子都没有戴。我不能在此久留，否则，我哥哥会担心我的。我想对您说，我犯了一个愚蠢的错误，把您当成了亨利爵士。我为此深表歉意，请您把我说过的话都忘了吧，那些话跟您毫无关系。"

"但是，我不能忘记啊，斯塔普尔顿小姐，"我说，"我是亨利爵士的朋友，关乎他安危的事情当然与我息息相关。请您告诉我，您那么急切地想让亨利爵士回伦敦去到底是什么原因。"

"女人的一时心血来潮而已，华生医生，等您对我有了进一步的了解之后，您就会明白，我的一言一行经常是没有什么来由的。"

"不，不，我记得您说话时的声音是颤抖的，神情急促恳切，斯塔普尔顿小姐，求求您，请您坦率地告诉我吧。从我到这里的那一刻起，我就感觉自己周围疑影重重。这里的生活也变得和格林彭泥潭一样到处都有陷阱。没有人引路，我们随时都会陷进去。请您告诉我吧，您说的那话是什么意思。我向您保证，一定会把您的忠告转述给亨利爵士的。"

一时间，她脸上显露出一丝迟疑的表情，但等到回

① tinge [tindʒ] v. 使带有…气息

② astound [ə'staund] v. 使震惊，使惊愕

③ cut sb off 截住

④ welfare [welfɛə] n. 康乐，安宁

⑤ whim [hwim] n. 狂想；幻想

An expression of **irresolution**① passed for an instant over her face, but her eyes had hardened again when she answered me.

"You make too much of it, Dr. Watson," said she. "My brother and I were very much shocked by the death of Sir Charles. We knew him very intimately, for his favourite walk was over the moor to our house. He was deeply impressed with the curse which hung over his family, and when this tragedy came I naturally felt that there must be some grounds for the fears which he had expressed. I was distressed therefore when another member of the family came down to live here, and I felt that he should be warned of the danger which he will run. That was all which I intended to convey."

"But what is the danger?"

"You know the story of the hound?"

"I do not believe in such nonsense."

"But I do. If you have any influence with Sir Henry, take him away from a place which has always been fatal to his family. The world is wide. Why should he wish to live at the place of danger?"

"Because it is the place of danger. That is Sir Henry's nature. I fear that unless you can give me some more definite information than this it would be impossible to get him to move."

"I cannot say anything definite, for I do not know anything definite."

"I would ask you one more question, Miss Stapleton. If you meant no more than this when you first spoke to me, why should you not wish your brother to **overhear**② what you said? There is nothing to which he, or anyone else, could object."

"My brother is very anxious to have the Hall inhabited, for he thinks that it is for the good of the poor folk upon the moor. He would be very angry if he knew that I had said anything which might induce Sir Henry to go away. But I have done my duty now and I will say no more. I must get back, or he will miss me and suspect that I have seen you. Good-bye!" She turned and had disappeared in a few minutes among the scattered boulders, while I, with my soul full of vague fears, pursued my way to Baskerville Hall.

① irresolution ['i,rezə'lju:ʃən]
n. 犹豫不决

答我的问题时，眼神便又坚定了起来。

"您想得太多了，华生医生，"她说，"我和哥哥两人对查尔斯爵士的猝亡都感到非常震惊。我们之间来往密切，因为他最喜欢步行穿过荒野到我们的住处。他时刻铭记着笼罩他们家族的灾祸根源，所以，当悲剧发生时，我自然而然地认为他所表现出来的恐惧一定是有某种缘由的。因此，当我发现这个家族的另一个成员要到这里来居住时，我就觉得应该有人向他发出警示，好叫他躲避可能的危险。这就是我所想传达的意思。"

"但是，是什么样的危险呢？"

"您知道那条猎犬的传说吧？"

"我并不相信那种无稽之谈。"

"但是，我相信，如果您真能影响亨利爵士，就请您领着他远离这儿吧，这个地方对他们整个家族来说永远是个要命之地。世界如此广阔，为何他偏偏想住在这个危险的地方呢？"

"他来这里住，正是因为这里是个危险的地方，亨利爵士的性格就是这样的。除非您能给我提供一些比您刚才说的更加确切的理由，否则，让他离开这里恐怕是根本不可能的事。"

"我无法说出任何确切的情况，因为我对此一无所知。"

"我想再请问您一个问题，斯塔普尔顿小姐，如果您刚开始对我说的话仅仅是这个意思，您为何不想让您哥哥听见您说的话呢？您的话里并不含有任何您哥哥或者别人会反感的东西啊。"

② overhear [,əuvə'hiə] *v.* 偶然听到；偷听到

"我哥哥非常急切地想让亨利爵士住到庄园里，他认为这会给荒原的穷人们带来好处。如果他知道我说过些可能会诱导亨利爵士离开的话，他一定会生气的。我的任务已经完成，没有别的要说了。我现在得回家了，不然我哥哥会担心我，会怀疑我跟您见过面的。再见！"她转身走了，几分钟的时间就消失在乱石之中。返回巴斯克维尔庄园的一路上，我心里充满了隐隐的担忧。

Chapter 8 First Report of Dr. Watson

From this point onward I will follow the course of events by **transcribing**[①] my own letters to Mr. Sherlock Holmes which lie before me on the table. One page is missing, but otherwise they are exactly as written and show my feelings and suspicions of the moment more accurately than my memory, clear as it is upon these tragic events, can possibly do.

Baskerville Hall, October 13th.

MY DEAR HOLMES:

My previous letters and telegrams have kept you pretty well up to date as to all that has occurred in this most God-forsaken corner of the world. The longer one stays here the more does the spirit of the moor sink into one's soul, its vastness, and also its grim charm. When you are once out upon its bosom you have left all traces of modern England behind you, but, on the other hand, you are conscious everywhere of the homes and the work of the prehistoric people. On all sides of you as you walk are the houses of these forgotten folk, with their graves and the huge **monoliths**[②] which are supposed to have marked their temples. As you look at their gray stone huts against the scarred hillsides you leave your own age behind you, and if you were to see a skin-clad, hairy man crawl out from the low door, fitting a flint-tipped arrow on to the string of his bow, you wouid feel that his presence there was more natural than your own. The strange thing is that they should have lived so thickly on what must always

第八章　华生医生的第一份报告

① transcribe [træn'skraib] *v.* 转录

从此处起，我要转录几封自己写给夏洛克·福尔摩斯先生的信件，信件就摆在我前面的桌上，以便叙述前前后后的事情。其中只有一页遗失了，但除此之外，其余部分保存得和我当初写信的时候一模一样。信件如实地记录了我当时的感受和疑惑。虽然我的记忆力也可以清晰地做到这点，但信件无疑比回忆要准确得多。

亲爱的福尔摩斯：

通过我先前的信件和电报，你已经及时知道了在世界上的这样一个荒凉偏僻的角落里所发生的一切了。一个人如果在此待的时间越长，荒原的气势便会更加深入地渗透到他的心灵。这儿广袤无垠，充满了恐怖的魔力。你一旦踏入荒原的中心地带，就丝毫看不到现代英国的痕迹了。而恰恰相反，你在那里到处都能看到史前人类的房舍和他们的劳动成果。你在行走的过程中，到处都可以看见早已被人遗忘的古人们的住房，他们的坟墓和巨大的石柱。那些石柱很可能是用来标明他们庙宇所在地的。当你站在斑驳的山坡上看着那一幢幢用灰色岩石砌成的小屋时，就会忘记自己现在所处的年代。如果此时你看到了一个身披兽皮、满身毛发的人从低矮的门洞里爬出来，把用燧石做的箭头的弓箭搭在弦上，你会感觉他的出现比你本人的要自然得多。让人感到奇怪的是，在这片一直都非常贫瘠的土地上，当时居住的人

② monolith ['mɒnəuliθ] *n.* 独块巨石

have been most unfruitful soil. I am no **antiquarian**①, but I could imagine that they were some unwarlike and harried race who were forced to accept that which none other would occupy.

All this, however, is foreign to the mission on which you sent me and will probably be very uninteresting to your severely practical mind. I can still remember your complete indifference as to whether the sun moved round the earth or the earth round the sun. Let me, therefore, return to the facts concerning Sir Henry Baskerville.

If you have not had any report within the last few days it is because up to to-day there was nothing of importance to relate. Then a very surprising circumstance occurred, which I shall tell you **in due course**②. But, first of all, I must keep you in touch with some of the other factors in the situation.

One of these, concerning which I have said little, is the escaped convict upon the moor. There is strong reason now to believe that he has got right away, which is a considerable relief to the lonely householders of this district. A fortnight has passed since his flight, during which he has not been seen and nothing has been heard of him. It is surely inconceivable that he could have **held out**③ upon the moor during all that time. Of course, so far as his concealment goes there is no difficulty at all. Any one of these stone huts would give him a hiding-place. But there is nothing to eat unless he were to catch and slaughter one of the moor sheep. We think, therefore, that he has gone, and the outlying farmers sleep the better in consequence.

We are four able-bodied men in this household, so that we could take good care of ourselves, but I confess that I have had uneasy moments when I have thought of the Stapletons. They live miles from any help. There are one maid, an old manservant, the sister, and the brother, the latter not a very strong man. They would be helpless in the hands of a desperate fellow like this Notting Hill criminal if he could once **effect**④ an entrance. Both Sir Henry and I were concerned at their situation, and it was suggested that Perkins the groom should go over to sleep there, but Stapleton would not hear of it.

The fact is that our friend, the baronet, begins to display a considerable interest in our fair neighbour. It is not to be wondered at, for time **hangs**⑤ heavily in this lonely spot to an active man like him, and she is a very

① antiquarian [ˌænti'kwɛə
riən] n. 古文物研究者

② in due course 到一定的时
候

③ hold out 继续生存，支撑

④ effect [i'fekt] v. 实现，达
到（目的等）

⑤ hang ['hæŋ] v. 悬挂，吊
着

口竟然那么密集。我不是考古学家，但可以想象一下，他们所属的那个种族不喜争斗，因而被人驱赶，被迫接受了这个谁也不愿居住的地方。

不过，所有这一切，与你派我来这里的使命毫无关系，很可能让你这样一个讲究实用的人感到乏味了吧。我至今仍记得，在谈论是太阳绕着地球转还是地球绕着太阳转的问题时，你表现出的那种漠不关心的态度。因此，还是让我回到和亨利·巴斯克维尔爵士有关的事情上来吧。

过去几天里，你没有收到我的报告，因为直到今天并没有什么重要的事情要报告的。后来，发生了一件令人倍感惊讶的事情，我现在就把它原原本本地告诉你。不过，首先，我得让你了解一些与此事相关的其他情况。

其中有一件事，我之前没有怎么提到，那就是荒原上那个逃犯。现在完全有理由相信，他已经跑掉了。本区域内零零散散居住着的居民们倒是大大松了一口气。在他逃出监狱的两个礼拜里，没有人看见过他，也没有人打听到他的消息。无法想象，他在荒原上能待这么长时间。当然，就藏身之处而言，这是绝对没有任何困难的。他可以藏匿在荒原上的任何一幢石头小屋里。但是，除非他能捕杀荒原上的绵羊，否则他什么吃的东西都没有。由此，我们认为他已经逃走了，那些住得边远一些的农夫们也因此睡得更踏实了。

庄园里住着我们四个身强力壮的男人，我们能照顾好自己。不过，我必须承认，自己一想起斯塔普尔顿一家人就觉得心里很不安。他们住的地方方圆几英里之内都找不到帮手，而且家里只有一个女仆，一个老男仆，再就是他们兄妹二人，当哥哥的也不是很强壮。那个来自诺丁山的亡命之徒一旦闯进门去，他们就会孤立无援，只能束手就擒。我和亨利爵士都很关心他们的处境，还提出一条建议：让马夫珀金斯晚上睡在他们那儿，但斯塔普尔顿根本听不进去。

事实上，我们的从男爵朋友已经开始对我们漂亮的女邻居表现出极大的好感。这原本也没有什么值得奇怪的，因为对他这样一个好动的年轻人来说，在偏僻寂

fascinating and beautiful woman. There is something tropical and exotic about her which forms a singular contrast to her cool and unemotional brother. Yet he also gives the idea of hidden fires. He has certainly a very marked influence over her, for I have seen her continually glance at him as she talked as if seeking **approbation**① for what she said. I trust that he is kind to her. There is a dry glitter in his eyes and a firm set of his thin lips, which goes with a positive and possibly a harsh nature. You would find him an interesting study.

He came over to call upon Baskerville on that first day, and the very next morning he took us both to show us the spot where the legend of the wicked Hugo is supposed to have had its origin. It was an excursion of some miles across the moor to a place which is so dismal that it might have suggested the story. We found a short valley between rugged tors which led to an open, grassy space **flecked**② over with the white cotton grass. In the middle of it rose two great stones, worn and sharpened at the upper end until they looked like the huge **corroding**③ fangs of some monstrous beast. In every way it corresponded with the scene of the old tragedy. Sir Henry was much interested and asked Stapleton more than once whether he did really believe in the possibility of the interference of the supernatural in the affairs of men. He spoke lightly, but it was evident that he was very much in earnest. Stapleton was **guarded**④ in his replies, but it was easy to see that he said less than he might, and that he would not express his whole opinion out of consideration for the feelings of the baronet. He told us of similar cases, where families had suffered from some evil influence, and he left us with the impression that he shared the popular view upon the matter.

On our way back we stayed for lunch at Merripit House, and it was there that Sir Henry made the acquaintance of Miss Stapleton. From the first moment that he saw her he appeared to be strongly attracted by her, and I am much mistaken if the feeling was not mutual. He referred to her again and again on our walk home, and since then hardly a day has passed that we have not seen something of the brother and sister. They dine here to-night, and there is some talk of our going to them next week. One would imagine that such a match would be very welcome to Stapleton, and yet I have more than once caught a look of the strongest disapprobation in his face when Sir Henry has been paying

① approbation [,æprəu'bei
ʃən] n. 批准，核准

② fleck [flek] v. 点缀

③ corrode [kə'rəud] v. 损
伤；使恶化

④ guarded ['gɑ:did] a. 谨慎
的；有保留的

窦的地方，生活实在是无聊，而且她又是美丽迷人的女子，身上有一种热带地区的人所特有的异国情调，这和她哥哥的冷淡、不动感情的状态形成了奇特的反差。不过，他也让人感觉他的内心热情似火。他一定具有某种左右她的能力，因为我观察到，她说话时眼睛总是朝他瞥，好像她说的每句话都要得到他的赞同似的。我确信他待她非常好。他两眼炯炯有神，双唇薄且坚定，具有这些特点的人往往性格果敢，也有可能是生性脾气粗暴。你可能会觉得他是个有趣的研究对象呢。

他在头一天就拜访了巴斯克维尔，翌日早晨，便领着我们两个人一同去查看了那个地点，据说，那就是恶人雨果传说的起因之地。我们穿过荒原漫步了几英里路程，最后到了一个异常阴森荒凉之处，一看就令人想到此处定会滋生这样的故事来的。我们在两座乱石冈之间发现了一段很短的谷地，尽头是一片开阔的空地，上面杂草丛生，其中夹杂着白色的羊胡子草。空地中间矗立着两块巨石，顶端因风吹雨打而成了尖形，看上去宛如巨型怪兽那被磨尖的大獠牙。那儿的一切同那个古老传说中的惨景非常相符。亨利爵士兴趣盎然，好几次问斯塔普尔顿，他是否真的相信某种超自然的力量会干预人间的事务。斯塔普尔顿回答得轻描淡写，但明显看得出来，他内心里非常地郑重其事。他回话时谨小慎微，但很容易看出，他为了顾及从男爵的感受，尽量缄口不言，不把自己的看法和盘托出。他给我们讲了几桩类似的案例，说有几户人家都遭受了邪恶力量的迫害。他给我们的印象是，自己在这件事情上与众人的观点是一致的。

返程途中，我们在梅里皮特别墅吃了午餐。亨利爵士和斯塔普尔顿小姐正是在那里互相认识的。爵士从看到她的第一眼起，似乎就被她深深地吸引住了。我丝毫没有看错，他们两人彼此都产生了好感。我们从那儿回家时，从男爵还一而再、再而三地提起她。随后，我们几乎每天都会看到他们兄妹二人。他们今晚在这儿用餐，席间谈到我们下个礼拜去他们那儿的打算。可想而知，如果这对年轻人结合在一起，斯塔普尔顿家一定会非常赞同的。但我却不止一次发现，每当亨利爵士对他

some attention to his sister. He is much attached to her, no doubt, and would lead a lonely life without her, but it would seem the height of selfishness if he were to stand in the way of her making so brilliant a marriage. Yet I am certain that he does not wish their intimacy to ripen into love, and I have several times observed that he has taken pains to prevent them from being **tete-a-tete**[①]. By the way, your instructions to me never to allow Sir Henry to go out alone will become very much more **onerous**[②] if a love affair were to be added to our other difficulties. My popularity would soon suffer if I were to carry out your orders to the letter.

The other day–Thursday, to be more exact–Dr. Mortimer lunched with us. He has been excavating a **barrow**[③] at Long Down and has got a prehistoric skull which fills him with great joy. Never was there such a single-minded enthusiast as he! The Stapletons came in afterwards, and the good doctor took us all to the yew alley at Sir Henry's request to show us exactly how everything occurred upon that fatal night. It is a long, dismal walk, the yew alley, between two high walls of clipped hedge, with a narrow band of grass upon either side. At the far end is an old **tumble-down**[④] summer-house. Halfway down is the moor-gate, where the old gentleman left his cigar-ash. It is a white wooden gate with a **latch**[⑤]. Beyond it lies the wide moor. I remembered your theory of the affair and tried to picture all that had occurred. As the old man stood there he saw something coming across the moor, something which terrified him so that he lost his wits and ran and ran until he died of sheer horror and exhaustion. There was the long, gloomy tunnel down which he fled. And from what? A sheep-dog of the moor? Or a **spectral**[⑥] hound, black, silent, and monstrous? Was there a human agency in the matter? Did the pale, watchful Barrymore know more than he cared to say? It was all dim and vague, but always there is the dark shadow of crime behind it.

One other neighbour I have met since I wrote last. This is Mr. Frankland, of Lafter Hall, who lives some four miles to the south of us. He is an elderly man, red-faced, white-haired, and **choleric**[⑦]. His passion is for the British law, and he has spent a large fortune in **litigation**[⑧]. He fights for the mere pleasure of fighting and is equally ready to take up either side of a question, so that it is no wonder that he has found it a costly amusement. Sometimes he will shut

① tete-a-tete ['teitɑ:'teit] *ad.* 两人私下地

② onerous ['ɔnərəs] *a.* 繁重的；麻烦的

③ barrow [bærəu] *n.* 古坟

④ tumble-down ['tʌmbldaun] *a.* 即将坍塌的

⑤ latch [lætʃ] *n.* 门闩

⑥ spectral ['spektrəl] *a.* 鬼怪似的，幽灵般的

⑦ choleric ['kɔlərik] *a.* （性情）暴躁的，易怒的

⑧ litigation [,liti'geiʃən] *n.* 打官司

妹妹表露出关切之情时，斯塔普尔顿的脸上就会露出非常反感的神情。毫无疑问，他和他这个妹妹的感情非常好，没有妹妹，他的生活就会寂寞无聊。不过，如果他因此而对妹妹的如此完美的婚姻加以阻拦，那他简直是自私到极点了。不过，我可以肯定，他并不希望他们的亲密关系进一步发展为爱情。我曾多次注意到，为了不让他们有单独密谈的机会，他费尽了心机。啊，对啦，你曾叮嘱我，绝对不许亨利爵士独自外出。现在看来，要做到这点恐怕越来越困难了，因为除了其他的种种困难，又增加了爱情问题。如果我不折不扣地按照你的嘱咐行事，那我很快就会变成不受欢迎的人了。

有一天——确切地说，是礼拜四——莫蒂默医生同我们共进午餐。他一直在长丘一带挖掘一座古冢，得到了一具史前人类的颅骨。他满心欢喜，还真没见过像他那样单纯的狂热分子呢！斯塔普尔顿兄妹稍晚一点也到了。应亨利爵士的要求，热心的医生把我们全都带到了紫杉树篱小道，给我们演示了出事那天晚上事情发生的整个过程。那是一条幽长阴森的紫杉树篱小道，夹在两行高高的修剪整齐的树篱中间。小道的两旁各有一片狭长的绿草带，远处的尽头是一座破旧的凉亭。小道的中间部分就是通向荒原的栅门，也就是老绅士留下雪茄烟灰的地方。栅门是用白色木头做的，上面装有门闩。推门向外就是广袤的荒原。我还记得你对此事的推测，便努力地想象事情发生的情形。老人站在栅门边时，他看见一个东西穿过荒原向他奔跑而来。那个东西把他吓得丧失了理智，令他只顾拼命地奔逃，直到自己心衰力竭，猝亡在地。他逃跑时正是沿着那条又长又阴森的小道。他要逃避什么呢？是荒原上的牧羊犬？还是一条悄无声息、魔鬼般的黑色大猎犬？这其中是否有人作祟呢？那个脸色苍白、眼神警觉的巴里摩尔是否知道很多，但却不肯说呢？整件事情扑朔迷离，但其背后始终隐藏着罪恶的阴影。

上次给你写完信后，我遇到了另一个邻居，即拉夫特尔庄园的弗兰克兰先生。他住在我们南面大概四英里处。他年岁较长，脸色红润，头发花白，脾气暴躁。他热心研究英国法律，为诉讼的事情花费了巨额财产。他

up a right of way and **defy**^① the parish to make him open it. At others he will with his own hands tear down some other man's gate and declare that a path has existed there from time immemorial, defying the owner to prosecute him for **trespass**^②. He is learned in old **manorial**^③ and communal rights, and he applies his knowledge sometimes in favour of the villagers of Fernworthy and sometimes against them, so that he is periodically either carried in triumph down the village street or else burned in **effigy**^④, according to his latest exploit. He is said to have about seven lawsuits upon his hands at present, which will probably swallow up the remainder of his fortune and so draw his **sting**^⑤ and leave him harmless for the future. Apart from the law he seems a kindly, good-natured person, and I only mention him because you were particular that I should send some description of the people who surround us. He is curiously employed at present, for, being an amateur astronomer, he has an excellent telescope, with which he lies upon the roof of his own house and sweeps the moor all day in the hope of catching a glimpse of the escaped convict. If he would confine his energies to this all would be well, but there are rumours that he intends to prosecute Dr. Mortimer for opening a grave without the consent of the next of kin because he dug up the neolithic skull in the barrow on Long Down. He helps to keep our lives from being monotonous and gives a little comic relief where it is badly needed.

And now, having brought you up to date in the escaped convict, the Stapletons, Dr. Mortimer, and Frankland, of Lafter Hall, let me end on that which is most important and tell you more about the Barrymores, and especially about the surprising development of last night.

First of all about the test telegram, which you sent from London in order to make sure that Barrymore was really here. I have already explained that the testimony of the postmaster shows that the test was worthless and that we have no proof one way or the other. I told Sir Henry how the matter stood, and he at once, in his **downright**^⑥ fashion, had Barrymore up and asked him whether he had received the telegram himself. Barrymore said that he had.

"Did the boy deliver it into your own hands?" asked Sir Henry.

Barrymore looked surprised, and considered for a little time.

"No," said he, "I was in the box-room at the time, and my wife brought it

① defy [di'fai] v.（对权势的公然）违抗

② trespass ['trespəs] n. 未经许可进入私人土地
③ manorial [mə'nɔːriəl] a. 庄园的
④ effigy ['efidʒi] n. 模拟像

⑤ sting [stiŋ] n. 蜇

与人争执就是为了享受争执的乐趣，遇到诉讼时，自己无所谓做原告还是被告。所以，毫不奇怪，他发现诉讼是一种昂贵的消遣。他有时候会拦断一条道路，不准人家通行，并且拒不执行教区要他撤除路障的命令。有时候会亲手把别人家的大门拆除，并且声称，道路从远古时期就已存在，反驳房主对他提起的非法入侵私宅的诉讼。他对古旧的采邑权法和公共权法都很精通，经常运用这方面的知识，有时是为弗恩沃西村村民的利益争讼，有时是用法律来反对他们。因此，根据他的所作所为，他时而是胜利者被人抬着招摇过市，时而被人把他的模拟人像当街烧毁。据说，眼下他手上仍有七宗讼案，很可能会把他仅剩的财产消耗殆尽，到时他就会像一只被拔掉蜇刺的黄蜂那样于人无害了。除了法律争讼问题，他看上去是一位和蔼可亲、心地善良的老人。我之所以提及他，仅仅是因为你特意吩咐过，对于我们周围所有人的情况，我都得向你汇报。弗兰克兰眼下又忙得不可开交了，因为他是个业余的天文爱好者，有一架性能优异的望远镜，所以，成天趴在自家的屋顶上用望远镜扫视整个荒原，以期发现逃犯的蛛丝马迹。如果他把全部精力都放在此事上，那一切都会平安无事。不过有传言说，他此举的用意是想控告莫蒂默医生未经死者近亲的许可便私掘坟墓，因为医生在长丘挖掘古冢时发现了一具新石器时代的古人颅骨。他让人们的生活脱离了单调与无聊，并在人们迫切需要的时候给人一些快乐的调剂。

好啦，我已经向你汇报了有关那名逃犯、斯塔普尔顿兄妹、莫蒂默医生和拉夫特尔庄园的弗兰克兰的最新动态。此信结束之际，还有一件非常重要的事情，我要告诉你关于巴里摩尔的情况，尤其是昨天晚上的惊人情形。

首先要说的是，你从伦敦发出的那封旨在确认巴里摩尔当时确实在此地的试探性电报。我已经向你解释过，通过对邮政所所长的询问，说明那封电报没起到任何作用，我们没有证据证明他当时不是在此地。我把事情的原委告诉了亨利爵士。他是直来直去的脾气，便立刻把巴里摩尔叫过来，问他是否亲手接收了那封电报。巴里摩尔回答说是。

⑥ downright ['daunrait] a. 爽快的，直率的

"那个男孩直接把电报送到你手上了吗？"亨利爵士问。

up to me."

"Did you answer it yourself?"

"No; I told my wife what to answer and she went down to write it."

In the evening he **recurred**[①] to the subject **of his own accord**[②].

"I could not quite understand the object of your questions this morning, Sir Henry," said he. "I trust that they do not mean that I have done anything to **forfeit**[③] your confidence?"

Sir Henry had to assure him that it was not so and pacify him by giving him a considerable part of his old wardrobe, the London **outfit**[④] having now all arrived.

Mrs. Barrymore is of interest to me. She is a heavy, solid person, very **limited**[⑤], intensely respectable, and inclined to be **puritanical**[⑥]. You could hardly conceive a less emotional subject. Yet I have told you how, on the first night here, I heard her sobbing bitterly, and since then I have more than once observed traces of tears upon her face. Some deep sorrow gnaws ever at her heart. Sometimes I wonder if she has a guilty memory which haunts her, and sometimes I suspect Barrymore of being a domestic tyrant. I have always felt that there was something singular and questionable in this man's character, but the adventure of last night **brings**[⑦] all my suspicions to a head.

And yet it may seem a small matter in itself. You are aware that I am not a very sound sleeper, and since I have been on guard in this house my **slumbers**[⑧] have been lighter than ever. Last night, about two in the morning, I was aroused by a stealthy step passing my room. I rose, opened my door, and peeped out. A long black shadow was trailing down the corridor. It was thrown by a man who walked softly down the passage with a candle held in his hand. He was in shirt and trousers, with no covering to his feet. I could merely see the outline, but his height told me that it was Barrymore. He walked very slowly and **circumspectly**[⑨], and there was something indescribably guilty and furtive in his whole appearance.

I have told you that the corridor is broken by the balcony which runs round the hall, but that it is resumed upon the farther side. I waited until he had passed out of sight and then I followed him. When I came round the balcony he had reached the end of the farther corridor, and I could see from the glimmer of

① recur [ri'kə:] v.（谈话时）回到…话题
② of one's own accord 主动地
③ forfeit ['fɔ:fit] v. 丧失

④ outfit ['autfit] n. 服装

⑤ limited ['limitid] a. 拘谨的
⑥ puritanical [,pjuəri'tænikəl] a. 宗教（或道德）上极端拘谨的

⑦ bring...to a head 使…得到解决
⑧ slumber ['slʌmbə] n. 睡眠

⑨ circumspectly ['sə:kəmspektli] ad. 谨慎地，小心地

巴里摩尔显得很惊讶，思忖了片刻。

"没有，我当时正好在储藏室里，是我太太收下后送上来的。"

"是你亲自去发的回电吗？"

"也不是。我告诉了她该怎么回复，她便下楼去拟电文了。"

当晚，巴里摩尔主动挑起了这个话题。

"对今天早上你们问我那些问题，意欲如何，我没有弄明白，亨利爵士，"他说，"我觉得，自己没有做错什么事情让您对我失去信任了吧？"

亨利爵士不得不向他保证，说事情绝非如此。为了安抚他，还把自己大部分的旧衣服送给了他，因为在伦敦新添置的衣服已经全部运到了。

巴里摩尔的太太也引起了我的注意。她是严肃庄重的人，行事拘谨，显得很体面，像清教徒那样严峻。你几乎想象不出，会有人比她更不易动感情。不过，我已经告诉过你在我们到达这儿的第一个晚上，就听见她哭得很伤心。此后，我好几次看到她脸上带着泪痕，肯定有什么令人伤痛欲绝的事情在折磨着她的内心。我有时想，她是不是有什么内疚感在心里挥之不去啊。有时还怀疑，巴里摩尔是个家庭暴君。我始终觉得这个人的性格中有古怪、可疑之处，但昨晚发生的事情却让我疑虑全消了。

不过，事情本身可能是微不足道的。你知道，我睡觉睡得不是很沉，况且我住在庄园宅邸里要时刻保持警惕，因此，睡眠时比任何时候都更加警觉。昨天夜间的凌晨两点钟左右，我被经过房外的鬼鬼祟祟的脚步声惊醒了。我便起床，打开房门，悄悄往外看。一个长长的黑影投射在走廊里。一个身影手里拿着蜡烛，轻轻地顺着走廊走过去。他穿着衬衫和长裤，光着双脚。我只看得到他的轮廓，但从那人的身高就可以知道，他就是巴里摩尔。他步伐缓慢，小心翼翼，浑身上下透着某种无法形容的恶意，一副不可告人的样子。

我曾告诉过你，走廊的中间是被一段环绕大厅的露台隔断了的，不过在露台的另一端又接下去了。我在门口等待着，直到看不见他了才跟踪过去。等我走近露台

light through an open door that he had entered one of the rooms. Now, all these rooms are unfurnished and unoccupied, so that his expedition became more mysterious than ever. The light shone steadily as if he were standing motionless. I crept down the passage as noiselessly as I could and peeped round the corner of the door.

Barrymore was crouching at the window with the candle held against the glass. His profile was half turned towards me, and his face seemed to be rigid with expectation as he stared out into the blackness of the moor. For some minutes he stood watching intently. Then he gave a deep groan and with an impatient gesture he put out the light. Instantly I made my way back to my room, and very shortly came the stealthy steps passing once more upon their return journey. Long afterwards when I had fallen into a light sleep I heard a key turn somewhere in a lock, but I could not tell whence the sound came. What it all means I cannot guess, but there is some secret business going on in this house of gloom which sooner or later we shall **get to the bottom of**[1]. I do not trouble you with my theories, for you asked me to furnish you only with facts. I have had a long talk with Sir Henry this morning, and we have made a plan of **campaign**[2] founded upon my observations of last night. I will not speak about it just now, but it should make my next report interesting reading.

的时候，他已经走到了走廊另一侧的尽头。我看到昏暗的灯光从一扇敞开的门里射出来，知道他走进了一个房间。目前，那些房间既无陈设，也无人居住，因此，他的举止就愈发显得诡秘怪异。灯光非常稳定，好像他正一动不动地站着。我蹑手蹑脚，尽量不弄出动静，顺着走廊走了过去，站在房门的一角向室内窥测。

巴里摩尔蹲伏在窗户跟前，举起蜡烛靠近玻璃。他的头侧面对着我，当他盯着那片漆黑的荒原凝望时，面部好像因为焦虑而变得僵硬。他站在那里专心专意地察看了几分钟，然后低沉地呻吟了一声，用极不耐烦的动作把蜡烛掐灭了。我急忙回到了卧室。随后不久，门外又一次传来了潜行回去的脚步声。过了很长一段时间，就在我刚刚蒙眬入睡的时候，听到某个地方有钥匙插进锁孔的声音，但我说不出声音究竟来自何方，无法猜透这一切到底意味着什么。不过，心里面觉得，这座阴森诡秘的宅邸里正在进行着某种秘密的活动，而我们对此迟早会弄个水落石出的。我不愿用自己的推断来干扰你，因为你曾要求我只给你提供事实。今天上午，我和亨利爵士谈了很长时间，并根据昨晚我观察到的事情制定了一个行动计划。我现在暂时保密，等下次写信时再向你报告，想必会很有意思的。

① get to the bottom of 弄清…的真相

② campaign [kæm'pein] *n.*（专为某一目的的）活动

Chapter 9　Second Report of Dr. Watson

THE LIGHT UPON THE MOOR

Baskerville Hall, Oct. 15th.

MY DEAR HOLMES:

If I was compelled to leave you without much news during the early days of my mission you must **acknowledge**[1] that I am making up for lost time, and that events are now crowding **thick and fast**[2] upon us. In my last report I ended upon my top note with Barrymore at the window, and now I have quite a **budget**[3] already which will, unless I am much mistaken, considerably surprise you. Things have taken a turn which I could not have anticipated. In some ways they have within the last forty-eight hours become much clearer and in some ways they have become more complicated. But I will tell you all and you shall judge for yourself.

Before breakfast on the morning following my adventure I went down the corridor and examined the room in which Barrymore had been on the night before. The western window through which he had stared so intently has, I noticed, one peculiarity above all other windows in the house–it commands the nearest outlook on to the moor. There is an opening between two trees which enables one from this point of view to look right down upon it, while from all the other windows it is only a distant glimpse which can be obtained. It follows, therefore, that Barrymore, since only this window would serve the purpose, must have been looking out for something or somebody upon the moor. The night was very dark, so that I can hardly imagine how he could have hoped to see anyone. It had struck me that it was possible that some love intrigue was **on foot**[4]. That would have accounted

第九章 华生医生的第二份报告

荒原上的灯光

① acknowledge [ək'nɔlidʒ] v.
承认
② thick and fast 接二连三
地
③ budget ['bʌdʒit] n. 一组
（新闻、信件等）

亲爱的福尔摩斯：

　　我遵嘱执行此次使命，如果说在最初时日里没有什么情况要报告给你，也是迫不得已。但是，你现在得承认，我正在弥补时间上的损失，况且，这儿也接二连三出现新情况，变化迅速。上次汇报时，我在结尾处只写到巴里摩尔站在窗口。现在，我已经掌握了更多情况。如果我估计得没错，你肯定会对此大为惊讶的。情况发生了转折，这是我始料未及的。在过去的48小时里，有些方面已经明朗多了，而另外一些方面却变得更加扑朔迷离。我现在把一切都报告给你，然后由你自己去做出判断。

　　我的那次奇遇之后的那个早晨，早餐之前，我顺着走廊察看了头天夜间巴里摩尔待的那个房间。我注意到，他当时是透过西面的窗户神情专注地向外观望的，那扇窗户有一个奇特之处，整个宅邸的其他窗户都不具备——它能近距离地看到荒原。窗户前面有两棵树，透过树中间的空隙便可把荒原尽收眼底，而从别的窗户却只能远远地看到一点点。因此，既然只有这扇窗户才能达到巴里摩尔的要求，我便推测，他当时一定是在寻找荒原上的什么东西或者什么人。夜色昏暗，我很难想象他指望着要看到什么人。但我突然又想到，说不定正在发生着男女偷情的事情。他行动诡秘，还有他妻子心神不宁，这样就说得通了。他长得一表人才，相貌出众，赢得某个乡村姑娘的欢心很容易。因此，这种说法是站

④ on foot 在进行中

for his stealthy movements and also for the uneasiness of his wife. The man is a striking-looking fellow, very well equipped to steal the heart of a country girl, so that this theory seemed to have something to support it. That opening of the door which I had heard after I had returned to my room might mean that he had gone out to keep some **clandestine**[①] appointment. So I reasoned with myself in the morning, and I tell you the direction of my suspicions, however much the result may have shown that they were unfounded.

But whatever the true explanation of Barrymore's movements might be, I felt that the responsibility of keeping them to myself until I could explain them was more than I could bear. I had an **interview**[②] with the baronet in his study after breakfast, and I told him all that I had seen. He was less surprised than I had expected.

"I knew that Barrymore walked about nights, and I had a mind to speak to him about it," said he. "Two or three times I have heard his steps in the passage, coming and going, just about the hour you name."

"Perhaps then he pays a visit every night to that particular window," I suggested.

"Perhaps he does. If so, we should be able to shadow him and see what it is that he is after. I wonder what your friend Holmes would do if he were here."

"I believe that he would do exactly what you now suggest," said I. "He would follow Barrymore and see what he did."

"Then we shall do it together."

"But surely he would hear us."

"The man is rather deaf, and in any case we must take our chance of that. We'll sit up in my room to-night and wait until he passes." Sir Henry rubbed his hands with pleasure, and it was evident that he **hailed**[③] the adventure as a relief to his somewhat quiet life upon the moor.

The baronet has been in communication with the architect who prepared the plans for Sir Charles, and with a contractor from London, so that we may expect great changes to begin here soon. There have been decorators and furnishers up from Plymouth, and it is evident that our friend has large ideas and means to spare no pains or expense to restore the grandeur of his family. When the house is **renovated**[④] and refurnished, all that he will need will be a wife to make it

得住脚的。我晚上回到卧室之后听到的开门声说明，他出去秘密幽会了。到了早晨，我就是这样说服自己的。我还是要把这些大致的猜测告诉给你，既使到头来我的结论可能被证明毫无根据也罢。

　　然而，不管对巴里摩尔的行为该做怎么样的解释，我觉得，如果要等到真相大白之后，我才能透露出去，这个责任未免过于重大，我承受不了。早晨过后，我去从男爵的书房同他会过面，我把自己亲眼看到的情况全部告诉了他，但他并没有我预想的那样惊讶。

　　"我知道巴里摩尔夜里经常四处走动，曾想过要找他谈一谈的，"他说，"就在您说的那个时间段，我曾两三次听到他在过道里走来走去的脚步声。"

　　"这么说，他可能每天夜间都要到那个窗口去走走了。"我提示说。

　　"或许是这样的。如果情况确实如此，我们倒可以跟踪他，看看他到底在寻找什么。我在想，如果您的朋友福尔摩斯在这儿，他会怎么办呢？"

　　"我觉得，他一定会像您现在所提议的这样做，"我说，"他会跟踪巴里摩尔，看看他究竟做过些什么。"

　　"那么，我们就一同行动吧。"

　　"但是，毫无疑问，他一定会听到动静的。"

　　"那人耳朵很背，不管怎么说，我们得抓住这个机会。今晚待在我房间里别睡，一直等到他从那儿经过。"亨利爵士兴致勃勃，搓着双手。很显然，他对这次冒险感到很开心，认为这可以消解他在荒原地带的孤寂感。

　　从男爵已经联系了曾帮助查尔斯爵士拟订修缮计划的建筑师，还联系了伦敦的承建商，所以，我们可以期待，这儿很快就会有变化了。还有来自普利茅斯的装饰师和家具商，显而易见，我们的朋友心中有了宏伟的计划，并要不遗余力，或者不惜代价，定要重现家族昔日的辉煌。等到宅邸重新翻修和布置之后，万事俱备，就差一位夫人了。我们私下里说说，有显而易见的迹象表明，只要那位小姐乐意，这一点是不成问题的。我很少看到过哪位男士像他对我们漂亮的邻居斯塔普尔顿小姐那样着迷的。不过，在这种情况下，真正的爱情发展得

① clandestine [klæn'destin] *a.* 秘密的

② interview ['intəvju:] *n.* 会谈

③ hail [heil] *v.* 对…表示欢迎

④ renovate ['renəuveit] *v.* 整修；翻修

complete. Between ourselves there are pretty clear signs that this will not be **wanting**[①] if the lady is willing, for I have seldom seen a man more **infatuated**[②] with a woman than he is with our beautiful neighbour, Miss Stapleton. And yet the course of true love does not run quite as smoothly as one would under the circumstances expect. To-day, for example, its surface was broken by a very unexpected ripple, which has caused our friend considerable perplexity and annoyance.

After the conversation which I have quoted about Barrymore, Sir Henry put on his hat and prepared to go out. As a matter of course I did the same.

"What, are *you* coming, Watson?" he asked, looking at me in a curious way.

"That depends on whether you are going on the moor," said I.

"Yes, I am."

"Well, you know what my instructions are. I am sorry to intrude, but you heard how earnestly Holmes insisted that I should not leave you, and especially that you should not go alone upon the moor."

Sir Henry put his hand upon my shoulder with a pleasant smile.

"My dear fellow," said he, "Holmes, with all his wisdom, did not foresee some things which have happened since I have been on the moor. You understand me? I am sure that you are the last man in the world who would wish to be a **spoil-sport**[③]. I must go out alone."

It put me in a most awkward position. I was at a loss what to say or what to do, and before I had made up my mind he picked up his cane and was gone.

But when I came to think the matter over my conscience reproached me bitterly for having **on any pretext**[④] allowed him to go out of my sight. I imagined what my feelings would be if I had to return to you and to confess that some misfortune had occurred through my disregard for your instructions. I assure you my cheeks flushed at the very thought. It might not even now be too late to overtake him, so I set off at once in the direction of Merripit House.

I hurried along the road at the top of my speed without seeing anything of Sir Henry, until I came to the point where the moor path branches off. There, fearing that perhaps I had come in the wrong direction after all, I mounted a hill from which I could command a view–the same hill which is cut into the dark quarry. Thence I saw him at once. He was on the moor path, about a quarter of a mile off,

① wanting ['wɔntiŋ] *a.* 缺少
的
② infatuated [in'fætjueitid] *a.*
着迷的，迷恋的

③ spoilsport ['spɔilspɔ:t] *n.*
扫兴者，败兴者

④ on any pretext 以任何借
口

并非像人们预料的那样一帆风顺。就拿今天来说吧，爱
情之海平静的水面就被一阵出人意料的波澜给扰乱了，
这给我们的朋友造成了巨大的困惑和烦恼。

在结束了我刚才记录下来的这段关于巴里摩尔的谈
话之后，亨利爵士戴好帽子准备出门了。当然了，我也
准备出去。

"什么，您也一起去，华生？"他问了一句，一边
看着我，一副好奇的样子。

"这就要看您是不是要去荒原了。"我说。

"对啊，我是去那儿。"

"那行啊，我所接受的指令您是知道的。干预了您
的行动，我很抱歉，但是，您听说了，福尔摩斯郑重其
事，坚持要我不能离开您，尤其是，您不能单独一人到
荒原去。"

亨利爵士把一只手搭在我肩膀上，脸上露出了愉悦
的笑容。

"亲爱的伙计，"他说，"即使福尔摩斯聪明透顶，
他对我到荒原后所发生的一些事情也是无法预料到的。
您明白我的意思吗？我敢肯定，您是决不愿意做一个让
人扫兴的人，我一定要单独出去。"

这件事让我陷入了尴尬的境地，我一时不知道该说什
么，该做什么。还没等我拿定主意，他便拿起手杖走了。

但是，当我把事情重新斟酌了一番之后，自己的良
心受到了强烈的谴责，因为他找了个托词，我便允许他
从自己的视线中消失了。一旦因为我不按你的嘱咐行事
而发生了什么不测，结果我得跑回来向你求助、认错，
到时，心里面是怎么个滋味儿那就很难说了。说实在
的，想到这点，我的脸上就觉得火辣辣的。或许现在去
追他也还为时未晚呢。于是，我立刻动身朝梅里皮特别
墅的方向走去。

我步伐匆匆，奋力追赶，一直跑到了荒原的岔路口
处，依然不见亨利爵士的踪影。这时，我担心起来，怀
疑自己跑错了方向。为了能观望到远处，我爬上了一座
小山冈——就是那座被开辟成采石场的黑色小山。到了
那儿之后，我立刻就看见了他。他走在荒原的小路上，
离我大概有四分之一英里的距离，身边还有一位女士，无

and a lady was by his side who could only be Miss Stapleton. It was clear that there was already an understanding between them and that they had met by appointment. They were walking slowly along in deep conversation, and I saw her making quick little movements of her hands as if she were very earnest in what she was saying, while he listened intently, and once or twice shook his head in strong **dissent**[①]. I stood among the rocks watching them, very much puzzled as to what I should do next. To follow them and break into their intimate conversation seemed to be an outrage, and yet my clear duty was never for an instant to let him out of my sight. To act the spy upon a friend was a hateful task. Still, I could see no better course than to observe him from the hill, and to clear my conscience by confessing to him afterwards what I had done. It is true that if any sudden danger had threatened him I was too far away to be of use, and yet I am sure that you will agree with me that the position was very difficult, and that there was nothing more which I could do.

Our friend, Sir Henry, and the lady had halted on the path and were standing deeply absorbed in their conversation, when I was suddenly aware that I was not the only witness of their interview. A **wisp**[②] of green floating in the air caught my eye, and another glance showed me that it was carried on a stick by a man who was moving among the broken ground. It was Stapleton with his butterfly-net. He was very much closer to the pair than I was, and he appeared to be moving in their direction. At this instant Sir Henry suddenly drew Miss Stapleton to his side. His arm was round her, but it seemed to me that she was **straining**[③] away from him with her face **averted**[④]. He stooped his head to hers, and she raised one hand as if in protest. Next moment I saw them spring apart and turn hurriedly round. Stapleton was the cause of the interruption. He was running wildly towards them, his absurd net **dangling**[⑤] behind him. He gesticulated and almost danced with excitement in front of the lovers. What the scene meant I could not imagine, but it seemed to me that Stapleton was **abusing**[⑥] Sir Henry, who offered explanations, which became more angry as the other refused to accept them. The lady stood by in **haughty**[⑦] silence. Finally Stapleton turned upon his heel and beckoned in a **peremptory**[⑧] way to his sister, who, after an irresolute glance at Sir Henry, walked off by the side of her brother. The naturalist's angry gestures showed that the lady was included in his displeasure. The baronet stood for a minute looking after them, and then he walked slowly back the way that he had come, his head

① dissent [di'sent] *n.* 不赞同

疑就是斯塔普尔顿小姐。很显然，他们之间已经形成了一种默契，这次会面也是早已约定好了的。两人一边并肩缓缓而行，一边窃窃私语。我看见她不停地打着手势，让人觉得她对自己所说的话很当真。与此同时，爵士也专注地倾听着，有一两次还摇头表示不认同。我站在岩石中间，注视着他们的一举一动，不知道接下去该如何做好。如果走上前去打断他们亲密的谈话，那未免显得唐突无礼。然而，我肩负着非常明确的责任，即片刻也不能让他离开我的视线。秘密监视自己的朋友可是一桩令人鄙视的差事啊。尽管如此，我想不出什么更好的办法，只能站在山岗上监视着，事后再向他坦白自己的行为，以求良心上的清白。老实说，如果当时突然发生了危及他生命的险情，我离他的距离就太远了，根本帮不上他的忙。不过我相信，你也会认同我的看法的。处于这种境地是非常为难的，我也确实没有其他的办法了。

② wisp [wisp] *n.* 一缕；一片

我们的朋友亨利爵士和那位小姐在小路上停下了脚步，完全沉浸在私语之中。这时，我突然发觉窥探他们俩幽会的不只是我一个人。我看到某个绿色的东西在空中晃动着，定神一看，发现那东西是装在一根木棒上的，而举着木棒的人正在崎岖不平的路上走动。来者正是拿着扑蝶网兜的斯塔普尔顿。同我所处的位置相比，他所

③ strain [strein] *v.* 尽力，努力
④ averted [ə'vəːtid] *a.* 转到一边去的

处的与那男女二人要近很多，他似乎朝着他们的方向走过去。就在那个当儿，亨利爵士突然一把将斯塔普尔顿小姐拉到自己的身边，用胳膊把她环抱着。但是，我看见她把脸转过去，好像要奋力挣脱他似的。他俯下身去碰她的头，而她则举起一只手，像是在反抗。随即，我

⑤ dangle ['dæŋgl] *v.* 悬荡

⑥ abuse [ə'bjuːz] *v.* 辱骂

看见他们受惊吓似的一跃身子分开了，并且慌忙转过身。原来是斯塔普尔顿打搅了他们。他正发疯似的向他们跑去，那个扑蝶网兜在他背后乱晃。他在那对情侣面前发怒，激动得手舞足蹈起来。我很难想象当时那个场景到

⑦ haughty ['hɔːti] *a.* 傲慢的
⑧ peremptory [pə'remptəri] *a.* 专横的

底是怎么回事。不过在我看来，斯塔普尔顿正在责骂亨利爵士，爵士则不断地向他解释，但他听不进任何辩解，反而更加怒火中烧了。小姐站立在一旁，态度傲慢，缄口不言。最后，斯塔普尔顿猛地转过身，态度专横地朝着妹妹招了招手。妹妹迟疑地瞥了亨利爵士一眼，然后同哥哥一道并肩走了。那个生物学家暴怒的手势说明，

hanging, the very picture of dejection.

What all this meant I could not imagine, but I was deeply ashamed to have witnessed so intimate a scene without my friend's knowledge. I ran down the hill therefore and met the baronet at the bottom. His face was flushed with anger and his brows were wrinkled, like one who is at his wit's ends what to do.

"Halloa, Watson! Where have you dropped from?" said he. "You don't mean to say that you came after me in spite of all?"

I explained everything to him: how I had found it impossible to remain behind, how I had followed him, and how I had witnessed all that had occurred. For an instant his eyes blazed at me, but my frankness disarmed his anger, and he broke at last into a rather rueful laugh.

"You would have thought the middle of that prairie a fairly safe place for a man to be private," said he, "but, by thunder, the whole countryside seems to have been out to see me do my **wooing**①-and a mighty poor wooing at that! Where had you engaged a seat?"

"I was on that hill."

"Quite in the back row, eh? But her brother was well up to the front. Did you see him come out on us?"

"Yes, I did."

"Did he ever strike you as being crazy–this brother of hers?"

"I can't say that he ever did."

"I dare say not. I always thought him sane enough until to-day, but you can take it from me that either he or I ought to be in a **strait-jacket**②. What's the matter with me, anyhow? You've lived near me for some weeks, Watson. Tell me straight, now! Is there anything that would prevent me from making a good husband to a woman that I loved?"

"I should say not."

"He can't object to my worldly position, so it must be myself that he has this **down**③ on. What has he against me? I never hurt man or woman in my life that I know of. And yet he would not so much as let me touch the tips of her fingers."

"Did he say so?"

"That, and a deal more. I tell you, Watson, I've only known her these few weeks, but from the first I just felt that she was made for me, and she, too–she was

他也迁怒于自己的妹妹。从男爵站在那里，对着他们的背影看了一会儿，然后便缓缓地沿着来时的小路往回走。只见他耷拉着脑袋，完全是一副沮丧落魄的模样。

这一切都是怎么一回事，我无法想象，只不过，自己在朋友不知情的情况下，目睹了如此私密的一幕，感到羞愧难当。我于是跑着到了山下，在山脚处遇上了从男爵。他气得满脸通红，眉头紧锁，一副不知所措的样子。

"嘿，华生！您是从哪儿掉下来的？"他问，"您不会是说，您不顾一切还是跟着我来了吧？"

我把全部情况解释给他听：我如何觉得自己无法留在家里，如何跟随着他，如何目睹了刚才发生的一幕。有一瞬间，他火冒三丈地逼视着我，但我坦诚的态度平息了他的怒气，他最终懊恼地哈哈大笑了起来。

"如果是您，也会觉得，荒原的中心地带是个安全的所在，男人可以干点私密的事情，"他说，"但是，天哪！整个地区的人都好像跑出来看我向人家求爱来了——多么糟糕透顶的求爱表演啊！您当时是在哪儿呢？"

① woo [wu:] v. 求爱；求婚

"我在那个山丘上。"

"位置有点靠后了吧，呃？但是，她哥哥倒是挺靠前的。您看见他冲到我们跟前了吗？"

"是啊，看见了。"

"您先前是否发觉他很疯狂——就是那位做哥哥的？"

"没有啊，我没有发觉。"

"我敢说，他没有。直到今天，我一直都觉得他是个精神很正常的人。但是，您尽管相信我好了，我们两个人之间总会有一个得穿上束身衣。说来说去，我有什么问题吗？您与我共同生活已经有几个礼拜了，华生。您就直率地告诉我吧！我有什么地方不正常，让我无法成为自己所爱的女人的理想丈夫吗？"

② strait-jacket [streit'dʒækit] n. 约束衣

"我看没有。"

"对于我的家世地位，他没有什么可说的，因此，一定是我身上的什么缺点让他看不起我。他对我的哪一点反感呢？我长到这么大，认识的男男女女很多，但从未伤害过他们中的任何人。然而，他却几乎连我碰一碰她的手指都不允许！"

③ down [daun] n. 恶感，恶意

"他说过这种话吗？"

happy when she was with me, and that I'll swear. There's a light in a woman's eyes that speaks louder than words. But he has never let us get together, and it was only to-day for the first time that I saw a chance of having a few words with her alone. She was glad to meet me, but when she did it was not love that she would talk about, and she wouldn't have let me talk about it either if she could have stopped it. She kept coming back to it that this was a place of danger, and that she would never be happy until I had left it. I told her that since I had seen her I was in no hurry to leave it, and that if she really wanted me to go, the only way to work it was for her to arrange to go with me. With that I offered in as many words to marry her, but before she could answer, down came this brother of hers, running at us with a face on him like a madman. He was just white with rage, and those light eyes of his were blazing with fury. What was I doing with the lady? How dared I offer her attentions which were **distasteful**[1] to her? Did I think that because I was a baronet I could do what I liked? If he had not been her brother I should have known better how to answer him. As it was I told him that my feelings towards his sister were such as I was not ashamed of, and that I hoped that she might honour me by becoming my wife. That seemed to make the matter no better, so then I lost my temper too, and I answered him rather more **hotly**[2] than I should perhaps, considering that she was standing by. So it ended by his going off with her, as you saw, and here am I as badly puzzled a man as any in this county. Just tell me what it all means, Watson, and I'll owe you more than ever I can hope to pay."

I tried one or two explanations, but, indeed, I was completely puzzled myself. Our friend's title, his fortune, his age, his character, and his appearance are all in his favour, and I know nothing against him unless it be this dark fate which runs in his family. That his advances should be rejected so **brusquely**[3] without any reference to the lady's own wishes and that the lady should accept the situation without protest is very amazing. However, our conjectures were set at rest by a visit from Stapleton himself that very afternoon. He had come to offer apologies for his rudeness of the morning, and after a long private interview with Sir Henry in his study the **upshot**[4] of their conversation was that the breach is quite healed, and that we are to dine at Merripit House next Friday as a sign of it.

"I don't say now that he isn't a crazy man," said Sir Henry; "I can't forget the look in his eyes when he ran at me this morning, but I must allow that no man

"说了，还说了很多别的呢。我告诉您，华生，我和她相识才不过几个礼拜而已，但是，从一开始看见她，我就感觉到，她就是为我而生的，而她也有这样的感觉——她同我在一块儿时，感到心情愉快，这个我可以发誓。她的眼睛闪闪发亮，这比她用语言表达还要有力。但她哥哥根本不让我们会面，我今天唯一一次有个机会和她单独说说话。她见到我非常高兴，但她高兴的原因不是因为可以同我谈情说爱，而且，她如果能制止得了我说话，甚至会不让我说到爱情上面去。她反复提到这个地方充满了危险，我若是不离开此地，她就永远都不会开心。我告诉她说，从我见到她时起，我就不再急着要离开此地了。使我离开的唯一办法是，她愿意同我一道离开。后来，我说了很多，向她求婚。但是，还没等她做出回答，她哥哥就朝着我们冲过来了，脸上的表情像是发了疯似的。他怒不可遏，脸色煞白，那双浅色的眼睛充满了怒火。我对那位小姐做了什么呢？我怎么敢冒昧提一些让她厌烦的建议呢？难道我自认为是个从男爵就可以随心所欲吗？如果他不是她的哥哥，要对付他倒是不成什么问题的。我当时对他说，自己并不认为同他妹妹产生感情是什么见不得人的事情，况且我还希望她能屈尊做我的夫人呢。我的这番话似乎并没有能够使事态有什么好转，我于是也发起脾气来了。在回答他的时候，言语好像有些过分，毕竟她还站在旁边呢。最后，正如您所看到的，他和她一道离开了，我一个人站在这儿，被弄得云里雾里，不知所措。就告诉我这是怎么回事吧，华生，我会对您感激不尽的。"

我尝试着做出了一两种解释，不过，事实上，我自己也是完全迷惑不解。我们这位朋友在身世、财产、年龄、性格和外貌方面拥有巨大的优势，除了一直笼罩着他家族的那个祸根之外，我找不出他的任何劣势。令人感到异常震惊的是，他哥哥丝毫不考虑小姐本人的意愿，便对追求她的人如此这般地粗暴拒绝，而小姐对此却毫不抗议，坦然接受一切。然而，斯塔普尔顿当天下午亲自登门了，从而消除了我们心中的种种猜测。他是专程来为自己上午的粗鲁态度道歉的。他们在书房里进行了长时间的密谈。谈话的结果是：两人之间尽释前

① distasteful [dis'teistful] a. 令人反感的

② hotly [hɔtli] ad. 激动地，急躁地

③ brusquely ['brʌskli] ad. 粗暴地

④ upshot ['ʌpʃɔt] n. 结局；结论

could make a more handsome apology than he has done."

"Did he give any explanation of his conduct?"

"His sister is everything in his life, he says. That is natural enough, and I am glad that he should understand her value. They have always been together, and according to his account he has been a very lonely man with only her as a companion, so that the thought of losing her was really terrible to him. He had not understood, he said, that I was becoming attached to her, but when he saw with his own eyes that it was really so, and that she might be taken away from him, it gave him such a shock that for a time he was not responsible for what he said or did. He was very sorry for all that had passed, and he recognized how foolish and how selfish it was that he should imagine that he could hold a beautiful woman like his sister to himself for her whole life. If she had to leave him he had rather it was to a neighbour like myself than to anyone else. But in any case it was a blow to him and it would take him some time before he could prepare himself to meet it. He would withdraw all opposition upon his part if I would promise for three months to let the matter rest and to be content with cultivating the lady's friendship during that time without claiming her love. This I promised, and so the matter rests."

So there is one of our small mysteries cleared up. It is something to have touched bottom anywhere in this bog in which we are **floundering**[①]. We know now why Stapleton looked with disfavour upon his sister's suitor–even when that suitor was so **eligible**[②] a one as Sir Henry. And now I pass on to another thread which I have **extricated**[③] out of the tangled **skein**[④], the mystery of the sobs in the night, of the tear-stained face of Mrs. Barrymore, of the secret journey of the butler to the western lattice window. Congratulate me, my dear Holmes, and tell me that I have not disappointed you as an agent–that you do not regret the confidence which you showed in me when you sent me down. All these things have by one night's work been thoroughly cleared.

I have said "by one night's work," but, in truth, it was by two nights' work, for on the first we drew entirely blank. I sat up with Sir Henry in his rooms until nearly three o'clock in the morning, but no sound of any sort did we hear except the chiming clock upon the stairs. It was a most melancholy **vigil**[⑤] and ended by each of us falling asleep in our chairs. Fortunately we were not discouraged, and we determined to try again. The next night we lowered the lamp and sat smoking

嫌，而且我们大家礼拜五到梅里皮特别墅去吃了饭，以此作为友好的开端。

"我不能说他现在就不是个疯狂之徒，"亨利爵士说，"我无法忘记他今天上午向我跑来时的那种眼神，但我又必须得承认，他那道歉的态度显得很是诚恳自然，没人比得上。"

"他对自己的行为做过什么解释吗？"

"他说，他妹妹是他生命的全部。这再自然不过了，而且，他能如此看重她，我打心眼儿里高兴。他们一直生活在一起，据他自己说，他是个很孤单寂寞的人，只有妹妹陪伴在身边，因此，一想到要失去她，心里就会很难受。他说，他之前并不知道我已经爱上了她，但当他亲眼看到事实确实如此，并且感觉到我会把她从他身边带走时，他便惊愕不已，以致一时间无法控制自己的言谈举止。他对已发生的事情感到十分抱歉。同时也意识到，自己曾妄想把像自己妹妹那样漂亮的姑娘终生束缚在自己的身边，那是多么愚蠢，多么自私。如果她一定要离开他的话，那他情愿把她嫁给像我这样的邻居，而不是其他任何人。但无论如何，这件事情对他是个打击，他需要一段时间做好思想准备，以便接受这个事实。如果我答应在今后的三个月内暂且搁下此事，只同那位小姐发展友谊，而不是爱情，他本人不会反对。我向他保证了这一点，事情就此平息下来了。"

这样一来，我们面临的几个小谜团中的一个就解开了。这就好像人在泥潭中挣扎时，终于在某处碰到了硬底似的。现在，我们明白了斯塔普尔顿为何对妹妹的追求者如此反感——就算是一位像亨利爵士这样不可多得的人。现在，我要转到从一团乱线中抽出的另一个线头上了——夜半哭声之谜，巴里摩尔太太脸上的泪痕之谜，还有管家夜间潜行去西面窗口之谜。亲爱的福尔摩斯，祝贺我吧，对我说，我接受你的委派后没有辜负你的嘱托——你在派我来这儿时，对我寄予的信任没有白费，因为我用一夜工夫就把所有谜团都彻底解开了。

我刚才说"一夜工夫"，但事实上，是花了两夜的工夫，因为第一天夜间几乎毫无结果。当夜，我和亨利爵士一同待在他的卧室里，一直等到将近凌晨三点，但

① flounder ['flaundə] v. 挣扎

② eligible ['elidʒəbl] a. 有条件被选上的

③ extricate ['ekstrikeit] v. 解脱

④ skein ['skein] n.（纱、线等的）一束

⑤ vigil ['vidʒil] n. 守夜，值夜

cigarettes without making the least sound. It was incredible how slowly the hours crawled by, and yet we were helped through it by the same sort of patient interest which the hunter must feel as he watches the trap into which he hopes the game may wander. One struck, and two, and we had almost for the second time given it up in despair when in an instant we both sat **bolt upright**[①] in our chairs with all our weary senses keenly on the alert once more. We had heard the creak of a step in the passage.

Very stealthily we heard it pass along until it **died away**[②] in the distance. Then the baronet gently opened his door and we set out in pursuit. Already our man had gone round the gallery, and the corridor was all in darkness. Softly we stole along until we had come into the other wing. We were just in time to catch a glimpse of the tall, black-bearded figure, his shoulders rounded, as he tiptoed down the passage. Then he passed through the same door as before, and the light of the candle framed it in the darkness and shot one single yellow beam across the gloom of the corridor. We **shuffled**[③] cautiously towards it, trying every **plank**[④] before we dared to put our whole weight upon it. We had taken the precaution of leaving our boots behind us, but, even so, the old boards snapped and creaked beneath our tread. Sometimes it seemed impossible that he should fail to hear our approach. However, the man is fortunately rather deaf, and he was entirely preoccupied in that which he was doing. When at last we reached the door and peeped through we found him crouching at the window, candle in hand, his white, intent face pressed against the pane, exactly as I had seen him two nights before.

We had arranged no plan of campaign, but the baronet is a man to whom the most direct way is always the most natural. He walked into the room, and as he did so Barrymore sprang up from the window with a sharp hiss of his breath and stood, livid and trembling, before us. His dark eyes, glaring out of the white mask of his face, were full of horror and astonishment as he gazed from Sir Henry to me.

"What are you doing here, Barrymore?"

"Nothing, sir." His agitation was so great that he could hardly speak, and the shadows sprang up and down from the shaking of his candle. "It was the window, sir. I go round at night to see that they are fastened."

"On the second floor?"

"Yes, sir, all the windows."

除了楼梯口上大钟报时的声音，什么都没听见。熬夜的滋味不好受，挺沉闷乏味的，最后我们两个人都倒在椅子上睡着了。所幸的是，我们非但没因此而泄气，而且还决心要再试一次。次日晚上，我们把灯弄得很暗，坐在房间里抽烟，没有弄出半点动静来。时间一点一点过去，慢得让人难以置信。不过，我们都耐着性子，饶有兴致地熬了过来，就像猎人守着陷阱等待猎物过来自投罗网一样。一点的钟声敲响了，两点的钟声又响起了。我们感到绝望，几乎准备再次放弃。就在那个当儿，我们两个不约而同地从椅子上腾地坐起身来，全身感官倦意顿消，立刻警惕了起来，因为我们听到走廊上传来的嘎吱嘎吱的脚步声。

　　脚步鬼鬼祟祟，我们听见它经过了走廊，最后消失在了远处。然后，从男爵轻轻地打开他的房门，我们开始跟踪。那人拐了个弯转入了露台，走廊里漆黑一片。我们放轻脚步，走到了露台的另一侧，正好看见那个高高的、蓄着黑胡子的人影。他弯腰屈背，踮着脚尖走过长廊，随后走进了上次进去过的那扇门。漆黑的夜色中，烛光把门框的轮廓照得清晰可见，给昏暗的走廊留下了唯一的一道黄光。我们小心翼翼地迈着小步向那扇门靠近，每次在把全身的重量压在地板之前都要先踩下试一试。为了谨慎起见，我们都把鞋给脱了，扔在了房间里。即便如此，老旧的地板还是在脚底下嘎吱作响。我们有时候会觉得，他不可能听不到我们走近的声音。不过幸运的是，那个人的耳朵很背，而且正全神贯注于自己的事情。我们终于走到了门口，朝着里面窥测了一下，看到他正弯腰站在窗前，手举蜡烛，那张苍白而神色紧张的面孔紧贴着窗玻璃，和我前天晚上看到的情形一模一样。

　　我们事先没有制定什么行动计划，但从男爵始终认为，最直截了当的办法就是最自然有效的办法。于是，他径直走进了房里，巴里摩尔被吓了一跳，他倒吸了一口冷气，猛地一下离开了窗口，站到了我们跟前。他面如死灰，浑身颤抖。他那苍白的脸上，两只黑色的眼睛充满了恐惧和惊讶，目光在亨利爵士和我身上打转。

　　"巴里摩尔，你在这儿干什么？"

　　"没有干什么，先生，"他被惊吓得几乎说不出话来

① bolt upright 笔直地，僵直地
② die away 渐渐消失

③ shuffle ['ʃʌfl] v. 轻轻地走
④ plank [plæŋk] n. 木板

"Look here, Barrymore," said Sir Henry sternly, "we have made up our minds to have the truth out of you, so it will save you trouble to tell it sooner rather than later. Come, now! No lies! What were you doing at that window?"

The fellow looked at us in a helpless way, and he wrung his hands together like one who is in the last **extremity**① of doubt and misery.

"I was doing no harm, sir. I was holding a candle to the window."

"And why were you holding a candle to the window?"

"Don't ask me, Sir Henry–don't ask me! I give you my word, sir, that it is not my secret, and that I cannot tell it. If it concerned no one but myself I would not try to keep it from you."

A sudden idea occurred to me, and I took the candle from the trembling hand of the butler.

"He must have been holding it as a signal," said I. "Let us see if there is any answer." I held it as he had done, and stared out into the darkness of the night. Vaguely I could discern the black bank of the trees and the lighter expanse of the moor, for the moon was behind the clouds. And then I gave a cry of **exultation**②, for a tiny pin-point of yellow light had suddenly **transfixed**③ the dark veil, and glowed steadily in the centre of the black square framed by the window.

"There it is!" I cried.

"No, no, sir, it is nothing–nothing at all!" the butler broke in; "I assure you, sir ––"

"Move your light across the window, Watson!" cried the baronet. "See, the other moves also! Now, you rascal, do you deny that it is a signal? Come, speak up! Who is your **confederate**④ out yonder, and what is this conspiracy that is going on?"

The man's face became openly defiant.

"It is my business, and not yours. I will not tell."

"Then you leave my employment right away."

"Very good, sir. If I must I must."

"And you go in disgrace. By thunder, you may well be ashamed of yourself. Your family has lived with mine for over a hundred years under this roof, and here I find you deep in some dark plot against me."

"No, no, sir; no, not against you!" It was a woman's voice, and Mrs. Barrymore, paler and more horror-struck than her husband, was standing at the

了，手上的蜡烛不断地抖动，人的影子也随之上下跳动，"是窗户，先生，我晚上常来看看它们是否关好了。"

"是三楼上的窗户吗？"

"对，先生，所有窗户。"

"看看这儿，巴里摩尔，"亨利爵士说着，语气很严厉，"我们已经下定决心，一定要你把实话说出来。你晚说还不如早说，这样也省得麻烦。说吧，快说！不要说谎！你到那扇窗前干什么？"

他无可奈何地看着我们，双手扭在一起，神情完全像个陷入了极端疑惑和痛苦中的人。

"我没做害人的事，先生，刚才只是关窗而已。"

"你为什么要举着蜡烛靠近窗口？"

"亨利爵士，您就别问了——快别问了！我跟您说吧，爵士，这不是我自己的什么秘密，我不能泄露出去。如果这事只关系到我一个人，那我是绝对不会对您有任何隐瞒的。"

这时，我突然灵机一动，一把从管家颤抖的手里夺过蜡烛。

"他举着蜡烛一定是把它当信号用，"我说，"我们看看是否有回应。"我按照他的做法举着蜡烛，而且注视着漆黑一团的窗外。因为云朵挡住了月亮，我只能模模糊糊地看到一排黑色的树影和颜色略淡的漫漫荒原。随即，我高兴得大声欢呼，因为在窗户正对着的远方，忽然出现了一个黄色的大头针般大小的光点，其亮光穿透了漆黑的夜幕。

"就在那边！"我大声说着。

"不，不，先生，那儿没什么——什么都不是！"管家脱口说，"我向您保证，先生——"

"华生，把蜡烛在窗前四处移动一下，"从男爵大声说，"看，那边的亮光也在移动。好啊，你这无赖，还要嘴硬说不是信号吗？哼，快说！你那边的同伙是什么人？你们现在搞的是什么阴谋？"

管家脸上的表情简慢无礼起来了。

"这是我个人的私事，跟您无关，我是不会说的。"

"那么，你就立刻走人吧。"

"很好，先生，如果我非走不可，那我就一定会走。"

① extremity [ik'stremiti] n. 尽头；终极

② exultation [ˌegzʌl'teiʃən] n. 狂喜
③ transfix [træns'fiks] v. 刺穿

④ confederate [kən'fedərit] n. 同党，共犯

door. Her **bulky**[①] figure in a shawl and skirt might have been comic were it not for the intensity of feeling upon her face.

"We have to go, Eliza. This is the end of it. You can pack our things," said the butler.

"Oh, John, John, have I brought you to this? It is my doing, Sir Henry–all mine. He has done nothing except for my sake, and because I asked him."

"Speak out, then! What does it mean?"

"My unhappy brother is starving on the moor. We cannot let him **perish**[②] at our very gates. The light is a signal to him that food is ready for him, and his light out yonder is to show the spot to which to bring it."

"Then your brother is --"

"The escaped convict, sir–Selden, the criminal."

"That's the truth, sir," said Barrymore. "I said that it was not my secret and that I could not tell it to you. But now you have heard it, and you will see that if there was a plot it was not against you."

This, then, was the explanation of the stealthy expeditions at night and the light at the window. Sir Henry and I both stared at the woman in amazement. Was it possible that this **stolidly**[③] respectable person was of the same blood as one of the most notorious criminals in the country?

"Yes, sir, my name was Selden, and he is my younger brother. We **humoured**[④] him too much when he was a lad and gave him his own way in everything until he came to think that the world was made for his pleasure, and that he could do what he liked in it. Then as he grew older he met wicked companions, and the devil entered into him until he broke my mother's heart and dragged our name in the dirt. From crime to crime he sank lower and lower until it is only the mercy of God which has snatched him from the **scaffold**[⑤]; but to me, sir, he was always the little curly-headed boy that I had nursed and played with as an elder sister would. That was why he broke prison, sir. He knew that I was here and that we could not refuse to help him. When he dragged himself here one night, weary and starving, with the warders **hard**[⑥] at his heels, what could we do? We took him in and fed him and cared for him. Then you returned, sir, and my brother thought he would be safer on the moor than anywhere else until the **hue and cry**[⑦] was over, so he lay in hiding there. But every second night we made sure if he was still there by putting a light

① bulky ['bʌlki] a. 肥胖的；
粗壮的

"而且，你走得很没有面子。天哪，你会对自己感到羞耻的。你的家人和我的家人在这个屋檐下一起生活了一百多年，而现在我却发现，你居然处心积虑地玩弄阴谋来坑害我。"

"不，不，先生，不是这么回事，不是要坑害您啊！"有个女人的声音传过来了，巴里摩尔太太站在了门口，脸色比丈夫的更苍白，看上去也更加惶恐不安。要不是她脸上那种极度紧张的神态，她那庞大的身躯配上裙子和披肩一定会显得很好笑。

② perish ['periʃ] v. 死去

"我们必须离开，伊丽莎。事情总算结束了，你可以去收拾我们的东西了。"管家说。

"噢，约翰，约翰，我真的把你连累到这种地步了吗？亨利爵士，这是我的事情——完全是我的事情。他这样做完全是因为我的原因，是我请求他这样做的。"

"那么，快说出来吧，这到底是怎么回事？"

"我那不幸的弟弟正在荒原上饿肚子，我们总不能让他饿死在自家门口吧。这烛光就是一个信号，告诉他食物已经准备好了，而那远处的亮光则是告知我们送饭地点的。"

③ stolidly ['stɒlidli] ad. 不动感情地

"这么说，你弟弟就是……"

④ humour ['hjuːmə] v. 纵容

"就是那个越狱犯，先生——罪犯塞尔登。"

"是这么回事，先生，"巴里摩尔说，"我说过，这不是我个人的秘密，而且，我不能向您泄露。不过，您现在都听到了，您也会明白，如果说这是个阴谋，那也不是针对您的啊。"

那么，这样就解开了深夜潜行和窗前烛光的谜团了。我和亨利爵士都感到很惊讶，瞪大眼睛盯着那个女人。顽强而可敬的女人竟然和本区最声名狼藉的罪犯来自同一血脉，这可能吗？

⑤ scaffold ['skæfəld] n. 断头台

"是啊，先生，我姓塞尔登，而他就是我的弟弟。他小时候，我们对他过分纵容，任何事情上都让他任性妄为，结果，他认为世界就是为了使他快乐而存在的，他在这个世界上可以为所欲为。等到长大成人之后，他遇上了一些品行不端的同伴，自己便也变坏了，我母亲最终被弄得心力交瘁，家庭的名声也被玷污了。

⑥ hard [hɑːd] ad. 接近地，紧随地

⑦ hue and cry 追捕犯人时的叫喊声

他屡次犯罪，越陷越深，直到落得只有上帝的仁慈才

in the window, and if there was an answer my husband took out some bread and meat to him. Every day we hoped that he was gone, but as long as he was there we could not desert him. That is the whole truth, as I am an honest Christian woman, and you will see that if there is blame in the matter it does not lie with my husband but with me, for whose sake he has done all that he has."

The woman's words came with an intense earnestness which carried conviction with them.

"Is this true, Barrymore?"

"Yes, Sir Henry. Every word of it."

"Well, I cannot blame you for **standing by**[①] your own wife. Forget what I have said. Go to your room, you two, and we shall talk further about this matter in the morning."

When they were gone we looked out of the window again. Sir Henry had flung it open, and the cold night wind beat in upon our faces. Far away in the black distance there still glowed that one tiny point of yellow light.

"I wonder he dares," said Sir Henry.

"It may be so placed as to be only visible from here."

"Very likely. How far do you think it is?"

"Out by the Cleft Tor, I think."

"Not more than a mile or two off."

"Hardly that."

"Well, it cannot be far if Barrymore had to carry out the food to it. And he is waiting, this villain, beside that candle. By thunder, Watson, I am going out to take that man!"

The same thought had crossed my own mind. It was not as if the Barrymores had taken us into their confidence. Their secret had been forced from them. The man was a danger to the community, an **unmitigated**[②] **scoundrel**[③] for whom there was neither pity nor excuse. We were only doing our duty in taking this chance of putting him back where he could do no harm. With his brutal and violent nature, others would have to pay the price if we held our hands. Any night, for example, our neighbours the Stapletons might be attacked by him, and it may have been the thought of this which made Sir Henry so keen upon the adventure.

"I will come," said I.

能使他免于上断头台的地步。但是，对于我这个做姐姐的来说，先生，他毕竟是我曾经用心照料过的、一起嬉戏过的那个卷发的孩子。先生，这就是他从监狱里逃出来的原因。他知道我们住在这儿，而且知道我们无法拒绝帮助他。一天晚上，他拖着疲倦而饥饿的身子到了这里，与此同时，监狱看守们在他后面紧追不放，我们还能怎么做呢？我们把他领进屋，给他饭吃，照顾他。先生，后来您回来了。我弟弟认为，在风声过去之前，他到荒原上去比在其他任何地方都要安全，因此，他就跑到那里藏匿了起来。但是，每隔一晚，我们就在窗前放一个烛光，以此确定他还待在那里。如果我们的信号有回应，我丈夫就会拿些面包和肉给他送去。我们每天都希望他走掉了，但只要他还在那里，我们就不能对他置之不理。这就是全部的实情。我是个虔诚的基督徒，您会明白，如果这样做有什么罪过的话，那也不能惩罚我丈夫，而应该惩罚我，因为他所做的这一切都是为了我。"

女人的话说得很诚恳，说明她说的是实情。

"这是真的吗，巴里摩尔？"

"是啊，亨利爵士，句句属实。"

① stand by 支持（某人）

"那行，我不能责怪你这样支持自己的太太。忘了我刚才说过的话吧。回屋去吧，你们二位，明天上午我们再来深谈此事。"

夫妇二人离开之后，我们再次走到窗前向外张望。亨利爵士一把推开窗户，深夜冰冷的寒风向我们迎面吹来。在漆黑的远方，那个黄色的小亮点仍在发光。

"真奇怪，他胆敢这么做。"亨利爵士说。

"或许蜡烛放置的位置只有我们这里才看得见。"

"很有可能。您看离这儿有多远？"

"我看，就在裂开岩那边。"

② unmitigated [ˌʌnˈmitigeitid] a. 十足的
③ scoundrel [ˈskaundrəl] n. 流氓，恶棍，无赖

"不过一两英里的距离吧。"

"没有那么远吧。"

"是啊，既然巴里摩尔要去那儿送吃的，那肯定就不太远了。那个坏蛋，他正在蜡烛边等着呢。天哪，华生，我要去把他抓起来！"

我的脑海掠过了同样的想法。看起来，巴里摩尔

"Then get your revolver and put on your boots. The sooner we start the better, as the fellow may put out his light and be off."

In five minutes we were outside the door, starting upon our expedition. We hurried through the dark shrubbery, amid the dull moaning of the autumn wind and the rustle of the falling leaves. The night air was heavy with the smell of damp and decay. Now and again the moon peeped out for an instant, but clouds were driving over the face of the sky, and just as we came out on the moor a thin rain began to fall. The light still burned steadily in front.

"Are you armed?" I asked.

"I have a hunting-crop."

"We must **close in on**[1] him rapidly, for he is said to be a desperate fellow. We shall take him by surprise and have him at our mercy before he can resist."

"I say, Watson," said the baronet, "what would Holmes say to this? How about that hour of darkness in which the power of evil is exalted?"

As if in answer to his words there rose suddenly out of the vast gloom of the moor that strange cry which I had already heard upon the borders of the great Grimpen Mire. It came with the wind through the silence of the night, a long, deep **mutter**[2], then a rising howl, and then the sad moan in which it died away. Again and again it sounded, the whole air throbbing with it, **strident**[3], wild, and **menacing**[4]. The baronet caught my sleeve and his face glimmered white through the darkness.

"My God, what's that, Watson?"

"I don't know. It's a sound they have on the moor. I heard it once before."

It died away, and an absolute silence closed in upon us. We stood straining our ears, but nothing came.

"Watson," said the baronet, "it was the cry of a hound."

My blood ran cold in my veins, for there was a **break**[5] in his voice which told of the sudden horror which had seized him.

"What do they call this sound?" he asked.

"Who?"

"The folk on the countryside."

"Oh, they are ignorant people. Why should you mind what they call it?"

"Tell me, Watson. What do they say of it?"

夫妇对我们并不信任，他们的秘密是被迫说出来的。对于这个地区的人来说，此人是一个祸害，一个罪大恶极的惯犯。对这样的人既不能同情，也不能原谅。我们若趁此机会把他缉拿归案，让他不再危害别人，那也只不过是尽了我们应尽的责任。他那种人本性恶劣，性情残暴，如果我们甩手不管，那别人就要付出代价了。比如我们的邻居斯塔普尔顿兄妹，说不定哪天夜间就会遭到他的袭击。或许因为亨利爵士正好想到了这一点，他坚持非去冒这个险不可。

"我也要去。"我说。

"那好，那就带上手枪，穿好靴子吧。我们动身越快越好，因为那家伙随时都可能吹灭蜡烛逃跑。"

① close in on 围住；接近

五分钟之后，我们便到了门外，开始了我们的探险之旅。秋风低吟，落叶沙沙，我们匆匆地穿过幽黑的矮树丛。深夜的空气中弥漫着浓稠的潮湿和腐烂的气味。月亮不时地从云缝里探出头来偷看一两秒钟，云朵在天空中翻腾。我们刚刚一脚踏进荒原，天就开始下起丝丝细雨来。前方的烛光仍然一动不动地亮着。

"您带了武器吗？"我问。

"我带了根猎鞭。"

② mutter ['mʌtə] n. 持续的低沉声音
③ strident ['straidənt] a. 尖声的，刺耳的
④ menacing ['menəsiŋ] a. 威胁的；险恶的

"我们必须迅速把他围住，因为大家都说他是个亡命之徒。我们要出其不意，让他没有时间反抗，然后一把逮住他。"

"我说啊，华生，"从男爵说，"福尔摩斯对此会说什么呢？他会不会说：这是'邪恶势力甚嚣尘上的黑暗时刻'？"

突然间，从广阔而阴森的荒原上传来一阵怪叫，好像是在回答他的问话似的。那声音我以前在格林彭大泥潭附近听到过。声音随风飘过寂静的夜空，先是一声悠长而深沉的低鸣，继而是高亢的吼叫，随后又变成凄惨的呻吟消逝而去。声音一次又一次地响起，它尖锐、狂野、吓人，整个空气都为之战栗。从男爵一把抓住我的袖子，他的脸在黑暗的夜色中惨白得发亮。

⑤ break [breik] n. 中断，中止

"天哪，华生，那是什么声音啊？"

"不知道。是荒原上发出的，前些日子我听到过。"

怪声消失了，周围一片寂静。我们停下脚步，竖起

I hesitated but could not escape the question.

"They say it is the cry of the Hound of the Baskervilles."

He groaned and was silent for a few moments.

"A hound it was," he said at last, "but it seemed to come from miles away, over yonder, I think."

"It was hard to say whence it came."

"It rose and fell with the wind. Isn't that the direction of the great Grimpen Mire?"

"Yes, it is."

"Well, it was up there. Come now, Watson, didn't you think yourself that it was the cry of a hound? I am not a child. You need not fear to speak the truth."

"Stapleton was with me when I heard it last. He said that it might be the calling of a strange bird."

"No, no, it was a hound. My God, can there be some truth in all these stories? Is it possible that I am really in danger from so dark a cause? You don't believe it, do you, Watson?"

"No, no."

"And yet it was one thing to laugh about it in London, and it is another to stand out here in the darkness of the moor and to hear such a cry as that. And my uncle! There was the footprint of the hound beside him as he lay. It all fits together. I don't think that I am a coward, Watson, but that sound seemed to freeze my very blood. Feel my hand!"

It was as cold as a block of marble.

"You'll be all right to-morrow."

"I don't think I'll get that cry out of my head. What do you advise that we do now?"

"Shall we turn back?"

"No, by thunder; we have come out to get our man, and we will do it. We after the convict, and a hell-hound, as likely as not, after us. Come on! We'll see it through if all the fiends of the pit were **loose**① upon the moor."

We stumbled slowly along in the darkness, with the black **loom**② of the craggy hills around us, and the yellow speck of light burning steadily in front. There is nothing so deceptive as the distance of a light upon a **pitch-dark**③ night, and

耳朵倾听，但什么声音都没有听到。

"华生，"从男爵说，"那是猎犬的叫声。"

我浑身的血液都冰凉了，因为他说话时声音发抖，说明他突然感到恐惧起来。

"他们把这称作什么声音？"他问。

"谁？"

"乡下的民众。"

"噢，他们都没什么知识。您何必关心他们把那个声音叫什么呢？"

"告诉我，华生，他们是怎么说的？"

我犹豫了一下，但还是无法回避这个问题。

"他们说，这就是巴斯克维尔猎犬的叫声。"

他嘀咕了一声，然后沉默了片刻。

"是条猎犬，"他最后开口说，"但我觉得，那声音是从好几英里以外的地方传来的，好像是来自那边。"

"很难说清到底是从哪边传过来的。"

"声音随风飘荡，忽高忽低。那边不就是格林彭大泥潭的方向吗？"

"对，是这样的。"

"对啦，就在那边。是啊，华生，您自己难道不认为那是猎犬的叫声吗？我不是个孩子，您用不着担心，就实话实说吧。"

"我上次听到那声音时，斯塔普尔顿正好和我在一块儿。他说这有可能是一种怪鸟的叫声。"

"不，不对，是猎犬的叫声。天哪，那些传说中难道真可能有真实的成分吗？有没有可能，我确实处在邪恶势力的包围当中呢？您不相信这一点，对吧，华生？"

"说得对，我不相信。"

"不过，这样的事情若是在伦敦会被当成笑料的，但在这漆黑的荒原上站立着，听到如此这般的叫声，那可又是另外一件事情了。还有我伯父！他躺着的地点旁边出现了猎犬的爪印。这都凑到一块儿来了。我认为，自己并不是个懦夫，华生，但是，那声音似乎令我浑身的血液都凝固了。摸摸我的手看看！"

他的手像一块大理石一样冰凉。

"您明天就会好起来的。"

① loose [lu:s] *a.* 自由的；不加限制的

② loom [lu:m] *n.* 隐约出现的巨大的影子

③ pitch-dark ['pitʃ'dɑ:k] *a.* 极黑的，漆黑的

sometimes the glimmer seemed to be far away upon the horizon and sometimes it might have been within a few yards of us. But at last we could see whence it came, and then we knew that we were indeed very close. A **guttering**[①] candle was stuck in a crevice of the rocks which flanked it on each side so as to keep the wind from it and also to prevent it from being visible, save in the direction of Baskerville Hall. A boulder of granite concealed our approach, and crouching behind it we gazed over it at the signal light. It was strange to see this single candle burning there in the middle of the moor, with no sign of life near it–just the one straight yellow flame and the gleam of the rock on each side of it.

"What shall we do now?" whispered Sir Henry.

"Wait here. He must be near his light. Let us see if we can get a glimpse of him."

The words were hardly out of my mouth when we both saw him. Over the rocks, in the crevice of which the candle burned, there was thrust out an evil yellow face, a terrible animal face, all **seamed**[②] and **scored**[③] with vile passions. Foul with mire, with a **bristling**[④] beard, and hung with **matted**[⑤] hair, it might well have belonged to one of those old savages who dwelt in the burrows on the hillsides. The light beneath him was reflected in his small, cunning eyes which peered fiercely to right and left through the darkness like a crafty and savage animal who has heard the steps of the hunters.

Something had evidently aroused his suspicions. It may have been that Barrymore had some private signal which we had neglected to give, or the fellow may have had some other reason for thinking that all was not well, but I could read his fears upon his wicked face. Any instant he might dash out the light and vanish in the darkness. I sprang forward therefore, and Sir Henry did the same. At the same moment the convict screamed out a curse at us and hurled a rock which **splintered**[⑥] up against the boulder which had sheltered us. I caught one glimpse of his short, squat, strongly built figure as he sprang to his feet and turned to run. At the same moment by a lucky chance the moon broke through the clouds. We rushed over the brow of the hill, and there was our man running with great speed down the other side, **springing**[⑦] over the stones in his way with the activity of a mountain goat. A lucky long shot of my revolver might have crippled him, but I had brought it only to defend myself if attacked and not to shoot an unarmed man

"我恐怕永远都忘不掉那个叫声了。您看我现在该怎么办啊？"

"我们回去吧？"

① guttering ['gʌtəriŋ] a.（烛光等）即将熄灭的

"不，不行。我们出来是要抓住那个人的，而且一定要抓住才是。我们在抓罪犯，而魔鬼猎犬，可能存在，也可能不存在，在后面追赶着我们呢。来吧！哪怕所有的妖魔鬼怪全部都释放到荒原上来了，我们也要坚持到底。"

黑暗中，我们跌跌撞撞地缓慢前行，周围全是一座座参差不齐的山岗的轮廓。正前方，黄色的光点一直亮着。漆黑一团的夜晚，灯光的距离极具欺骗性。闪烁的亮光时而仿佛远在天边，时而又好似近在咫尺。不过，我们终于看清了亮光所在的位置，我们知道自己离它已经很近了。那支蜡烛被嵌在石头缝里，三面都被石头挡住了，这样不但挡住了风，还可以避免亮光被从巴斯克维尔庄园以外的其他方向看见。一块花岗岩巨石隐蔽住了我们的行踪。我们猫着腰躲在巨石的后面，从石头上探头看着那盏信号灯。令我们感到莫名其妙的是，荒原的中间只有一支孤零零的蜡烛在亮着，旁边连一个人影都没有——只有一股笔直的黄色火苗，还有周围岩石上的亮光。

② seam [si:m] v. 使缝合
③ score [skɔ:] v. 在…上刻痕
④ bristling ['brisliŋ] a. 毛发直立的
⑤ matted ['mætid] a. 缠结的

"我们现在怎么办？"亨利爵士低声说。

"在这儿等着吧，他一定在离灯光的不远处，我们到处找找，看能否见到他。"我的话刚刚说出口，霎时间，我们都看见他了。燃放蜡烛的石缝上面的岩石后面探出了一张吓人的黄色面孔——一张狰狞的面孔，满是横肉，肮脏邋遢，长着粗硬的胡须，头发乱蓬蓬的，和古时候住在山边洞穴里的野人倒很相像。他那细小而狡猾的眼睛里映出了下方的烛光，在黑暗中敏锐地左顾右盼，就像一只听到了猎人脚步声的狡黠的猛兽。

⑥ splinter ['splintə] v. 裂成碎片

很显然，有什么东西引起了他的怀疑。他和巴里摩尔之间有可能约定了某种秘密暗号，而我们之前却未能发出。或者说，那家伙根据其他迹象感觉到了事情不妙，因为我从他那邪恶的脸上看到了恐惧的神色。考虑到他随时都可能蹿离亮处，消失在漆黑的夜色之中，我因此一跃身子向前，亨利爵士也同样行动了。就在同一时刻，罪犯尖声咒骂了我们一句，搬起一块石头砸过

⑦ spring [spriŋ] v. 跳跃

who was running away.

We were both swift runners and in fairly good training, but we soon found that we had no chance of overtaking him. We saw him for a long time in the moonlight until he was only a small speck moving swiftly among the boulders upon the side of a distant hill. We ran and ran until we were completely blown, but the space between us grew ever wider. Finally we stopped and sat panting on two rocks, while we watched him disappearing in the distance.

And it was at this moment that there occurred a most strange and unexpected thing. We had risen from our rocks and were turning to go home, having abandoned the hopeless chase. The moon was low upon the right, and the jagged **pinnacle**[①] of a granite tor stood up against the lower curve of its silver disc. There, outlined as black as an **ebony**[②] statue on that shining background, I saw the figure of a man upon the tor. Do not think that it was a delusion, Holmes. I assure you that I have never in my life seen anything more clearly. As far as I could judge, the figure was that of a tall, thin man. He stood with his legs a little separated, his arms folded, his head bowed, as if he were brooding over that enormous wilderness of **peat**[③] and granite which lay before him. He might have been the very spirit of that terrible place. It was not the convict. This man was far from the place where the latter had disappeared. Besides, he was a much taller man. With a cry of surprise I pointed him out to the baronet, but in the instant during which I had turned to grasp his arm the man was gone. There was the sharp pinnacle of granite still cutting the lower edge of the moon, but its peak bore no trace of that silent and motionless figure.

I wished to go in that direction and to search the tor, but it was some distance away. The baronet's nerves were still quivering from that cry, which recalled the dark story of his family, and he was not in the mood for fresh adventures. He had not seen this lonely man upon the tor and could not feel the thrill which his strange presence and his commanding attitude had given to me. "A warder, no doubt," said he. "The moor has been thick with them since this fellow escaped." Well, perhaps his explanation may be the right one, but I should like to have some further proof of it. To-day we mean to communicate to the Princetown people where they should look for their missing man, but it is **hard lines**[④] that we have not actually had the triumph of bringing him back as our own prisoner. Such are the adventures of last

来。石头碰到遮挡我们的大石上，被摔得粉碎。当他霍地站立起来转身逃跑时，正巧月亮从云层后钻了出来，我一眼看到了他那矮墩而强壮的身躯。我们冲过小山头，那家伙则从山的另一侧向下跑去。一路上，他在乱石上跳来跳去，简直和山羊的动作如出一辙。如果运气好的话，我用那把手枪远射就可以把他打残。但是，我带上它的唯一目的，是在受人攻击时可以自卫，而不是要枪杀一个手无寸铁的逃犯。

我们两个人都是快跑高手，而且都经历过良好的训练。但我们很快发现，不可能追赶得上他。我们凭借着月光长时间看着他，一直到他变成了一个小黑点，在远处小山一侧的乱石丛中快速移动。我们跑啊跑，直到完全筋疲力尽，但我们之间的距离越来越远了。最后，我们停了下来，一边坐在两块大石头上喘着粗气，一边眼睁睁地看着他消失在远方。

而就在那个当儿，发生了一件极为不可思议而又在预料之外的事情。我们当时已经失望了，不再追赶，从石头上站起身，打算转身回家了。月亮低垂在右侧的天空，银盘的下方衬托着一座花岗石岩岗嶙峋的尖顶。明亮的背景下，我看到了一个男人的身影，他站在岩岗上，犹如一座漆黑的铜像。你可不要认为那是一个幻影啊，福尔摩斯。我可以保证，自己一生中可从未看东西看得如此真真切切过。根据我的判断，那是个高高瘦瘦的男人。他在那里站着，两腿稍稍分开，双臂交叉，头低垂着，正对着眼前广阔的而又满是泥炭和岩石的荒野，像是在思索着问题。他说不定就是那恐怖地带的精灵呢。他不是那个罪犯，距离那个罪犯逃遁的地方还很远。再说了，他的身材也高了很多。我不由得惊叫了一声，并要指给从男爵看，但就在我转身抓他手臂的一瞬间，那人不见了。此时花岗岩的尖顶仍然遮盖着月亮的下半部，但其顶上却没有了任何那静立不动之人的踪迹。

我本想朝着那个方向走，对那处岩岗搜寻一番，但距离太远了。那个叫声让从男爵想起了涉及到他家族的那个恐怖的故事，自听到之后，他一直感到很紧张，浑身颤抖，没有了再进行探险的心情。他没有看到那个独自站在岩顶上的人，无法体会他的奇异现身和威风凛凛

① pinnacle ['pinəkl] *n.* 山顶；山峰
② ebony ['ebəni] *a.* （漆）黑色的

③ peat [pi:t] 泥炭

④ hard lines 坏运气；厄运

night, and you must acknowledge, my dear Holmes, that I have done you very well in the matter of a report. Much of what I tell you is no doubt quite irrelevant, but still I feel that it is best that I should let you have all the facts and leave you to select for yourself those which will be of most service to you in helping you to your conclusilons. We are certainly making some progress. So far as the Barrymores go we have found the motive of their actions, and that has cleared up the situation very much. But the moor with its mysteries and its strange inhabitants remains as **inscrutable**[①] as ever. Perhaps in my next I may be able to throw some light upon this also. Best of all would it be if you could come down to us. In any case you will hear from me again in the course of the next few days.

的神气所带给我的不寒而栗的感觉。"是个狱警，毫无疑问，"他说，"那家伙越狱后，荒原上到处都是狱警。"是啊，他的解释或许是正确的，但我还想找到进一步的证据。我们打算今天告诉王子镇的居民，让他们知道逃犯的下落和去向。不过，遗憾的是，我们并没有获得真正的胜利，即把他缉拿归案。以上就是我们昨晚探险的全过程。你得承认，亲爱的福尔摩斯，就一封信中涉及到的情况而言，我对你还是有一个挺不错的交代的。毋庸置疑，我向你叙述的这些情况大都与案件没有多大关系。不过，我仍然还是觉得，最好还是要让你掌握全部事实，由你自己从中取舍，判断出有用的信息。我们现在确实取得了一些进展。对巴里摩尔一家人，我们已经发现了他们行动的动机，整个事态也得到了澄清。但同时，神秘的荒原，还有上面住着的那些奇特的居民依然是一如既往，神秘莫测。下次的报告中，我或许能对此澄清一二。你最好能够亲自来我们这儿一趟。不管怎样说，你很快就会收到我的来信的。

① inscrutable [in'skru:təbl]
　a. 神秘的；谜一般的

Chapter 10　Extract from the Diary of Dr. Watson

So far I have been able to quote from the reports which I have **forwarded**[①] during these early days to Sherlock Holmes. Now, however, I have arrived at a point in my narrative where I am compelled to abandon this method and to trust once more to my recollections, aided by the diary which I kept at the time. A few extracts from the latter will carry me on to those scenes which are **indelibly**[②] fixed in every detail upon my memory. I proceed, then, from the morning which followed our **abortive**[③] chase of the convict and our other strange experiences upon the moor.

October 16th. A dull and foggy day with a drizzle of rain. The house is **banked**[④] in with rolling clouds, which rise now and then to show the dreary curves of the moor, with thin, silver **veins**[⑤] upon the sides of the hills, and the distant boulders gleaming where the light strikes upon their wet faces. It is melancholy outside and in. The baronet is in a black reaction after the excitements of the night. I am conscious myself of a weight at my heart and a feeling of impending danger—ever present danger, which is the more terrible because I am unable to define it.

And have I not cause for such a feeling? Consider the long sequence of incidents which have all pointed to some sinister influence which is at work around us. There is the death of the last occupant of the Hall, fulfilling so exactly the conditions of the family legend, and there are the repeated reports from peasants of the appearance of a strange creature upon the moor. Twice I have with my own ears heard the sound which resembled the distant baying of a hound. It is

第十章 华生医生的日记摘抄

① forward ['fɔ:wəd] v. 转交
（信件等）

② indelible [in'deləbl] a. 去
不掉的
③ abortive [ə'bɔ:tiv] a. 失败
的

④ bank [bæŋk] v. （雪）堆
积起来
⑤ vein [vein] n. 纹理

迄今为止，我叙述的这些情况，选自自己到庄园后的最初日子里写给夏洛克·福尔摩斯的报告中的内容。然而，现如今，情况叙述至此，我就不得不放弃那种方法，再次依赖自己的记忆，借助当时保存下来的日记。通过摘录一些日记片断，我便可以回忆起当时的一些情景，因为那些东西深深地铭刻在了我的记忆当中。我就从那天早上开始吧，也就是我们去追捕逃犯却毫无所获，同时还有在荒原上其他种种奇遇之后的那个早晨。

10月16日，阴天多雾，伴有蒙蒙细雨。宅邸云遮雾罩，云雾涌动，时而升腾，显露出阴郁起伏的荒原。山丘斜坡面上银色的裂纹，还有远处那些潮湿的表面闪闪发亮的巨石。室内室外弥漫着忧郁的氛围。昨夜的惊恐之后，从男爵情绪不佳。我内心也感到极为沉重，觉得有一种危险即将降临——这种危险自始至终都存在着，但我对此却无法形容，便觉得更加不寒而栗了。

难道说我的这种感觉没有来由吗？想一想一连串接踵而至的怪事情，全都指向一点：我们身边有一种极为凶狠的罪恶势力在作祟。庄园的上一任主人猝亡，完全应验了这个家族的种种传说，农夫们反复声称有怪兽出现在荒原。我本人就曾两次亲耳听见那种极像从远处传来的猎犬的狂吠声。说这真正是超乎自然的现象，令人难以置信，根本不可能。一只妖魔猎犬竟会留下实实在在的爪印，空中会回荡着吼叫声，那是无法想象的事情。斯塔普尔顿或许会相信这套迷信，莫蒂默也是如

incredible, impossible, that it should really be outside the ordinary laws of nature. A spectral hound which leaves material footmarks and fills the air with its howling is surely not to be thought of. Stapleton may fall in with such a superstition, and Mortimer also; but if I have one quality upon earth it is common sense, and nothing will persuade me to believe in such a thing. To do so would be to descend to the level of these poor peasants, who are not content with a mere fiend dog but must needs describe him with hell-fire shooting from his mouth and eyes. Holmes would not listen to such fancies, and I am his agent. But facts are facts, and I have twice heard this crying upon the moor. Suppose that there were really some huge hound loose upon it; that would go far to explain everything. But where could such a hound lie concealed, where did it get its food, where did it come from, how was it that no one saw it by day? It must be confessed that the natural explanation offers almost as many difficulties as the other. And always, apart from the hound, there is the fact of the human agency in London, the man in the cab, and the letter which warned Sir Henry against the moor. This at least was real, but it might have been the work of a protecting friend as easily as of an enemy. Where is that friend or enemy now? Has he remained in London, or has he followed us down here? Could he—could he be the stranger whom I saw upon the tor?

It is true that I have had only the one glance at him, and yet there are some things to which I am ready to swear. He is no one whom I have seen down here, and I have now met all the neighbours. The figure was far taller than that of Stapleton, far thinner than that of Frankland. Barrymore it might possibly have been, but we had left him behind us, and I am certain that he could not have followed us. A stranger then is still dogging us, just as a stranger dogged us in London. We have never shaken him off. If I could lay my hands upon that man, then at last we might find ourselves at the end of all our difficulties. To this one purpose I must now devote all my energies.

My first **impulse**[1] was to tell Sir Henry all my plans. My second and wisest one is to play my own game and speak as little as possible to anyone. He is silent and **distrait**[2]. His nerves have been strangely shaken by that sound upon the moor. I will say nothing to add to his anxieties, but I will take my own steps to attain my own end.

此。但是，如果要说我活在世上有什么优点的话，那就是常识，因此，任凭是谁都无法劝说我相信那样的鬼话。如果真的相信，那就等于把自己降低到了那些可怜的农夫的水平。他们并不满足于把那条猎犬描述成单纯的妖魔鬼怪犬，还要添油加醋地把它描绘成嘴巴和眼睛都能够喷出地狱之火。对这些异想天开的事情，福尔摩斯是绝对不会听信的，而我就是他的代理人。不过，事实终归是事实，我在荒原上已经两次听到那个声音了。如果确实有一条大猎犬跑到了荒原上，那一切就都能解释清楚了。但是，这样的猎犬能藏身何处呢？从何处弄到食物？又是从何处跑来的？怎么就没有人光天化日之下看到呢？必须承认，这个合乎自然的解释和那个超乎自然的解释一样，都难以说得通。除了猎犬，还有伦敦马车里的那个男人，还有那封提醒亨利爵士不要去荒原的信件，这都表明有人插手其中。最起码那封信是真实的，不过，这其中存在着两种可能性：有可能是朋友保护他的行为，也完全可能是坏人的伎俩。朋友也好，恶人也罢，他们现在都在哪儿呢？是留在伦敦，还是跟踪我们到了这里？会不会——会不会他就是我在突岩上看见的那个陌生人？

确实，我同他只是打了照面，但是，有些情况还是绝对有把握的。那个人绝对不是本地人，我见过了这儿的所有邻居，但从未看见过他。此人身材比斯塔普尔顿要高出很多，比弗兰克兰要瘦削很多，看上去倒有点像巴里摩尔的。不过，我们之前把巴里摩尔留在了家里，我敢肯定，他一定没有跟踪我们。这么看来，那就一直有个陌生人在跟踪着我们，就像我们在伦敦时遇到的情形一样。我们无法把他甩掉。如果我能亲手抓住那个人，那我们的问题最终就迎刃而解了。而要达到这一目的，我现在必须把全部的精力都投入上去。

我最初的想法是把自己的计划一五一十告诉亨利爵士。但后来想一想，最明智的做法是自己干，对其他人缄口不言。他没吭一声，一脸茫然。荒原上的叫声令他的神经受到了莫名其妙的震撼。我不会说任何让他更紧张的话，但同时，我会按照自己的安排一步步地达到自己既定的目标。

① impulse ['impʌls] n. 冲动

② distrait [di:s'trei] a. 心不在焉的

Chapter 10   Extract from the Diary of Dr. Watson

We had a small **scene**[①] this morning after breakfast. Barrymore asked leave to speak with Sir Henry, and they were **closeted**[②] in his study some little time. Sitting in the billiard-room I more than once heard the sound of voices raised, and I had a pretty good idea what the point was which was under discussion. After a time the baronet opened his door and called for me.

"Barrymore considers that he has a **grievance**[③]," he said. "He thinks that it was unfair on our part to hunt his brother-in-law down when he, of his own free will, had told us the secret."

The butler was standing very pale but very **collected**[④] before us.

"I may have spoken too warmly, sir," said he, "and if I have, I am sure that I beg your pardon. At the same time, I was very much surprised when I heard you two gentlemen come back this morning and learned that you had been chasing Selden. The poor fellow has enough to fight against without my putting more upon his track."

"If you had told us of your own free will it would have been a different thing," said the baronet, "you only told us, or rather your wife only told us, when it was forced from you and you could not help yourself."

"I didn't think you would have taken advantage of it, Sir Henry–indeed I didn't."

"The man is a public danger. There are lonely houses scattered over the moor, and he is a fellow who would stick at nothing. You only want to get a glimpse of his face to see that. Look at Mr. Stapleton's house, for example, with no one but himself to defend it. There's no safety for anyone untill he is under lock and key."

"He'll break into no house, sir. I give you my solemn word upon that. But he will never trouble anyone in this country again. I assure you, Sir Henry, that in a very few days the necessary arrangements will have been made and he will be on his way to South America. For God's sake, sir, I beg of you not to let the police know that he is still on the moor. They have given up the chase there, and he can lie quiet until the ship is ready for him. You can't **tell on**[⑤] him without getting my wife and me into trouble. I beg you, sir, to say nothing to the police."

"What do you say, Watson?"

I shrugged my shoulders. "If he were safely out of the country it would

① scene [si:n] *n.* 事件
② closet ['klɔzit] *v.* 关在私室里与人密谈

③ grievance ['gri:vəns] *n.* 不满的理由

④ collected [kə'lektid] *a.* 镇定的，泰然自若的

早餐过后，出现了一个小插曲。巴里摩尔离开时提出要跟亨利爵士谈一谈，他们便去了书房，关起门来谈了好一阵子。我坐在弹子房里，好几次听到他们的嗓门高了起来。我很清楚，他们在谈的是什么问题。过了一会儿，从男爵打开门叫我进去。

"巴里摩尔对我们表示不满，"从男爵说，"他认为，是他自觉自愿把那个秘密告诉给我们的，而我们却去追捕他的内弟，这样做显得不厚道。"

管家站在我们跟前，脸色苍白，但神情显得很镇定。

"我的话或许说得过头了些，先生，"他说，"如果真是这样，那请您一定多包涵。但是，今天早上我听见你们二位回家，得知你们昨晚一直在追捕塞尔登，我感到非常意外。那个可怜的家伙，即便我不给他添什么麻烦，他要受的罪也已经够多的了。"

"如果真是如你所说，你是自愿交代的，事情或许就不会是这样了，"从男爵说，"但事实上，你，准确地说你太太，是在我们强迫的情况下不得已才说的。"

"但亨利爵士啊，我没想到您竟会趁此机会去缉拿他——说真格的，我一点儿也没有想到啊。"

"那家伙对于公众是个祸害。荒原上零零散散地住着一些孤立无援的人家，而他却是个亡命之徒。只要一看他那张脸，你就能明白这点。比如斯塔普尔顿家，看家护院的就只有他一个人而已。因此，不把他缉拿归案，没有什么安全可言。"

"他不会私闯民宅的，爵士，这一点我可以郑重地向您保证。反正他不会再次骚扰这儿的任何人了。我向您保证，亨利爵士。几天之后就会安排好一切的，让他出发到南美洲去。看在上帝的份儿上，爵士，我求求您，请不要让狱警知道他还藏匿在荒原上。他们本来都已经放弃了，不去那儿追捕他了，如此一来，他便可以不声不响地藏匿起来，一直等待到上船。如果您现在告发他，就必定会让我和我妻子陷入麻烦。我求求您，爵士，千万不要把这事告诉狱警啊。"

⑤ tell on 告发

"您怎么看，华生？"

我耸了耸肩膀。"如果他安全地离开这个国家，那倒能给纳税人减去一笔负担。"

relieve the tax-payer of a burden."

"But how about the chance of his **holding someone up**① before he goes?"

"He would not do anything so mad, sir. We have provided him with all that he can want. To commit a crime would be to show where he was hiding."

"That is true," said Sir Henry. "Well, Barrymore --"

"God bless you, sir, and thank you from my heart! It would have killed my poor wife had he been taken again."

"I guess we are aiding and **abetting**② a **felony**③, Watson? But, after what we have heard, I don't feel as if I could give the man up, so there is an end of it. All right, Barrymore, you can go."

With a few broken words of gratitude the man turned, but he hesitated and then came back.

"You've been so kind to us, sir, that I should like to do the best I can for you in return. I know something, Sir Henry, and perhaps I should have said it before, but it was long after the inquest that I found it out. I've never breathed a word about it yet to mortal man. It's about poor Sir Charles's death."

The baronet and I were both upon our feet. "Do you know how he died?"

"No, sir, I don't know that."

"What then?"

"I know why he was at the gate at that hour. It was to meet a woman."

"To meet a woman! He?"

"Yes, sir."

"And the woman's name?"

"I can't give you the name, sir, but I can give you the initials. Her initials were L. L."

"How do you know this, Barrymore?"

"Well, Sir Henry, your uncle had a letter that morning. He had usually a great many letters, for he was a public man and well known for his kind heart, so that everyone who was in trouble was glad to turn to him. But that morning, as it chanced, there was only this one letter, so I took the more notice of it. It was from Coombe Tracey, and it was addressed in a woman's hand."

"Well?"

① hold sb up 拦劫，抢劫

"但是，万一他在临走之前遇上谁挟持一下怎么办呢？"

"他不可能会有如此疯狂的行为的，先生，我们给他备齐了他所需要的全部物品。他若是犯案，那会泄露他藏匿的地点的。"

"这倒是事实，"亨利爵士说，"那行啊，巴里摩尔——"

"愿上帝保佑您，爵士，我由衷地感激您！如果他再度被逮住了，那会要了我那可怜的太太的命的。"

② abet [ə'bet] v. 怂恿（犯罪）
③ felony ['feləni] n. 重罪

"我怎么觉得我们这是在纵容一桩重罪呢，华生？但是，听了他刚才的话，我又觉得自己不能再去检举那个人了，这件事就到此结束吧！行啊，巴里摩尔，你可以走了。"

对方断断续续地说着感激的话，一边转过身，但迟疑了片刻后，又转回身来。

"您对我们真是太好了，先生，我愿尽我最大的努力来报答您。亨利爵士；我知道一件事，也许本来早该说出来的，但事情也是我在验尸过了很久后才发现的。我还没跟任何人透露过一点口风。事情与查尔斯爵士的猝死有关。"

我和从男爵同时站起身。"你知道他是怎么死的？"

"不，先生，这个我可不知道。"

"那你知道什么呢？"

"我知道他为何在那个时刻站在栅门边，那是要去同一个女人会面。"

"去和女人会面！他吗？"

"没错，先生。"

"那个女人叫什么名字？"

"我无法告诉您她的姓名，先生，不过，我可以把她姓名的首字母告诉您，是L.L.。"

"你是怎么知道这个情况的，巴里摩尔？"

"是啊，亨利爵士，您伯父当天早晨收到了一封信。他平时信件很多，因为他是个知名人士，而且以心地善良著称，所以，但凡有难处的人都会乐意向他求助。但是，事有凑巧，他那天早晨就只收到了一封信，因此，我就比平时多看了一眼。信是从库姆特雷西寄过来的，信封上的字迹出自一位女士之手。"

"呃？"

"Well, sir, I thought no more of the matter, and never would have done had it not been for my wife. Only a few weeks ago she was cleaning out Sir Charles's study–it had never been touched since his death-and she found the ashes of a burned letter in the back of the **grate**①. The greater part of it was **charred**② to pieces, but one little slip, the end of a page, hung together, and the writing could still be read, though it was gray on a black ground. It seemed to us to be a postscript at the end of the letter, and it said: 'Please, please, as you are a gentleman, burn this letter, and be at the gate by ten o'clock.' Beneath it were signed the initials L. L."

"Have you got that slip?"

"No, sir, it crumbled all to bits after we moved it."

"Had Sir Charles received any other letters in the same writing?"

"Well, sir, I took no particular notice of his letters. I should not have noticed this one, only it happened to come alone."

"And you have no idea who L. L. is?"

"No, sir. No more than you have. But I expect if we could lay our hands upon that lady we should know more about Sir Charles's death."

"I cannot understand, Barrymore, how you came to conceal this important information."

"Well, sir, it was immediately after that our own trouble came to us. And then again, sir, we were both of us very fond of Sir Charles, as we well might be considering all that he has done for us. To **rake this up**③ couldn't help our poor master, and it's well to go carefully when there's a lady in the case. Even the best of us --"

"You thought it might injure his reputation?"

"Well, sir, I thought no good could come of it. But now you have been kind to us, and I feel as if it would be treating you unfairly not to tell you all that I know about the matter."

"Very good, Barrymore; you can go." When the butler had left us Sir Henry turned to me. "Well, Watson, what do you think of this new light?"

"It seems to leave the darkness rather blacker than before."

"So I think. But if we can only trace L. L. it should clear up the whole business. We have gained that much. We know that there is someone who has

"是啊，先生，我当时没有多想此事。如果不是我太太的关系，我也不可能再想起它来。就在几个礼拜之前，她去收拾查尔斯爵士的书房——那个房间自他去世后，还一直没人动过，看到壁炉格子后面有烧过的信纸灰烬。信纸的大部分已经烧成了灰烬，但下端的一小块地方还保留完整，不过也已烧焦了，但上面的字迹还能够辨认得出来。我们觉得那是信件结尾处的附笔，内容是，'您是位正人君子，请您，请您一定要把信烧掉，并在十点时到栅门旁等候。'下面就是落款姓氏的首字母L.L.。"

"那张纸条还在你手上吗？"

"不在，先生，我们的手碰一下，它就变成碎屑了。"

"查尔斯爵士还收到过同样笔迹的来信吗？"

"呃，先生，我没有特别注意他的信件。那封信是因为它刚好是单独寄过来的，我这才留意了一下。"

"你知道那个署名L.L.的人是谁吗？"

"不知道，爵士。我知道的并不比您多。不过，我觉得，如果我们能找到那位女士的话，那就可以多了解一些查尔斯爵士去世时的情况。"

"我不理解，巴里摩尔，你怎么会把这么重要的信息隐瞒下来啊。"

"是啊，先生，我刚知道这个情况，自己就遇上麻烦了。还有就是因为，我们夫妻二人都非常喜欢查尔斯爵士，一直念着爵士对我们的好。即便提起那件事情，对于我们故去的主人也是无济于事的，况且这其中还牵扯到一位女士，最好是谨慎行事。即便我们中间最好的人——"

"你觉得，这样可能会有损于他的声誉吗？"

"是啊，先生，我想这事说出来也没有任何益处。但是，现在，您对我们这么好，我觉得如果不把自己知道的所有情况都告诉您，那就有愧于您了。"

"很好，巴里摩尔，你可以走了。"管家离开后，亨利爵士转身对着我。"对了，华生，您对这个新出现的情况怎么看？"

"事情本来就扑朔迷离，现在看起来更甚了。"

"我也是这么看来着，但是，只要我们能够查找到L.L.那位女士，那整件事情就水落石出了。我们就了解了这么多。如果能够找到她，我们就能够知道，是谁掌

the facts if we can only find her. What do you think we should do?"

"Let Holmes know all about it at once. It will give him the clue for which he has been seeking. I am much mistaken if it does not bring him down."

I went at once to my room and drew up my report of the morning's conversation for Holmes. It was evident to me that he had been very busy of late, for the notes which I had from Baker Street were few and short, with no comments upon the information which I had supplied and hardly any reference to my mission. No doubt his blackmailing case is absorbing all his **faculties**①. And yet this new factor must surely arrest his attention and renew his interest. I wish that he were here.

October 17th. All day to-day the rain poured down, rustling on the ivy and dripping from the eaves. I thought of the convict out upon the bleak, cold, shelterless moor. Poor devil! Whatever his crimes, he has suffered something to **atone**② for them. And then I thought of that other one–the face in the cab, the figure against the moon. Was he also out in that **deluge**③–the unseen watcher, the man of darkness? In the evening I put on my waterproof and I walked far upon the **sodden**④ moor, full of dark imaginings, the rain beating upon my face and the wind whistling about my ears. God help those who wander into the great mire now, for even the firm **uplands**⑤ are becoming a **morass**⑥. I found the black tor upon which I had seen the solitary watcher, and from its craggy summit I looked out myself across the melancholy downs. Rain **squalls**⑦ drifted across their russet face, and the heavy, slate-coloured clouds hung low over the landscape, trailing in gray **wreaths**⑧ down the sides of the fantastic hills. In the distant hollow on the left, half hidden by the mist, the two thin towers of Baskerville Hall rose above the trees. They were the only signs of human life which I could see, save only those prehistoric huts which lay thickly upon the slopes of the hills. Nowhere was there any trace of that lonely man whom I had seen on the same spot two nights before.

As I walked back I was overtaken by Dr. Mortimer driving in his dog-cart over a rough moorland track which led from the outlying farmhouse of Foulmire. He has been very **attentive**⑨ to us, and hardly a day has passed that he has not called at the Hall to see how we were getting on. He insisted upon

握着真相。您认为我们该怎么办呢？"

"得立刻让福尔摩斯知道全部情况才是啊，这就能给他提供一条他始终在寻找的线索。如果这还不能把他引到这儿来，那我的判断可就大错特错了。"

我立刻返回到了自己的房间，起草报告，把早上交谈的情况报告给福尔摩斯。我很清楚，他最近非常忙碌，因为我很少收到来自贝克大街的信件，即便有也很简短，对我提供的情况没有作任何评论，关于我的使命几乎只字未提。毫无疑问，他把全部精力都用在那桩敲诈勒索案上了。不过，这个新的情况定会引起他的注意的，并且重新唤起他的兴趣。他若是现在在这里该有多好啊。

10月17日，今天一整天都大雨倾盆，雨水落在常青藤上发出簌簌声，屋檐上的流水滴答落下。我想起了那个逃犯，正身处荒凉寒冷、毫无遮蔽的荒原上。可怜的魔鬼！无论他犯下了什么罪，但眼下这番痛苦多少有了一定的补偿了。然后，我又想起了另一个人——马车里的那张面孔，月亮下的那个身影。那位隐秘的监视者，那位神秘莫测的人物——难道他也同样处在倾盆大雨之中吗？傍晚时分，我穿上防雨衣裤，在湿软的荒原上走了很远。雨点打在我的脸上，风在我的耳畔呼啸，我心里充满了各种可怕的想象。但愿上帝伸出援手，帮助那些流落在大泥潭里的人们，因为此时连坚硬的高地都成沼泽了。我找到了那座孤零零的监视人站立过的黑色岩岗，走到了怪石嶙峋的山顶。亲眼看到了那一片阴郁的丘陵。狂风暴雨冲刷着赤褐色的地表。密集的深蓝灰色的云层低垂着笼罩大地，缓慢地飘出一个个灰色的云团，在奇形怪状的山边涌动。左手边远处的山涧里，巴斯克维尔庄园内的两座细长的塔楼穿透雾气，若隐若现地凸立在树梢上。除了那些密布在山坡上的史前期留下小屋之外，那是我能够看到的唯一一个人类生活的痕迹。我到前天夜间那个孤独人站立的同一地点寻找，但没发现他的任何踪迹。

我步行着返回时，莫蒂默医生追赶了上来。他驾着一辆双轮马车行进在一条崎岖不平的荒原小道上，那是一条通向边远的富尔米尔农舍的路。他一直非常关心我们，几乎每天都要去一趟庄园，看看我们情况怎么样。他

① faculty ['fækəlti] *n.* 能力，才能

② atone [ə'təun] *v.* 赎罪

③ deluge ['delju:dʒ] *v.* 淹没，使泛滥

④ sodden ['sɔdən] *a.* 湿透的

⑤ upland ['ʌplənd] *n.* 高地

⑥ morass [mə'ræs] *n.* 沼泽

⑦ squall [skwɔ:l] *n.* 暴风

⑧ wreath [ri:θ] *n.* 圈状物

⑨ attentive [ə'tentiv] *a.* 关心的，关怀的

my climbing into his dog-cart, and he gave me a lift homeward. I found him much troubled over the disappearance of his little spaniel. It had wandered on to the moor and had never come back. I gave him such consolation as I might, but I thought of the pony on the Grimpen Mire, and I do not fancy that he will see his little dog again.

"By the way, Mortimer," said I as we jolted along the rough road, "I suppose there are few people living within driving distance of this whom you do not know?"

"Hardly any, I think."

"Can you, then, tell me the name of any woman whose initials are L. L.?"

He thought for a few minutes.

"No," said he. "There are a few gipsies and labouring folk for whom I can't answer, but among the farmers or gentry there is no one whose initials are those. Wait a bit though," he added after a pause. "There is Laura Lyons–her initials are L. L.–but she lives in Coombe Tracey."

"Who is she?" I asked.

"She is Frankland's daughter."

"What! Old Frankland the **crank**①?"

"Exactly. She married an artist named Lyons, who came sketching on the moor. He proved to be a **blackguard**② and deserted her. The fault from what I hear may not have been entirely on one side. Her father refused to have anything to do with her because she had married without his consent and perhaps for one or two other reasons as well. So, between the old sinner and the young one the girl has had a pretty bad time."

"How does she live?"

"I fancy old Frankland allows her a **pittance**③, but it cannot be more, for his own affairs are considerably involved. Whatever she may have deserved one could not allow her to go hopelessly to the bad. Her story got about, and several of the people here did something to enable her to earn an honest living. Stapleton did for one, and Sir Charles for another. I gave a trifle myself. It was to set her up in a typewriting business."

He wanted to know the object of my inquiries, but I managed to satisfy his curiosity without telling him too much, for there is no reason why we

坚持要我坐他的马车，因此，我就搭他的车往回赶了。我发现，他对自己那只小长耳猎犬的失踪非常烦恼。那只小狗有一回跑到荒原上后就一直没有回来。我想方设法安慰他，但同时，我想起了格林彭泥潭里的小马驹，因此，心里面不再抱有什么幻想，他不可能再找回小狗了。

"啊，对啦，莫蒂默，"我们在路上颠簸着前行时，我说，"我看，这儿凡是您的马车能跑到的人家，里面住的人您差不多都认识了吧？"

"我认为，几乎没有不认识的。"

"那么，请您告诉我们，有没有哪个女人的名字首字母是L.L.的？"

他思忖了片刻。

"没有，"他说，"有几个吉卜赛人和几个做苦力活儿的，这个我就说不准。但是，庄稼人或乡绅中间，没有哪个女人的姓名首字母是L.L.的。等一下，"他停顿了一下，然后接着说，"有个叫劳拉·莱昂斯的——她的姓名首字母就是L.L.，不过她住在库姆特雷西。"

"她是谁？"我问。

"她是弗兰克兰的女儿。"

"什么啊！就是那个行为古怪的老弗兰克兰吗？"

"一点不错。她嫁给了一个名叫莱昂斯的艺术家，他是来荒原上写生的。那家伙是个坏蛋，他把劳拉给遗弃了。从我听说的情况看，或许不完全是一方的过错。她父亲对她不管不问，因为她结婚前没有得到父亲的同意。说不定还有别的原因吧。所以，姑娘夹在一老一少两个恶棍中间，日子过得可艰难了。"

"她怎么生活啊？"

"我猜想，老弗兰克兰给她提供了一点生活费用，但数额不会很大，因为他自己摊上了一大堆事情，够伤脑筋的。虽说她这是自找的，但不能眼看着她无依无靠，每况愈下。她的事情广为人们所知，这儿有几个人给她提供了帮助，使她能够过上正常的生活。斯塔普尔顿是一个，查尔斯爵士也是一个。我自己也曾给过她一些钱，让她做点打字的活儿。"

他想要知道我打听情况的目的，我设法满足了他的好奇心，不过没有说得太多。我没有理由随便相信

① crank [kræŋk] *n.* 怪人

② blackguard ['blægɑ:d] *n.* 坏蛋，恶棍

③ pittance ['pitəns] *n.* 微薄的津贴

should take anyone into our confidence. To-morrow morning I shall find my way to Coombe Tracey, and if I can see this Mrs. Laura Lyons, of **equivocal**① reputation, a long step will have been made towards clearing one incident in this chain of mysteries. I am certainly developing the wisdom of the serpent, for when Mortimer pressed his questions to an inconvenient extent I asked him casually to what type Frankland's skull belonged, and so heard nothing but **craniology**② for the rest of our drive. I have not lived for years with Sherlock Holmes for nothing.

I have only one other incident to record upon this **tempestuous**③ and melancholy day. This was my conversation with Barrymore just now, which gives me one more strong card which I can play in due time.

Mortimer had stayed to dinner, and he and the baronet played écarté afterwards. The butler brought me my coffee into the library, and I took the chance to ask him a few questions.

"Well," said I, "has this precious relation of yours departed, or is he still lurking out yonder?"

"I don't know, sir. I hope to heaven that he has gone, for he has brought nothing but trouble here! I've not heard of him since I left out food for him last, and that was three days ago."

"Did you see him then?"

"No, sir, but the food was gone when next I went that way."

"Then he was certainly there?"

"So you would think, sir, unless it was the other man who took it."

I sat with my coffee-cup halfway to my lips and stared at Barrymore.

"You know that there is another man then?"

"Yes, sir; there is another man upon the moor."

"Have you seen him?"

"No, sir."

"How do you know of him then?"

"Selden told me of him, sir, a week ago or more. He's in hiding, too, but he's not a convict as far as I can make out. I don't like it, Dr. Watson—I tell you straight, sir, that I don't like it." He spoke with a sudden passion of earnestness.

① equivocal [i'kwivəkəl]
   a. 有问题的

② craniology [ˌkreini'ɔlədʒi]
   n. 颅骨学

③ tempestuous [tem'pestjuəs]
   a. 暴风雨的

一个人。明天上午，我就要去一趟库姆特雷西，如果能够见到那位劳拉·莱昂斯太太，即那位名声存疑的女士，那对于解开一系列谜团中的一个可就迈出了一大步了。我已经变得像蛇一样精明了，因为当莫蒂默问题弄得我很尴尬，不好回答时，我便故意漫不经心，向他打听弗兰克兰的颅骨属于何种类型。因此，在剩下的行程中，我就没有听到过关于颅相学之外的东西了。我在夏洛克·福尔摩斯身边待了这么多年，日子没有白过啊。

这是个暴风骤雨、阴郁寒冷的日子，只有另外一件事情值得一记。那就是我刚才同巴里摩尔之间的一席交谈，这又给了我一张王牌，适当的时候就可以打出去。

莫蒂默留下来吃晚饭了，随后便同从男爵一道玩牌。管家给我把咖啡送到了图书室，我便趁此机会问了他一些问题。

"对了，"我说，"你的那位至亲已经离开了呢，还是仍然藏匿在那边？"

"我不知道啊，先生，愿上帝保佑，他已经离开了。他在这儿好事没做一件，麻烦倒是惹了不少！我上次给他送食物后一直没有他的音讯，那是三天前的事了。"

"你当时见到他人了吗？"

"没有，先生。但我第二天再去时，那里已经没有食物了。"

"那就是说，他一定还在那儿了？"

"如果不是别的什么人取走了食物，先生，您当然可以这么认为。"

我坐着，咖啡杯还未送到嘴边，便打量起巴里摩尔来。

"这么说，你知道荒原上还有另一个人？"

"是这样的，先生，荒原上还有另外一个人。"

"你见到过那个人吗？"

"没有啊，先生。"

"那你是如何知道他的呢？"

"是塞尔登告诉我的，先生。那是在一个礼拜之前，或者更早一点。那人也藏匿在荒原上，但据我判断，他不是犯人。我被这件事弄得很烦，华生医生——我就直说了吧，我对此厌烦极了。"霎时间，他说话的语气变

"Now, listen to me, Barrymore! I have no interest in this matter but that of your master. I have come here with no object except to help him. Tell me, frankly, what it is that you don't like."

Barrymore hesitated for a moment, as if he regretted his **outburst**① or found it difficult to express his own feelings in words.

"It's all these goings-on, sir," he cried at last, waving his hand towards the rain-lashed window which faced the moor. "There's **foul play**② somewhere, and there's black **villainy**③ brewing, to that I'll swear! Very glad I should be, sir, to see Sir Henry on his way back to London again!"

"But what is it that alarms you?"

"Look at Sir Charles's death! That was bad enough, for all that the coroner said. Look at the noises on the moor at night. There's not a man would cross it after sundown if he was paid for it. Look at this stranger hiding out yonder, and watching and waiting! What's he waiting for? What does it mean? It means no good to anyone of the name of Baskerville, and very glad I shall be to be quit of it all on the day that Sir Henry's new servants are ready to take over the Hall."

"But about this stranger," said I. "Can you tell me anything about him? What did Selden say? Did he find out where he hid, or what he was doing?"

"He saw him once or twice, but he is a deep one and gives nothing away. At first he thought that he was the police, but soon he found that he had some **lay**④ of his own. A kind of gentleman he was, as far as he could see, but what he was doing he could not make out."

"And where did he say that he lived?"

"Among the old houses on the hillside–the stone huts where the old folk used to live."

"But how about his food?"

"Selden found out that he has got a lad who works for him and brings all he needs. I dare say he goes to Coombe Tracey for what he wants."

"Very good, Barrymore. We may talk further of this some other time." When the butler had gone I walked over to the black window, and I looked through a blurred pane at the driving clouds and at the tossing outline of the wind-swept trees. It is a wild night indoors, and what must it be in a stone hut

得非常恳切了。

"是啊，听我说，巴里摩尔！我对此事毫无兴趣，但我要替你家主人着想。除了为你的主人排忧解难，我到这儿来没有别的任何目的。因此，请你坦率地告诉我，你究竟为什么烦恼？"

巴里摩尔迟疑了片刻，好像是觉得自己刚才不该口无遮拦说出那些话，又好像是觉得很难用言语来表达自己的感受。"对于这儿发生的一切，先生，"他最后大声说着，一只手朝正对着荒原方向的窗户挥了挥，"那儿的某个角落里，一定有坏蛋正在策划着什么害人的勾当，我敢发誓！先生，如果能亲眼看到亨利爵士重新回到伦敦，我会非常高兴的！"

"但是，究竟是什么情况让你这样惊恐不安呢？"

"想想查尔斯爵士的死亡！验尸官所说的那些话就已经够吓人的了。您再想想夜晚荒原上种种怪异的声音。日落之后，即便是给钱也没有人愿意穿过荒原的。想想那个藏匿在远处的人，他正在窥探和等待着呢！他在等待着什么呢？那是什么用意啊？对巴斯克维尔家族的任何人来说，这都不是什么好兆头。因此，我很高兴自己将要把这一切都抛之脑后了，只等待着亨利爵士的新仆人们能够接管庄园的那一天。"

"但是，有关那个陌生人的事情，"我说，"你能告诉我一点儿关于他的情况吗？塞尔登是怎么说的？他发现了那人藏匿在哪儿，或者有什么行动了吗？"

"他见过那人一两次，但那人隐藏得很深，没暴露任何情况。一开始，他认为那人是个狱警，但他不久便发现，那人自己另有图谋。据他观察，那人属于上流社会的人物，不过他也搞不清他到底在干些什么。"

"他说过那人住在什么地方吗？"

"住在山坡上那些古老的房子里——就是那些古人居住过的石头房子。"

"但是，他怎么弄到食物的？"

"塞尔登发现，他雇了个小男孩来伺候他，替他送必需品。我敢说，那小孩是去库姆特雷西给他弄必需品的。"

"很好，巴里摩尔。你说的这个情况我们改天再详谈吧。"管家离开后，我走到漆黑的窗户前，透过模糊

① outburst ['autbə:st] n.（情感的）爆发

② foul play 暴行（尤指谋杀）

③ villainy ['viləni] n. 邪恶，恶行

④ lay [lei] n. 企图；计划

upon the moor. What passion of hatred can it be which leads a man to lurk in such a place at such a time! And what deep and earnest purpose can he have which calls for such a trial! There, in that hut upon the moor, seems to lie the very centre of that problem which has vexed me so **sorely**[①]. I swear that another day shall not have passed before I have done all that man can do to reach the heart of the mystery.

不清的窗玻璃，看到天上的云朵正在翻腾，树影被风吹得左右摇晃。这样的夜晚对待在家里的人来说都很恶劣，而对于藏匿在荒原上石屋里的人来说更加如此了。能让人在这种地方、这种时候藏匿起来，那该是怎样的深仇大恨啊！到底是什么深厚而迫切的目标令他能够经受住如此的艰难困苦！看来解开令我困扰不已的难题的关键就在荒原上的那个小屋里。我发誓，明天一定要像那人一样排除万难，直捣那谜团的中心。

① sorely ['sɔ:li] *ad.* 严厉地，剧烈地

Chapter 11   The Man on the Tor

The extract from my private diary which forms the last chapter has brought my narrative up to the eighteenth of October, a time when these strange events began to move swiftly towards their terrible conclusion. The incidents of the next few days are indelibly **graven**[①] upon my recollection, and I can tell them without reference to the notes made at the time. I start them from the day which succeeded that upon which I had established two facts of great importance, the one that Mrs. Laura Lyons of Coombe Tracey had written to Sir Charles Baskerville and made an appointment with him at the very place and hour that he met his death, the other that the lurking man upon the moor was to be found among the stone huts upon the hillside. With these two facts in my possession I felt that either my intelligence or my courage must be **deficient**[②] if I could not throw some further light upon these dark places.

I had no opportunity to tell the baronet what I had learned about Mrs. Lyons upon the evening before, for Dr. Mortimer remained with him at cards until it was very late. At breakfast, however, I informed him about my discovery and asked him whether he would care to accompany me to Coombe Tracey. At first he was very eager to come, but on second thoughts it seemed to both of us that if I went alone the results might be better. The more formal we made the visit the less information we might obtain. I left Sir Henry behind, therefore, not without some **prickings**[③] of conscience, and drove off upon my new quest.

When I reached Coombe Tracey I told Perkins to put up the horses, and I made inquiries for the lady whom I had come to interrogate. I had no difficulty

第十一章　岩岗上的男子

① grave [greiv] *v.* 铭记，牢记（在心头）

② deficient [di'fiʃənt] *a.* 不足的

③ pricking ['prikiŋ] *n.* 刺痛感

上一章的内容是从我的私人日记摘录的。我叙述的时间进入到了10月18日，从此，那些不可思议的怪事情便开始接二连三地发生，迅速接近那个可怕的结局。随后数日发生的事情深深地印刻在我的脑海里，我无需翻看当时所做的任何记录，就可以直接叙述出来。那就从我弄清了两个非常重要的事实之后的第二天说起吧。其中一件是，库姆特雷西的劳拉·莱昂斯太太曾经给查尔斯·巴斯克维尔爵士写过信，信中约定的见面地点和时间正是爵士死亡的地点和时间。另一件是，藏匿在荒原上的那个人可以在山边的石头房里找到。掌握这两个情况之后，我觉得，如果自己不能让这些谜团显露端倪的话，那就要么是自己不够聪明，要么就是缺乏勇气。

头天晚上，我没有机会把自己了解到的有关莱昂斯太太的情况告诉从男爵，因为莫蒂默医生和他玩牌玩到很晚。不过，当天早餐时，我把自己的发现全都告诉了他，并问他是否愿意陪我一同去一趟库姆特雷西。刚一开始时，他很乐意前往，但仔细一想，我们又都觉得，我单独前往效果会更加好些。我们把走访的事情越是弄得郑重其事，可能掌握到的情况反而会越少。因此，我让亨利爵士留在家里后，便怀着一颗忐忑不安的心，独自驱车出发，去进行一番新的探索了。

我到达了库姆特雷西之后，便吩咐珀金斯安顿好马匹，自个儿去打听此行所要寻访的那位女士的住所。我轻而易举就找到了她的住所。她家坐落在村庄的中心，

· 207 ·

in finding her rooms, which were central and well appointed. A maid showed me in without ceremony, and as I entered the sitting-room a lady, who was sitting before a Remington typewriter, sprang up with a pleasant smile of welcome. Her face fell, however, when she saw that I was a stranger, and she sat down again and asked me the object of my visit.

The first impression left by Mrs. Lyons was one of extreme beauty. Her eyes and hair were of the same rich hazel colour, and her cheeks, though considerably freckled, were flushed with the exquisite bloom of the brunette, the dainty pink which lurks at the heart of the **sulphur**[1] rose. Admiration was, I repeat, the first impression. But the second was criticism. There was something subtly wrong with the face, some coarseness of expression, some hardness, perhaps, of eye, some looseness of lip which marred its perfect beauty. But these, of course, are after-thoughts. At the moment I was simply conscious that I was in the presence of a very handsome woman, and that she was asking me the reasons for my visit. I had not quite understood until that instant how **delicate**[2] my mission was.

"I have the pleasure," said I, "of knowing your father."

It was a clumsy introduction, and the lady made me feel it.

"There is nothing in common between my father and me," she said. "I owe him nothing, and his friends are not mine. If it were not for the late Sir Charles Baskerville and some other kind hearts I might have starved for all that my father cared."

"It was about the late Sir Charles Baskerville that I have come here to see you."

The freckles started out on the lady's face.

"What can I tell you about him?" she asked, and her fingers played nervously over the **stops**[3] of her typewriter.

"You knew him, did you not?"

"I have already said that I owe a great deal to his kindness. If I am able to support myself it is largely due to the interest which he took in my unhappy situation."

"Did you correspond with him?"

The lady looked quickly up with an angry gleam in her hazel eyes.

里面陈设很好。有位女仆没行任何礼节就把我领进了门。我进入客厅时，坐在雷明顿打字机前的女士迅速站起身。她脸上露着愉快的笑容，表示欢迎。然而，当她看到我是个陌生人时，脸便耷拉下来了，重新坐下，问我上门有什么事情。

莱昂斯太太给我的第一个印象是美丽绝伦，眼睛和头发都是深棕色的，脸颊上虽有雀斑，但色泽红润得恰到好处，就像硫磺色玫瑰花蕾中那娇艳欲滴的粉色。我要重申一下，倾慕是第一印象，而第二印象就是非议。那张脸上隐隐显出有不对劲的地方，表情略嫌粗俗，眼神或许有点生硬，嘴唇略显放荡，这一切瑕疵令她的绝伦美貌打了折扣。但是，这些当然都是后来的想法。我当时只知道，自己站在一个非常漂亮的女人面前，而对方正在询问我上门的缘由。直到那一刻，我才真正认识到我的任务有多么棘手。

"我很有幸，"我说，"认识您父亲。"

这样的介绍显得很愚笨，对方的反应让我有了这种感觉。

"我和我父亲之间毫无共同之处，"她说，"我对他没有任何亏欠，他的朋友并不是我的朋友。如果不是已故的查尔斯·巴斯克维尔爵士和另外的几个好心人，我早就已经饿死了。我父亲才不会管我的死活呢。"

"我到这儿来，就是想向您打听一些有关已故查尔斯·巴斯克维尔爵士的事情。"

女人脸上的雀斑显得更加清晰了。

"有关他的事情，我又能告诉您些什么呢？"她问了一声，手指头紧张地敲打着打字机上的标点符号键。

"您认识他，对吧？"

"我已经说过了，他心地善良，我非常感谢他。如果说我现在能自食其力的话，那也主要是因为他怜悯我可悲的处境。"

"您给他写过信吗？"

女士迅速抬起头，棕褐色的眼睛里闪烁着愤怒的光芒。

"您问这些是什么目的？"她反问着，语气尖锐。

① sulphur ['sʌlfə] *n.* 硫黄色，柠檬色

② delicate ['delikət] *a.* 微妙的；棘手的

③ stop [stɔp] *n.* 标点符号，（尤指）句号

"What is the object of these questions?" she asked sharply.

"The object is to avoid a public scandal. It is better that I should ask them here than that the matter should pass outside our control."

She was silent and her face was still very pale. At last she looked up with something reckless and defiant in her manner.

"Well, I'll answer," she said. "What are your questions?"

"Did you correspond with Sir Charles?"

"I certainly wrote to him once or twice to acknowledge his **delicacy**[①] and his generosity."

"Have you the dates of those letters?"

"No."

"Have you ever met him?"

"Yes, once or twice, when he came into Coombe Tracey. He was a very retiring man, and he preferred to do good **by stealth**[②]."

"But if you saw him so seldom and wrote so seldom, how did he know enough about your affairs to be able to help you, as you say that he has done?"

She met my difficulty with the utmost **readiness**[③].

"There were several gentlemen who knew my sad history and united to help me. One was Mr. Stapleton, a neighbour and intimate friend of Sir Charles's. He was exceedingly kind, and it was through him that Sir Charles learned about my affairs."

I knew already that Sir Charles Baskerville had made Stapleton his **almoner**[④] upon several occasions, so the lady's statement bore the impress of truth upon it.

"Did you ever write to Sir Charles asking him to meet you?" I continued.

Mrs. Lyon flushed with anger again.

"Really, sir, this is a very extraordinary question."

"I am sorry, madam, but I must repeat it."

"Then I answer, certainly not."

"Not on the very day of Sir Charles's death?"

The flush had faded in an instant, and a deathly face was before me. Her dry lips could not speak the "No" which I saw rather than heard.

"Surely your memory deceives you," said I. "I could even quote a passage

"目的就是要避免公开的丑闻。我到这儿来问这些问题，比在外面议论纷纷，弄得不可收拾要好一些。"

她缄口不言，脸色依然苍白。最后，她抬起了头，态度显得不顾一切，傲慢自大。

"得了，我来回答吧，"她说，"您有什么要问的？"

"您给查尔斯爵士写过信吗？"

"我确实给他写过一两次，目的是感谢他体贴入微，慷慨大度。"

"您还记得写信的日期吗？"

"不记得了。"

"您同他见过面吗？"

"见过，他到库姆特雷西来时，我们见过一两次。他是个不喜欢张扬的人，喜欢不声不响地做好事。"

"但是，如果您很少见他，又不常给他写信，那他是怎样了解您那么多事情，从而像您所说的那样来帮助您呢？"

她毫不犹豫地回答了我认为是很难回答的问题。"有好几位绅士知道我悲惨的经历，他们联合起来帮助我。一位是斯塔普尔顿先生，他是查尔斯爵士的邻居兼密友。他心肠极好，查尔斯爵士正是通过他才了解到我的情况。"

我已经知道了，查尔斯·巴斯克维尔爵士曾经几次让斯塔普尔顿负责帮他分发救济金，因此，女士说的让我感觉是实话。

"您曾经给查尔斯爵士写过一封信，请求他同您见面，对吧？"我接着问。

莱昂斯太太又一次气得满脸通红。

"事实上，先生，这是一个非同寻常的问题。"

"对不起，太太，但我必须再问您一遍。"

"那我就答复您吧，一定没有过。"

"查尔斯爵士死亡的那天您没给他写信？"

她脸上的血色霎时消失了，我眼前出现了一张死人般的面孔。她那干燥的嘴唇连"没有"二字都说不出声来，我只看到有了个这样的形状。

"您肯定是记错了，"我说，"我甚至能摘录您信中的一段，上面写着：'您是一位正人君子，请您，请您

① delicacy ['delikəsi] *n.* 体谅，体贴

② by stealth 偷偷地，暗中地

③ readiness ['redinis] *n.* 迅速

④ almoner ['ɑ:mənə] *n.* （富户的）救济品分发人员

of your letter. It ran 'Please, please, as you are a gentleman, burn this letter, and be at the gate by ten o'clock.' "

I thought that she had fainted, but she recovered herself by a **supreme**① effort.

"Is there no such thing as a gentleman?" she gasped.

"You do Sir Charles an injustice. He *did* burn the letter. But sometimes a letter may be legible even when burned. You acknowledge now that you wrote it?"

"Yes, I did write it," she cried, pouring out her soul in a torrent of words. "I did write it. Why should I deny it? I have no reason to be ashamed of it. I wished him to help me. I believed that if I had an interview I could gain his help, so I asked him to meet me."

"But why at such an hour?"

"Because I had only just learned that he was going to London next day and might be away for months. There were reasons why I could not get there earlier."

"But why a **rendezvous**② in the garden instead of a visit to the house?"

"Do you think a woman could go alone at that hour to a bachelor's house?"

"Well, what happened when you did get there?"

"I never went."

"Mrs. Lyons!"

"No, I swear it to you on all I hold sacred. I never went. Something **intervened**③ to prevent my going."

"What was that?"

"That is a private matter. I cannot tell it."

"You acknowledge then that you made an appointment with Sir Charles at the very hour and place at which he met his death, but you deny that you kept the appointment."

"That is the truth."

Again and again I cross-questioned her, but I could never get past that point.

"Mrs. Lyons," said I as I rose from this long and **inconclusive**④ interview, "you are taking a very great responsibility and putting yourself in a very false

① supreme [sjuːˈpriːm] *a*. 最大的；极度的

② rendezvous [ˈrɒndivuː] *n*. 约会

③ intervene [ˌintəˈviːn] *v*. 干涉；干预

④ inconclusive [ˌinkənˈkluːsiv] *a*. 无结果的

一定把信烧掉，并在十点时到栅门旁等候。'"

我觉得，她听后晕过去了，但又竭尽全力地恢复了平静。

"这世界上难道就没有真正的君子了吗？"她说着，呼吸急促。

"您错怪查尔斯爵士了，他确实把信烧了。但有时候，信件烧毁后上面的内容还是可以看得出来。您现在承认，您那天确实给他写过信吧？"

"没错，我确实写了，"她提高嗓门，言辞激烈，一五一十地把话全都说了出来，"我确实写了信，我为何要否认呢？我没理由因此觉得羞耻。我就是希望他能帮帮我。我觉得，如果自己同他见个面，就能够从他那儿得到帮助，于是写信请求同他见面。"

"但是，为何要选在那个时刻呢？"

"因为我当时刚知道，他次日要去伦敦，并且有可能去很长时间。而我不能早一点赶到他那里也是事出有因的。"

"但是，会面的地点为何是在花园里，而不是在室内呢？"

"您觉得一个女人在那个时刻单独到一个单身男人家里去合适吗？"

"对啊，那您到那里后发生了什么事情？"

"我根本没去。"

"莱昂斯太太！"

"没去，我以我视为神圣的一切向您发誓，根本没去。中间出了点别的事情，弄得我没有去成。"

"什么事呢？"

"是件私事，我不能告诉您。"

"这么说，您承认您和查尔斯爵士约好的会面时间和地点，正是他去世的时间和地点，但同时又否认自己曾如约前往。"

"这是实情。"

我反复询问她，但都未能了解到更多情况。

"莱昂斯太太，"我一边说，一边站起身，结束了这次漫长而毫无结果的会面，"您没有把自己知道的事情全部说出来，这样做不仅要承担很大的责任，还会将您

position by not **making an absolutely clean breast of**[①] all that you know. If I have to call in the aid of the police you will find how seriously you are **compromised**[②]. If your position is innocent, why did you in the first instance deny having written to Sir Charles upon that date?"

"Because I feared that some false conclusion might be drawn from it and that I might find myself involved in a scandal."

"And why were you so **pressing**[③] that Sir Charles should destroy your letter?"

"If you have read the letter you will know."

"I did not say that I had read all the letter."

"You quoted some of it."

"I quoted the postscript. The letter had, as I said, been burned and it was not all legible. I ask you once again why it was that you were so pressing that Sir Charles should destroy this letter which he received on the day of his death."

"The matter is a very private one."

"The more reason why you should avoid a public investigation."

"I will tell you, then. If you have heard anything of my unhappy history you will know that I made a rash marriage and had reason to regret it."

"I have heard so much."

"My life has been one incessant **persecution**[④] from a husband whom I **abhor**[⑤]. The law is upon his side, and every day I am faced by the possibility that he may force me to live with him. At the time that I wrote this letter to Sir Charles I had learned that there was a prospect of my regaining my freedom if certain expenses could be met. It meant everything to me–peace of mind, happiness, self-respect–everything. I knew Sir Charles's generosity, and I thought that if he heard the story from my own lips he would help me."

"Then how is it that you did not go?"

"Because I received help in the interval from another source."

"Why, then, did you not write to Sir Charles and explain this?"

"So I should have done had I not seen his death in the paper next morning."

The woman's story hung coherently together, and all my questions were unable to shake it. I could only check it by finding if she had, indeed, **instituted**[⑥] divorce **proceedings**[⑦] against her husband at or about the time of

① make a clean breast of
把…和盘托出

② compromise ['kɔmprəm
aiz] v. 损害（名声等）

③ pressing ['presiŋ] a. 热切
的；坚持的

④ persecution [,pə:si'kju:ʃən]
n. 虐待
⑤ abhor [əb'hɔ:] v. 憎恶

⑥ institute ['institjut] v. 着
手，开始
⑦ proceedings [prəu'si:diŋs]
n. 诉讼程序；诉讼

自己置于非常不利的境地。如果到了非要警方出面干预不可的地步，那您就会发现自己的麻烦大了。如果您在本案中是清白无辜的，那为何一开始否认自己出事那天给查尔斯爵士写过信呢？"

"因为我担心，人们会因此产生某种错误的推论，同时，也担心自己被卷入到一桩丑闻中去。"

"您为何迫切要求查尔斯爵士把您写给他的信毁掉呢？"

"如果您看过那信，就会知道原因了。"

"我并没有说自己看过整封信啊。"

"您引用了其中的一部分。"

"我引用了信的附笔。我说过了，信被烧毁了，上面的内容不能全部看出来。我再问您一遍，您究竟为何如此迫切要求查尔斯爵士毁掉他在猝死当天收到的来信？"

"这纯属我个人的私事。"

"那您就更要避免公开调查了。"

"那行，我就告诉您吧。如果您听说过我的悲惨经历，您就会知道，我结婚时太过草率，并因此懊悔不已。"

"这些我都听说过。"

"我那令人厌恶的丈夫不时地虐待我，我的日子不好过。法律也站在他那边，我每天都要面临被迫和他同房的可能性。写信的当天，我听人说只要我能付清几笔费用，就能重获自由。对我来说，自由简直代表着一切——心平气和，幸福美满，充满自尊——一切的一切。我知道，查尔斯爵士慷慨大方，心里想着，如果我亲口把自己的苦处告诉他，他就会帮助我的。"

"那您怎么又没去成呢？"

"因为当时，我从其他人那里得到了援助。"

"那么，您为什么不写信告诉查尔斯爵士，向他解释一下呢？"

"我本来是打算这么做的，但次日早上我就从报纸上看到了他的死讯。"

女人所说的情况前后相符，我把所想到的问题都提出来了，但毫无纰漏。我只能去核实一下，她向她丈夫

the tragedy.

It was unlikely that she would dare to say that she had not been to Baskerville Hall if she really had been, for a trap would be necessary to take her there, and could not have returned to Coombe Tracey until the early hours of the morning. Such an excursion could not be kept secret. The probability was, therefore, that she was telling the truth, or, at least, a part of the truth. I came away baffled and disheartened. Once again I had reached that dead wall which seemed to be built across every path by which I tried to get at the object of my mission. And yet the more I thought of the lady's face and of her manner the more I felt that something was being held back from me. Why should she turn so pale? Why should she fight against every admission until it was forced from her? Why should she have been so **reticent**[①] at the time of the tragedy? Surely the explanation of all this could not be as innocent as she would have me believe. For the moment I could proceed no farther in that direction, but must turn back to that other clue which was to be sought for among the stone huts upon the moor.

And that was a most vague direction. I realized it as I drove back and noted how hill after hill showed traces of the ancient people. Barrymore's only indication had been that the stranger lived in one of these abandoned huts, and many hundreds of them are scattered throughout the length and breadth of the moor. But I had my own experience for a guide since it had shown me the man himself standing upon the summit of the Black Tor. That, then, should be the centre of my search. From there I should explore every hut upon the moor until I lighted upon the right one. If this man were inside it I should find out from his own lips, at the point of my revolver if necessary, who he was and why he had dogged us so long. He might slip away from us in the crowd of Regent Street, but it would puzzle him to do so upon the lonely moor. On the other hand, if I should find the hut and its tenant should not be within it I must remain there, however long the vigil, until he returned. Holmes had missed him in London. It would indeed be a triumph for me if I could run him to earth where my master had failed.

Luck had been against us again and again in this inquiry, but now at last it came to my aid. And the messenger of good fortune was **none other than**[②] Mr.

提出离婚诉讼是否确实在悲剧发生的时候，或者查一查悲剧发生的时间。

如果她真的到过巴斯克维尔庄园，那她可能不会有胆量说自己没有去过，因为她要是去了那儿，那就一定得乘马车，而且在第二天清早前是无法返回库姆特雷西的。这样的远行很难不被人发现。因此，她很可能说的是实话，或者说，她至少说出了一部分实情。

我返回了，态度茫然，神情沮丧。再次碰了壁，好像在每一条能让我到达任务终点的路上都有这么一堵墙壁似的。不过，当我回想她的面容和举止时，我越来越觉得她还有些情况瞒着我。她的脸色为何变得那么苍白？她为何每次都先是矢口否认，继而迫不得已时又会承认呢？悲剧发生之后，她为何会如此三缄其口①？所有这些问题的答案绝非像她让我相信的那样清白无辜。眼下我无法沿此方向继续前进，而必须返回到荒原上的石屋去寻找别的线索了。

但是，这条线索也是十分含糊不清的。我在驱车返回的途中意识到了这一点，而且注意到，群山连绵，显露着古人生活的痕迹。巴里摩尔就只说明了一点，即那个陌生人住在那些遗弃的小屋中的一幢里，这儿一带的荒原上，零零散散有成百上千幢小屋。但是，我亲眼见识过的，那人站立在黑色的岩岗上，可以以此作为参照。如此说来，我应该以此为中心展开搜寻。一幢一幢地查看过去，直到找到那一幢为止。如果那人在里面，我就会要他亲口说出他是谁，为何这么长时间以来一直跟踪我们。必要时，我甚至会用手枪逼着他说。在熙熙攘攘的摄政街上，他可能从我们面前溜走，但在人烟稀少的荒原上，他恐怕会感到逃跑无路吧。如果我找到了那幢小屋而那人又不在里面，无论要熬到多晚，我都一定会在守在那里，一直等到他回来为止。在伦敦，福尔摩斯让他溜掉了。我如果能在自己的大师同伴失败后逮住他，那对我来说确实是一个很大的胜利啊。

调查过程中，我们的运气一直不佳，但是，现如今，我终于时来运转了。给我带来好运的不是别人，正是弗兰克兰先生②。他胡子花白，脸色红润，正站在他家

① reticent ['retisənt] *a.* 沉默的；有保留的

② none other than 不是别的而正是

Frankland, who was standing, gray-whiskered and red-faced, outside the gate of his garden, which opened on to the highroad along which I travelled.

"Good-day, Dr. Watson," cried he with **unwonted**[1] good humour, "you must really give your horses a rest and come in to have a glass of wine and to congratulate me."

My feelings towards him were very far from being friendly after what I had heard of his treatment of his daughter, but I was anxious to send Perkins and the wagonette home, and the opportunity was a good one. I **alighted**[2] and sent a message to Sir Henry that I should walk over in time for dinner. Then I followed Frankland into his dining-room.

"It is a great day for me, sir—one of the **red-letter**[3] days of my life," he cried with many chuckles. "I have brought off a double event. I mean to teach them in these parts that law is law, and that there is a man here who does not fear to **invoke**[4] it. I have established a right of way through the centre of old Middleton's park, slap across it, sir, within a hundred yards of his own front door. What do you think of that? We'll teach these **magnates**[5] that they cannot **ride roughshod over**[6] the rights of the commoners, confound them! And I've closed the wood where the Fernworthy folk used to picnic. These **infernal**[7] people seem to think that there are no rights of property, and that they can swarm where they like with their papers and their bottles. Both cases decided, Dr. Watson, and both in my favour. I haven't had such a day since I had Sir John Morland for trespass because he shot in his own **warren**[8]."

"How on earth did you do that?"

"Look it up in the books, sir. It will repay reading—Frankland v. Morland, Court of Queen's Bench. It cost me £200, but I got my verdict."

"Did it do you any good?"

"None, sir, none. I am proud to say that I had no interest in the matter. I act entirely from a sense of public duty. I have no doubt, for example, that the Fernworthy people will burn me in effigy to-night. I told the police last time they did it that they should stop these disgraceful exhibitions. The County Constabulary is in a scandalous state, sir, and it has not afforded me the protection to which I am entitled. The case of Frankland v. Regina will bring the matter before the attention of the public. I told them that they would have

面朝我要经过的大路的花园门口。

"您好啊，华生医生，"他异常亲切地跟我打着招呼，"您确实得让您的马匹休息一会儿才是啊，进来喝一杯，庆贺一下我吧！"

我在听说了他对待自己女儿的态度之后，对他就没有什么好感。不过，我当时正急于要打发珀金斯赶着马车回家去，因而这是一个好机会。我下了马车，给亨利爵士写了个便条，说我步行着回去，应该刚好能赶上晚饭。然后，我就跟在弗兰克兰先生后面，走进他家的餐厅。

"对我而言，这是个很了不起的日子啊，先生——是我人生中的一个大喜日子，"他大声说着，咯咯地笑个不停，"我了却了两桩事情，就是要好好教训一下这个地方的那些人，让他们知道法律就是法律，这儿还真就有这么一个不害怕诉诸法律的人。我已经确认了一项道路通行的权利，道路穿过老米德尔顿家园林的中心，正好从里面穿过，先生，离他家前门不超过一百码。对这事，您是怎么看的？我们要好好教训教训那帮大人物，要让他们知道，平民的权利是不能任意践踏的，那些混蛋！还有就是，我把那片弗恩沃西人常去野餐的树林给封闭掉了。那些人无法无天，好像觉得世界上压根就不存在什么产权问题，感觉他们想去哪儿就去哪儿，带着报纸和酒瓶。这两桩事情都有了结果了，华生医生，都是判我胜诉。自从约翰·莫兰爵士因在自己的鸟兽畜养场开枪而被我告发以来，我还没有哪天过得像今天这么开心呢。"

"您是如何做到这一点的呢？"

"请您查看一下这些法庭记录簿吧，先生，很值得一看的——弗兰克兰诉莫兰，女王法庭。这场诉讼案花费了我二百英镑，不过最后还是我胜诉了。"

"它给您带来了什么好处吗？"

"没有啊，先生，什么好处都没有。我可以很自豪地说，自己这样做完全是处于一种公共责任感。比如说吧，我毫不怀疑，弗恩沃西的人今晚肯定会烧毁我的模拟人像。他们上次这样做时，我报了警，建议制止那些不雅的行为。郡警察局太丢人了，他们无力给我提供应

---

① unwonted [ʌn'wəuntid] *a.* 不寻常的；少有的

② alight [ə'lait] *v.* 下车

③ red-letter ['red'letə] *a.* 值得纪念的；喜庆的

④ invoke [in'vəuk] *v.* 行使（法权等）

⑤ magnate ['mægneit] *n.* 巨头；大资本家；要人；富豪

⑥ ride roughshod over 欺凌

⑦ infernal [in'fə:nəl] *a.* [口语] 可恨的，坏透的，该死的

⑧ warren ['wɔrən] *a.* 小猎物繁殖场

occasion to regret their treatment of me, and already my words have come true."

"How so?" I asked.

The old man put on a very **knowing**① expression.

"Because I could tell them what they are dying to know; but nothing would induce me to help the rascals in any way."

I had been **casting round for**② some excuse by which I could get away from his gossip, but now I began to wish to hear more of it. I had seen enough of the contrary nature of the old sinner to understand that any strong sign of interest would be the surest way to stop his confidences.

"Some **poaching**③ case, no doubt?" said I with an indifferent manner.

"Ha, ha, my boy, a very much more important matter than that! What about the convict on the moor?"

I started. "You don't mean that you know where he is?" said I.

"I may not know exactly where he is, but I am quite sure that I could help the police to lay their hands on him. Has it never **struck**④ you that the way to catch that man was to find out where he got his food and so trace it to him?"

He certainly seemed to be getting uncomfortably near the truth. "No doubt," said I; "but how do you know that he is anywhere upon the moor?"

"I know it because I have seen with my own eyes the messenger who takes him his food."

My heart sank for Barrymore. It was a serious thing to be in the power of this **spiteful**⑤ old **busybody**⑥. But his next remark took a weight from my mind.

"You'll be surprised to hear that his food is taken to him by a child. I see him every day through my telescope upon the roof. He passes along the same path at the same hour, and to whom should he be going except to the convict?"

Here was luck indeed! And yet I suppressed all appearance of interest. A child! Barrymore had said that our unknown was supplied by a boy. It was on his track, and not upon the convict's, that Frankland had stumbled. If I could get his knowledge it might save me a long and weary hunt. But **incredulity**⑦ and indifference were evidently my strongest cards.

"I should say that it was much more likely that it was the son of one of the

有的保护。弗兰克兰诉女王政府一案，很快就会引起社会公众的注意的。我告诉过他们，他们总有一天会后悔自己曾经那样对待我的，现在，我的话已经应验了。"

"怎么会这样呢？"我问。

老人摆出一副老奸巨猾的样子。

"因为我掌握了他们拼命想要知道的东西，但是，无论如何，任何情况都不可能诱使我给那帮恶棍提供什么帮助。"

我之前一直在找借口脱身，不想再听他闲扯，但是，我现在表现得想要多听一听。我对老恶棍的脾气观察得差不多了，知道只要表示出强烈兴趣，他立刻就会闭口不谈。

"您所说的毫无疑问是一桩偷猎的案件吧？"我说，一副漫不经心的样子。

"哈，哈，伙计啊，是一件比这个更加严重得多的事情啊！藏匿在荒原上的那个逃犯怎么样了呢？"

我怔了一下。"您不会是说，您知道他在哪儿吧？"

"我或许不知道他藏匿的确切地点，但我非常肯定，我能协助狱警把他逮住。您难道没有想到过，缉拿那个家伙的办法就是查清他获得食物的来源，然后顺藤摸瓜再去抓他吗？"

他似乎真的快要接近那个令人不安的事实了。"当然了，"我说，"但是，您是怎样知道他藏匿在荒原的某个角落里的呢？"

"我知道，因为我亲眼看到了那个给他送食物的使者。"

我替巴里摩尔担心起来了，如果落在了这样一个好惹是生非而且爱管闲事的老家伙手上，事态可就严重了。但他随后的那句话令我如释重负。

"他的食物是由一个小男孩送过去的，您听了肯定觉得惊讶吧。我每天都通过屋顶上的那架望远镜观察他。他每天都是在同一时间经过同一条路，除了那个罪犯那里，他还能到什么地方去呢？"

这可真是运气啊！不过，我还是控制住了自己，不表露一点兴趣。一个小孩！巴里摩尔也曾说过，那个陌生人的食物就是由一个小男孩递送的。弗兰克兰误打误撞上的是寻找那陌生人的线索，而不是抓捕那罪犯的线

① knowing ['nəuiŋ] *a.* 狡猾的；精明的

② cast round for 寻找

③ poaching ['pəutʃiŋ] *n.* 非法狩猎

④ strike [straik] *v.* 使突然想到

⑤ spiteful ['spaitful] *a.* 怀有恶意的

⑥ busybody ['bizi,bɔdi] *n.* 爱管闲事的人

⑦ incredulity [,inkri'djuːləti] *n.* 怀疑

moorland shepherds taking out his father's dinner."

The least appearance of opposition struck fire out of the old **autocrat**①. His eyes looked **malignantly**② at me, and his gray whiskers bristled like those of an angry cat.

"Indeed, sir!" said he, pointing out over the wide-stretching moor. "Do you see that Black Tor over yonder? Well, do you see the low hill beyond with the thornbush upon it? It is the stoniest part of the whole moor. Is that a place where a shepherd would be likely to take his station? Your suggestion, sir, is a most absurd one."

I meekly answered that I had spoken without knowing all the facts. My submission pleased him and led him to further confidences.

"You may be sure, sir, that I have very good grounds before I come to an opinion. I have seen the boy again and again with his bundle. Every day, and sometimes twice a day, I have been able–but wait a moment, Dr. Watson. Do my eyes deceive me, or is there at the present moment something moving upon that hillside?"

It was several miles off, but I could distinctly see a small dark dot against the dull green and gray.

"Come, sir, come!" cried Frankland, rushing upstairs. "You will see with your own eyes and judge for yourself."

The telescope, a formidable instrument mounted upon a tripod, stood upon the flat **leads**③ of the house. Frankland **clapped**④ his eye to it and gave a cry of satisfaction.

"Quick, Dr. Watson, quick, before he passes over the hill!"

There he was, sure enough, a small **urchin**⑤ with a little bundle upon his shoulder, toiling slowly up the hill. When he reached the crest I saw the ragged **uncouth**⑥ figure outlined for an instant against the cold blue sky. He looked round him with a furtive and stealthy air, as one who dreads pursuit. Then he vanished over the hill.

"Well! Am I right?"

"Certainly, there is a boy who seems to have some secret errand."

"And what the errand is even a county **constable**⑦ could guess. But not one word shall they have from me, and I **bind**⑧ you to secrecy also, Dr. Watson.

① autocrat ['ɔ:təukræt] *n.* 专横霸道的人
② malignantly [mə'lignəntli] *ad.* 怀有恶意地

索。如果他能把掌握的情况告诉我，那我就不用花那么长的时间，那么辛苦地去追查了。但是，表示怀疑和漠不关心显然是我手上的两张王牌。

"要我说，那更有可能是某个荒原牧羊人的儿子在给他父亲送饭呢。"

态度专横的老家伙听出了一丝不同意的表示，顿时冒起火来。他的两只眼睛恶狠狠地看着我，灰白的胡须就像猫发怒时那样直竖起来。

"确确实实，先生！"他说，一边指向宽阔的荒原，"您看到远处那座黑色的岩岗了吗？啊，您看到那边长满荆棘的矮山了吗？那是整个荒原上岩石最为密布的地方。那个地方难道会有牧人居住吗？您的说法，先生，真是荒谬透顶啊。"

我态度温和地回答说，自己是因为不了解情况才这么说的。我表现出的软弱屈从，令他很是开心，结果便使得他愿意接着说下去。

"您可以肯定，先生，我在形成这种看法之前就已经掌握了充分证据。我好几次看到过那个孩子提着一包东西。一天一次，有时候一天两次，我都能——请等一等，华生医生。是我的眼睛花了，还是那山坡上现在确实有什么东西在移动呢？"

大概有几英里远的距离，但在暗绿和灰色背景的衬托之下，我能清楚地看到一个小黑点。

③ leads [ledz] *n.* （铺屋顶用的）薄铅板；铅板屋顶
④ clap [klæp] *v.* 迅速地放置
⑤ urchin ['ə:tʃin] *n.* 顽童，淘气鬼
⑥ uncouth [ʌn'ku:θ] *a.* 陌生的

"来吧，先生，快来！"弗兰克兰大声呼喊着，一边冲上楼，"您亲眼看一看，然后做出自己的判断吧。"

望远镜是个庞然大物，安装在一个三脚架上，立在房顶的铅板平台上。弗兰克兰把眼睛凑了上去，随即发出了满意的欢呼声。

"快点，华生医生，快来看，要赶在他翻过山之前啊！"

那就是他，千真万确，一个肩背着一小包东西的孩子，正费力地慢慢往山上爬。当他走到山顶时，我看到那个衣衫凌乱的陌生人在暗蓝色的天空下闪现了一下。他神色诡异地环顾了一下四周，好像是害怕有人跟踪。然后，便消失在山边了。

⑦ constable ['kʌnstəbl] *n.* 警察
⑧ bind [baind] *v.* 使成为义务

"是啊！我说得没错吧？"

Not a word! You understand!"

"Just as you wish."

"They have treated me shamefully–shamefully. When the facts come out in Frankland v. Regina I venture to think that a thrill of indignation will run through the country. Nothing would induce me to help the police in any way. For all they cared it might have been me, instead of my effigy, which these rascals burned at the stake. Surely you are not going! You will help me to empty the **decanter**[①] in honour of this great occasion!"

But I resisted all his **solicitations**[②] and succeeded in dissuading him from his announced intention of walking home with me. I kept the road as long as his eye was on me, and then I struck off across the moor and made for the stony hill over which the boy had disappeared. Everything was working in my favour, and I swore that it should not be through lack of energy or **perseverance**[③] that I should miss the chance which fortune had thrown in my way.

The sun was already sinking when I reached the summit of the hill, and the long slopes beneath me were all golden-green on one side and gray shadow on the other. A haze lay low upon the farthest sky-line, out of which jutted the fantastic shapes of Belliver and Vixen Tor. Over the wide expanse there was no sound and no movement. One great gray bird, a gull or **curlew**[④], soared aloft in the blue heaven. He and I seemed to be the only living things between the huge arch of the sky and the desert beneath it. The barren scene, the sense of loneliness, and the mystery and urgency of my task all struck a chill into my heart. The boy was nowhere to be seen. But down beneath me in a cleft of the hills there was a circle of the old stone huts, and in the middle of them there was one which retained sufficient roof to act as a screen against the weather. My heart leaped within me as I saw it. This must be the burrow where the stranger lurked. At last my foot was on the threshold of his hiding place–his secret was within my grasp.

As I approached the hut, walking as warily as Stapleton would do when with poised net he drew near the settled butterfly, I satisfied myself that the place had indeed been used as a habitation. A vague pathway among the boulders led to the **dilapidated**[⑤] opening which served as a door. All was silent within. The unknown might be lurking there, or he might be **prowling**[⑥] on

"毫无疑问，那个男孩看上去正在执行什么秘密差事。"

"连一般的乡下警察都能猜出那是什么样的差事。但是，我决不会向他们吭一声的。华生医生，我希望您也能保守秘密，不要露一点口风，您明白吧！"

"我一定按照您的意思办。"

"他们对待我有愧——有愧啊。等到弗兰克兰诉女王政府的诉讼案的内情传出时，我敢说，全国上下都会为之轰动，为之激愤。我无论如何都不会帮警察的忙，因为他们专门管住我，而对烧毁我的模拟人像的那些流氓恶棍却放任自流。您可千万别走开！您要帮我把这一瓶酒都喝光，以此来庆贺这个伟大的时刻！"

我谢绝了他的好意，同时也成功地说服了他放弃同我一道步行着回去的想法。他看到我之前，我一直走的是大路。但之后，我便离开了大路，转到了荒原上，朝那个孩子消失的那座石头山上走去。一切都对我非常有利，我对天发誓，一定不会因为自己身疲力乏和缺少毅力而错过这天赐良机。

我登上山顶时，太阳已经落山了，脚下那长长的山坡，一边是金黄草绿，一边是灰暗阴郁。苍凉的暮色笼罩着远方的天际，上面屹立着形状古怪的贝利弗岩岗和维克森岩冈。在这片广阔的地面上，毫无声息，毫无动静。一只或是鸥、或是麻鹬的大灰鸟在高高的蓝天上翱翔。在苍穹和荒原之间，似乎只有它和我两个生命体存在。荒芜的景色，孤独的感觉，加上我神秘而又紧迫的使命，令我的内心颤抖。那孩子毫无踪影了。但是，我身下的一道山沟里，一些古老的石屋围成的圆圈里，正中间，有一座石屋还保有着屋顶，足以为人避风挡雨的。我一看到屋子，心便狂跳了起来。这一定是那个可疑人的藏身之处了。我的脚步终于踏进了他藏身处的门槛——他的秘密已经在我控制的范围之内了。

我向小屋靠近时，行动谨小慎微，如同斯塔普尔顿高举捕蝶网慢慢接近停落稳当的蝴蝶。令我感到满意的是，石屋确实曾被用作居住之地。乱石间隐约可

① decanter [di'kæntə] *n.* 酒瓶

② solicitation [sə,lisi'teiʃən] *n.* 请求，恳求

③ perseverance [,pə:si'viərəns] *n.* 耐性；毅力

④ curlew ['kə:lju:] *n.* 麻鹬

⑤ dilapidated [di'læpideitid] *a.* 倾坍的

⑥ prowl [praul] *v.* （暗中）巡行于

the moor. My nerves tingled with the sense of adventure. Throwing aside my cigarette, I closed my hand upon the butt of my revolver and, walking swiftly up to the door, I looked in. The place was empty.

But there were ample signs that I had not come upon a false scent. This was certainly where the man lived. Some blankets rolled in a waterproof lay upon that very stone slab upon which neolithic man had once slumbered. The ashes of a fire were heaped in a rude grate. Beside it lay some cooking utensils and a bucket half-full of water. A litter of empty tins showed that the place had been occupied for some time, and I saw, as my eyes became accustomed to the checkered light, a **pannikin**[1] and a half-full bottle of spirits standing in the corner. In the middle of the hut a flat stone served the purpose of a table, and upon this stood a small cloth bundle–the same, no doubt, which I had seen through the telescope upon the shoulder of the boy. It contained a loaf of bread, a tinned tongue, and two tins of preserved peaches. As I set it down again, after having examined it, my heart leaped to see that beneath it there lay a sheet of paper with writing upon it. I raised it, and this was what I read, roughly scrawled in pencil: "Dr. Watson has gone to Coombe Tracey."

For a minute I stood there with the paper in my hands thinking out the meaning of this **curt**[2] message. It was I, then, and not Sir Henry, who was being dogged by this secret man. He had not followed me himself, but he had set an agent–the boy, perhaps–upon my track, and this was his report. Possibly I had taken no step since I had been upon the moor which had not been observed and reported. Always there was this feeling of an unseen force, a fine net drawn round us with infinite skill and delicacy, holding us so lightly that it was only at some supreme moment that one realized that one was indeed entangled in its **meshes**[3].

If there was one report there might be others, so I looked round the hut in search of them. There was no trace, however, of anything of the kind, nor could I discover any sign which might indicate the character or intentions of the man who lived in this singular place, save that he must be of Spartan habits and cared little for the comforts of life. When I thought of the heavy rains and looked at the gaping roof I understood how strong and **immutable**[4] must be the purpose which had kept him in that inhospitable abode. Was he our malignant

见一条小路，通向那破烂不堪、即将倒塌的当作门用的缺口，里面一片寂静。那人可能正藏匿在那里，也可能正在荒原上游荡。冒险带来的刺激令我精神为之一振。我把烟头往旁边一扔，用手紧紧地握住手枪的枪柄，迅速走到门口，朝着室内看了看，里面空空如也。

但是，室内有足够迹象说明，我并没有找错地方，这里一定是那个人的安身之所。那块新石器时代人曾经睡过的石板上，放着几条用防雨布卷包着的毛毯。在一个粗陋的石框里，烧过的灰烬堆成了堆。旁边还放着一些厨房用具，装着一半水的水桶，摆放得乱七八糟的空罐头盒。这一切都说明，那人在这个石屋里已经住了一段时间了。我的眼睛慢慢地习惯了斑驳的光线之后，看到室内的一角还立着一个金属小杯和半瓶酒。屋子的中间有一块平坦的当桌子用的石头，上面放着一个小布包，无疑就是我从望远镜里看到的小孩肩背着的那个包。包里面有一块面包，一听牛舌和两听蜜桃罐头。我把东西重新放下时，心都快跳到嗓子眼了，因为我看到下面还放着一张写了字的纸条。我把字条举起，上面用铅笔潦草地写着："华生医生已经去过库姆特雷西了。"

我手里拿着纸条足足站立了一分钟光景，心里思忖着纸条上文字的真正含义。如此看来，那个神秘的男人所要跟踪的人不是亨利爵士，而是我本人。而且，还不是他本人跟踪我，而是指派了另外一个人——说不定就是那个孩子——来跟踪我，纸条就是孩子写的报告。很有可能自从我到荒原以来，我的一举一动都在他的监视之下，都被他报告上去了。我一直有一种感觉，觉得有一股看不见的力量像一张紧密的网把我们团团包围住，手法精湛娴熟，神奇微妙，令我们感觉不到巨大的约束力，以致只有到了极其紧要的时刻，我们才知道自己确实被缠在网中了。

既然有了这么一份报告，那就可能还有另外一些，因此，我就把屋子找了个遍。但是，没有发现任何纸条一类的东西，也没有发现任何能够显示住在这个奇怪地方的人的性格特点和意图的痕迹。我只能确定一点：他

① pannikin ['pænikin] *n.* 金属小杯

② curt [kə:t] *a.* 简短的

③ mesh [meʃ] *n.* 网眼

④ immutable [i'mju:təbl] *a.* 不可改变的

enemy, or was he by chance our guardian angel? I swore that I would not leave the hut until I knew.

Outside the sun was sinking low and the west was blazing with scarlet and gold. Its reflection was shot back in ruddy patches by the distant pools which lay amid the great Grimpen Mire. There were the two towers of Baskerville Hall, and there a distant blur of smoke which marked the village of Grimpen. Between the two, behind the hill, was the house of the Stapletons. All was sweet and mellow and peaceful in the golden evening light, and yet as I looked at them my soul shared none of the peace of Nature but quivered at the vagueness and the terror of that interview which every instant was bringing nearer. With tingling nerves but a fixed purpose, I sat in the dark recess of the hut and waited with sombre patience for the coming of its tenant.

And then at last I heard him. Far away came the sharp clink of a boot striking upon a stone. Then another and yet another, coming nearer and nearer. I shrank back into the darkest corner and **cocked**^① the pistol in my pocket, determined not to discover myself until I had an opportunity of seeing something of the stranger. There was a long pause which showed that he had stopped. Then once more the footsteps approached and a shadow fell across the opening of the hut.

"It is a lovely evening, my dear Watson," said a well-known voice. "I really think that you will be more comfortable outside than in."

一定有个斯巴达人式的习惯，几乎不在意生活是否舒适。我想起那天的倾盆大雨，看了看这张着大口的屋顶，便知道他能在这种条件恶劣的地方住下来，一定有一个异常强烈的矢志不移的目标。他是我们凶狠的敌人，还是我们的保护天使呢？我暗自发誓，在调查清楚之前，绝不离开这座石屋。

室外，太阳已经落下山了，西边的天际闪烁着金色的落日余晖，洒落在远处格林彭大泥潭中的水洼上，水面反射出点点红光。可以看到巴斯克维尔庄园的两幢塔楼，看到远处一片标示着格林彭村所在地的朦胧的烟雾。斯塔普尔顿家的别墅就在这两者之间的一座小山后面。在金黄色余晖的照耀下，一切都是那样美好宜人，平和静谧。但是，当我看着眼前的景物时，心里非但感受不到一点大自然的宁静，相反，因为与那人的会面越来越近，我心里不禁茫然，害怕得发颤。神情紧张，但目标坚定，我坐在小屋里一个黑暗的角落，耐心地等待主人的归来。

后来，我终于听到他的动静了。他的皮靴踩在石头上发出的嘎吱声，一声接一声，越来越近。我蜷缩在室内一个黑暗的角落里，手伸进口袋扳起手枪的扳机，决定在看到陌生人之前不暴露自己。这时，脚步声停顿了好一阵子，说明那人站住不动了。后来，脚步声再次响起，一个黑影投射在石屋的开口处。

"这真是个美丽的黄昏啊，亲爱的华生，"一个熟悉的声音说，"我真的认为，你到外面来会比待在里面舒服得多啊。"

① cock[kɔk] v. 扣扳机准备发射

Chapter 12   Death on the Moor

For a moment or two I sat breathless, hardly able to believe my ears. Then my senses and my voice came back to me, while a **crushing**[①] weight of responsibility seemed in an instant to be lifted from my soul. That cold, **incisive**[②], ironical voice could belong to but one man in all the world.

"Holmes!" I cried–"Holmes!"

"Come out," said he, "and please be careful with the revolver."

I stooped under the rude lintel, and there he sat upon a stone outside, his gray eyes dancing with amusement as they fell upon my astonished features. He was thin and worn, but clear and alert, his keen face bronzed by the sun and roughened by the wind. In his tweed suit and cloth cap he looked like any other tourist upon the moor, and he had contrived, with that **catlike**[③] love of personal cleanliness which was one of his characteristics, that his chin should be as smooth and his linen as perfect as if he were in Baker Street.

"I never was more glad to see anyone in my life," said I as I wrung him by the hand.

"Or more astonished, eh?"

"Well, I must confess to it."

"The surprise was not all on one side, I assure you. I had no idea that you had found my occasional **retreat**[④], still less that you were inside it, until I was within twenty paces of the door."

"My footprint, I presume?"

"No, Watson; I fear that I could not **undertake**[⑤] to recognize your footprint

第十二章 命丧荒原

一时间，我坐着喘不过气来，简直无法相信自己的耳朵。然后才恢复了神智，能够说话了，同时感觉到，一直压在自己心头的重任好像顷刻间给卸了下来。刚才的声音只能属于世界上唯一的一个人，沉静冷漠，深沉尖锐，嘲讽揶揄。

"福尔摩斯！"我大声喊着——"福尔摩斯！"

"出来吧，"他说，"当心手枪啊。"

我弓着身子走出简陋的门楣，一眼看见福尔摩斯坐在屋外的石头上。他看见我惊讶的表情时，灰色的眼睛里充满了欢快的神色。他又瘦又憔悴，但仍然清醒而机警。他的脸被太阳晒成了古铜色，被风吹得粗糙了。他身穿格子呢套装，头戴布帽，看上去和荒原上的旅行者没有什么两样。他依旧像猫爱整洁那样保持个人的卫生，这是他的一个性格特点。他的下巴光溜溜的，身上的亚麻布衬衣笔挺，同他住在贝克大街时完全一样。

"我生平见了谁，都没有像此时见你这么高兴啊。"我说着，一边紧紧地握着他的手。

"也从来没有感觉这样惊讶吧，呃？"

"是啊，这一点我必须承认。"

"惊讶可不是单方面的，我实话告诉你。没想到，你竟然找到了我的临时栖身处，更想不到你会躲在里面，直到我离门口不到二十步远的时候，我才发现呢。"

"我猜，是因为我的脚印吧？"

"不，华生，世界上有的是脚印，我恐怕还不能从中

① crushing ['krʌʃiŋ] *a.* 压倒的；使人受不了的

② incisive [in'saisiv] *a.* 敏锐的，尖锐的

③ catlike ['kætlaik] *a.* 似猫的

④ retreat [ri'tri:t] *n.* 隐居处

⑤ undertake [ˌʌndə'teik] *v.* 许诺；保证

amid all the footprints of the world. If you seriously desire to deceive me you must change your **tobacconist**①; for when I see the stub of a cigarette marked Bradley, Oxford Street, I know that my friend Watson is in the neighbourhood. You will see it there beside the path. You threw it down, no doubt, at that supreme moment when you charged into the empty hut."

"Exactly."

"I thought as much–and knowing your admirable **tenacity**② I was convinced that you were sitting in ambush, a weapon within reach, waiting for the tenant to return. So you actually thought that I was the criminal?"

"I did not know who you were, but I was determined to find out."

"Excellent, Watson! And how did you **localize**③ me? You saw me, perhaps, on the night of the convict hunt, when I was so imprudent as to allow the moon to rise behind me?"

"Yes, I saw you then."

"And have no doubt searched all the huts until you came to this one?"

"No, your boy had been observed, and that gave me a guide where to look."

"The old gentleman with the telescope, no doubt. I could not make it out when first I saw the light flashing upon the lens." He rose and peeped into the hut. "Ha, I see that Cartwright has brought up some supplies. What's this paper? So you have been to Coombe Tracey, have you?"

"Yes."

"To see Mrs. Laura Lyons?"

"Exactly."

"Well done! Our researches have evidently been running on parallel lines, and when we unite our results I expect we shall have a fairly full knowledge of the case."

"Well, I am glad from my heart that you are here, for indeed the responsibility and the mystery were both becoming too much for my nerves. But how in the name of wonder did you come here, and what have you been doing? I thought that you were in Baker Street working out that case of blackmailing."

"That was what I wished you to think."

"Then you use me, and yet do not trust me!" I cried with some bitterness. "I think that I have deserved better at your hands, Holmes."

① tobacconist [təˈbækənist]
　　n. 烟草制品零售商

② tenacity [tiˈnæsiti] *n.* 坚
　　持，固执，顽强

③ localize [ˈləukəlaiz] *v.* 确
　　定…的地点

把你的辨认出来。如果你真的想要蒙混我，你就得把自己抽的香烟牌子换一换，因为我一看到牛津大街的布莱德雷商行的标识，就知道我的朋友华生就在附近。在小路边发现了烟头，毫无疑问，那是你冲进这幢空屋时扔下的。"

"一点没错。"

"我就觉得是这样的——由于知道你有坚韧不拔的性格，令人敬佩，我坚信，你一定坐在暗处，还带着手枪，等待着主人返回。这么说，你真的认为我就是那逃犯了？"

"我并不知道你是什么人，但决心要查个究竟。"

"好极了，华生！你是如何确定我的位置的？可能是你们抓逃犯的那天晚上你看到我了吧？我当晚太大意了，让身后升起的月亮照着了我。"

"是啊，我当时看见你了。"

"你肯定找遍了所有石屋，这才找到了这一座吧？"

"不，你雇的那个男孩被人发现了，我也因而知道了寻找的范围。"

"毫无疑问，是那个有架望远镜的老绅士。我最初看见镜片的反光时，还弄不清是怎么回事。"他站起身，朝小屋里瞥了一眼。"哈，我看卡特赖特又给我送吃用物品了。纸条上写了什么？这么说，你已经去过库姆特雷西了，对吧？"

"对啊。"

"去见劳拉·莱昂斯太太吗？"

"一点不错。"

"干得漂亮！很显然，我们两个人的调查是平行进行的。我认为，只要我们把结果汇总一下，就能对本案有个比较全面的了解。"

"对啊，你到这儿来了，我感到由衷地高兴，因为本案确实扑朔迷离，而且我肩负的责任重大，感觉自己的神经都受不了了。不过，你究竟是怎样神奇地降临到这个地方来的呢？你来后都干了什么呢？我以为你还在贝克大街处理那件敲诈勒索案呢。"

"我就是希望你这样想。"

"这么说来，你用我，但又不信任我！"我觉得很委屈，便大声说着，"我认为，自己在你手下应该得到更多的赏识才是啊，福尔摩斯。"

"My dear fellow, you have been invaluable to me in this as in many other cases, and I beg that you will forgive me if I have seemed to play a trick upon you. In truth, it was partly for your own sake that I did it, and it was my appreciation of the danger which you ran which led me to come down and examine the matter for myself. Had I been with Sir Henry and you it is confident that my point of view would have been the same as yours, and my presence would have warned our very **formidable**① opponents to be **on their guard**②. As it is, I have been able to get about as I could not possibly have done had I been living in the Hall, and I remain an unknown factor in the business, ready to **throw in all my weight**③ at a critical moment."

"But why keep me in the dark?"

"For you to know could not have helped us and might possibly have led to my discovery. You would have wished to tell me something, or in your kindness you would have brought me out some comfort or other, and so an unnecessary risk would be run. I brought Cartwright down with me–you remember the little chap at the express office–and he has seen after my simple wants: a loaf of bread and a clean collar. What does man want more? He has given me an extra pair of eyes upon a very active pair of feet, and both have been invaluable."

"Then my reports have all been wasted!"–My voice trembled as I recalled the pains and the pride with which I had composed them.

Holmes took a bundle of papers from his pocket.

"Here are your reports, my dear fellow, and very well **thumbed**④, I assure you. I made excellent arrangements, and they are only delayed one day upon their way. I must compliment you exceedingly upon the zeal and the intelligence which you have shown over an extraordinarily difficult case."

I was still rather **raw**⑤ over the deception which had been practised upon me, but the warmth of Holmes's praise drove my anger from my mind. I felt also in my heart that he was right in what he said and that it was really best for our purpose that I should not have known that he was upon the moor.

"That's better," said he, seeing the shadow rise from my face. "And now tell me the result of your visit to Mrs. Laura Lyons–it was not difficult for me to guess that it was to see her that you had gone, for I am already aware that she is

"亲爱的朋友啊，你在本案中对我的帮助和你在其他案件中的一样，都是无法估量的。如果说这一次你觉得，我在你面前玩了心眼儿，请你务必原谅。实际上，我这么做的一部分原因是替你考虑，正因为我意识到了你所面临的危险，这才亲自赶过来调查案情的。如果我和亨利爵士还有你待在一块儿的话，那我的看法就会和你们的一样，而且我的出现无疑会提醒我们那可怕的对手，让他提高警惕。实际上，我一直在四处走动，但如果我住在庄园里，那我就可能根本做不到。此外，我在这件事情中始终是个不为人知的角色，在紧要关头时我随时可以全力以赴。"

"但是，你为何让我也蒙在鼓里呢？"

"因为即便你知道了，那也对我们不会有什么帮助，说不定还会把我给暴露出来。你可能会想把一些情况告诉我，或者是出于好心，想给我送点这样或那样的东西，以便让我过得更加舒适一些，这样势必会带来不必要的风险。我带来了卡特赖特——你记得的，那个信差事务所送信的少年，要他满足我的简单需求：一块面包，一套干净衣服。除此之外，一个男人还需要什么呢？有了他，我就等于多了两只眼睛，多了一双勤快的脚，他简直是个无价之宝啊。"

"这么说来，我给你写的报告全都白费力气了！"——我回想起写报告时的艰辛与自豪，说话的声音不禁有些颤抖。

福尔摩斯从自己的衣服口袋里掏出一卷信件。

"这就是你报告的信件，好伙计，我可以向你保证，我反复看了好多遍呢。我做了精心的安排，信件在路上只会耽搁一天的时间。这是一桩古怪离奇的疑难案件，你在其中表现出了满腔热忱和聪明才智，我要向你表示崇高的敬意。"

我还在为自己受到蒙骗而愤愤不平。但是，福尔摩斯的这番赞扬却令我倍感温馨，驱散了心中的怨气。我打心眼里觉得，他的话很有道理，他没有把自己到达荒原的事告诉给我，对我们实现自己的目标大有好处。

"这样反而更好，"他看到我脸上的阴云消散后说，"你这就把你去库姆特雷西寻访劳拉·莱昂斯太太的情

① formidable ['fɔ:midəbl] a. 可怕的，令人畏惧的
② on one's guard 警惕，提防
③ throw in all one's weight 全力以赴
④ thumb [θʌm] v. 用拇指翻动（书页）
⑤ raw [rɔ:] a. 刺痛的

the one person in Coombe Tracey who might be of service to us in the matter. In fact, if you had not gone to-day it is exceedingly probable that I should have gone to-morrow."

The sun had set and dusk was settling over the moor. The air had turned chill and we withdrew into the hut for warmth. There, sitting together in the twilight, I told Holmes of my conversation with the lady. So interested was he that I had to repeat some of it twice before he was satisfied.

"This is most important," said he when I had concluded. "It fills up a gap which I had been unable to bridge in this most complex affair. You are aware, perhaps, that a close intimacy exists between this lady and the man Stapleton?"

"I did not know of a close intimacy."

"There can be no doubt about the matter. They meet, they write, there is a complete understanding between them. Now, this puts a very powerful weapon into our hands. If I could only use it to **detach**[①] his wife ——"

"His wife?"

"I am giving you some information now, in return for all that you have given me. The lady who has **passed**[②] here as Miss Stapleton is in reality his wife."

"Good heavens, Holmes! Are you sure of what you say? How could he have permitted Sir Henry to fall in love with her?"

"Sir Henry's falling in love could do no harm to anyone except Sir Henry. He took particular care that Sir Henry did not *make* love to her, as you have yourself observed. I repeat that the lady is his wife and not his sister."

"But why this **elaborate**[③] deception?"

"Because he foresaw that she would be very much more useful to him in the character of a free woman."

All my unspoken instincts, my vague suspicions, suddenly took shape and centred upon the naturalist. In that impassive, colourless man, with his straw hat and his butterfly-net, I seemed to see something terrible–a creature of infinite patience and craft, with a smiling face and a murderous heart.

"It is he, then, who is our enemy–it is he who dogged us in London?"

"So I read the riddle."

况同我说说吧。我毫不费力就猜到了，你去那里就是去找她的，因为我已经意识到了：在整个库姆特雷西，这件事情能够帮上忙的就只有她了。实际上，如果你今天没去见她，我很可能明天就该去找她了。"

太阳已经落山了，荒原上暮色四合。空气变得凛冽了起来，我们退回到了小屋取暖。暮色中，我们一同坐着，我把同那位女士交谈的内容全部告诉了福尔摩斯。他兴致勃勃，有些情况我还得重复说，他才满意。

"这个情况十分重要，"我刚一说完，他就说，"正好把这桩异乎寻常的案件中我无法连接的缺口给填补上了。你或许已经知道了，那位女士和斯塔普尔顿之间关系很亲密，对吧？"

"我并不知道他们之间关系亲密。"

"这个情况确切无疑，他们平常见面，书信来往，达成了某种默契。我们现在掌握了这一点，就等于手上多了一件利器。如果我利用这一点来离间他和他夫人——"

"他夫人？"

"你给我提供了那么多的信息，作为回报，我也告诉你一些情况。那个在这儿充当斯塔普尔顿小姐的女士实际上是他夫人。"

"天哪，福尔摩斯！你确定你刚才说的是真实的吗？那他怎么可能允许亨利爵士爱上自己的夫人呢？"

"亨利爵士坠入情网这件事情伤不着别的任何人，只会伤到亨利爵士本人。他特别小心提防着，不让亨利爵士对自己的夫人求爱。这一点想必你已经注意到了吧。我再说一遍，那位女士不是他的妹妹，而是他夫人。"

"但是，他为何要处心积虑设置这样一场骗局呢？"

"因为他预想到了，让她充当一个未婚女子对他更有帮助。"

突然之间，我的种种无法言说的感觉，模模糊糊的疑惑，全都明朗起来，全都集中在了那位生物学家的身上，正是他，头戴着草帽，手拿着扑蝶网兜，不动声色，毫无个性。我从他身上似乎看到了某种可怕的东西——充满耐心，诡异狡诈，笑里藏刀，口蜜腹剑。

"这么说来，他就是我们的对手——在伦敦盯我们

① detach [di'tætʃ] v. 使分离

② pass [pɑ:s] v. 被接受；被承认

③ elaborate [i'læbərət] a. 精心设计的

"And the warning–it must have come from her!"

"Exactly."

The shape of some monstrous villainy, half seen, half guessed, loomed through the darkness which had **girt**① me so long.

"But are you sure of this, Holmes? How do you know that the woman is his wife?"

"Because he so far forgot himself as to tell you a true piece of autobiography upon the occasion when he first met you, and I dare say he has many a time regretted it since. He was once a schoolmaster in the north of England. Now, there is no one more easy to trace than a schoolmaster. There are **scholastic**② agencies by which one may identify any man who has been in the profession. A little investigation showed me that a school had come to grief under **atrocious**③ circumstances, and that the man who had owned it–the name was different–had disappeared with his wife. The descriptions agreed. When I learned that the missing man was devoted to **entomology**④ the identification was complete."

The darkness was rising, but much was still hidden by the shadows.

"If this woman is in truth his wife, where does Mrs. Laura Lyons come in?" I asked.

"That is one of the points upon which your own researches have shed a light. Your interview with the lady has cleared the situation very much. I did not know about a **projected**⑤ divorce between herself and her husband. In that case, regarding Stapleton as an unmarried man, she counted no doubt upon becoming his wife."

"And when she is undeceived?"

"Why, then we may find the lady of service. It must be our first duty to see her–both of us–to-morrow. Don't you think, Watson, that you are away from your charge rather long? Your place should be at Baskerville Hall."

The last red streaks had faded away in the west and night had settled upon the moor. A few faint stars were gleaming in a violet sky.

"One last question, Holmes," I said as I rose. "Surely there is no need of secrecy between you and me. What is the meaning of it all? What is he after?"

Holmes's voice sank as he answered:

① girt [gə:t] v. 围绕，包围

② scholastic [skə'læstik] a. 学校的；学术的

③ atrocious [ə'trəuʃəs] a. 恶劣的，差的，次的

④ entomology [,entə'mɔlədʒi] n. 昆虫学

⑤ projected ['prɔdʒektid] a. 计划中的

梢的也正是他啦？"

"我认为，这就是谜底。"

"还有那道警示———一定是她发的！"

"一点没错。"

这么长时间以来，我被若隐若现、半蒙半猜的鬼魅般的罪行所蒙蔽，它现在终于透过重重黑暗慢慢地露出了原形。

"但是，你对此有把握吗，福尔摩斯？你怎么知道那个女人就是他夫人呢？"

"因为他头一次遇见你时，便得意忘形了，竟然给你讲了他自己的一段真实经历。我敢说，他事后对此肯定是后悔不已。他从前曾在英格兰北部地区当过一所学校的校长。现在要查个学校校长，可比查什么人都更容易啊。通过教育机构，就能查出任何做过教育工作的人。我稍稍调查了一下，就了解到曾有一所学校，由于管理不善倒闭了，而那个学校的校长——是另外一个名字，同他的夫人一同不见了人影。夫妇两人的相貌特征和我们看到的这对夫妇也很吻合。当我获悉那个失踪的男人也热衷于昆虫学时，鉴定身份的工作至此就圆满结束了。"

云雾已经开始消散，但许多真相依旧隐藏在阴影之中。

"如果那个女人真是他夫人，那劳拉·莱昂斯太太又怎么会涉足进来呢？"我问。

"这是你自己的调查已经解释清楚了的问题之一。你对她的走访已经把事情搞得很明了了。我之前不知道她和她的丈夫有离婚的企图。如果确有其事，而且她以为斯塔普尔顿未婚，那她无疑指望自己能够做他的夫人。"

"但是，一旦她明白了真相呢？"

"啊，到那时，那位女士就可能会为我们所用了。我们当务之急就是明天去看她——我们两人都去。你难道不觉得，华生，自己离开岗位太久了吗？你本应该待在巴斯克维尔庄园的。"最后一道红光消失在了西边，夜幕已经笼罩在荒原上了。紫色的天空中微微地闪烁着几颗星星。

"最后一个问题，福尔摩斯，"我说，一边站起身，"我们之间肯定是没必要保密的。他这么做到底是什么意思？他究竟想要得到什么呢？"

福尔摩斯回答时声音低沉：

"It is murder, Watson–refined, cold-blooded, deliberate murder. Do not ask me for particulars. My nets are closing upon him, even as his are upon Sir Henry, and with your help he is already almost at my mercy. There is but one danger which can threaten us. It is that he should strike before we are ready to do so. Another day–two at the most–and I have my case complete, but until then guard your charge as closely as ever a fond mother watched her ailing child. Your mission to–day has justified itself, and yet I could almost wish that you had not left his side. Hark!"

A terrible scream–a prolonged yell of horror and anguish burst out of the silence of the moor. That frightful cry turned the blood to ice in my veins.

"Oh, my God!" I gasped. "What is it? What does it mean?"

Holmes had sprung to his feet, and I saw his dark, athletic outline at the door of the hut, his shoulders stooping, his head thrust forward, his face peering into the darkness.

"Hush!" he whispered. "Hush!"

The cry had been loud on account of its **vehemence**[①], but it had **pealed out**[②] from somewhere far off on the shadowy plain. Now it burst upon our ears, nearer, louder, more urgent than before.

"Where is it?" Holmes whispered; and I knew from the thrill of his voice that he, the man of iron, was shaken to the soul. "Where is it, Watson?"

"There, I think." I pointed into the darkness.

"No, there!"

Again the agonized cry swept through the silent night, louder and much nearer than ever. And a new sound mingled with it, a deep, muttered **rumble**[③], musical and yet menacing, rising and falling like the low, constant murmur of the sea.

"The hound!" cried Holmes. "Come, Watson, come! Great heavens, if we are too late!"

He had started running swiftly over the moor, and I had followed at his heels. But now from somewhere among the broken ground immediately in front of us there came one last despairing yell, and then a dull, heavy thud. We halted and listened. Not another sound broke the heavy silence of the windless night.

"这是桩谋杀案，华生——设计巧妙，残忍无情，处心积虑。具体的细节就别再问我了。正如他的网兜罩住了亨利爵士一样，我的网也紧紧地围住了他。加上你的协助，他几乎已经是我的瓮中之鳖了。我们担心出现的危险就只有一个了，那就是他会在我们采取行动之前先行下手。还有一天——最多两天——我这边的准备工作就会完成。但在此之前，你要像慈爱的母亲看护自己生病的孩子那样紧紧地看好你所要保护的人。事实证明，你今天所做的事是没有错的。但我还是不禁想到，如果你没有离开他就好了。听！"

一声可怕的尖叫——声音拖得很长，惊恐而愤怒，打破了荒原的寂静。尖叫声令我全身的血液都凝固了。

"噢，上帝啊！"我喘不过气来，"那是什么声音？怎么回事？"

福尔摩斯霍地站起身，我随即便看到他运动员般的身影冲到了石屋门口，他压低双肩，把头往前探，朝着黑暗中张望。

"嘘！"他低声说，"不要出声！"

刚才的声音之所以响亮，是因为发出时声嘶力竭。但是，听起来像是从黑暗的荒原远处传来的。此时，叫声又在我们的耳畔响起，比先前更加临近，更加响亮，更加急促。

"哪边传过来的？"福尔摩斯低声问了一句，我听到他的声音发颤，就明白尽管他平时是个具有钢铁般意志的人，但此时，他也深受震撼了，"华生，哪边传过来的？"

"我觉得，是那边。"我指向黑暗之中。

"我看是那边！"

痛苦的惨叫声再一次响彻了静谧的夜空，声音越来越响亮，比先前临近了很多。其中混杂着一种新的声音，低沉含混的咕哝声，听起来虽然悦耳，但充满了阴险，一起一落的，犹如大海低沉持续的低吟声。

"是猎犬！"福尔摩斯大喊着，"快来，华生，快来，天哪，我们要赶不及了！"

他急忙冲向荒原，我则紧跟其后。就在这个当儿，我们正前方不远处的坑洼不平的小路上，传来了最后一声令人撕心裂肺的惨叫，接着便是沉闷的重物倒地的声

① vehemence ['vi:iməns] n. 剧烈，激烈
② peal out 发出响亮的声音

③ rumble ['rʌmbl] n. 咕哝声

I saw Holmes put his hand to his forehead like a man distracted. He stamped his feet upon the ground.

"He has beaten us, Watson. We are too late."

"No, no, surely not!"

"Fool that I was to **hold my hand**①. And you, Watson, see what comes of abandoning your charge! But, by Heaven, if the worst has happened we'll avenge him!"

Blindly we ran through the gloom, **blundering**② against boulders, forcing our way through **gorse**③ bushes, panting up hills and rushing down slopes, heading always in the direction whence those dreadful sounds had come. At every rise Holmes looked eagerly round him, but the shadows were thick upon the moor, and nothing moved upon its dreary face.

"Can you see anything?"

"Nothing."

"But, hark, what is that?"

A low moan had fallen upon our ears. There it was again upon our left! On that side a ridge of rocks ended in a sheer cliff which overlooked a stone-strewn slope. On its jagged face was **spread-eagled**④ some dark, irregular object. As we ran towards it the vague outline hardened into a definite shape. It was a **prostrate**⑤ man face downward upon the ground, the head doubled under him at a horrible angle, the shoulders rounded and the body hunched together as if in the act of throwing a **somersault**⑥. So **grotesque**⑦ was the attitude that I could not for the instant realize that that moan had been the passing of his soul. Not a whisper, not a rustle, rose now from the dark figure over which we stooped. Holmes laid his hand upon him and held it up again with an exclamation of horror. The gleam of the match which he struck shone upon his **clotted**⑧ fingers and upon the ghastly pool which widened slowly from the crushed skull of the victim. And it shone upon something else which turned our hearts sick and faint within us–the body of Sir Henry Baskerville!

There was no chance of either of us forgetting that peculiar ruddy tweed suit–the very one which he had worn on the first morning that we had seen him in Baker Street. We caught the one clear glimpse of it, and then the match flickered and went out, even as the hope had gone out of

音。我们停下脚步，仔细聆听。但无风的夜晚恢复了其深沉的寂静，毫无半点声息。

我看到福尔摩斯神色紧张，把手摁在前额上，两脚拼命跺着地。

"他击败我们了，华生，我们晚了一步。"

"不，不会的，一定不会的！"

"我迟迟没有动手，真是个笨蛋。还有你，华生，你现在明白擅离职守酿成什么后果了吧！但是，天哪！如果发生了最坏的事情，我们一定要对他施行报复！"

我们在黑暗中向前乱跑，撞到乱石上，强行穿过荆棘丛，气喘吁吁地跑上一个山坡，再沿着另一个斜坡往下冲。但我们一直向着那些恐怖声音传来的方向。每次一到山顶，福尔摩斯总是焦急地四处张望。但荒原上漆黑异常，没有任何东西在这荒凉的地面上移动。

"你看到什么了吗？"

"没有。"

"但是，你听，那是什么声音？"

低沉的呻吟声传到了我们的耳畔。那声音又是在我们的左边！那边有一条岩脊，尽头处是陡直的悬崖，从那往下可以看到一个多石的山坡。在那高低不平的地面上，平躺着一堆黑乎乎的形状不规则的东西。我们跑近时，模糊的轮廓越来越明确。原来是个脸朝下倒在地上的人，他的头折叠在身体下面，惨不忍睹，肩膀和身体蜷缩成一团，就像正在做翻跟斗的动作似的。如此怪异的姿势，我一时间没有反应过来，我们刚才听到的呻吟声表示他已魂魄归天了。我们弓身看着眼前黑乎乎的躯体，一声不响，一动不动。福尔摩斯用手碰了碰尸体，接着又缩了回来，惊恐地大叫了一声。他擦亮了一根火柴，亮光照出了他瘦骨嶙峋的手指，也照亮了一滩可怕的东西，因死者的颅骨被击碎，那滩东西慢慢扩大了。火柴的亮光还照亮了另外一件东西，令我们痛心疾首，几乎晕倒——亨利·巴斯克维尔爵士的尸体！

我们两个人都不可能忘记那身款式奇特、略带红色的苏格兰粗呢套装——那正是我们在贝克大街第一次见到他时，他穿在身上的衣服。我们刚看清楚了一眼，火柴的亮光闪烁了几下便熄灭了，就像我们心中的希望之

---

① hold one's hand 迟迟不动手

② blunder ['blʌndə] v. 慌乱地走

③ gorse [gɔ:s] n. 金雀花；荆豆

④ spread-eagle ['spred,i:gl] v. 四肢张开着躺卧

⑤ prostrate ['prɔstreit] a. 俯卧的

⑥ somersault ['sʌməsɔ:lt] n. 筋斗

⑦ grotesque [grəu'tesk] a. 怪异的

⑧ clotted [klɔtid] v. 凝结的

our souls. Holmes groaned, and his face glimmered white through the darkness.

"The brute! the brute!" I cried with **clenched**^① hands. "Oh Holmes, I shall never forgive myself for having left him to his fate."

"I am more to blame than you, Watson. In order to have my case well rounded and complete, I have thrown away the life of my client. It is the greatest blow which has befallen me in my career. But how could I know–how could l know–that he would risk his life alone upon the moor in the face of all my warnings?"

"That we should have heard his screams–my God, those screams!–and yet have been unable to save him! Where is this brute of a hound which drove him to his death? It may be lurking among these rocks at this instant. And Stapleton, where is he? He shall **answer for**^② this deed."

"He shall. I will see to that. Uncle and nephew have been murdered– the one frightened to death by the very sight of a beast which he thought to be supernatural, the other driven to his end in his wild flight to escape from it. But now we have to prove the connection between the man and the beast. Save from what we heard, we cannot even swear to the existence of the latter, since Sir Henry has evidently died from the fall. But, by heavens, cunning as he is, the fellow shall be in my power before another day is past!"

We stood with bitter hearts on either side of the **mangled**^③ body, overwhelmed by this sudden and **irrevocable**^④ disaster which had brought all our long and weary labours to so piteous an end. Then as the moon rose we climbed to the top of the rocks over which our poor friend had fallen, and from the summit we gazed out over the shadowy moor, half silver and half gloom. Far away, miles off, in the direction of Grimpen, a single steady yellow light was shining. It could only come from the lonely abode of the Stapletons. With a bitter curse I shook my fist at it as I gazed.

"Why should we not seize him at once?"

"Our case is not complete. The fellow is wary and cunning to the last degree. It is not what we know, but what we can prove. If we make one false move the villain may escape us yet."

① clenched [klentʃt] *a.*握紧的

② answer for 为…受罚

③ mangled ['mæŋgld] *a.* 血肉模糊的
④ irrevocable [i'revəkəbl] *a.* 不能挽回的

光熄灭了一样。福尔摩斯呻吟着，脸色煞白，在黑暗中若隐若现。

"畜生！畜生！"我大声诅咒着，紧握着双拳，"啊，福尔摩斯，我永远都无法原谅自己，我竟然离开了他，让他惨遭厄运。"

"我的过错比你的还要大呢，华生。我为了全方位地做好侦破的准备工作，竟然将自己嘱托人的性命弃之不顾。这是我整个事业中受到的最惨重的打击。但是，我怎么能想到——我怎么能想到——他会对我所有的警示置若罔闻，竟然冒着生命危险独自跑到荒原上来呢？"

"真没有想到，我们竟然听到了他凄惨的喊叫声——上帝啊，那要命的喊叫声——但我们竟然救不了他！那条把他置于死地的猎犬到哪儿去了呢？那畜生此刻可能就潜藏在这乱石堆里呢。还有斯塔普尔顿，他现在在哪里呢？他一定要为此付出代价。"

"那是一定的。我保证找他算账。伯侄二人都惨遭谋害——一个是亲眼看到了那条畜生，以为那是魔怪化身，被活活吓死了。另一个是拼命逃跑，最终也难逃死亡的厄运。不过现在，我们必须要证明那人和那畜生之间的关系。要不是我们听到了声音，我们甚至都无法肯定那条畜生的存在，因为亨利爵士显然是摔死的。不过，上帝有眼，即便他再狡猾，我也要让他在明天之内落入我的手掌！"

我们两个人伫立在血肉模糊的尸体两边，痛心疾首，目睹着眼前突如其来的不可逆转的惨剧。没想到我们这么长时间以来奔波劳累竟然落得个如此悲惨的结局。少顷，月亮升起来了，我们爬上了我们不幸的朋友摔倒的岩岗顶端，站在最高处，眺望着幽暗的荒原，黑暗中亮着些许银色的月光。几英里外格林彭的方向，亮着唯一一点橘黄色的灯光。只有一种可能性：那是孤单的斯塔普尔顿家的灯火。我看着那灯光，不由得对它挥舞着拳头，恶狠狠地诅咒着。

"我们为何不立刻把他抓起来呢？"

"本案揭底的时机还不成熟。那家伙精明狡诈，关键不在于我们掌握了什么情况，而是我们能够拿出什么样的证据。我们一旦走错了一步，那恶棍就会从我们手

"What can we do?"

"There will be plenty for us to do to-morrow. To-night we can only perform the last offices to our poor friend."

Together we made our way down the **precipitous**① slope and approached the body, black and clear against the silvered stones. The agony of those contorted limbs struck me with a **spasm**② of pain and blurred my eyes with tears.

"We must send for help, Holmes! We cannot carry him all the way to the Hall. Good heavens, are you mad?"

He had uttered a cry and bent over the body. Now he was dancing and laughing and wringing my hand. Could this be my stern, self-contained friend? These were hidden fires, indeed!

"A beard! A beard! The man has a beard!"

"A beard?"

"It is not the baronet–it is–why, it is my neighbour, the convict!"

With feverish haste we had turned the body over, and that dripping beard was pointing up to the cold, clear moon. There could be no doubt about the **beetling**③ forehead, the sunken animal eyes. It was indeed the same face which had glared upon me in the light of the candle from over the rock–the face of Selden, the criminal.

Then in an instant it was all clear to me. I remembered how the baronet had told me that he had handed his old wardrobe to Barrymore. Barrymore had passed it on in order to help Selden in his escape. Boots, shirt, cap–it was all Sir Henry's. The tragedy was still black enough, but this man had at least deserved death by the laws of his country. I told Holmes how the matter stood, my heart bubbling over with thankfulness and joy.

"Then the clothes have been the poor devil's death," said he. "It is clear enough that the hound has been laid on from some article of Sir Henry's–the boot which was abstracted in the hotel, in all probability–and so ran this man down. There is one very singular thing, however: How came Selden, in the darkness, to know that the hound was **on his trail**④?"

"He heard him."

"To hear a hound upon the moor would not work a hard man like this

上逃脱。"

"那我们能怎么办？"

"我们明天有很多事情要做。今晚就只能给这位不幸的朋友料理后事了。"

我们一同择路从陡坡上下来，走到尸体旁边，在反射着银光的石头的衬托下，黑色的尸身显得更加清晰了。他的四肢扭曲变形，当时一定痛苦异常了。我看后痛心疾首，双眼噙满了泪水，视线模糊。

"我们必须得叫人来帮忙，福尔摩斯，我们两个人没法把他一路抬回庄园。天啊，你疯了吗？"

我话还没说完，福尔摩斯早已大叫一声，弯身对着尸体。一时间，他手舞足蹈，哈哈大笑，拽着我的手不停地摇晃。眼前是我那位态度严肃、稳健持重的朋友吗？真正是蕴藏在内心的怒火迸发了啊！

"胡子！胡子！此人蓄着胡子！"

"蓄着胡子？"

"这么说来，他不是从男爵——那他是——天哪，他是我的邻居，那个犯人！"

我们心急火燎，迅速把尸体翻转过来，鲜血淋淋的胡须正对着清冷的月亮翘起。毫无疑问，看那凸出的前额，深陷的恶毒的眼睛。确实，曾经在烛光之下，从岩石上面注视着我的就是这张面孔——逃犯塞尔登的面孔。

霎时间，我全明白了。我记得，从男爵先前告诉过我，他把自己的旧衣服全都送给了巴里摩尔。巴里摩尔准是把衣服又转送给了塞尔登，以便有助于他逃跑。靴子，衬衣，帽子——全都是亨利爵士的。这场悲剧仍然是够悲惨的，但是，按照英国的法律，此人被处死至少也是罪有应得。我把事情的原委告诉了福尔摩斯，心里洋溢着感恩之情和快乐之意。

"这么说来，这些衣物便成了这个可怜鬼的死因了，"他说，"事情已经很清楚了，亨利爵士的某件衣物被拿给那条猎犬闻过了——最有可能是在旅馆里被人盗走的那只靴子——因此，猎犬才对此人紧追不放。不过，还有一点很离奇：塞尔登为何能在一片漆黑中知道有条猎犬在背后追他呢？"

"他听见了声音吧。"

① precipitous [pri'sipitəs] a. 陡峭的；险峻的

② spasm ['spæzəm] n. 痉挛；抽搐

③ beetling ['bi:tliŋ] a. 突出的

④ on one's trail 追猎

convict into such a **paroxysm**[①] of terror that he would risk recapture by screaming wildly for help. By his cries he must have run a long way after he knew the animal was on his track. How did he know?"

"A greater mystery to me is why this hound, presuming that all our conjectures are correct --"

"I presume nothing."

"Well, then, why this hound should be loose to-night. I suppose that it does not always run loose upon the moor. Stapleton would not let it go unless he had reason to think that Sir Henry would be there."

"My difficulty is the more formidable of the two, for I think that we shall very shortly get an explanation of yours, while mine may remain forever a mystery. The question now is, what shall we do with this poor **wretch's**[②] body? We cannot leave it here to the foxes and the ravens."

"I suggest that we put it in one of the huts until we can communicate with the police."

"Exactly. I have no doubt that you and I could carry it so far. Halloa, Watson, what's this? It's the man himself, by all that's wonderful and audacious! Not a word to show your suspicions–not a word, or my plans crumble to the ground."

A figure was approaching us over the moor, and I saw the dull red glow of a cigar. The moon shone upon him, and I could distinguish the **dapper**[③] shape and **jaunty**[④] walk of the naturalist. He stopped when he saw us, and then came on again.

"Why, Dr. Watson, that's not you, is it? You are the last man that I should have expected to see out on the moor at this time of night. But, dear me, what's this? Somebody hurt? Not–don't tell me that it is our friend Sir Henry!" He hurried past me and stooped over the dead man. I heard a sharp intake of his breath and the cigar fell from his fingers.

"Who–who's this?" he stammered.

"It is Selden, the man who escaped from Princetown."

Stapleton turned a ghastly face upon us, but by a supreme effort he had overcome his amazement and his disappointment. He looked sharply from Holmes to me.

① paroxysm ['pærəksizəm]
n. （疾病等的）突然发
作；阵发

② wretch [retʃ] n. 不幸的人

③ dapper ['dæpə] a. 短小精
悍的
④ jaunty ['dʒɔːnti] a. 轻快的

"像他那样残忍的逃犯，仅仅听到荒原上有猎犬的
声音，还不至于惊吓到这种地步，以致冒着再度被抓住
的危险而疯狂地高声呼救的。根据他的喊声来判断，他
在知道了有动物追他后，还跑了很长的一段路。他又是
怎么知道的呢？"

"如果我们的推测完全正确，那就还有一个更大的
谜团，那条猎犬为何——"

"我不做任何推测。"

"对啊，那条猎犬为何今天晚上被放出来了？我想
它总不至于经常被放到荒原上来吧。斯塔普尔顿一定
是以为亨利爵士在荒原上，否则，他是不会把猎犬放
出来的。"

"这两个问题中，我的那个更加难于回答，因为我
认为，你的那个问题的答案，我们马上就可以找到了。
而我要的答案恐怕永远是个谜。我们面临的问题是，该
如何处理这个死者的尸体呢？我们总不能置之不管，让
狐狸、老鸦把它吃掉吧！"

"我建议，把它放在一座小屋里，然后通知警察来
处理。"

"一点没错。毫无疑问，你我两个人抬着他走这么
一段距离是没有问题的。嗨，华生，那是谁？是他本人
吗？胆子够大的啊！千万别说什么你有所怀疑的话——
一声都不要吭，不然，我们的整个计划就泡汤了。"

我看到一个身影正在荒原上移动，离我们越来越
近，还看抽雪茄冒出的暗淡红光。月光照在他的身上，
我辨认出了生物学家那短小的身材和轻快的步伐。他看
到我们后便停下了脚步，然后继续向我们走过来。

"哎呀，华生医生，不会是您吧？都这么晚了，我
万万没想到会在这荒原上见到您呢。但是，天哪，这是
怎么啦？是有人受伤了吗？不，千万别对我说这是我们
的朋友亨利爵士！"他匆匆忙忙从我们身边走过，弯下
腰面对着死者。我听到他猛然倒吸了一口冷气，雪茄烟
也从指缝中掉了下来。

"谁？——这是谁？"他说话语无伦次。

"他叫塞尔登，是从王子镇跑出来的那个逃犯。"

斯塔普尔顿转向我们，脸色煞白。但是，他极力地

"Dear me! What a very shocking affair! How did he die?"

"He appears to have broken his neck by falling over these rocks. My friend and I were strolling on the moor when we heard a cry."

"I heard a cry also. That was what brought me out. I was uneasy about Sir Henry."

"Why about Sir Henry in particular?" I could not help asking.

"Because I had suggested that he should come over. When he did not come I was surprised, and I naturally became alarmed for his safety when I heard cries upon the moor. By the way"–his eyes darted again from my face to Holmes's–"did you hear anything else besides a cry?"

"No," said Holmes; "did you?"

"No."

"What do you mean, then?"

"Oh, you know the stories that the peasants tell about a **phantom**① hound, and so on. It is said to be heard at night upon the moor. I was wondering if there were any evidence of such a sound to-night."

"We heard nothing of the kind," said I.

"And what is your theory of this poor fellow's death?"

"I have no doubt that anxiety and exposure have driven him off his head. He has rushed about the moor in a crazy state and eventually fallen over here and broken his neck."

"That seems the most reasonable theory," said Stapleton, and he gave a sigh which I took to indicate his relief. "What do you think about it, Mr. Sherlock Holmes?"

My friend **bowed**② his compliments.

"You are quick at identification," said he.

"We have been expecting you in these parts since Dr. Watson came down. You are in time to see a tragedy."

"Yes, indeed. I have no doubt that my friend's explanation will cover the facts. I will take an unpleasant remembrance back to London with me to-morrow."

"Oh, you return to-morrow?"

"That is my intention."

克制住了自己惊恐和失望的情绪，犀利的目光在我和福尔摩斯身上游离。

"天哪！这太令人震惊了！他是怎么死的？"

"看样子，他从山岩上摔下来，把脖子摔断了。我正和我的朋友在荒原上散步，突然听到了一声凄惨的叫喊。"

"我也是听到了叫喊声，就跑出来了。我还担心是亨利爵士呢！"

"您为何特别担心亨利爵士呢？"我忍不住问了一句。

"因为我曾建议他来我家，但他没有来，我感觉奇怪。当我听到荒原上传来的叫喊声时，自然就担心起他的安全来了。啊，对了，"——他的目光再次离开我转到福尔摩斯身上——"除了喊叫外，您还听到了别的声音吗？"

"没有，"福尔摩斯说，"您呢？"

"没有。"

"那么，您这话是什么意思呢？"

"噢，您知道那些庄稼人传说的关于鬼怪猎犬之类的故事吧。据说，夜间在荒原上就能听见它发出的声音。我刚才还以为今天晚上有人听到了那种声音呢。"

"我们没有听见什么。"我说。

"那您推测，这个可怜家伙是怎么死的？"

"我肯定，紧张焦虑和风餐露宿的生活把他逼得发疯了。他神经错乱，在荒原上到处乱跑，最终摔倒在这里，摔断了脖子。"

"这似乎是最合理的推测了，"斯塔普尔顿说，又叹息了一声，我感觉他已经放宽心了，"这个事情您是怎么看的呢，夏洛克·福尔摩斯先生？"

我朋友欠了欠身子，算是打招呼了。

"您很善于认人啊，"他说。

"自从华生医生到这儿以后，我们这儿的人就一直期待着您的到来。您来得正是时候，目睹了这场悲剧。"

"是啊，确实如此。我确信，我朋友所做的解释能说明所有的问题。我明天回伦敦时，脑子里面还得想着这件不愉快的事情呢。"

"噢，您明天就会回去？"

"我是这样打算的。"

"但愿您的到来能够廓清我们迷惑不解的情况啊。"

① phantom ['fæntəm] a. 幽灵似的；鬼怪的

② bow [bau] v. 欠身（表示赞同、招呼等）

· 251

"I hope your visit has cast some light upon those occurrences which have puzzled us?"

Holmes shrugged his shoulders.

"One cannot always have the success for which one hopes. An investigator needs facts and not legends or rumours. It has not been a satisfactory case."

My friend spoke in his frankest and most unconcerned manner. Stapleton still looked hard at him. Then he turned to me.

"I would suggest carrying this poor fellow to my house, but it would give my sister such a fright that I do not feel **justified**① in doing it. I think that if we put something over his face he will be safe until morning."

And so it was arranged. Resisting Stapleton's offer of hospitality, Holmes and I set off to Baskerville Hall, leaving the naturalist to return alone. Looking back we saw the figure moving slowly away over the broad moor, and behind him that one black **smudge**② on the silvered slope which showed where the man was lying who had come so horribly to his end.

福尔摩斯耸了耸肩膀。

"人们希望的事情并不总能获得成功啊。调查案件的人需要的是事实，而不是什么传说或者谣言。本案办得不怎么令人满意。"

我朋友说话时，态度直率，显得漫不经心。斯塔普尔顿仍然目不转睛地看着他，然后目光又移到了我的身上。

"我本想提议把死者抬到我家里去的，但是，那样的话，我妹妹一定会大受惊吓的，因此还是觉得不要这样做为好。我认为，我们先拿东西盖住他的脸，明天天亮之前应该不会有问题的。"

事情就这样安排好了。我和福尔摩斯拒绝了斯塔普尔顿热情的邀请，动身回巴斯克维尔庄园，让生物学家独自一人回家。我们回头看了看，看到那个身影在宽阔的荒原上慢慢前行，渐行渐远，而在他身后，在那个月光照着的斜坡上，黑乎乎的一堆仍然看得见。那个人躺在那儿，结局悲惨。

① justified ['dʒʌstifaid] a. 有
正当理由的

② smudge [smʌdʒ] n. 污
迹；污点

Chapter 13　Fixing the Nets

"We're at close grips at last," said Holmes as we walked together across the moor. "What a **nerve**[①] the fellow has! How he pulled himself together in the face of what must have been a paralyzing shock when he found that the wrong man had fallen a victim to his plot. I told you in London, Watson, and I tell you now again, that we have never had a foeman more worthy of our steel."

"I am sorry that he has seen you."

"And so was I at first. But there was no getting out of it."

"What effect do you think it will have upon his plans now that he knows you are here?"

"It may cause him to be more cautious, or it may drive him to desperate measures at once. Like most clever criminals, he may be too confident in his own cleverness and imagine that he has completely deceived us."

"Why should we not arrest him at once?"

"My dear Watson, you were born to be a man of action. Your instinct is always to do something energetic. But supposing, for argument's sake, that we had him arrested to-night, what on earth the better off should we be for that? We could prove nothing against him. There's the **devilish**[②] cunning of it! If he were acting through a human agent we could get some evidence, but if we were to drag this great dog to the light of day it would not help us in putting a rope round the neck of its master."

"Surely we have a case."

第十三章 布下罗网

① nerve [nə:v] *n.* 精神力量，胆量

"我们终于要同他面对面较量了，"我们一同走过荒原时，福尔摩斯说，"那家伙的内心可是够强大的啊！当他发现自己的阴谋导致了错误的对象遇害时，本应惊慌失措，震惊不已，但他却表现得十分镇静！我在伦敦时就告诉过你的，华生，现在还要对你重申一次，我们从未遇到过比这个更加值得较量的对手。"

"我感到遗憾的是，他已经看见你了。"

"我开始也是这么想来着，但是，这是没有办法的事情。"

"他现在既然知道你来了，你认为这样对于他的计划会有什么影响吗？"

"他可能会更加谨慎从事，或者铤而走险。像大多数聪明的罪犯一样，他可能会高估自己的智慧，心里会以为自己的伎俩已经蒙蔽住了我们。"

"我们为何不立刻逮捕他呢？"

"亲爱的华生啊，你天生就是个爱行动的人，你的本能总是促使你淋漓尽致地采取行动。但是，我们可以探讨一下，如果我们今晚把他给逮捕了，那我们究竟能够取得什么进展呢？我们没有任何可以控告他的证据。这其中施用了魔鬼一样狡猾的伎俩，如果他是通过人来进行犯罪活动的，那我们倒还可以获得一些证据。但我们如果在光天化日之下把那条打猎犬拉出来，对我们是毫无作用的，我们根本无法把绳索捆在其主人的脖子上。"

② devilish ['deviliʃ] *ad.* 极端，非常

"我们肯定有证据的。"

"Not a shadow of one—only **surmise**① and conjecture. We should be laughed out of court if we came with such a story and such evidence."

"There is Sir Charles's death."

"Found dead without a mark upon him. You and I know that he died of sheer fright, and we know also what frightened him; but how are we to get twelve **stolid**② jurymen to know it? What signs are there of a hound? Where are the marks of its fangs? Of course we know that a hound does not bite a dead body and that Sir Charles was dead before ever the brute overtook him. But we have to *prove* all this, and we are not in a position to do it."

"Well, then, to-night?"

"We are not much better off to-night. Again, there was no direct connection between the hound and the man's death. We never saw the hound. We heard it, but we could not prove that it was running upon this man's trail. There is a complete absence of motive. No, my dear fellow; we must reconcile ourselves to the fact that we have no case at present, and that it is worth our while to run any risk in order to establish one."

"And how do you propose to do so?"

"I have great hopes of what Mrs. Laura Lyons may do for us when the position of affairs is made clear to her. And I have my own plan as well. Sufficient for to-morrow is the evil **thereof**③; but I hope before the day is past to have the upper hand at last."

I could draw nothing further from him, and he walked, lost in thought, as far as the Baskerville gates.

"Are you coming up?"

"Yes; I see no reason for further concealment. But one last word, Watson. Say nothing of the hound to Sir Henry. Let him think that Selden's death was as Stapleton would have us believe. He will have a better nerve for the ordeal which he will have to undergo to-morrow, when he is engaged, if I remember your report **aright**④, to dine with these people."

"And so am I."

"Then you must excuse yourself and he must go alone. That will be easily arranged. And now, if we are too late for dinner, I think that we are both ready for our suppers."

① surmise ['sə:maiz] *n.* 猜测，臆测

② stolid ['stɔlid] *a.* 古板的，固执的

③ thereof [,ðɛə'ɔv] *ad.* 关于那

④ aright [ə'rait] *ad.* 正确地

"连个影儿都没有啊——只不过是一些主观臆断和猜测而已。如果我们在法庭上就只呈现这么一段故事和这么一个证据，那我们一定会受到人们的嘲笑，让人给轰出来的。"

"查尔斯爵士的猝死就是证据啊。"

"他被人发现死亡时，身上没有一点儿痕迹。你我都知道他纯粹是被吓死的，也知道了是什么东西使他感到恐惧的，但是，我们怎样才能让十二位顽固不化的陪审员也相信呢？猎犬留下了什么痕迹？犬牙印子在哪儿呢？我们当然清楚，猎犬是不会咬尸体的，而且查尔斯爵士早在那畜生追上之前就已经死了。我们必须把这一切都加以证明，但是，我们眼下还无法证明啊。"

"是啊，那么，今天晚上的事情呢？"

"今天晚上，我们的状况也好不到哪儿去。还是老问题，那人的死和猎犬之间没有什么直接关联。我们都没看见那条猎犬。我们确实听到了声音，但也无法证明它就在那人身后追赶，而且毫无杀人动机。亲爱的伙计啊，那是行不通的，我们必须让自己认清现实：我们目前还没有证据。而为了寻找到证据，任何冒险行动都是值得我们试一试的。"

"你觉得我们该怎么办呢？"

"我对劳拉·莱昂斯太太抱有很大的希望，只要我们把实情对她讲清楚，她便可能帮上我们的大忙。此外，我也做好了计划，那就让罪恶势力明天再猖狂一天，但愿明天结束前，我们能够控制住局势。"

我从他嘴里根本再问不出什么东西来了，他一边走一边陷入沉思，就这样一直走到了巴斯克维尔庄园的大门口。

"你也进去吗？"

"对，我看没有什么理由再躲躲藏藏了。不过，华生，我还有最后一句话：猎犬的事你对亨利爵士要缄口不言。让他把塞尔登死因想成斯塔普尔顿希望我们相信的那样。这样一来，他将会以更加坚强的意志来经受明天的苦难了。如果我没把你的报告记错的话，他已经约好明天去斯塔普尔顿家去吃晚饭的。"

"他们也约了我。"

Sir Henry was more pleased than surprised to see Sherlock Holmes, for he had for some days been expecting that recent events would bring him down from London. He did raise his eyebrows, however, when he found that my friend had neither any luggage nor any explanations for its absence. Between us we soon supplied his wants, and then over a belated supper we explained to the baronet as much of our experience as it seemed desirable that he should know. But first I had the unpleasant duty of breaking the news to Barrymore and his wife. To him it may have been an **unmitigated**[①] relief, but she wept bitterly in her apron. To all the world he was the man of violence, half animal and half demon; but to her he always remained the little wilful boy of her own girlhood, the child who had clung to her hand. Evil indeed is the man who has not one woman to mourn him.

"I've been **moping**[②] in the house all day since Watson went off in the morning," said the baronet. "I guess I should have some credit, for I have kept my promise. If I hadn't sworn not to go about alone I might have had a more lively evening, for I had a message from Stapleton asking me over there."

"I have no doubt that you would have had a more lively evening," said Holmes drily. "By the way, I don't suppose you appreciate that we have been mourning over you as having broken your neck?"

Sir Henry opened his eyes. "How was that?"

"This poor wretch was dressed in your clothes. I fear your servant who gave them to him may get into trouble with the police."

"That is unlikely. There was no mark on any of them, as far as I know."

"That's lucky for him—in fact, it's lucky for all of you, since you are all on the wrong side of the law in this matter. I am not sure that as a conscientious detective my first duty is not to arrest the whole household. Watson's reports are most **incriminating**[③] documents."

"But how about the case?" asked the baronet. "Have you made anything out of the tangle? I don't know that Watson and I are much the wiser since we came down."

"I think that I shall be in a position to make the situation rather more clear to you before long. It has been an exceedingly difficult and most complicated business. There are several points upon which we still want light—but it is

"那你得替自己找个理由推辞掉，让他一个人独自前往。这个事情很容易办成。对了，如果我们错过了吃晚饭的时间的话，那我们两个人就一同吃点夜宵吧。"

亨利爵士见到夏洛克·福尔摩斯后，与其说是惊讶，还不如说是高兴，因为几天来，他一直在盼望着，近来发生了这么些事情，希望他会从伦敦赶过来。不过，当他看到我的朋友既没有带任何行李，又没有对此作任何解释的时候，他倒是真的扬起了眉头。我们很快就给他提供了生活必需品，然后，我们在吃推迟了的晚餐时，把我们的遭遇中从男爵似乎应该知道的那部分向他作了解释。不过在此之前，我还履行了令人沮丧的责任：把情况告诉了巴里摩尔夫妇。对巴里摩尔说来，这或许是一件让人如释重负的事，但他太太听后便用围裙捂着脸，失声痛哭了起来。对整个社会来说，他是个凶狠残暴之徒，半是动物半是魔鬼。但在她的心目中，他永远都是她童年记忆中的那个任性的、紧抓着她的手不放的小孩子。这个人确实罪孽深重，死后连个替他守丧的女人都没有。

"华生医生一早就出门了，我在家里苦闷了一整天，"从男爵说，"我觉得自己应该受到赞扬才是，因为我遵守了诺言。如果不是因为我起过誓，保证绝不单独外出，我这个晚上也许能过得愉快得多，因为我收到了斯塔普尔顿捎过来的信，他邀请我上他那儿去。"

"我相信，如果您去了，那确实会是一个比较愉快的夜晚，"福尔摩斯说着，态度显得很冷淡，"啊，对了，我们刚才一直以为是您摔断了脖子而伤心不已呢，我想您不会因此而感到不愉快吧？"

亨利爵士睁大了眼睛，"怎么回事啊？"

"那个死去的坏蛋穿的是您的衣服，可能是您家的仆人送过去的吧，恐怕警察会来找他的麻烦呢。"

"这不可能，那些衣服没有一件上面有记号，这我是知道的。"

"那算他运气——事实上，你们都有运气，因为从法律角度来说，你们在这件事情上是有过错的。作为一个公正的侦探，我可以肯定，我的首要职责就是把你们

① unmitigated [ˌʌn'mitigeitid] a. 全然的，十足的

② mope [məup] v. 没精打采地度过

③ incriminate [in'krimineit] v. 控告；控诉

coming all the same."

"We've had one experience, as Watson has no doubt told you. We heard the hound on the moor, so I can swear that it is not all empty superstition. I had something to do with dogs when I was out West, and I know one when I hear one. If you can muzzle that one and put him on a chain I'll be ready to swear you are the greatest detective of all time."

"I think I will muzzle him and chain him all right if you will give me your help."

"Whatever you tell me to do I will do."

"Very good; and I will ask you also to do it blindly, without always asking the reason."

"Just as you like."

"If you will do this I think the chances are that our little problem will soon be solved. I have no doubt ——"

He stopped suddenly and stared fixedly up over my head into the air. The lamp beat upon his face, and so intent was it and so still that it might have been that of a clear-cut classical statue, a personification of alertness and expectation.

"What is it?" we both cried.

I could see as he looked down that he was repressing some internal emotion. His features were still composed, but his eyes shone with amused exultation.

"Excuse the admiration of a **connoisseur**[①]," said he as he waved his hand towards the line of portraits which covered the opposite wall. "Watson won't allow that I know anything of art, but that is mere jealousy because our views upon the subject differ. Now, these are a really very fine series of portraits."

"Well, I'm glad to hear you say so," said Sir Henry, glancing with some surprise at my friend. "I don't pretend to know much about these things, and I'd be a better judge of a horse or a **steer**[②] than of a picture. I didn't know that you found time for such things."

"I know what is good when I see it, and I see it now. That's a Kneller, I'll swear, that lady in the blue silk over yonder, and the stout gentleman with the wig ought to be a Reynolds. They are all family portraits, I presume?"

全家逮捕。华生的报告就是非常有力的定罪证明。"

"但是，案件进展如何啊？"从男爵问，"在这一团乱麻里，您理出了些头绪吗？我觉得，我和华生两个人到这儿后并没有掌握更多情况。"

"我认为，我不久就可以把案情向您讲述清楚的。这确实是一桩难度极大而且极为复杂的案件。我们现在还有一些问题没有弄明白——但不久就会全明白的。"

"我们曾经亲身体验过一次，这点华生无疑早就告诉您了吧。我们有一次在荒原上听到了猎犬的叫声，所以我敢保证，那个传说不完全是空穴来风。我在美国西部时，跟犬类有过一些接触，我听到它们的声音可以辨认出来。如果您能够给犬戴上笼头，套上铁链，那我就可以起誓作证，您是有史以来最最伟大的大侦探。"

"我觉得，我一定能给它戴上笼头，套上铁链的，前提是您要给我一些帮助。"

"不管您叫我做什么，我都一定照办。"

"很好，我还要请您不折不扣地服从我，不要老是问为什么。"

"全听您的。"

"如果您愿意这样做，我想我们的小问题很快就能解决了。我深信——"

他突然打住不说了，眼睛牢牢盯着我的头的上方。灯光照在他的脸上，那样专注，纹丝不动，就像是一尊经典的线条清晰的雕像——纯粹就是机敏和期待的化身。

① connoisseur [ˌkɔnəˈsəː] n.
（艺术品等的）鉴赏家

"什么东西？"我们两人齐声问。

当他朝下看时，我看得出，他正在抑制着自己内在的情感。他的表情仍然非常镇定，但是，他的眼睛里充满了喜悦的神情。

② steer[stiə] n. 肉用公牛，
菜牛

"请原谅，我在鉴赏画作呢，"他说着，一边挥手指着对面墙上挂着的那排肖像画，"华生认为，我不懂艺术。但是，这纯粹是心理不平衡，因为我们对艺术的看法大不相同。是啊，这些人物肖像画很有水平啊。"

"啊，听到您这么说，我很高兴，"亨利爵士说，同时目光惊讶地看了看我朋友，"关于这些画作，我不敢

· 261 ·

"Every one."

"Do you know the names?"

"Barrymore has been coaching me in them, and I think I can say my lessons fairly well."

"Who is the gentleman with the telescope?"

"That is Rear-Admiral Baskerville, who served under Rodney in the West Indies. The man with the blue coat and the roll of paper is Sir William Baskerville, who was Chairman of Committees of the House of Commons under Pitt."

"And this Cavalier opposite to me—the one with the black velvet and the lace?"

"Ah, you have a right to know about him. That is the cause of all the mischief, the wicked Hugo, who started the Hound of the Baskervilles. We're not likely to forget him."

I gazed with interest and some surprise upon the portrait.

"Dear me!" said Holmes, "he seems a quiet, meek-mannered man enough, but I dare say that there was a lurking devil in his eyes. I had pictured him as a more robust and **ruffianly**[①] person."

"There's no doubt about the **authenticity**[②], for the name and the date, 1647, are on the back of the canvas."

Holmes said little more, but the picture of the old **roysterer**[③] seemed to have a fascination for him, and his eyes were continually fixed upon it during supper. It was not until later, when Sir Henry had gone to his room, that I was able to follow the trend of his thoughts. He led me back into the banqueting-hall, his bedroom candle in his hand, and he held it up against the time-stained portrait on the wall.

"Do you see anything there?"

I looked at the broad plumed hat, the curling **love-locks**[④], the white lace collar, and the straight, severe face which was framed between them. It was not a brutal **countenance**[⑤], but it was prim, hard, and stern, with a firm-set, thin-lipped mouth, and a coldly intolerant eye.

"Is it like anyone you know?"

"There is something of Sir Henry about the jaw."

冒充内行。我对马或牛知道得比较多,对画不懂。我先前真不知道,您竟然会有工夫关注这些东西。"

"我只要看一眼,就能看出好坏来。我敢发誓,那边那幅穿着蓝色绸缎衣服的女性画像出自内勒爵士之手,而那个结实的戴着假发的绅士画像应该是雷诺兹画的。我看,这些都是您家族成员的画像吧?"

"每一幅都是。"

"您知道他们的名字吗?"

"巴里摩尔一直在给我介绍他们,我认为,自己还是记得很熟的。"

"那位手拿望远镜的绅士是谁?"

"他是巴斯克维尔海军少将,在西印度群岛任职于罗德尼的麾下。那个身穿蓝色大衣、拿着纸卷的是威廉·巴斯克维尔爵士,在皮特任首相的内阁里,任下议院委员会的主席。"

"还有我正对面的那位保王党成员——就是那位身穿黑色天鹅绒礼服、身披绶带的绅士是谁啊?"

"啊,您可得了解他——品性恶劣的雨果。他是一切灾难的源头,巴斯克维尔猎犬的传说就是从他开始的。我们不可能忘记他。"

我目不转睛地盯着肖像画看,充满了兴趣,还带着几分惊奇。

"天哪!"福尔摩斯说,"他看上去是个态度平静、性格温和的人啊,但我可以说,他的眼睛里暗藏着乖戾的神色。我先前把他想象成是一个更加壮实和凶残的人。"

"这幅画像的真实性是毋庸置疑的,因为在画布的背面还写有画中人物的姓名和年代'1647'。"

福尔摩斯没再多说什么,但是,他对那张老酒鬼的肖像画好像着了迷似的。我们用餐时,他的眼睛仍然不停地盯着它看。直到后来,亨利爵士回自己房间去了,我才跟上了他的思路。他手里拿着卧室里的蜡烛把我领回到餐厅,随后,便把蜡烛高高地举起,照着墙上一张因年代久远而略微褪色的肖像画上。

"你从那上面看出了什么吗?"

我看着那饰有羽毛的宽檐帽,卷曲的发穗,镶着白

① ruffianly ['rʌfiənli] *a.* 凶狠的;残暴的

② authenticity [,ɔ:θen'tisəti] *n.* 可靠性;真实性

③ roysterer ['rɔistərər] *n.* 喝酒喧闹者

④ love-lock ['lʌvlɔk] *n.* 前额卷发

⑤ countenance ['kauntənəns] *n.* 面容

"Just a suggestion, perhaps. But wait an instant!" He stood upon a chair, and, holding up the light in his left hand, he curved his right arm over the broad hat and round the long **ringlets**①.

"Good heavens!" I cried in amazement.

The face of Stapleton had sprung out of the canvas.

"Ha, you see it now. My eyes have been trained to examine faces and not their **trimmings**②. It is the first quality of a criminal investigator that he should see through a disguise."

"But this is marvellous. It might be his portrait."

"Yes, it is an interesting instance of a **throwback**③, which appears to be both physical and spiritual. A study of family portraits is enough to convert a man to the doctrine of reincarnation. The fellow is a Baskerville—that is evident."

"With designs upon the succession."

"Exactly. This chance of the picture has supplied us with one of our most obvious missing links. We have him, Watson, we have him, and I dare swear that before to-morrow night he will be fluttering in our net as helpless as one of his own butterflies. A pin, a cork, and a card, and we add him to the Baker Street collection!" He burst into one of his rare fits of laughter as he turned away from the picture. I have not heard him laugh often, and it has always **boded ill**④ to somebody.

I was up **betimes**⑤ in the morning, but Holmes was **afoot**⑥ earlier still, for I saw him as I dressed, coming up the drive.

"Yes, we should have a full day to-day," he remarked, and he rubbed his hands with the joy of action. "The nets are all in place, and the **drag**⑦ is about to begin. We'll know before the day is out whether we have caught our big, lean-jawed **pike**⑧, or whether he has got through the meshes."

"Have you been on the moor already?"

"I have sent a report from Grimpen to Princetown as to the death of Selden. I think I can promise that none of you will be troubled in the matter. And I have also communicated with my faithful Cartwright, who would certainly have **pined**⑨ away at the door of my hut, as a dog does at his master's grave, if I had not set his mind at rest about my safety."

蕾丝的领口，还有饰物中间的那张严肃刻板的面孔。面孔虽说不上残忍，却也显得古板、僵硬、严峻，上面单薄的双唇紧闭着，眼神显得冷漠无情而又愤世嫉俗。

"他像不像你认识的某个人？"

"他的下巴有点像亨利爵士。"

"或许有那么一点点吧。不过，稍等一下！"他站立在一把椅子上，左手举着蜡烛，右臂弯曲成弧形，遮住了宽檐帽和长长的发卷。

"天哪！"我大叫了起来，很是吃惊。

斯塔普尔顿的面孔跃然出现在画布上。

"哈，你现在看出来了。我的眼睛是经受过训练的，专注于画面中面孔，而不是面孔周围的装饰物。刑事侦探的首要素质就是要善于识破伪装。"

"但是，这事真是神了，有可能就是他的肖像画啊。"

"对啊，这是返祖现象中一个很有意思的例子，神形兼备啊。如果对家族的肖像进行一番研究，那就可以证明转世轮回的说法是站得住脚的。很显然，那家伙是巴斯克维尔家族中的一员。"

"图谋攫取继承权。"

"一点不错。幸运的是，这幅肖像画替我们提供了一个最明显缺失的环节。我们逮着他了，华生，我们逮着他了。我敢保证，明晚结束之前，他就会像他自己捕到的蝴蝶那样在我们布下的罗网中无助地拍打着翅膀了。用一根针、一块软木和一张卡片，我们就可以把他做成标本，添加到贝克大街的标本中去！"他转身离开那张画像时，突然发出了一阵少有的哈哈大笑声。我并不常听到他的这种笑声，而他这么一笑就会有人要倒霉了。

翌日早晨，我一早就起床了，但福尔摩斯起得还要更早，因为我在穿衣时看到他正在车道上往回走。

"是啊，我们今天可要忙碌了！"他说着，一面因行动在即而兴奋得搓着双手，"罗网已经布好了，马上就要收了。今天结束之前，我们就能知道，是我们把那条尖嘴大狗鱼逮住了，还是他从我们的网眼里溜掉了。"

"你已经去过荒原了吗？"

"我到了格林盆邮局，把塞尔登死亡的消息发到王子

---

① ringlet ['riŋlit] *n.* 长鬈发

② trimming ['trimiŋ] *n.* 修饰物

③ throwback ['θrəubæk] *n.* 隔世遗传

④ bode ill 是不好的预兆
⑤ betimes [bi'taimz] *ad.* 很早
⑥ afoot [ə'fut] *a.* 活动着（的）

⑦ drag [dræg] *n.* 拖，拉

⑧ pike [paik] *n.* 大狗鱼

⑨ pine [pain] *v.* 衰弱；憔悴

"What is the next move?"

"To see Sir Henry. Ah, here he is!"

"Good-morning, Holmes," said the baronet. "You look like a general who is planning a battle with his chief of the staff."

"That is the exact situation. Watson was asking for orders."

"And so do I."

"Very good. You are engaged, as I understand, to dine with our friends the Stapletons to-night."

"I hope that you will come also. They are very hospitable people, and I am sure that they would be very glad to see you."

"I fear that Watson and I must go to London."

"To London?"

"Yes, I think that we should be more useful there at the present **juncture**[①]."

The baronet's face perceptibly lengthened.

"I hoped that you were going to see me through this business. The Hall and the moor are not very pleasant places when one is alone."

"My dear fellow, you must trust me **implicitly**[②] and do exactly what I tell you. You can tell your friends that we should have been happy to have come with you, but that urgent business required us to be in town. We hope very soon to return to Devonshire. Will you remember to give them that message?"

"If you insist upon it."

"There is no alternative, I assure you."

I saw by the baronet's clouded brow that he was deeply hurt by what he regarded as our desertion.

"When do you desire to go?" he asked coldly.

"Immediately after breakfast. We will drive in to Coombe Tracey, but Watson will leave his things as a **pledge**[③] that he will come back to you. Watson, you will send a note to Stapleton to tell him that you regret that you cannot come."

"I **have a good mind to**[④] go to London with you," said the baronet. "Why should I stay here alone?"

"Because it is your post of duty. Because you gave me your word that you

镇去了。我觉得，我可以保证，你们中的任何人都不会被这件事打扰了。我也和忠心耿耿的卡特莱特联系了一下，如果他不能确认我安然无恙，那他肯定会像守在主人坟旁的老犬那样在我那小屋门口憔悴而死的。"

"下一步怎么办呢？"

"去看看亨利爵士。啊，他来了！"

"早上好，福尔摩斯，"从男爵说，"您看上去真像个正在和参谋长筹划一次战役的将军啊。"

"情形正是如此，华生正在向我请令呢。"

"我也一样。"

"很好，据我了解，您今晚应邀要去我们的朋友斯塔普尔顿家吃饭吧。"

"我希望您也一同去。他们非常好客，而且我肯定，他们看到您一定会非常高兴的。"

"我和华生恐怕得去趟伦敦啊。"

"去伦敦？"

"对啊，我认为我们这个时候去伦敦会比待在这儿更加有利。"

从男爵的脸明显拉长了。

"我本来指望着你们陪同我渡过这个难关的。一个人孤零零地待着，庄园和荒原可都不是什么令人愉快的地方啊。"

"亲爱的朋友，您一定要完全信任我，不折不扣地按照我的吩咐去做。您可以告诉您的朋友，说我们本来是很乐意同您一道前往的，但发生了一件紧急事件，我们迫不得已要回伦敦去，但愿我们很快就能返回德文郡。您会记住把这个信息传递给他们吧？"

"如果您坚持这样要求的话。"

"我实话告诉您，别无选择了。"

从男爵紧锁眉头，我知道，他以为我们丢下他一人不管了，因而感到很沮丧。

"你们打算什么时间动身呢？"他问了一声，态度显得很冷漠。

"用过早餐就立刻出发。我们要乘马车到库姆特雷西去。不过，华生会把他的行李物品留在这里，以此当作他会返回您这儿来的保证。华生，你还要给斯塔普尔

① juncture ['dʒʌŋktʃə] n. 时机

② implicitly [im'plisitli] ad. 无保留地；绝对地

③ pledge [pledʒ] n. 保证

④ have a good mind 很想（做某事）

would do as you were told, and I tell you to stay."

"All right, then, I'll stay."

"One more direction! I wish you to drive to Merripit House. Send back your trap, however, and let them know that you intend to walk home."

"To walk across the moor?"

"Yes."

"But that is the very thing which you have so often cautioned me not to do."

"This time you may do it with safety. If I had not every confidence in your nerve and courage I would not suggest it, but it is essential that you should do it."

"Then I will do it."

"And as you value your life do not go across the moor in any direction save along the straight path which leads from Merripit House to the Grimpen Road, and is your natural way home."

"I will do just what you say."

"Very good. I should be glad to get away as soon after breakfast as possible, so as to reach London in the afternoon."

I was much astounded by this programme, though I remembered that Holmes had said to Stapleton on the night before that his visit would **terminate**[①] next day. It had not crossed my mind, however, that he would wish me to go with him, nor could I understand how we could both be absent at a moment which he himself declared to be critical. There was nothing for it, however, but implicit obedience; so we bade good-bye to our rueful friend, and a couple of hours afterwards we were at the station of Coombe Tracey and had dispatched the trap upon its return journey. A small boy was waiting upon the platform.

"Any orders, sir?"

"You will take this train to town, Cartwright. The moment you arrive you will send a wire to Sir Henry Baskerville, in my name, to say that if he finds the pocketbook which I have dropped he is to send it by registered post to Baker Street."

"Yes, sir."

顿写个便条，说明你不能赴约，并表达歉意。"

"我也很想同你们一道回伦敦去，"从男爵说，"我为何就该一个人待在这儿呢？"

"因为这是您的责任，因为您答应过我，会不折不扣按照我的吩咐去做，而我现在就要求您待在这儿。"

"那好吧，我留下来。"

"再提一个要求！我希望您坐马车去梅里皮特别墅，不过，您到达后要把马车打发回来，并且让他们知道，您打算走路回家。"

"要穿过荒原吗？"

"要啊。"

"但是，这正是您经常警示我，叫我不要那么做啊！"

"您这一回那么做会很安全的。如果我对您的意志和勇气没有信心，那我是不会建议您这样做的。总之，您一定要这样做啊。"

"那我就这样做吧。"

"如果您珍惜自己的生命，您横穿荒原时，千万不要朝其他方向走，只走那条从梅里皮特别墅通向格林彭大路的直路，那也是您回家的必经之路。"

"我一定按照您吩咐的去做。"

"很好，为了能赶在下午到达伦敦，我很乐意在早饭之后尽快动身。"

我对他的行程计划感到很是吃惊，因为我记得福尔摩斯昨晚对斯塔普尔顿说过，他的到访要到次日才结束。我压根儿没有想到他会要求我一同前往，也不明白，在这样一个他所谓的关键时刻，我们两个人怎么能够不在场呢。不过，我无可奈何，只能不折不扣服从。因此，我们和我们神情沮丧的朋友告了别。两个小时后，我们到达了库姆特雷西车站，打发马车往回赶。一个小男孩正在站台上等着我们。

"有什么吩咐吗，先生？"

"卡特莱特，你马上乘坐这趟火车到伦敦。车一到站，你就用我的名字给亨利·巴斯克维尔爵士发一封电报，说如果他找到了我遗落在他那里的记事本的话，请他用挂号信帮我把它寄到贝克大街去。"

"好的，先生。"

① terminate ['tə:mineit] *v.* 结束

"And ask at the station office if there is a message for me."

The boy returned with a telegram, which Holmes handed to me. It ran:

> Wire received. Coming down with unsigned warrant. Arrive five-forty.
> LESTRADE.

"That is in answer to mine of this morning. He is the best of the professionals, I think, and we may need his assistance. Now, Watson, I think that we cannot employ our time better than by calling upon your acquaintance, Mrs. Laura Lyons."

His plan of campaign was beginning to be evident. He would use the baronet in order to convince the Stapletons that we were really gone, while we should actually return at the instant when we were likely to be needed. That telegram from London, if mentioned by Sir Henry to the Stapletons, must remove the last suspicions from their minds. Already I seemed to see our nets drawing closer around that lean-jawed pike.

Mrs. Laura Lyons was in her office, and Sherlock Holmes opened his interview with a frankness and directness which considerably amazed her.

"I am investigating the circumstances which **attended**[①] the death of the late Sir Charles Baskerville," said he. "My friend here, Dr. Watson, has informed me of what you have communicated, and also of what you have withheld in connection with that matter."

"What have I withheld?" she asked defiantly.

"You have confessed that you asked Sir Charles to be at the gate at ten o'clock. We know that that was the place and hour of his death. You have withheld what the connection is between these events."

"There is no connection."

"In that case the coincidence must indeed be an extraordinary one. But I think that we shall succeed in establishing a connection, after all. I wish to be perfectly frank with you, Mrs. Lyons. We regard this case as one of murder, and the evidence may **implicate**[②] not only your friend Mr. Stapleton but his wife as well."

The lady sprang from her chair.

"你现在到车站的邮局去打听一下，看是否有我的电报。"

小男孩回来时手里拿着一封电报，福尔摩斯把它递给了我。上面写道：

电报收悉，即带空白拘票前往。五点四十分到。

莱斯特雷德

"这就是我今早发的电报的回复。我认为他是官方侦探中最能干的一位，我们可能需要他的帮助。现在，华生，我觉得我们可以去拜访一下你的老熟人劳拉·莱昂斯太太了，这样我们就能够充分利用好时间。"

他的行动方案开始变得明晰起来了。他利用从男爵，让斯塔普尔顿确信我们出发去了伦敦，而实际上，我们将随时在有可能需要我们的时刻返回。从伦敦发来的电报，如果亨利爵士向斯塔普尔顿夫妇提起的话，一定会打消他们心中的最后一丝疑虑。我好像已经看到，我们围着那条尖嘴狗鱼撒下的网正越拉越紧了。

劳拉·莱昂斯太太正在自己的工作室里。夏洛克·福尔摩斯开始询问时，态度坦诚直率，令她感到非常诧异。

① attend [ə'tend] v. 伴随

"我正在调查导致已故查尔斯·巴斯克维尔爵士死亡的原因，"他说，"我的这位朋友，华生医生，已经把你们之间的谈话内容全部告诉我了，而且他还说了，您对与那件事情相关的情况还有所隐瞒。"

"我隐瞒什么了？"她问了一句，态度显得简慢。

"您已经承认了，您请求过查尔斯爵士，要他十点钟的时候到栅门口去。据我们所知，那正好是他死亡的时间和地点。您隐瞒了这些情况之间的关联。"

"毫无关联。"

"这么看来，这确实是个非同寻常的巧合啊。但是，我认为，我们一定能够建立起某种联系来的。我想要完全坦诚地对您说，莱昂斯太太。我们认为，这是一件谋杀案，而且有证据表明，您的朋友斯塔普尔顿先生和他夫人都被牵连进去了。"

② implicate ['implikeit] v. 使牵连其中

女士猛然从坐着的椅子上一跃起身。

"His wife!" she cried.

"The fact is no longer a secret. The person who has passed for his sister is really his wife."

Mrs. Lyons had resumed her seat. Her hands were grasping the arms of her chair, and I saw that the pink nails had turned white with the pressure of her grip.

"His wife!" she said again. "His wife! He is not a married man."

Sherlock Holmes shrugged his shoulders.

"Prove it to me! Prove it to me! And if you can do so --!" The fierce flash of her eyes said more than any words.

"I have come prepared to do so," said Holmes, drawing several papers from his pocket. "Here is a photograph of the couple taken in York four years ago. It is **indorsed**[1] 'Mr. and Mrs. Vandeleur,' but you will have no difficulty in recognizing him, and her also, if you know her by sight. Here are three written descriptions by trustworthy witnesses of Mr. and Mrs. Vandeleur, who at that time kept St. Oliver's private school. Read them and see if you can doubt the identity of these people."

She glanced at them, and then looked up at us with the set, rigid face of a desperate woman.

"Mr. Holmes," she said, "this man had offered me marriage on condition that I could get a divorce from my husband. He has lied to me, the villain, in every conceivable way. Not one word of truth has he ever told me. And why-why? I imagined that all was for my own sake. But now I see that I was never anything but a tool in his hands. Why should I preserve faith with him who never kept any with me? Why should I try to shield him from the consequences of his own wicked acts? Ask me what you like, and there is nothing which I shall hold back. One thing I swear to you, and that is that when I wrote the letter I never dreamed of any harm to the old gentleman, who had been my kindest friend."

"I entirely believe you, madam," said Sherlock Holmes. "The **recital**[2] of these events must be very painful to you, and perhaps it will make it easier if I tell you what occurred, and you can check me if I make any **material**[3] mistake. The sending of this letter was suggested to you by Stapleton?"

"她夫人！"她大声说。

"这个事情已经不是什么秘密了，被当作他妹妹的那位女士实际上就是他夫人。"

莱昂斯太太重新坐到了椅子上，两只手紧紧抓住扶手。我看到她那粉红色的指甲都变成了白色，抓得太用力了。

"他夫人！"她重复说，"他夫人！他还未婚呢。"

夏洛克·福尔摩斯耸了耸肩膀。

"给我拿出证据来！给我拿出证据来！如果您真的能证明——！"她愤怒的目光胜过千言万语。

"我来到这儿，就是要准备拿出证据，"福尔摩斯说着，一面从口袋里掏出几页纸，"这儿有一张他们夫妇二人四年前在约克拍的照片，背面的署名①是'范德勒先生和夫人'。但您很容易就能把他认出来。还有她，如果您见过她人的话。这里有三份关于范德勒先生和夫人的书面材料，是几个可靠的证人寄过来的，他们当时开办了一所名叫圣·奥利弗的私立学校。看一看吧，看您是否还会怀疑他们就是这两个人。"

她看了看照片中的两个人，然后抬起头看着我们，板着面孔，露出一副绝望的神情。

"福尔摩斯先生，"她说，"此人曾经向我求过婚，前提是我能和我丈夫离婚。那个混蛋，他想尽一切办法来欺骗我。他对我说过的话没有一句是真实的。但为什么———到底为什么呢？我先前以为一切都是为了我好。我现在总算明白了，自己只不过是他手里的一件道具而已。既然他对我从来就没有过什么意思，那我凭什么要对他保持忠诚呢？我为何要竭力袒护他，让他逃脱因自己所犯的罪行而应受到的惩罚呢？您想要问什么就问吧，我不会有一丝一毫的隐瞒了。有一点我可以向您发誓，那就是，我写那封信的时候，从没想到会加害那位老绅士，因为他是对我最好的朋友。"

"太太，我完全相信您的话，"夏洛克·福尔摩斯说，"要您复述②那些事情，您一定会感到非常痛苦。不如让我来述说事情的原委吧，遇到我说错了的地方，您再帮我指正，这样您或许会好受一些。是斯塔普尔顿建议您写那封信的吧？"

---

① indorse [in'dɔːs] v. 在背面签名

② recital [ri'saitəl] n. 叙述

③ material [mə'tiəriəl] a. 重要的，重大的

"He dictated it."

"I presume that the reason he gave was that you would receive help from Sir Charles for the legal expenses connected with your divorce?"

"Exactly."

"And then after you had sent the letter he dissuaded you from keeping the appointment?"

"He told me that it would hurt his self-respect that any other man should find the money for such an object, and that though he was a poor man himself he would devote his last penny to removing the obstacles which divided us."

"He appears to be a very consistent character. And then you heard nothing until you read the reports of the death in the paper?"

"No."

"And he made you swear to say nothing about your appointment with Sir Charles?"

"He did. He said that the death was a very mysterious one, and that I should certainly be suspected if the facts came out. He frightened me into remaining silent."

"Quite so. But you had your suspicions?"

She hesitated and looked down.

"I knew him," she said. "But if he had kept faith with me I should always have done so with him."

"I think that on the whole you have had a fortunate escape," said Sherlock Holmes. "You have had him in your power and he knew it, and yet you are alive. You have been walking for some months very near to the edge of a **precipice**①. We must wish you good-morning now, Mrs. Lyons, and it is probable that you will very shortly hear from us again."

"Our case becomes **rounded off**②, and difficulty after difficulty **thins away**③ in front of us," said Holmes as we stood waiting for the arrival of the express from town. "I shall soon be in the position of being able to put into a single connected narrative one of the most singular and **sensational**④ crimes of modern times. Students of criminology will remember the **analogous**⑤ incidents in Godno, in Little Russia, in the year'66, and of course there are the Anderson murders in North Carolina, but this case possesses some features

"是他口述的。"

"我猜想，他给的理由是：您将从查尔斯爵士那里获得离婚诉讼所需的相关费用，对吧？"

"一点没错。"

"而在您把信寄出去后，他又劝阻您不要前去赴约，对吧？"

"他告诉我，为了这样的目的而叫别的男人出钱帮忙会伤害他的自尊心，而且，虽然他自己也没钱，但他会用尽自己最后的一个便士，来消除挡在我们之间的障碍。"

"他看上去是一个言行一致的人。此后，您除了从报上看到有关死亡案的报道外，就什么都没听说过吗？"

"没有。"

"而且他还要您发誓，关于您和查尔斯爵士约定见面的事情，决不对外人吭一声，对吧？"

"对，他说那是一桩非常神秘的死亡案，如果约定见面的事情传出去了，我一定会被人怀疑的。他把我吓得不敢说话了。"

"差不多是这样，但您应该也有所怀疑吧？"

她犹豫了一下，低下了头。

"我了解他的为人，"她说，"但是，如果他一直对我真诚的话，我就会始终对他忠贞不贰的。"

"我认为，总体上来说，您算是逃脱了厄运，这是很庆幸的事情，"夏洛克·福尔摩斯说，"他知道自己的命运攥在您的手上，而您现在竟然还活着。这几个月来，您一直徘徊在悬崖边上呢。我们现在必须要同您告别了，莱昂斯太太，或许您很快就会再次听到我们的消息。"

"我们侦破案件的各项准备工作已经圆满完成了，困难一个接着一个在我们面前排除了，"我们站着等候从伦敦开来的快车时，福尔摩斯说，"我不久就能写出一部完整的近代最离奇、最惊人的犯罪小说了。研究犯罪学的学者们会记得1866年在小俄罗斯的格罗德诺发生过相似的案件，当然还会记得北卡罗来纳州发生的安德森谋杀案，但本案具有一些与众不同的特点。即使到了这个时候，我们都还没有掌握确切的证据来控诉那个诡

① precipice ['presipis] n. 悬崖
② round off 圆满结束
③ thin away 变薄；变瘦；变淡
④ sensational [sen'seiʃənəl] a. 耸人听闻的
⑤ analogous [ə'næləgəs] a. 类似的，相似的

which are entirely its own. Even now we have no clear case against this very wily man. But I shall be very much surprised if it is not clear enough before we go to bed this night. "

The London express came roaring into the station, and a small, wiry bulldog of a man had sprung from a first-class carriage. We all three shook hands, and I saw at once from the **reverential**[①] way in which Lestrade gazed at my companion that he had learned a good deal since the days when they had first worked together. I could well remember the scorn which the theories of the reasoner used then to excite in the practical man.

"Anything good?" he asked.

"The biggest thing for years," said Holmes. "We have two hours before we need think of starting. I think we might employ it in getting some dinner, and then, Lestrade, we will take the London fog out of your throat by giving you a breath of the **pure**[②] night air of Dartmoor. Never been there? Ah, well, I don't suppose you will forget your first visit."

计多端的人。不过，如果今晚我们睡觉之前，事情还没弄清楚的话，那才叫非常奇怪呢。"

从伦敦开来的快车高声鸣笛驶入车站，一个像斗牛犬一般矮小结实的男子从头等车厢里跳了出来。我们三个人互相握了手。我看见莱斯特雷德看着我同伴时样子非常谦恭，便立刻明白了，自从他们首次合作以来，他已经学到了很多东西。我还清楚地记得，这位喜欢推理的人那时对这位讲求实际的人总是冷嘲热讽。

"有什么好事吗？"他问。

"是多年来最最重大的案件，"福尔摩斯说，"从现在到考虑动手之前，我们有两个小时时间。我看，我们可以利用这段时间先吃顿晚饭，然后，莱斯特雷德，我们将带您去达特穆尔高地呼吸一下夜晚纯净的空气，把您喉咙里的伦敦雾气清除干净。您从没到过那儿吧？啊，这是您第一次出游，我想，您一辈子都不会忘记的。"

① reverential [ˌrevəˈrenʃəl] a. 虔诚的；尊敬的

② pure [pjuə] a. 纯净的，洁净的

Chapter 14   The Hound of the Baskervilles

One of Sherlock Holmes's defects–if, indeed, one may call it a defect–
was that he was exceedingly **loath**[①] to communicate his full plans to any
other person until the instant of their fulfilment. Partly it came no doubt from
his own masterful nature, which loved to dominate and surprise those who
were around him. Partly also from his professional caution, which urged him
never to take any chances. The result, however, was very trying for those
who were acting as his agents and assistants. I had often suffered under it,
but never more so than during that long drive in the darkness. The great
ordeal was in front of us; at last we were about to make our final effort, and
yet Holmes had said nothing, and I could only surmise what his course of
action would be. My nerves thrilled with anticipation when at last the cold
wind upon our faces and the dark, void spaces on either side of the narrow
road told me that we were back upon the moor once again. Every stride of
the horses and every turn of the wheels was taking us nearer to our supreme
adventure.

Our conversation was **hampered**[②] by the presence of the driver of the
hired wagonette, so that we were forced to talk of trivial matters when our
nerves were tense with emotion and anticipation. It was a relief to me, after
that unnatural restraint, when we at last passed Frankland's house and knew
that we were drawing near to the Hall and to the scene of action. We did not
drive up to the door but got down near the gate of the avenue. The wagonette
was paid off and ordered to return to Coombe Tracey **forthwith**[③], while we

第十四章　巴斯克维尔的猎犬

① loath [ləuθ] *a.* 不愿意的

福尔摩斯有一个缺点——事实上，如果人们可以把它称作是缺点的话——那就是，其完整的行动计划不等到圆满实施的那一刻，他是决不会向任何人透露的。其原因一方面无疑是，他本人生性高傲，喜欢控制一切，让他周围的人感到惊讶。另一方面因为，他出于职业上的谨慎，决不会焦躁从事，去冒什么风险。不过，这样一来，他的委托人和助手就常常感到非常痛苦了。我本人就有过几次类似的痛苦经历，但都没有哪一次像这次一样，长时间驱车在黑暗中行进，难熬极了。严峻的考验就在我们的面前，我们的行动终于进入了最后阶段，但是，福尔摩斯却缄口不言，而我只能猜测他的行动方案到底是怎么一回事。最后，冰冷刺骨的寒风吹打在我们的脸上，狭窄的车道两边漆黑一片，空无一物，我这才意识到，我们又回到荒原上了。想到即将发生的事情，我感到异常激动。马匹每前行一步，车轮每转动一圈，我们就离命运攸关的历险更加接近一步了。

② hamper ['hæmpə] *v.* 束缚，限制

由于有雇来的马车夫在场，我们的谈话内容便受到限制了，只得聊些鸡毛蒜皮的小事。但这期间，我们的神经绷得很紧，内心激动，充满了期待。我们好不容易经过了弗兰克兰的家，知道自己已经临近巴克斯维尔庄园，临近行动的现场了，这时候，我总算挨过了不自然的紧张状态，心里松了一口气。我们没有让马车驶到庄园门口，而是在通向庄园的小路附近下了车。付过车费，吩咐马车立刻回库姆特雷西后，我们开始步行去梅

③ forthwith ['fɔ:θ'wið] *ad.* 立刻，马上

started to walk to Merripit House.

"Are you armed, Lestrade?"

The little detective smiled.

"As long as I have my trousers I have a hip-pocket, and as long as I have my hip-pocket I have something in it."

"Good! My friend and I are also ready for emergencies."

"You're mighty **close**[①] about this affair, Mr. Holmes. What's the game now?"

"A waiting game."

"My word, it does not seem a very cheerful place," said the detective with a shiver, glancing round him at the gloomy slopes of the hill and at the huge lake of fog which lay over the Grimpen Mire. "I see the lights of a house ahead of us."

"That is Merripit House and the end of our journey. I must request you to walk on tiptoe and not to talk above a whisper."

We moved cautiously along the track as if we were **bound for**[②] the house, but Holmes halted us when we were about two hundred yards from it.

"This will do," said he. "These rocks upon the right make an admirable screen."

"We are to wait here?"

"Yes, we shall make our little ambush here. Get into this hollow, Lestrade. You have been inside the house, have you not, Watson? Can you tell the position of the rooms? What are those latticed windows at this end?"

"I think they are the kitchen windows."

"And the one beyond, which shines so brightly?"

"That is certainly the dining-room."

"The blinds are up. You know the lie of the land best. Creep forward quietly and see what they are doing–but for heaven's sake don't let them know that they are watched!"

I tiptoed down the path and stooped behind the low wall which surrounded the stunted orchard. Creeping in its shadow I reached a point whence I could look straight through the uncurtained window.

There were only two men in the room, Sir Henry and Stapleton. They sat

里皮特别墅。

"您带武器了吗，莱斯特雷德？"

小个子侦探露出了微笑。

"只要我穿了裤子，裤子后面就会有个口袋。只要有个口袋，我就会往里面放点东西。"

"很好啊！我和我朋友也做好了应急的准备。"

"您在这件事情上口风把得可真严啊，福尔摩斯先生，我们现在该做什么呢？"

"等待猎物出现啊。"

"哎呀，看起来，这可不是个让人感觉舒心的所在啊，"侦探说着，一边环顾着四周。他看到了一道道阴暗的山坡和笼罩在格林彭泥潭上的雾海，不禁打了个寒战。"我看到了我们前方住房里的灯光了。"

"那幢住宅就是梅里皮特别墅，也是我们今天行程的终点站。我现在要求，你们必须用足尖走路，说话只能低声耳语。"

我们小心翼翼地顺着小路前行，好像马上就要到达那所房子似的，但是，在离住房大概有二百码处时，福尔摩斯把我们叫住了。

"待在这儿就行了，"他说，"右侧这些山石是绝妙的屏障。"

"我们就在这里等待吗？"

"对啊，我们要在此地展开一场小规模的伏击。快到这道沟里来，莱斯特雷德。你已经进去过那幢别墅，对吧，华生？能说出每个房间的具体位置吗？这一侧的那几个格子窗是什么房间？"

"我觉得，那应该是厨房的窗户。"

"再过去的那个很敞亮的窗户呢？"

"那一定是餐室。"

"百叶窗拉起来了。那儿的地形你清楚，请你悄悄地爬过去，看看他们在干什么。但看在上帝的份儿上，千万别让他们觉察到了。"

我蹑手蹑脚地顺着小路走了过去，猫着腰躲在一堵矮墙的后面。矮墙周围种着长势不佳的果木林。我在阴影处慢慢爬行，爬到了一个较高处，由此可以通过没有挂窗帘的窗户直接看到室内的情况。

① close [kləuz] a. 守口如瓶的

② bound for 以…为目的地

with their profiles towards me on either side of the round table. Both of them were smoking cigars, and coffee and wine were in front of them. Stapleton was talking with animation, but the baronet looked pale and distrait. Perhaps the thought of that lonely walk across the ill-omened moor was weighing heavily upon his mind.

As I watched them Stapleton rose and left the room, while Sir Henry filled his glass again and leaned back in his chair, puffing at his cigar. I heard the creak of a door and the crisp sound of boots upon gravel. The steps passed along the path on the other side of the wall under which I crouched. Looking over, I saw the naturalist pause at the door of an **out-house**[①] in the corner of the orchard. A key turned in a lock, and as he passed in there was a curious **scuffling**[②] noise from within. He was only a minute or so inside, and then I heard the key turn once more and he passed me and reentered the house. I saw him rejoin his guest, and I crept quietly back to where my companions were waiting to tell them what I had seen.

"You say, Watson, that the lady is not there?" Holmes asked when I had finished my report.

"No."

"Where can she be, then, since there is no light in any other room except the kitchen?"

"I cannot think where she is."

I have said that over the great Grimpen Mire there hung a dense, white fog. It was drifting slowly in our direction and banked itself up like a wall on that side of us, low but thick and well defined. The moon shone on it, and it looked like a great shimmering ice-field, with the heads of the distant tors as rocks borne upon its surface. Holmes's face was turned towards it, and he muttered impatiently as he watched its **sluggish**[③] drift.

"It's moving towards us, Watson."

"Is that serious?"

"Very serious, indeed–the one thing upon earth which could have disarranged my plans. He can't be very long, now. It is already ten o'clock. Our success and even his life may depend upon his coming out before the fog is over the path."

室内只坐着两个人，亨利爵士和斯塔普尔顿。他们在圆桌两边面对面地坐着，侧对着我。两人都在吸雪茄烟，前面摆着咖啡和葡萄酒。斯塔普尔顿正兴致勃勃地说着话，但从男爵却脸色苍白，一副魂不守舍的样子。说不定是因为他想到要独自一人跨过那片不祥的荒原，所以才忧心忡忡的吧。

正当我监视他们的时候，斯塔普尔顿站起身，走出了餐厅，而在这个当儿，亨利爵士又把酒杯斟满了，向后斜靠在椅背上，吸着雪茄烟。我听到了门发出的吱吱声，随后又是皮靴踩在石子路上清脆的声音。脚步在我所蹲的那堵墙的另一侧的小路上走过。从墙头看去，我看到生物学家在果木林一角的小屋门口停了下来。他掏出钥匙在锁孔里转一下，进门后，里面传出一阵奇怪的扭打声。他只在里面待了一分钟左右，我便再次听到了转动钥匙的声音。随后，他从我身旁走过，又进到室内去了。我看到他和客人又坐在了一起后，便悄悄地爬回到我朋友身边，把自己看到的情况告诉给了他们。

"你是说，那位女士不在场，对吧，华生？"我报告完毕后，福尔摩斯问。

"对啊。"

"既然除了厨房，别处都没有灯光，那她可能在哪儿呢？"

"我想象不出她会在哪儿。"

我已经说过了，格林彭大泥潭上笼罩着浓密的白雾。雾气正慢慢地向我们这边飘过来，越聚越多，就像在我们这边竖了一堵墙似的，虽然不高，但很厚实，而且界限分毭。月亮照在上面，厚墙看上去就是一片闪闪发光的冰原，远处突起的岩冈就像是冰原上生出的岩石一样。福尔摩斯扭过头朝着那边看了看，当他看着它缓慢前移时，不耐烦地咕哝着。

"雾气正朝着我们移动呢，华生。"

"这很严重吗？"

"非常严重，确实严重——只有这种情况会打乱我的计划。他不能待很长时间了，现在已经十点钟了。我们能否成功，甚至他的性命是否安全，都取决于他是否会在浓雾笼罩在路面之前出来。"

① outhouse ['authaus] *n.* 附属建筑，外屋

② scuffle ['skʌfl] *v.* 扭打

③ sluggish ['slʌgiʃ] *a.* 缓慢的

The night was clear and fine above us. The stars shone cold and bright, while a half-moon bathed the whole scene in a soft, uncertain light. Before us lay the dark bulk of the house, its **serrated**① roof and bristling chimneys hard outlined against the silver-spangled sky. Broad bars of golden light from the lower windows stretched across the orchard and the moor. One of them was suddenly shut off. The servants had left the kitchen. There only remained the lamp in the dining-room where the two men, the murderous host and the unconscious guest, still chatted over their cigars.

Every minute that white woolly plain which covered one-half of the moor was drifting closer and closer to the house. Already the first thin wisps of it were curling across the golden square of the lighted window. The farther wall of the orchard was already invisible, and the trees were standing out of a swirl of white vapour. As we watched it the fog-wreaths came crawling round both corners of the house and rolled slowly into one dense bank, on which the upper floor and the roof floated like a strange ship upon a shadowy sea. Holmes struck his hand passionately upon the rock in front of us and stamped his feet in his impatience.

"If he isn't out in a quarter of an hour the path will be covered. In half an hour we won't be able to see our hands in front of us."

"Shall we move farther back upon higher ground?"

"Yes, I think it would be as well."

So as the fog-bank flowed onward we fell back before it until we were half a mile from the house, and still that dense white sea, with the moon silvering its upper edge, swept slowly and **inexorably**② on.

"We are going too far," said Holmes. "We dare not take the chance of his being overtaken before he can reach us. At all costs we must hold our ground where we are." He dropped on his knees and clapped his ear to the ground. "Thank God, I think that I hear him coming."

A sound of quick steps broke the silence of the moor. Crouching among the stones we stared intently at the silver-tipped bank in front of us. The steps grew louder, and through the fog, as through a curtain, there stepped the man whom we were awaiting. He looked round him in surprise as he emerged into the clear, starlit night. Then he came swiftly along the path, passed close to where we lay,

① serrated ['seritid] *a.* 有锯
　齿的

② inexorablely [in'eksərəbli]
　ad. 不可阻挡地

我们头顶上的夜空明朗而美好。星星闪烁着清冷而
明亮的光芒，半圆的月亮高挂在空中，让一切景致都沐
浴在柔和而朦胧的光线中。我们面前屹立着的是房屋的
主体，它那锯齿状的屋顶和挺拔的烟囱的轮廓，都被银
光璀璨的天空清晰地映衬了出来。几道宽阔的金黄色光
束从下面的窗户里射出来，穿过了果木林，朝荒原的方
向照去。其中的一道突然熄灭了，看来仆人们已经离开
厨房。只有餐厅里的灯光仍然亮着，里面的两个男人，
一个是蓄意杀人的别墅主人，一个是蒙在鼓里的客人，
还在一边抽着雪茄一边闲聊着。

白茫茫像羊毛一样的大雾已经把荒原遮住了一半，
此时正争分夺秒地向房屋这边飘过来，越飘越近。透着亮
光的金色窗框上已经迎来了第一片薄薄的雾气，果木林后
面的那堵墙已经看不清了，果树的下半部分已经被白色水
汽形成的涡流遮掩了，只露出上半部分。就在我们守望着
的当儿，滚滚浓雾已经爬上了房屋的两角，慢慢地堆积成
了一个厚实的堤坝，二楼和屋顶看上去就像一艘形状古怪
的漂浮在朦胧海面上的船只。福尔摩斯心急火燎，焦躁不
安，手击打着我们面前的岩石，脚跺着地面。

"如果他在一刻钟之内还不出来，路面就完全被遮住
了。再过半个小时，我们就会伸手不见五指了。"

"我们要不要往后退，到高一点的地方去呢？"

"对，我觉得这样也行。"

因此，当浓雾不断向我们涌来的时候，我们就不断
地后退，一直退到了离别墅半英里外的地方。但是，浓
密的白茫茫雾海上银色的月光闪耀，仍然在缓慢而又不
依不饶地向我们袭来。

"我们退得距离太远了，"福尔摩斯说，"他还没有
到达我们这儿就会被别人赶上的，我们不能冒这个风险
啊，所以要不惜一切代价坚守住眼下这块阵地才是。"
他双膝着地，把一只耳朵贴近地面。"感谢上帝，感觉
他好像过来了。"

一阵急促的脚步声打破了荒原的寂静。我们蜷缩在
乱石之间，牢牢地盯着前方那道银白色的雾墙。脚步声越
来越响，我们等待着的那个人穿过纱帘般的浓雾，走过来
了。他进入到明朗的星光照耀的夜幕中后，惊恐不安地朝

and went on up the long slope behind us. As he walked he glanced continually over either shoulder, like a man who is ill at ease.

"Hist!" cried Holmes, and I heard the sharp click of a cocking pistol. "Look out! It's coming!"

There was a thin, crisp, continuous patter from somewhere in the heart of that crawling bank. The cloud was within fifty yards of where we lay, and we glared at it, all three, uncertain what horror was about to break from the heart of it. I was at Holmes's elbow, and I glanced for an instant at his face. It was pale and **exultant**①, his eyes shining brightly in the moonlight. But suddenly they started forward in a rigid, fixed stare, and his lips parted in amazement. At the same instant Lestrade gave a yell of terror and threw himself face downward upon the ground. I sprang to my feet, my **inert**② hand grasping my pistol, my mind paralyzed by the dreadful shape which had sprung out upon us from the shadows of the fog. A hound it was, an enormous coal-black hound, but not such a hound as mortal eyes have ever seen. Fire burst from its open mouth, its eyes glowed with a **smouldering**③ glare, its muzzle and **hackles**④ and **dewlap**⑤ were outlined in flickering flame. Never in the **delirious**⑥ dream of a disordered brain could anything more savage, more appalling, more hellish be conceived than that dark form and savage face which broke upon us out of the wall of fog.

With long bounds the huge black creature was leaping down the track, following hard upon the footsteps of our friend. So paralyzed were we by the **apparition**⑦ that we allowed him to pass before we had recovered our nerve. Then Holmes and I both fired together, and the creature gave a hideous howl, which showed that one at least had hit him. He did not pause, however, but bounded onward. Far away on the path we saw Sir Henry looking back, his face white in the moonlight, his hands raised in horror, glaring helplessly at the frightful thing which was hunting him down.

But that cry of pain from the hound had blown all our fears to the winds. If he was vulnerable he was mortal, and if we could wound him we could kill him. Never have I seen a man run as Holmes ran that night. I am reckoned fleet of foot, but he outpaced me as much as I outpaced the little professional. In front of us as we flew up the track we heard scream after

着四周环顾了一番。接着便顺着小路疾速前行，经过了我们藏身之处的附近，朝着我们背后的长山坡继续前行。他一边走，一边不断地朝两侧看，一副心绪不宁的样子。

"嘘！"福尔摩斯叫了一声，我便听到了一声清脆的扳动手枪扳手的声音，"注意点！来了！"

涌动着的雾墙之中传来了尖细、清脆、连续不断的啪嗒声。浓雾离我们所处的地方还不到五十码的距离了。我们三个人都目不转睛地盯着，不知道会有什么恐怖的东西从里面冒出来。此时，我正待在福尔摩斯的胳膊肘边，便不时地瞥一眼他的脸庞。只见他脸色苍白，情绪激动，两眼在月光下闪闪发亮。突然，他看着前方，目不转睛地盯着，惊恐地张开着嘴唇。就在这个当儿，莱斯特雷德恐惧地大喊了一声，随即便脸朝下匍匐在地上。我一跃身子站立起来，动作迟缓的手握住了手枪，迷雾之中蹿出一个可怕的东西，我脑子一片空白，人都吓傻了。原来是一条猎犬，一条体形巨大全身漆黑的猎犬，但绝非世人见过的那种。只见它那张大嘴向外喷火，眼睛闪烁着闷火一样的幽光，闪烁的火光下，现出了鼻口部分、竖起的颈背部毛和颈部的垂皮的轮廓。其幽黑的躯体和狰狞的面目冲出雾墙呈现在我们面前，比神经错乱时所做的噩梦中出现的任何怪物都更加凶狠野蛮，更加恐怖可怕，更加穷凶极恶。

体形巨大的黑色畜生大步向前跳跃着，顺着小路，紧紧跟随在我们的朋友身后。我们被眼前的幽灵吓得动弹不得，竟然眼睁睁地看着它从我们身边跑了。等到我们镇定下来之后，我和福尔摩斯一同开了枪，那东西发出了一声恐怖的哀叫，说明至少有一发子弹已经打中了它。但是，它并没有停下脚步，而是继续向前追去。在小路的远处，我们看到亨利爵士扭头向后看。他的脸在月光下显得煞白，双手吓得不停地挥舞，眼睛绝望地盯着对他穷追不舍的可怕的畜生。

但是，猎犬痛苦的叫声驱散了我们心中的恐惧。如果它受到了伤害，那就说明是肉体凡胎。如果我们可以击伤它，那就说明我们可以击毙它。我从未见过福尔摩斯跑得像当晚那么快过。我是公认的跑起来快步如飞的人，但他竟然超过了我，同时也超过了那位小个子官方

---

① exultant [ig'zʌltənt] a. 欢腾的，狂喜的

② inert [i'nəːt] a. 呆滞的；迟钝的

③ smoulder ['sməuldə] v. （无火苗地）闷烧

④ hackles ['hæklz] n. 狗颈背部竖起的毛

⑤ dewlap ['djuːlæp] n. （颈部下面的）垂肉，垂皮

⑥ delirious [di'liriəs] a. 发狂的；神志昏迷的

⑦ apparition [ˌæpə'riʃən] n. 幽灵

scream from Sir Henry and the deep roar of the hound. I was in time to see the beast spring upon its victim, hurl him to the ground, and **worry**① at his throat. But the next instant Holmes had emptied five barrels of his revolver into the creature's flank. With a last howl of agony and a vicious snap in the air, it rolled upon its back, four feet **pawing**② furiously, and then fell **limp**③ upon its side. I stooped, panting, and pressed my pistol to the dreadful, shimmering head, but it was useless to press the trigger. The giant hound was dead.

Sir Henry lay insensible where he had fallen. We tore away his collar, and Holmes breathed a prayer of gratitude when we saw that there was no sign of a wound and that the rescue had been in time. Already our friend's eyelids shivered and he made a feeble effort to move. Lestrade thrust his brandy-flask between the baronet's teeth, and two frightened eyes were looking up at us.

"My God!" he whispered. "What was it? What, in heaven's name, was it?"

"It's dead, whatever it is," said Holmes. "We've **laid**④ the family ghost once and forever."

In mere size and strength it was a terrible creature which was lying stretched before us. It was not a pure bloodhound and it was not a pure mastiff; but it appeared to be a combination of the two–**gaunt**⑤, savage, and as large as a small lioness. Even now, in the stillness of death, the huge jaws seemed to be dripping with a bluish flame and the small, deep-set, cruel eyes were ringed with fire. I placed my hand upon the glowing muzzle, and as I held them up my own fingers smouldered and gleamed in the darkness.

"**Phosphorus**⑥," I said.

"A cunning preparation of it," said Holmes, sniffing at the dead animal. "There is no smell which might have interfered with his power of scent. We owe you a deep apology, Sir Henry, for having exposed you to this fright. I was prepared for a hound, but not for such a creature as this. And the fog gave us little time to receive him."

"You have saved my life."

"Having first endangered it. Are you strong enough to stand?"

"Give me another mouthful of that brandy and I shall be ready for anything.

① worry ['wʌri] v. （狗等）
撕碎；啮咬

② paw [pɔ:] v. 用爪子抓
③ limp [limp] a. 无生气
的；软绵绵的

④ lay [lei] v. 打倒，击倒

⑤ gaunt [gɔ:nt] a. 可怕的；
令人生畏的

⑥ phosphorus ['fɔsfərəs] n.
磷

侦探。我们顺着小路向前奔跑的当儿，听到了前方亨利爵士发出的一声声尖叫，还有那猎犬低沉的狂吠。我们赶到现场时，正好看到野兽一跃而起向从男爵身上扑去，把他碰翻在地，正要撕咬他的喉咙。千钧一发之际，福尔摩斯连开五枪，子弹击中畜生的侧腹。猎犬发出最后一声痛苦的吠叫，并向空中恶狠狠地咬了一口，随后便倒在了地上，四脚疯狂地乱蹬了一阵后不再动弹了。我喘着粗气，躬下身子，手枪顶着可怕的闪闪发光的畜生的头，但已经没有必要扣动扳机了。巨型猎犬死了。

亨利爵士躺在他摔倒的地方，失去了知觉。我们扯开他的衣领，看到爵士身上没有任何伤痕，意识到此次救援还算及时。福尔摩斯这时才舒了一口气，口里低声念叨着谢天谢地。我们那位朋友的眼睑轻微地抖动了一下，还有气无力地挪了挪身子。莱斯特雷德把他的白兰地酒瓶塞进从男爵的上下牙齿之间，他抬头看了看我们，眼神里充满了惊恐。

"天哪！"他轻声说，"那是什么？看在上帝的分儿上，请告诉我那是什么东西啊？"

"不管是什么，它反正都已经死了，"福尔摩斯说，"我们已经彻底消灭了侵害您的家族的恶魔。"

就其体形和力量而言，四肢笔挺地躺在我们面前的畜生是很可怕的。它既不是纯种血狸，也不是纯种獒犬，看上去却像是这两个物种的杂交。它的外表恐怖凶狠，而且体形大得像牝狮。即便是现在，它死了，无法动弹了，那巨型大嘴似乎仍然在喷射着蓝色的火焰，那细小、深陷且凶残的眼睛四周仍有一圈火环。我摸了摸那张发光的嘴，然后把手举起来一看，我自己的手指也在黑暗中发起光来。

"是磷，"我说。

"策划得真是诡秘啊，"福尔摩斯说，同时嗅了嗅亡犬。

"它身上没有会影响其嗅觉的气味。我们非常抱歉，亨利爵士，让您受惊吓了。我原本以为要对付的是一条普通猎犬，但万万没想到竟会是这样的一条畜生。此外，由于浓雾的缘故，我们无法早一点儿消灭它。"

"你们救了我的命。"

"那也是在让您的生命承受了一次危险之后啊，您

So! Now, if you will help me up. What do you propose to do?"

"To leave you here. You are not fit for further adventures to-night. If you will wait, one or other of us will go back with you to the Hall."

He tried to stagger to his feet; but he was still ghastly pale and trembling in every limb. We helped him to a rock, where he sat shivering with his face buried in his hands.

"We must leave you now," said Holmes. "The rest of our work must be done, and every moment is of importance. We have our case, and now we only want our man.

"It's a thousand to one against our finding him at the house," he continued as we retraced our steps swiftly down the path. "Those shots must have told him that the game was up."

"We were some distance off, and this fog may have deadened them."

"He followed the hound to call him off–of that you may be certain. No, no, he's gone by this time! But we'll search the house and make sure."

The front door was open, so we rushed in and hurried from room to room to the amazement of a **doddering**[①] old manservant, who met us in the passage. There was no light save in the dining-room, but Holmes caught up the lamp and left no corner of the house unexplored. No sign could we see of the man whom we were chasing. On the upper floor, however, one of the bedroom doors was locked.

"There's someone in here," cried Lestrade. "I can hear a movement. Open this door!"

A faint moaning and rustling came from within. Holmes struck the door just over the lock with the flat of his foot and it flew open. Pistol in hand, we all three rushed into the room.

But there was no sign within it of that desperate and defiant villain whom we expected to see. Instead we were faced by an object so strange and so unexpected that we stood for a moment staring at it in amazement.

The room had been **fashioned**[②] into a small museum, and the walls were lined by a number of glass-topped cases full of that collection of butterflies and moths the formation of which had been the relaxation of this complex and dangerous man. In the centre of this room there was an upright beam, which

现在能站立起来吗？"

"再给我喝一大口白兰地酒，我就什么都能受得了了。啊，请扶我起来吧。您打算怎么办呢？"

"把您留在这儿，您今晚不能再冒什么风险了。您稍等片刻，我们当中有个人送您回庄园去。"

他吃力地站立了起来，但仍然脸色煞白，手脚也在颤抖。我们把他扶到一块石头边坐下，他用颤抖的双手捂住脸。

"我们现在必须得离开您了，"福尔摩斯说，"我们必须把剩下的事情处理完，分秒必争。我们已经掌握了足够证据，现在只需要抓住那个人就可以了。"

"要想在室内抓住他，可能性微乎其微，"我们顺着小路迅速往回走时，福尔摩斯接着说，"几声枪响已经惊动了他，他知道，自己的诡计没能得逞。"

"我们当时离他还有一段距离，大雾说不定会消解枪声呢。"

"他跟随在猎犬的后面，以便指挥它——你们可以肯定这一点吧。不，不，他现在已经离开了！但是，我们还要去别墅查看一下，以便确认。"

别墅的前门敞开着，我们冲了进去，匆匆忙忙，挨个房间检查，令那位老态龙钟的男仆惊讶不已。除了餐室，到处都漆黑一团。福尔摩斯急忙点亮灯，找遍了整座别墅，任何角落都没有放过，但不见我们要寻找的人的踪影。不过，楼上有间卧室是锁着的。

"里面有人，"莱斯特雷德大声说，"我听见里面有动静，把这扇门打开！"

里面传来微弱的呻吟声和窸窣声。福尔摩斯用脚底板在门锁处踹了一脚，门瞬间就打开了。我们三个人手里握着枪，冲进了房间。

但是，里面根本没有我们想要找到的那个亡命之徒。相反，呈现在我们面前的却是一件非常奇怪而又出人意料的东西，我们伫立了片刻，惊恐地盯着看。

房间布置成了一座小型博物馆，墙上挂着一排排装着玻璃盖的小匣子，里边装满了蝴蝶和飞蛾。采集这些昆虫是那个诡计多端、充满危险的人的娱乐消遣。房间的中间有一根直立着的木柱，显然是某个时候支起来用

① doddering ['dɔdəriŋ] a. 老态龙钟的

② fashion ['fæʃən] v. 做成……的形状

had been placed at some period as a support for the old worm-eaten **baulk**[①] of timber which spanned the roof. To this post a figure was tied, so **swathed**[②] and muffled in the sheets which had been used to secure it that one could not for the moment tell whether it was that of a man or a woman. One towel passed round the throat and was secured at the back of the pillar. Another covered the lower part of the face, and over it two dark eyes–eyes full of grief and shame and a dreadful questioning–stared back at us. In a minute we had torn off the **gag**[③], unswathed the bonds, and Mrs. Stapleton sank upon the floor in front of us. As her beautiful head fell upon her chest I saw the clear red **weal**[④] of a whiplash across her neck.

"The brute!" cried Holmes. "Here, Lestrade, your brandy-bottle! Put her in the chair! She has fainted from ill-usage and exhaustion."

She opened her eyes again.

"Is he safe?" she asked. "Has he escaped?"

"He cannot escape us, madam."

"No, no, I did not mean my husband. Sir Henry? Is he safe?"

"Yes."

"And the hound?"

"It is dead."

She gave a long sigh of satisfaction.

"Thank God! Thank God! Oh, this villain! See how he has treated me!" She shot her arms out from her sleeves, and we saw with horror that they were all mottled with bruises. "But this is nothing–nothing! It is my mind and soul that he has tortured and **defiled**[⑤]. I could endure it all, ill-usage, solitude, a life of deception, everything, as long as I could still cling to the hope that I had his love, but now I know that in this also I have been his **dupe**[⑥] and his tool." She broke into passionate sobbing as she spoke.

"You bear him no good will, madam," said Holmes. "Tell us then where we shall find him. If you have ever aided him in evil, help us now and so atone."

"There is but one place where he can have fled," she answered. "There is an old tin mine on an island in the heart of the mire. It was there that he kept his hound and there also he had made preparations so that he might have a refuge. That is where he would fly."

① baulk [bɔːk] *n.* 梁木

② swathe [sweið; swɔð] *v.*
包，裹

③ gag [gæg] *n.* 塞口物

④ weal [wiːl] *n.* 鞭痕

⑤ defile [diˈfail] *v.* 玷污，弄
脏

⑥ dupe[djuːp] *n.* 被利用的
工具

以顶住被虫蛀过的旧梁木的。柱子上捆绑着一个人，被床单严严实实地捆住了，发不出声音，因而无法立刻知道是男是女。一条毛巾绕着脖子系在背后的柱子上，另一条毛巾蒙住了面孔的下半部，上面露出了两只黑眼睛——眼神中充满了悲伤和羞耻，还有极度的疑惑——直盯着我们看。我们立刻扯出塞在她嘴里的东西，解开捆绑在她身上的东西，斯塔普尔顿夫人的身子瘫了下来，坐在我们面前的地上。当她垂下那美丽的头颅时，我清楚地看到她脖子上有红色的鞭痕。

"真是个畜生啊！"福尔摩斯大声说，"过来，莱斯特雷德，快把您的白兰地酒瓶拿来！把她安置在椅子上！她受到了残暴的虐待，过度疲劳，已经昏迷过去了。"

她这时睁开了眼睛。

"他没事了吗？"她问，"他已经逃跑了吗？"

"他逃不掉的，夫人。"

"不，不，我问的不是我丈夫。亨利爵士呢？他平安无事了吗？"

"对啊。"

"那条猎犬呢？"

"死了。"

她这才欣喜地长叹了一声。

"感谢上帝！感谢上帝啊！噢，那个恶棍！看看他是如何对待我的吧！"她猛然把手臂从袖管里露了出来，我们惊恐地看到上面伤痕累累。"但是，这算不了什么——算不了什么啊！他真正折磨和玷污的是我的心灵。但凡我仍然抱有一线希望，那就是拥有着他的爱，一切都可以忍受，包括饱受虐待，孤独凄苦，掩人耳目过日子，一切的一切。但是，现如今，我明白了，连爱也没有了，我就是一枚任他摆布的棋子，一件任他利用的工具。"她说话时，情绪激动，哭泣了起来。

"您对他已经绝望了，夫人，"福尔摩斯说，"那就请告诉我们，我们在哪儿可以找到他。如果您曾经帮助过他作孽，那现在就助我们一臂之力，将功补过吧。"

"他逃去的地方只有一个，"她回答说，"泥潭中心地带有一个小岛，上面有一处旧的锡矿。那正是他藏匿猎犬的地方，他也在那儿做好了准备，以便藏身之用。

The fog-bank lay like white wool against the window. Holmes held the lamp towards it.

"See," said he. "No one could find his way into the Grimpen Mire to-night."

She laughed and clapped her hands. Her eyes and teeth gleamed with fierce merriment.

"He may find his way in, but never out," she cried. "How can he see the guiding wands to-night? We planted them together, he and I, to mark the pathway through the mire. Oh, if I could only have plucked them out to-day. Then indeed you would have had him at your mercy!"

It was evident to us that all pursuit was in vain until the fog had lifted. Meanwhile we left Lestrade in possession of the house while Holmes and I went back with the baronet to Baskerville Hall. The story of the Stapletons could no longer be withheld from him, but he took the blow bravely when he learned the truth about the woman whom he had loved. But the shock of the night's adventures had shattered his nerves, and before morning he lay delirious in a high fever under the care of Dr. Mortimer. The two of them were destined to travel together round the world before Sir Henry had become once more the **hale**[①], **hearty**[②] man that he had been before he became master of that ill-omened estate.

And now I come rapidly to the conclusion of this singular narrative, in which I have tried to make the reader share those dark fears and vague surmises which clouded our lives so long and ended in so tragic a manner. On the morning after the death of the hound the fog had lifted and we were guided by Mrs. Stapleton to the point where they had found a pathway through the bog. It helped us to realize the horror of this woman's life when we saw the eagerness and joy with which she laid us on her husband's track. We left her standing upon the thin **peninsula**[③] of firm, **peaty**[④] soil which **tapered**[⑤] out into the widespread bog. From the end of it a small wand planted here and there showed where the path zigzagged from tuft to tuft of **rushes**[⑥] among those green-scummed pits and foul **quagmires**[⑦] which barred the way to the stranger. Rank reeds and lush, slimy water-plants sent an odour of decay and a

他一定是跑到那里去了。"

白茫茫像羊毛一样的雾墙紧贴着窗户，福尔摩斯举着灯走向窗口。"你们看，"他说，"今晚没有人能找到进入格林彭泥潭的道路。"

她哈哈大笑起来，拍着手，眼睛里和牙齿上闪烁着狂喜的光芒。

"他或许可以找到进入的路，但绝对找不到出来的，"她大声说，"他今晚如何看得清那些指路的木桩啊？那是我们，他和我，一同竖立的桩子，为的是标出穿过泥潭的小路。噢，如果我今天把它们全部拔除了该有多好啊。那样的话，你们就确实可以任意处置他了！"

很显然，对于我们来说，如果大雾没有散尽，一切追踪搜寻的行动都是徒劳的。于是，我们留下莱斯特雷德把守住宅，我和福尔摩斯则陪同从男爵一同回巴斯克维尔庄园去了。斯塔普尔顿夫妇的事情不可能再向他隐瞒了。不过，当他得知自己深爱着的女人的真实身份后，勇敢地承受住了打击。但是，经受了夜间冒险的打击之后，他感到精神崩溃，所以，天还没有亮，他便发起了高烧，躺在床上神志不清，由莫蒂默医生照料着。他们两个人决定一同周游世界，以便让亨利爵士像先前一样精神饱满，健康爽朗，然后再返回来继承这笔不祥的遗产，成为庄园的主人。

现在，我要快速结束这个古怪离奇的故事了。故事叙述过程中，我试图营造出一种氛围，让读者感受阴郁的恐惧和种种模棱两可的猜测，这种氛围长时间笼罩在我们的生活中，而且最终以惨烈的悲剧结束。猎犬死亡后的那个早晨，大雾散去了，我们在斯塔普尔顿夫人的引导下，到达了那个他们夫妇发现通向泥潭的小路的地方。我们看到她带领我们追踪她丈夫时所表露出来的急切而又喜悦的情绪，更加觉得，眼前的女人过去的生活有多么悲惨。我们让她在一处留了下来，那儿空间很狭窄，形状像个半岛，表面是硬邦邦的泥煤。从这一处地方的尽头起，处处插着小木桩，标示出一条曲曲折折的小路。小路从一个乱树丛连到另一个，蜿蜒在漂着绿沫的水洼和污浊的泥坑之间，不熟悉地形的人根本无法通行。茂密的芦苇和葱郁多汁而又黏滑的水草散发出一股

① hale [heil] *a.*（特指老人）健壮的；矍铄的
② hearty ['hɑ:ti] *a.* 健壮的，精力充沛的

③ peninsula [pi'ninsjulə] *n.* 半岛
④ peaty [pi:ti] *a.* 泥炭的
⑤ taper ['teipə] *v.* 一头的宽度逐渐变尖细
⑥ rush[rʌʃ] *n.* 灯芯草科植物
⑦ quagmire ['kwægmaiə] *n.* 沼泽地；泥潭

heavy **miasmatic**① vapour onto our faces, while a false step plunged us more than once thigh-deep into the dark, quivering mire, which shook for yards in soft **undulations**② around our feet. Its tenacious grip plucked at our heels as we walked, and when we sank into it it was as if some malignant hand was tugging us down into those **obscene**③ depths, so grim and purposeful was the clutch in which it held us. Once only we saw a trace that someone had passed that perilous way before us. From amid a tuft of cotton-grass which bore it up out of the slime some dark thing was projecting. Holmes sank to his waist as he stepped from the path to seize it, and had we not been there to drag him out he could never have set his foot upon firm land again. He held an old black boot in the air. "Meyers, Toronto," was printed on the leather inside.

"It is worth a mud bath," said he. "It is our friend Sir Henry's missing boot."

"Thrown there by Stapleton in his flight."

"Exactly. He retained it in his hand after using it to set the hound upon the track. He fled when he knew the game was **up**④, still clutching it. And he hurled it away at this point of his flight. We know at least that he came so far in safety."

But more than that we were never destined to know, though there was much which we might surmise. There was no chance of finding footsteps in the mire, for the rising mud oozed swiftly in upon them, but as we at last reached firmer ground beyond the morass we all looked eagerly for them. But no slightest sign of them ever met our eyes. If the earth told a true story, then Stapleton never reached that island of refuge towards which he struggled through the fog upon that last night. Somewhere in the heart of the great Grimpen Mire, down in the foul slime of the huge morass which had sucked him in, this cold and cruel-hearted man is forever buried.

Many traces we found of him in the bog-girt island where he had hid his savage ally. A huge driving-wheel and a shaft half-filled with rubbish showed the position of an abandoned mine. Beside it were the crumbling remains of the cottages of the miners, driven away no doubt by the foul reek of the surrounding swamp. In one of these a **staple**⑤ and chain with a quantity of gnawed bones showed where the animal had been confined. A skeleton with a tangle of brown

① miasmatic [ˌmiəz'mætik] *a.* 毒气的；沼气的；瘴气造成的

② undulation [ˌʌndju'leiʃən] *n.* 波动；起伏

③ obscene [əb'si:n] *a.* 可憎的，令人讨厌的

④ up [ʌp] *ad.* 完成了，结束了

⑤ staple ['steipl] *n.* 马蹄铁

腐烂的臭味，浓重的秽气迎面扑来。我们走错一步，就会陷入那黝黑颤动着的泥坑，淤泥不止一次没过了我们的膝盖。即便走了好几码之后，淤泥还是黏黏糊糊地沾在我们脚上。我们行进当中，泥泞会牢牢地吸住我们的脚后跟，而当我们陷入其中时，它就像一只狠毒的手，把我们拽入污泥的深处，拽得很牢固，很坚决。只有一次，我们看到了一点迹象，说明先前有人经过了这条险象环生的小路。黏土地上生长着的一丛棉草中间，凸显出了一个黑色的物体。福尔摩斯朝着小路旁边迈了一步，想要抓住它，但他却陷入了泥潭，淹没到了齐腰处。要不是我们拼命拽着他，把他拖了出来，他的双脚恐怕再也不能在陆地上行走了。他把一只黑色的旧靴子举到空中。皮革的里面印着"多伦多的梅耶斯"字样。

"这个泥泞浴洗一洗也是很值得的啊，"他说，"这正是我们的朋友亨利爵士丢失的那只皮靴。"

"是斯塔普尔顿逃跑时丢弃的。"

"一点没错。为了让猎犬去追逐亨利爵士，他让它嗅了靴子上的气味。然后就一直把靴子拿在手上。他知道了自己的阴谋失败后，便逃跑了，手里依旧抓住靴子。他逃到这个地方后，便随手把它扔了出去。我们据此知道，他安全地逃逸到了这儿。"

尽管我们能够做出更多的猜测，但除了上述情况，我们无法知道得更多了。不可能在泥潭里寻找到脚印，因为不断涌动的污泥很快就会使脚印消失。不过，我们终于走出了泥潭，到达了更加坚硬的路面，然后急切地寻找脚印。但是，脚印的影子都没有看见，连最微弱的痕迹都没有。如果地面显示的情况属实，那说明斯塔普尔顿昨晚冒着浓雾拼命向着小岛逃跑时，并没有到达目的地，而是在格林彭大泥潭中心地带的某处地方，陷入到了泥浆之中。冷酷无情、心狠手辣的恶人永远葬身其中了。

在泥潭环绕着的小岛上，也就是他藏匿那条凶狠的帮凶之处，我们发现了大量他留下的痕迹。一个巨大的驱动轮和一口填了一半垃圾的竖井表明这儿是一处废弃的矿场。旁边是一些矿工们居住的坍塌了的小屋的遗址，矿工们毫无疑问是被周围泥潭的恶臭味熏跑的。在其中的一幢小屋里，有一只马蹄铁，一条锁链，还有一

hair adhering to it lay among the débris.

"A dog!" said Holmes. "By Jove, a curly-haired spaniel. Poor Mortimer will never see his pet again. Well, I do not know that this place contains any secret which we have not already fathomed. He could hide his hound, but he could not hush its voice, and hence came those cries which even in daylight were not pleasant to hear. On an emergency he could keep the hound in the out-house at Merripit, but it was always a risk, and it was only on the supreme day, which he regarded as the end of all his efforts, that he dared do it. This paste in the tin is no doubt the luminous mixture with which the creature was **daubed**①. It was suggested, of course, by the story of the family hell-hound, and by the desire to frighten old Sir Charles to death. No wonder the poor devil of a convict ran and screamed, even as our friend did, and as we ourselves might have done, when he saw such a creature bounding through the darkness of the moor upon his track. It was a cunning device, for, apart from the chance of driving your victim to his death, what peasant would venture to inquire too closely into such a creature should he get sight of it, as many have done, upon the moor? I said it in London, Watson, and I say it again now, that never yet have we helped to hunt down a more dangerous man than he who is lying yonder"–he swept his long arm towards the huge mottled expanse of green-splotched bog which stretched away until it merged into the russet slopes of the moor.

些啃咬过的骨头，可见这是关那条畜生的场所。瓦砾之中，有一具遗骨，上面还黏着一丛棕色的毛发。

"一条狗！"福尔摩斯说，"天哪，是条卷毛长耳猎犬。可怜的莫蒂默再也看不到他的宠物犬了。是啊，我看，这个地方再没有什么我们还没有弄明白的秘密啦。他可以把犬藏匿起来，但他不能使它不吠叫，因而才会传出那些即便是光天化日时听来都很可怕的声音。一旦出现了什么紧急情况，他可以把猎犬关在梅里皮特别墅外面的小屋里。但这样做毕竟有风险，所以只会在最关键的时刻，即他认为一切已经准备妥帖了之后，才会大胆那么做。装在铁罐里的糊状物无疑就是他涂抹在那畜生身上的能发光的混合物。当然，这是受了那个世代相传的魔鬼猎犬故事的启发，也是为了吓死老查尔斯爵士所需要的。毫无疑问，那个死去的恶魔般的逃犯看到这样一条畜生穿越漆黑的荒原，在他身后紧追不舍，这时候，他便会像我们的朋友一样，一面奔跑一面大叫，换成是我们，说不定也会如此呢。这真是个狡猾的设计，一方面，有机会把受害人吓死，另一方面，即便有农夫看见了猎犬，事实上有很多人确实看到了，又有哪个人胆敢对猎犬作深入调查呢？我在伦敦说过，华生，现在要再重复一遍，我们还从未协助追踪过任何一个比藏匿在那边的更加危险的人物呢"——他朝着广阔的泥潭地挥了挥自己修长的胳膊。上面点缀着绿色，向着远处延伸，直到同红褐色的荒原连成一片。

① daub [dɔːb] v. 涂抹

Chapter 15   A Retrospection

It was the end of November, and Holmes and I sat, upon a raw and foggy night, on either side of a blazing fire in our sitting-room in Baker Street. Since the tragic upshot of our visit to Devonshire he had been engaged in two affairs of the utmost importance, in the first of which he had exposed the atrocious conduct of Colonel Upwood in connection with the famous card scandal of the Nonpareil Club, while in the second he had defended the unfortunate Mme. Montpensier from the charge of murder which hung over her in connection with the death of her step-daughter, Mlle. Carere, the young lady who, as it will be remembered, was found six months later alive and married in New York. My friend was in excellent spirits over the success which had attended a succession of difficult and important cases, so that I was able to **induce**① him to discuss the details of the Baskerville mystery. I had waited patiently for the opportunity, for I was aware that he would never permit cases to **overlap**②, and that his clear and logical mind would not be drawn from its present work to dwell upon memories of the past. Sir Henry and Dr. Mortimer were, however, in London, on their way to that long voyage which had been recommended for the restoration of his shattered nerves. They had called upon us that very afternoon, so that it was natural that the subject should come up for discussion.

"The whole course of events," said Holmes, "from the point of view of the man who called himself Stapleton was simple and direct, although to us, who had no means in the beginning of knowing the motives of his actions and could only learn part of the facts, it all appeared exceedingly complex. I have

第十五章　回首案情

　　那是在11月底，一个阴郁寒冷、雾气弥漫的夜晚，我和福尔摩斯一边一个端坐在贝克大街我们起居室燃烧正旺的壁炉前。自从我们经历了德文郡那场悲剧的结局之后，他又忙着侦办了两桩重大案件。第一桩案件中，他揭露了厄普伍德上校涉嫌臭名昭著的"完美俱乐部"的纸牌作弊丑闻。第二桩案件中，他则保护了不幸的蒙庞西耶夫人，洗刷了她的谋杀罪名，因为她先前被指控谋杀了自己的继女卡雷尔小姐。但人们会记住，那位小姐在六个月之后被发现仍然活着，而且在纽约结婚嫁人了。我朋友因为连续成功破解了一系列扑朔迷离而又至关重要的案件，所以显得精神抖擞。因此，我这才引得他谈一谈巴斯克维尔庄园谜案的种种细节。我一直在耐心地等待着机会，因为我很清楚，他绝不愿意让案件相互搅合在一起，况且，他那清晰而富有逻辑性的头脑是不会脱离案件而去追忆过去的事情的。不过，亨利爵士和莫蒂默医生当时都在伦敦，正打算进行一次长途旅行，以便让爵士那几近崩溃的神经得到恢复。刚好在当天下午，他们登门来拜访我们，所以我们很自然地谈起了那桩案件。

　　"一系列事件的全过程，"福尔摩斯说，"在那个自称是斯塔普尔顿的人看来，再简单不过了。但对我们来说，一切都是那么错综复杂，因为我们刚开始时根本无法弄清他行动的动机，而且只掌握了一部分事实。后来，我和斯塔普尔顿夫人交谈过两次。通过交谈，我就

① induce [in'dju:s] v. 引诱，诱使
② overlap [,əuvə'læp] v. 重叠

had the advantage of two conversations with Mrs. Stapleton, and the case has now been so entirely cleared up that I am not aware that there is anything which has remained a secret to us. You will find a few notes upon the matter under the heading B in my indexed list of cases."

"Perhaps you would kindly give me a sketch of the course of events from memory."

"Certainly, though I cannot guarantee that I carry all the facts in my mind. Intense mental concentration has a curious way of **blotting out**[①] what has passed. The **barrister**[②] who has his case at his fingers' ends and is able to argue with an expert upon his own subject finds that a week or two of the courts will drive it all out of his head once more. So each of my cases displaces the last, and Mlle. Carere has blurred my recollection of Baskerville Hall. To-morrow some other little problem may be submitted to my notice which will in turn dispossess the fair French lady and the infamous Upwood. So far as the case of the hound goes, however, I will give you the course of events as nearly as I can, and you will suggest anything which I may have forgotten.

"My inquiries show beyond all question that the family portrait did not lie, and that this fellow was indeed a Baskerville. He was a son of that Rodger Baskerville, the younger brother of Sir Charles, who fled with a sinister reputation to South America, where he was said to have died unmarried. He did, as a matter of fact, marry, and had one child, this fellow, whose real name is the same as his father's. He married Beryl Garcia, one of the beauties of Costa Rica, and, having **purloined**[③] a considerable sum of public money, he changed his name to Vandeleur and fled to England, where he established a school in the east of Yorkshire. His reason for attempting this special line of business was that he had struck up an acquaintance with a **consumptive**[④] tutor upon the voyage home, and that he had used this man's ability to make the undertaking a success. Fraser, the tutor, died however, and the school which had begun well sank from disrepute into **infamy**[⑤]. The Vandeleurs found it convenient to change their name to Stapleton, and he brought the remains of his fortune, his schemes for the future, and his taste for entomology to the south of England. I learn at the British Museum that he was a recognized authority upon the subject, and that the name of Vandeleur has been permanently attached to a certain moth

意识到本案已经基本上不存在什么谜团了。在我那部案件目录索引栏的B字开头的栏目下面，你可以找到关于本案的详情记录。"

"你就行行好，根据回忆，给我讲述一下事情的大致情况吧。"

"当然可以，但是，我不能保证自己记住了全部事实，因为在思想高度集中的时候，往事常常会在记忆中消失。律师在处理手边的案件时，往往能够就该案的问题与专家展开辩论，但是，诉讼结束一两个礼拜之后，则又会把案情忘得一干二净。因此，后来的案件会不断地替代先前的案件在我脑海中所占据的位置，而卡雷尔小姐一案也就使我对巴斯克维尔庄园一案的记忆变得模糊起来了。等到了明天，说不定又会有某个案件交到我的手上，同样将会替代那法国姑娘和臭名昭著的厄普伍德两案的位置。不过，关于猎犬案，我会尽可能如实地向你讲述它的全部过程的，如果我遗忘了什么，你就提示一下吧。

"我的调查确凿无疑地表明，巴斯克维尔家族的画像是真实可信的，那个家伙确实是巴斯克维尔家族的成员。其父亲就是查尔斯爵士的弟弟罗杰·巴斯克维尔，他背负着一身臭名逃到了南美洲。传说他到了那儿后没结婚就去世了，但实际上，他结婚成了家，还生了一个孩子，孩子的真实姓名和他父亲的一样。他同一位哥斯达黎加的美女贝丽尔·迦洛茜娅结了婚。他在攫取了一大笔公款之后，改名换姓为范德勒，逃到了英格兰，并在约克郡的东部开办了一所学校。他之所以会想到从事这种特殊的事业，是因为他在乘船回国的途中，结识了一位罹患肺病的教师，他以为可以利用这位教师的力量成就一番事业。但是，那位名叫弗雷泽的教师亡故了，那所开始发展得很不错的学校便因此日渐衰败，从名誉不佳一直降落到臭名远扬。他们为了方便起见就改姓斯塔普尔顿，并带着所剩的财产，怀着对未来的设想，还有对昆虫学的爱好，移居到了英格兰南部。我在大英博物馆查阅资料得知，他是该领域内公认的权威。范德勒这个姓氏同某一种飞蛾产生了永久性的联系，因为那种飞蛾是他在约克郡首次发现的。

① blot out 抹掉，抹去
② barrister ['bæristə] n. 律师

③ purloin [pə:'lɔin] v. 偷窃

④ consumptive [kən'sʌmptiv] a. 患肺结核的

⑤ infamy ['infəmi] n. 声名狼藉

which he had, in his Yorkshire days, been the first to describe.

"We now come to that portion of his life which has proved to be of such intense interest to us. The fellow had evidently made inquiry and found that only two lives intervened between him and a valuable estate. When he went to Devonshire his plans were, I believe, exceedingly hazy, but that he meant mischief from the first is evident from the way in which he took his wife with him in the character of his sister. The idea of using her as a **decoy**^① was clearly already in his mind, though he may not have been certain how the details of his plot were to be arranged. He meant in the end to have the estate, and he was ready to use any tool or run any risk for that end. His first act was to establish himself as near to his ancestral home as he could, and his second was to cultivate a friendship with Sir Charles Baskerville and with the neighbours.

"The baronet himself told him about the family hound, and so prepared the way for his own death. Stapleton, as I will continue to call him, knew that the old man's heart was weak and that a shock would kill him. So much he had learned from Dr. Mortimer. He had heard also that Sir Charles was superstitious and had taken this grim legend very seriously. His ingenious mind instantly suggested a way by which the baronet could be done to death, and yet it would be hardly possible to bring home the guilt to the real murderer.

"Having conceived the idea he proceeded to carry it out with considerable **finesse**^②. An ordinary schemer would have been content to work with a savage hound. The use of artificial means to make the creature **diabolical**^③ was a flash of genius upon his part. The dog he bought in London from Ross and Mangles, the dealers in Fulham Road. It was the strongest and most savage in their possession. He brought it down by the North Devon line and walked a great distance over the moor so as to get it home without exciting any remarks. He had already on his insect hunts learned to penetrate the Grimpen Mire, and so had found a safe hiding-place for the creature. Here he **kennelled**^④ it and waited his chance.

"But it was some time coming. The old gentleman could not be decoyed outside of his grounds at night. Several times Stapleton lurked about with his hound, but without avail. It was during these fruitless quests that he, or rather his ally, was seen by peasants, and that the legend of the demon dog received

"我们现在要说到强烈吸引我们兴趣的那段生活了。很显然，那家伙进行了一番调查后发现，只有两个人阻碍他获得那笔庞大的财产。他去德文郡时，我认为他的种种计划还很模糊，但从他把自己的夫人说成是自己的妹妹这点来看，他显然从一开始就居心不良。很明显，他早就想好了要用她做诱饵，尽管他当时也不确定实施这个计划的具体细节。他的最终目的是攫取到财产，为此，他准备利用一切手段，或者甘冒任何风险。他首先要做的就是在尽可能靠近他祖上庄园的地方安置下来。其次是，同查尔斯·巴斯克维尔爵士以及邻居们友好交往。

"从男爵亲口告诉了他有关那条家族猎犬的传说，因而为自己铺下了一条通往死亡的道路。斯塔普尔顿，我将一直这样称呼他，知道老人的心脏很衰弱，只要一受惊吓就会死亡。他从莫蒂默医生那儿了解到了这些情况。此外，他还听说查尔斯爵士非常迷信，对那个恐怖的传说更是坚信不疑。他头脑精明，立刻就有了一个主意，既可以置查尔斯爵士于死地，又能够使人们几乎无法追查到真正的凶手。

"他想出了这样一个主意之后，便开始很精心地实施了。平常的阴谋者拥有了一条凶狠的猎犬也就心满意足了。但是，他却灵光一现，采用人为的手段，使那条畜生变得像恶魔一般令人恐惧。他从伦敦富勒姆大街的罗斯—曼格尔斯商行买了一条大猎犬。那是他们所有犬中最强壮和最凶恶的一条。他乘坐北德文郡线路的火车，为了掩人耳目，把猎犬弄回家，牵着猎犬在荒原上走了很远的路程。他先前在捕捉昆虫时，已经熟悉了如何穿过格林彭泥潭，同时也为那条畜生寻找了一个安全的藏匿地点。于是把猎犬关在那儿，等待时机。

"但是，过去了一段时间，无法把老绅士从自己的宅邸庭院里引诱出来。斯塔普尔顿几次牵着猎犬埋伏在他家附近，但都没有结果。就在这一系列毫无结果的跟踪过程中，它，准确地说是他的帮凶，被荒原上的农夫看见了，关于魔鬼猎犬的传说从此也得到了新的证实。他曾一度希望，自己的夫人可以去引诱查尔斯爵士，从而把他推向死亡，但出乎他的预料，她很不顺从。她不

① decoy ['diːkɔi] *n.* 诱饵

② finesse [fi'nes] *n.* 谋略，巧计
③ diabolical ['daiə'bɔlikəl] *a.* 恶魔似的

④ kennel['kenəl] *v.* 把（狗）关进狗窝

a new confirmation. He had hoped that his wife might lure Sir Charles to his ruin, but here she proved unexpectedly independent. She would not endeavour to entangle the old gentleman in a sentimental attachment which might deliver him over to his enemy. Threats and even, I am sorry to say, blows refused to move her. She would have nothing to do with it, and for a time Stapleton was **at a deadlock**①.

"He found a way out of his difficulties through the chance that Sir Charles, who had conceived a friendship for him, made him the minister of his charity in the case of this unfortunate woman, Mrs. Laura Lyons. By **representing**② himself as a single man he acquired complete influence over her, and he gave her to understand.that in the event of her obtaining a divorce from her husband he would marry her. His plans were suddenly brought to a head by his knowledge that Sir Charles was about to leave the Hall on the advice of Dr. Mortimer, with whose opinion he himself pretended to coincide. He must act at once, or his victim might get beyond his power. He therefore put pressure upon Mrs. Lyons to write this letter, imploring the old man to give her an interview on the evening before his departure for London. He then, by a **specious**③ argument, prevented her from going, and so had the chance for which he had waited.

"Driving back in the evening from Coombe Tracey he was in time to get his hound, to treat it with his infernal paint, and to bring the beast round to the gate at which he had reason to expect that he would find the old gentleman waiting. The dog, incited by its master, sprang over the wicket-gate and pursued the unfortunate baronet, who fled screaming down the yew alley. In that gloomy tunnel it must indeed have been a dreadful sight to see that huge black creature, with its flaming jaws and blazing eyes, bounding after its victim. He fell dead at the end of the alley from heart disease and terror. The hound had kept upon the grassy border while the baronet had run down the path, so that no track but the man's was visible. On seeing him lying still the creature had probably approached to sniff at him, but finding him dead had turned away again. It was then that it left the print which was actually observed by Dr. Mortimer. The hound was called off and hurried away to its lair in the Grimpen Mire, and a mystery was left which puzzled the authorities, alarmed the countryside, and

肯设法让老绅士坠入情网，因为那样很可能让他落入死敌的手里。威胁，甚至是我很不愿提起的殴打，都没能让她屈服。她根本不愿意涉及其中，因此，在一段时间里，斯塔普尔顿一筹莫展，计划受阻。

① at a deadlock 陷入困境

"后来，机会终于来了，查尔斯爵士同他建立起了良好的关系，委托他对那个名叫劳拉·莱昂斯太太的可怜女人实施慈善接济。这样一来，他在重重困境之中找到了一条出路。他对外声称自己是单身汉，所以，对她有了完全的影响力。他还使她相信，只要她能够同自己的丈夫离婚，他就会娶她为妻。他听说查尔斯爵士听从了莫蒂默医生的建议，正准备离开庄园，而他本人也假装完全同意。这时候，他的计划突然到了一个成败攸关的时刻。他必须立刻采取行动，否则，他对受害者可能就鞭长莫及了。因此，他给莱昂斯太太施加压力，让她给老绅士写信，恳求老人在他动身去伦敦的头天晚上与她见上一面。然后，他又用似乎说得过去的理由阻止她前去赴约，因此，迎来了一个他期待已久的机会。

② represent [,repri'zent] v. 陈述

③ specious ['spi:ʃəs] a. 似是而非的

"傍晚时分，他从库姆特雷西乘车返回，及时赶到了猎犬藏匿地，并把发光材料抹在它身上，然后牵着那条畜生绕到了庄园栅门附近，因为他有理由相信他会找到正在那儿等候的老绅士。猎犬在主人的怂恿下，一下跃过了栅门，对不幸的从男爵紧追不舍。老爵士尖叫着沿着紫杉树篱小道拼命逃跑。处在阴暗的树篱小道上，加上看见一条体形巨大、皮毛黝黑、嘴巴眼睛都冒着火光的畜生在身后跳跃着前行，确实会感到非常恐惧。因此，他跑到树篱小道尽头时，便因心脏病和恐惧而倒地身亡了。猎犬一直沿着小草茂盛的路边跑，而爵士是在小道上跑，所以道路除了人的脚印外看不到任何其他脚印。猎犬看到他躺倒后没有任何动静，或许还凑近去嗅了嗅，但当它发现他已死去后，便掉头走了。也正是在那个时候，它留下了一些爪印，后来确实被莫蒂默医生注意到了。猎犬被呼唤离开了，并匆忙地被赶回了设在格林彭泥潭的犬窝。这样一来，就留下了一个谜团，它让警方感到莫名其妙，让整个地区的人们感到惶恐不安，最后我们加入了对案情的调查。

finally brought the case within the scope of our observation.

"So much for the death of Sir Charles Baskerville. You perceive the devilish cunning of it, for really it would be almost impossible to make a case against the real murderer. His only **accomplice**[①] was one who could never give him away, and the grotesque, inconceivable nature of the device only served to make it more effective. Both of the women concerned in the case, Mrs. Stapleton and Mrs. Laura Lyons, were left with a strong suspicion against Stapleton. Mrs. Stapleton knew that he had designs upon the old man, and also of the existence of the hound. Mrs. Lyons knew neither of these things, but had been impressed by the death occurring at the time of an uncancelled appointment which was only known to him. However, both of them were under his influence, and he had nothing to fear from them. The first half of his task was successfully accomplished, but the more difficult still remained.

"It is possible that Stapleton did not know of the existence of an heir in Canada. In any case he would very soon learn it from his friend Dr. Mortimer, and he was told by the latter all details about the arrival of Henry Baskerville. Stapleton's first idea was that this young stranger from Canada might possibly be done to death in London without coming down to Devonshire at all. He distrusted his wife ever since she had refused to help him in laying a trap for the old man, and he dared not leave her long out of his sight for fear he should lose his influence over her. It was for this reason that he took her to London with him. They lodged, I find, at the Mexborough Private Hotel, in Craven Street, which was actually one of those called upon by my agent in search of evidence. Here he kept his wife imprisoned in her room while he, disguised in a beard, followed Dr. Mortimer to Baker Street and afterwards to the station and to the Northumberland Hotel. His wife had some **inkling**[②] of his plans; but she had such a fear of her husband—a fear founded upon brutal ill-treatment—that she dare not write to warn the man whom she knew to be in danger. If the letter should fall into Stapleton's hands her own life would not be safe. Eventually, as we know, she adopted the expedient of cutting out the words which would form the message, and addressing the letter in a disguised hand. It reached the baronet, and gave him the first warning of his danger.

"It was very essential for Stapleton to get some article of Sir Henry's attire

"关于查尔斯·巴斯克维尔爵士死亡的情况就讲述到这儿。你可以想象得到，案件中的手段有多么狠毒和狡诈，说实在的，我们几乎不可能对真正的凶手提起诉讼。他唯一的同谋是永远都不会把他的秘密泄露出去的，而他那奇特而难以想象的手法也让其阴谋更加高效地进行。两位与案件有关联的女人，斯塔普尔顿夫人和劳拉·莱昂斯太太，对斯塔普尔顿都极为怀疑。斯塔普尔顿夫人知道他在设计暗算老人，也知道那条猎犬的存在。莱昂斯太太对这两方面的情况都不知情，但她对爵士的猝死一定印象深刻，因为惨剧正好发生在自己爽约的时间里，而约会的事情只有他一个人知道，因此，她是心存怀疑的。不过，两个女人都受到了斯塔普尔顿的控制，而他对她们则有恃无恐。他那阴谋的前半部分成功地完成了，但留下了更加棘手的另一半。

① accomplice [əˈkʌmplis] n. 同谋，帮凶

"斯塔普尔顿可能并不知道，巴克斯维尔家族在加拿大还有一个继承人。但不管怎么说，他很快就从他的朋友莫蒂默医生那里得知了这一情况。莫蒂默医生把亨利·巴斯克维尔即将到来的种种细节全都告诉了他。斯塔普尔顿的第一反应就是，那个从加拿大来的陌生年轻人或许压根儿就到不了德文郡，他一到伦敦就可能把他给灭了。自从他夫人拒绝帮助他设陷阱谋害老爵士之后，他就不再信任她了，而且也不敢让夫人长时间离开自己的视线，担心会失去对她的控制。正因为如此，他便把她带在身边，一同到了伦敦。我发现，他们住在克雷文大街的梅克斯伯勒私人旅馆里，就是我曾经派人去寻找证据的那些旅馆中的一家。他把自己的夫人软禁在她的房间里，而他却乔装改扮蓄着胡子，尾随莫蒂默医生到了贝克大街，然后又去了车站，还到过诺森伯兰旅馆。他夫人对他的阴谋略知一二，但她很害怕丈夫——那是一种受过残暴虐待后产生的恐惧，以至于她不敢写信提醒那个她知道正处在危险之中的男人。如果那封信落到了斯塔普尔顿的手上，她自己也就性命难保了。最后，正如我们所知道的那样，她采用一种应急的办法：从报纸上剪下一些文字，拼凑成了那封短信，还用伪装的笔迹写下了收信人的地址。那封信被送到了从男爵手上，他因此得到了第一次危险的警示。

② inkling [ˈiŋkliŋ] n. 模糊的想法

so that, in case he was driven to use the dog, he might always have the means of setting him upon his track. With characteristic promptness and audacity he set about this at once, and we cannot doubt that the boots or chamber-maid of the hotel was well bribed to help him in his design. By chance, however, the first boot which was **procured**[1] for him was a new one and, therefore, useless for his purpose. He then had it returned and obtained another–a most **instructive**[2] incident, since it proved conclusively to my mind that we were dealing with a real hound, as no other supposition could explain this anxiety to obtain an old boot and this indifference to a new one. The more *outré* and **grotesque**[3] an incident is the more carefully it deserves to be examined, and the very point which appears to complicate a case is, when duly considered and scientifically handled, the one which is most likely to **elucidate**[4] it.

"Then we had the visit from our friends next morning, shadowed always by Stapleton in the cab. From his knowledge of our rooms and of my appearance, as well as from his general conduct, I am inclined to think that Stapleton's career of crime has been by no means limited to this single Baskerville affair. It is suggestive that during the last three years there have been four considerable burglaries in the west country, for none of which was any criminal ever arrested. The last of these, at Folkestone Court, in May, was remarkable for the cold-blooded **pistolling**[5] of the **page**[6], who surprised the masked and solitary burglar. I cannot doubt that Stapleton recruited his **waning**[7] resources in this fashion, and that for years he has been a desperate and dangerous man.

"We had an example of his readiness of resource that morning when he got away from us so successfully, and also of his audacity in sending back my own name to me through the cabman. From that moment he understood that I had taken over the case in London, and that therefore there was no chance for him there. He returned to Dartmoor and awaited the arrival of the baronet."

"One moment!" said I. "You have, no doubt, described the sequence of events correctly, but there is one point which you have left unexplained. What became of the hound when its master was in London?"

"I have given some attention to this matter and it is undoubtedly of importance. There can be no question that Stapleton had a confidant, though it is unlikely that he ever placed himself in his power by sharing all his plans

"对于斯塔普尔顿而言，很有必要弄到一件亨利爵士穿戴的物件，以便他在不得已的情况下要动用猎犬时，总能有办法追踪到他。他生性机敏，胆大妄为，于是说干就干起来了。毫无疑问，为了实现这个计划，他一定用很多钱贿赂了旅馆里的男女仆人。不过，事情很凑巧，他拿到的第一只靴子是新买来的，因此对他毫无用处。后来，他把靴子送了回去，顺手偷了另外一只——这件小事帮了我们的大忙，让我的心里有了一个结论：即我们真正要打交道的是一条猎犬，因为没有任何其他假设能够解释他为何要如此迫不及待地搞到一只旧靴子，而对那只新靴子却毫无兴趣。越是稀奇古怪的事情就越要耐心细致地加以研究，那些看来好像会使整个案件变得错综复杂的线索，只要我们进行适当的思索与科学的处理，往往是最有可能说明问题的。

"随后的第二天上午，我们的朋友上门来找我们，斯塔普尔顿始终在身后跟踪。从他对我们的住宅和对我的相貌的了解程度，还有他一贯的行为，我感觉，他的犯罪史绝对不仅仅局限于巴斯克维尔庄园这一桩案件。据说在过去三年里，西部地区已经发生了四起重大盗窃案，而且没有一桩案件是抓到了罪犯的。最后一桩是五月份在弗克斯通宅邸发生的，其独特之处在于：一个男仆被残暴地枪杀了，就因为他偶然看到了那个戴着面具的孤身盗贼。我肯定，斯塔普尔顿就是采用这样的方式来补充他那日益减少的财产的，这么多年来，他一直是肆无忌惮的亡命之徒。

"那天上午，他从我们面前成功逃脱，我就见识了他机敏应变的智慧。同时，他通过马车夫在我面前复述我的姓名，这也让我见识了他的胆大妄为。从那一刻起，他便知道，我已经在伦敦接下了本案，因此，他在伦敦没有下手的机会了，于是返回到达特穆尔荒原，等待着从男爵的到来。"

"等一等！"我说，"毫无疑问，你已经如实地描述了这一系列的事情，不过，还有一点你没有解释。那就是，主人在伦敦的那些日子里，那只猎犬该怎么办呢？"

"我曾注意了这个情况，无疑至关重要。毋庸置疑，斯塔普尔顿有一个心腹，不过好像还不至于把自己的计

① procure [prəu'kjuə] v. 获得，取得

② instructive [in'strʌktiv] a. 有益的

③ grotesque [grəu'tesk] a. 怪异的

④ elucidate [i'l(j)u:sideit] v. 阐明，说明

⑤ pistol ['pist(ə)l] v. 用手枪射击

⑥ page [peidʒ] n. 青年侍从

⑦ waning ['weiniŋ] a. 日益减少的

with him. There was an old manservant at Merripit House, whose name was Anthony. His connection with the Stapletons can be traced for several years, as far back as the school-mastering days, so that he must have been aware that his master and mistress were really husband and wife. This man has disappeared and has escaped from the country. It is suggestive that Anthony is not a common name in England, while Antonio is so in all Spanish or Spanish-American countries. The man, like Mrs. Stapleton herself, spoke good English, but with a curious lisping accent. I have myself seen this old man cross the Grimpen Mire by the path which Stapleton had marked out. It is very probable, therefore, that in the absence of his master it was he who cared for the hound, though he may never have known the purpose for which the beast was used.

"The Stapletons then went down to Devonshire, whither they were soon followed by Sir Henry and you. One word now as to how I stood myself at that time. It may possibly **recur**[①] to your memory that when I examined the paper upon which the printed words were fastened I made a close inspection for the water-mark. In doing so I held it within a few inches of my eyes, and was conscious of a faint smell of the scent known as white **jessamine**[②]. There are seventy-five perfumes, which it is very necessary that a criminal expert should be able to distinguish from each other, and cases have more than once within my own experience depended upon their prompt recognition. The scent suggested the presence of a lady, and already my thoughts began to turn towards the Stapletons. Thus I had made certain of the hound, and had guessed at the criminal before ever we went to the west country.

"It was my game to watch Stapleton. It was evident, however, that I could not do this if I were with you, since he would be keenly on his guard. I deceived everybody, therefore, yourself included, and I came down secretly when I was supposed to be in London. My hardships were not so great as you imagined, though such trifling details must never interfere with the investigation of a case. I stayed for the most part at Coombe Tracey, and only used the hut upon the moor when it was necessary to be near the scene of action. Cartwright had come down with me, and in his disguise as a country boy he was of great assistance to me. I was dependent upon him for food and clean linen. When I was watching Stapleton, Cartwright was frequently watching you, so that I was able to keep

划向他和盘托出，以免受到他的牵制。梅里皮特别墅里有个老男仆，他叫安东尼，同斯塔普尔顿夫妇的关系可以追溯到几年前，即斯塔普尔顿担任校长期间。因此，他对男女主人的夫妻关系一定心知肚明。那个人已经逃离了乡间，踪影全无了。据悉，'安东尼'这个名字在英格兰并不常见，而'安东尼奥'在所有西班牙语国家和西班牙语美洲国家里也同样如此。那个人像斯塔普尔顿夫人本人一样，英语说得不错，但奇怪的是，都带大舌头口音。我亲眼看到，那个老人顺着斯塔普尔顿做了记号的小路穿过了格林彭泥潭。因此，主人外出时，负责照料猎犬的人很可能就是他，不过他或许根本就不知道畜生是用来干什么的。

　　"后来，斯塔普尔顿夫妇到达了德文郡，紧接着，你和亨利爵士也到了那儿。讲述一下我本人当时的看法吧。你可能还记得，我在仔细查看上面贴着铅字的纸张时，近距离观察了上面的水印。当时，我把纸张拿到离眼睛只有几英寸的距离，闻到了一股淡淡的类似于一种叫作白迎春花的香味。一共有七十五种香水，犯罪学专家都应该能把它们区分出来。在我个人的经历中，根据本人迅速识别香水的能力而破解的案件不止一桩。那股香味表明该案涉及到一位女士，我当时心里面就开始怀疑上斯塔普尔顿夫妇了。这样一来，我们到达西部乡村之前，我就确定了猎犬的存在，猜出了该案的罪犯。

　　"我要玩的游戏就是监视斯塔普尔顿。不过，显而易见，如果我同你们待在一块儿，那就监视不了了，因为他十分警觉。因此，我蒙骗了所有人，包括你在内。人们都以为我在伦敦，其实我已经悄然到了那儿。我遇到的艰难险阻并不像你想象的那样不得了，不过那些琐碎的情况决不能干扰对一桩案件的调查。我大部分时间都待在库姆特雷西，只有在不得已要靠近犯罪现场时，才会利用荒原上的小屋。卡特莱特当时随我一道过去，他化装成一个乡下少年，给了我很大的帮助。我的食物和干净的衣服全靠他帮忙。我在监视斯塔普尔顿期间，卡特莱特也常常在监视你，所以我能够把全部线索都抓在手上。

① recur [ri'kə:] v. 借助于，诉诸

② jessamine ['dʒesəmin] n. 茉莉

my hand upon all the strings.

"I have already told you that your reports reached me rapidly, being forwarded instantly from Baker Street to Coombe Tracey. They were of great service to me, and especially that one incidentally truthful piece of biography of Stapleton's. I was able to establish the identity of the man and the woman and knew at last exactly how I stood. The case had been considerably complicated through the incident of the escaped convict and the relations between him and the Barrymores. This also you cleared up in a very effective way, though I had already come to the same conclusions from my own observations.

"By the time that you discovered me upon the moor I had a complete knowledge of the whole business, but I had not a case which could go to a jury. Even Stapleton's attempt upon Sir Henry that night which ended in the death of the unfortunate convict did not help us much in proving murder against our man. There seemed to be no alternative but to catch him **red-handed**[1], and to do so we had to use Sir Henry, alone and apparently unprotected, as a bait. We did so, and at the cost of a severe shock to our client we succeeded in completing our case and driving Stapleton to his destruction. That Sir Henry should have been exposed to this is, I must confess, a reproach to my management of the case, but we had no means of foreseeing the terrible and paralyzing spectacle which the beast presented, nor could we predict the fog which enabled him to burst upon us at such short notice. We succeeded in our object at a cost which both the specialist and Dr. Mortimer assure me will be a temporary one. A long journey may enable our friend to recover not only from his shattered nerves but also from his wounded feelings. His love for the lady was deep and sincere, and to him the saddest part of all this black business was that he should have been deceived by her.

"It only remains to indicate the part which she had played throughout. There can be no doubt that Stapleton exercised an influence over her which may have been love or may have been fear, or very possibly both, since they are by no means incompatible emotions. It was, at least, absolutely effective. At his command she consented to pass as his sister, though he found the limits of his power over her when he endeavoured to make her the direct **accessory**[2] to murder. She was ready to warn Sir Henry so far as she could without

"我已经对你说过了，你的报告很快就能送到我手上，因为立刻就可以从贝克大街迅速送往库姆特雷西。那些报告对我可起作用了，尤其是斯塔普尔顿讲述自己身世的那一份，其中碰巧有些情况是真实的。我能够确认那对男女的身份，并且最终确切知道了我该如何应对。由于发生了罪犯逃跑事件，再加上逃犯和巴里摩尔夫妇之间的关系，本案变得非常扑朔迷离，而对于这一点，你又是行之有效地给澄清了，尽管我依据自己的观察已经得出了同样的结论。

"在你发现我就在荒原一带时，我已经完全掌握了整个案情，但还没有一件能提供给陪审团的证据。即便是那天晚上斯塔普尔顿企图加害亨利爵士，结果却害死了那个倒霉的逃犯的事实，我们都还无法证明他犯了谋杀罪。看起来，除了当场把他抓住，我们根本没有其他更加有效的办法。为了实现这个目标，我们只好让亨利爵士处在孤立无援而且显然是毫无防备的境地，让他充当诱饵。我们确实这样做了，在付出了让我们的委托人受到严重惊吓的代价后，我们成功地获取了所需的证据，并把凶手斯塔普尔顿推向了毁灭之路。我必须承认，让亨利爵士经受这样的惊吓是我在处理本案中的一大缺陷。但是，我们无法预料，那条畜生看上去竟是那么凶狠可怕。我们也无法预知当晚会有那么浓的大雾，以致那条畜生突然就蹿到了我们面前，令我们措手不及。我们成功地完成了任务，但同时，也付出了代价。所幸的是，专家莫蒂默医生向我保证，这只是暂时的，一次长途旅行就可能让我们的朋友那几近崩溃的神经，以及那受到伤害的心灵都得以恢复。他对那位女士的爱是深沉的、真挚的，因而对他来说，这件倒霉的事件中最伤他心的莫过于他竟然被她给欺骗了。

"现在，就差她在整个案件中所扮演的角色没有说了。毋庸置疑，她受到了斯塔普尔顿的牵制，这或许由于爱情，或许由于恐惧，很可能两者兼而有之，因为这两种情感并不是彼此不能相容的。不管原因如何，那种牵制力至少是绝对有效的。她听从他的命令，同意在人前装作是他的妹妹。但当他逼迫她直接参与谋杀的时候，他发现他对她的牵制力也是有限度的。只

① red-handed ['red'hændid] a. 正在作案的

② accessory [ək'sesəri] n. 从犯；帮凶

implicating her husband, and again and again she tried to do so. Stapleton himself seems to have been capable of jealousy, and when he saw the baronet **paying court to**① the lady, even though it was part of his own plan, still he could not help interrupting with a passionate outburst which revealed the fiery soul which his self-contained manner so cleverly concealed. By encouraging the intimacy he made it certain that Sir Henry would frequently come to Merripit House and that he would sooner or later get the opportunity which he desired. On the day of the crisis, however, his wife turned suddenly against him. She had learned something of the death of the convict, and she knew that the hound was being kept in the out-house on the evening that Sir Henry was coming to dinner. She **taxed**② her husband with his intended crime, and a furious scene followed in which he showed her for the first time that she had a rival in his love. Her fidelity turned in an instant to bitter hatred, and he saw that she would betray him. He tied her up, therefore, that she might have no chance of warning Sir Henry, and he hoped, no doubt, that when the whole countryside put down the baronet's death to the curse of his family, as they certainly would do, he could win his wife back to accept an accomplished fact and to keep silent upon what she knew. In this I fancy that in any case he made a miscalculation, and that, if we had not been there, his doom would none the less have been sealed. A woman of Spanish blood does not **condone**③ such an injury so lightly. And now, my dear Watson, without referring to my notes, I cannot give you a more detailed account of this curious case. I do not know that anything essential has been left unexplained."

"He could not hope to frighten Sir Henry to death as he had done the old uncle with his bogie hound."

"The beast was savage and half-starved. If its appearance did not frighten its victim to death, at least it would paralyze the resistance which might be offered."

"No doubt. There only remains one difficulty. If Stapleton came into the succession, how could he explain the fact that he, the heir, had been living unannounced under another name so close to the property? How could he claim it without causing suspicion and inquiry?"

"It is a formidable difficulty, and I fear that you ask too much when you

要不把自己的丈夫牵连进去，她就准备向亨利爵士发出警告，而且她确实一次又一次地设法这样做了。看起来，斯塔普尔顿本人也会心怀妒意。当他看到亨利爵士对自己的夫人求婚时，尽管这是他计划之内的事，但他还是无法忍受，并脾气暴躁地加以干涉。这就暴露了他机智地用自制力掩盖着的凶残本性。通过拉近与亨利爵士的感情，他就能确保，爵士会经常去梅里皮特别墅。这样一来，他早晚有一天会有自己所期待的良机。但是，就在情况危急的那一天，他夫人突然同他对立起来了。她已经得知了逃犯死亡的情况，而且还知道，就在亨利爵士要来吃饭的当天晚上，那条猎犬被关在了别墅外面的房子里。她猜测到了丈夫图谋犯罪，并加以谴责，接着大吵了一场。争吵中，他第一次向她透露，自己已经另有所爱了。霎时间，她对他的忠贞演变成了强烈的仇恨。他心里明白，她一定会出卖自己，因此，便把她捆绑了起来，使她没有机会去向亨利爵士发出警示。毫无疑问，他心里指望着，整个地区的人都会把爵士的死亡归咎于其家族的厄运———他们一定会那样认为的。然后，他就可以设法赢回夫人的心，让她接受这个既定的事实，并对她所知道的一切保持沉默。在这件事情上，我认为，无论如何，他的如意算盘都落空了，即便我们没去那里，他的结局也是早已注定了的。一个具有西班牙血统的女人在受到这样的侮辱后，是断然不会轻而易举地饶恕他的。现在，亲爱的华生，如果我不看一看自己的笔记，便无法把这桩奇案给你讲述得更详细了。我不知道自己是否留下了什么重要细节没有解释清楚的。"

"那条凶狠的猎犬吓死了亨利爵士的大伯，他不可能同样指望着吓死亨利爵士吧。"

"那条猎犬生性凶狠，饥饿不已。即便其形象不把受害者吓死，至少也会令其失去抵抗力的。"

"毫无疑问。只剩下一个难题了。假设斯塔普尔顿果真继承了财产，那他如何能够对别人解释，他作为法定继承人为何要改名换姓隐居在离祖传地产那么近的地方？他又如何能够既继承财产，又不引起人们怀疑，从而招致调查呢？"

① pay court to 向…献殷勤；向…求爱

② tax [tæks] v. 谴责；责备

③ condone [kən'dəun] v. 宽恕，原谅

expect me to solve it. The past and the present are within the field of my inquiry, but what a man may do in the future is a hard question to answer. Mrs. Stapleton has heard her husband discuss the problem on several occasions. There were three possible courses. He might claim the property from South America, establish his identity before the British authorities there, and so obtain the fortune without ever coming to England at all; or he might adopt an elaborate disguise during the short time that he need be in London; or, again, he might **furnish**[1] an accomplice with the proofs and papers, putting him in as heir, and retaining a claim upon some **proportion**[2] of his income. We cannot doubt from what we know of him that he would have found some way out of the difficulty. And now, my dear Watson, we have had some weeks of severe work, and for one evening, I think, we may turn our thoughts into more pleasant channels. I have a box for 'Les Huguenots.' Have you heard the De Reszkes? Might I trouble you then to be ready in half an hour, and we can stop at Marcini's for a little dinner on the way?"

"这是一个莫大的难题啊。你指望我来解决，恐怕对我要求过于苛刻了吧。我只负责调查过去和现在发生的事情，而对一个人将来会做什么，很难给出答案的。斯塔普尔顿夫人有几次听他说到过这个问题，大概有三条途径，他可能会向在南美洲的英国当局证明自己的身份，然后在当地要求继承这份财产，这样，他就无须返回英格兰就能继承到财产。他也可能特意乔装改扮一番，以此度过必须待在伦敦的短暂时期。他还有可能找到一个同谋，给他提供所需的证据和文件，让他充当继承人，同时对他的部分收入保留所有权。根据我们对他的了解，他一定能想出一个办法来解决这个难题的。好了，亲爱的华生，我们已经紧张地工作了好几个礼拜了，我觉得，我们今晚可以换换环境，想点更加愉悦的事情了。今晚剧场演出歌剧《胡格诺派教徒》，我订了个包厢。你听过德·雷什克兄弟的演唱吗？请你在半小时内准备好，我们还可以顺道去玛齐尼餐厅吃点晚饭呢。"

① furnish ['fə:niʃ] v. 提供

② proportion [prəu'pɔ:ʃən] n. 比例